JESUS CHRIST
His Life and Teaching

VOLUME FOUR
The Parables of Jesus

The publication of this book was made possible
through a generous donation from
His Eminence Melchisedek,
Archbishop of Pittsburgh and Western Pennsylvania.

Metropolitan
HILARION ALFEYEV

JESUS CHRIST

His Life and Teaching

In Six Volumes

VOLUME FOUR

THE PARABLES
OF JESUS

ST VLADIMIR'S SEMINARY PRESS
YONKERS, NEW YORK
2021

Library of Congress Cataloging-in-Publication Data

Names: Ilarion, Metropolitan of Volokolamsk, 1966- author. | Kotar, Nicholas, translator.
Title: The parables of Jesus / Hilarion Alfeyev.
Other titles: Pritchi Iisusa. English
Description: Yonkers, NY : St Vladimir's Seminary Press, 2021. | Series: Jesus Christ: his
  life and teaching ; volume four | Includes bibliographical references. | Summary: "In
  this fourth volume of the series Jesus Christ: His Life and Teaching, Metropolitan
  Hilarion Alfeyev explores the parables of Jesus, drawing both on the Church's two
  millennia of interpretive history, as well as the most promising fruits of modern
  biblical scholarship. Every single parable is examined in this broad context, and
  profound meaning is found in the original context, in the Church's reception history,
  and in our own contemporary situation"—Provided by publisher.
Identifiers: LCCN 2021042626 (print) | LCCN 2021042627 (ebook) | ISBN
  9780881416985 (paperback) | ISBN 9780881416992 (kindle edition)
Subjects: LCSH: Jesus Christ--Parables.
Classification: LCC BT375.3 .I5313 2021 (print) | LCC BT375.3 (ebook) | DDC
  226.8/06—dc23
LC record available at https://lccn.loc.gov/2021042626
LC ebook record available at https://lccn.loc.gov/2021042627

COPYRIGHT © 2021

ST VLADIMIR'S SEMINARY PRESS
575 Scarsdale Road, Yonkers, NY 10707
1-800-204-2665
www.svspress.com

ISBN 978–088141–698–5 (paper)
ISBN 978–088141–699–2 (electronic)

Unless noted otherwise, scriptural quotations are taken from the King James Version,
with some modifications for accuracy or ease of comprehension. Psalm texts are
taken from a draft translation of the Psalter, edited by Hieromonk Herman (Majkrzak)
and Priest Ignatius Green, and used by permission. Psalms are cited according to the
Septuagint (LXX) numbering, which differs from the Hebrew numbering (used by most
English translations) in Pss 9–147: LXX Ps 9 = Heb. Pss 9–10; LXX Pss 10–112 = Heb.
11–113; LXX 113 = Heb. 114–115; LXX 114 = Heb. 116.1–9; LXX 115 = Heb. 116.10–19;
LXX 116–145 = Heb. 117–146; LXX 146 = Heb. 147.1–11; LXX 147 = Heb. 147.12–20.

TABLE OF CONTENTS

PREFACE

This book continues a series of studies dedicated to the life and teachings of Jesus Christ. The series is divided into the following thematic sections, each occupying its own volume: 1) the birth and childhood of Jesus, as well as the beginning of his ministry, 2) his Sermon on the Mount, 3) his miracles, 4) his parables, 5) Jesus in the Gospel of John, 6) the passion and the resurrection. This volume is dedicated to the parables of Jesus Christ, which are found in the three synoptic Gospels: Matthew, Mark, and Luke.

Christ Pantocrator,
Icon, 13th century

In the history of mankind, there has never been another teacher who used the genre of parables so extensively and consistently as did Jesus Christ. He inherited this genre from the tradition of the Old Testament, but he widened its potential and honed its artistry to such a degree of perfection that none of his successors—neither in the first generation nor in any other—has ever returned to the genre.[1] We do not find a single parable in the book of Acts, nor in any of the apostolic letters or epistles of Paul, nor in the writings of the Apostolic Fathers, nor even in the writings of the Fathers of the Church (except for rare cases that are more like similes or metaphors than true parables).

In his own public ministry, Jesus often used images and comparisons taken from everyday life or from the natural world. But, strictly speaking, not all of these similes are parables. For example, he calls the apostles the "salt of the earth" in his Sermon on the Mount (Mt 5.13–16). This is a metaphor,

[1]W. F. Albright and C. S. Mann, *Matthew: Introduction, Translation and Notes* (London: Doubleday & Company, Inc., 1971), 132.

not a parable. Later in the same sermon, Jesus suggests that his disciples look at the birds who "sow not, neither do they reap, nor gather into barns," and at the lilies of the field, who "toil not, neither do they spin" (Mt 6.26, 28). These images indicate God's care for man and illustrate the main point of the Sermon on the Mount: "Therefore take no thought, saying, 'What shall we eat?' Or, 'What shall we drink?' Or, 'Wherewithal shall we be clothed?' . . . Take therefore no thought for the morrow" (Mt 6.31.34). But these are not parables. Only the words that conclude the Sermon on the Mount constitute a parable—the story of the wise man who built his house on the rock, and the foolish man who built his house on sand (Mt 7.24–27).

In this book we will examine neither the images in the Sermon on the Mount,[2] nor the teachings about the Good Shepherd (Jn 10.1–16) and the grapevine (Jn 15.1–8) found in the Gospel of John. These teachings have some similarities to parables, since they both use metaphorical language.[3] But as a rule, they are not generally included in examinations of the parables. We will examine them in greater detail in the fifth book of this series, which is dedicated entirely to the Gospel of John.

Furthermore, this book will not deal with various short pronouncements of Jesus that have some similarity to parables, such as "They that be whole need not a physician, but they that are sick" (Mt 9.12; Mk 2.17; Luke 5.31).

The instruction concerning the dread judgment in the Gospel according to Matthew (Mt 25.31–46) is sometimes included in the list of parables because it begins with a simile comparing the righteous to sheep and all the others to goats. But this comparison does not continue in the rest of the account. From our point of view, this teaching is not a parable. It should be examined separately, as part of the series of Jesus' teachings in the Gospel of Matthew.[4]

---

[2]We have already examined these, in Metropolitan Hilarion Alfeyev, *Jesus Christ: His Life and Teaching*, vol. 2, *The Sermon on the Mount*: (Yonkers, NY: St Vladimir's Seminary Press, 2019).

[3]Concerning the metaphorical or parabolic character of Jesus's teachings in the Gospel of John, cf. C. H. Dodd, *Historical Tradition in the Fourth Gospel* (Cambridge: Cambridge University Press, 1976), 366–87.

[4]This will be examined in the sixth book of this series.

*Christ
Pantocrator,*
Mosaic,
12th century

In this volume, therefore, we will examine only those stories that are, strictly defined, parables. These are fables with a storyline and characters. We will discuss them in the order that they were spoken, as much as such a chronology can be reconstructed from the three synoptic Gospels. Consequently, these parables will be divided into three sections: 1) parables spoken during the Galilean ministry of Jesus, 2) parables spoken on the way from Galilee to Jerusalem, and 3) parables spoken in Jerusalem during the final days of Jesus' earthly life.

*Christ
Pantocrator*,
Mosaic,
20th century

Chapter 1

THE PARABLES OF JESUS AND THEIR INTERPRETATION

What is a parable? Scholars have debated this question for more than a century, and no easy answer has yet been offered. Nonetheless, practically all scholars agree that the essential element of all parables is metaphor.[1] Without a metaphor, there can be no parable, and every parable can also be called an extended metaphor. At the same time, of course, this does not mean that all metaphors are necessarily parables.

Scholars of literature usually define parables as short narratives that use metaphorical language for the purposes of expressing a moral truth.

Jesus often expressed his teaching in the form of parables. If we consider all of his instructions contained in the four Gospels, a third (or rather almost 35%) consists of parables.[2] It was so typical for Jesus to use the parable as the primary vehicle for transmitting his spiritual and moral truths that the evangelists made special note of it: "All these things spake Jesus unto the multitudes in parables; and without a parable spake he not unto them" (Mt 13.34); "And with many such parables spake he the word unto them, as they were able to hear it. But without a parable spake he not unto them: and when they were alone, he expounded all things to his disciples" (Mk 4.33–34). When Jesus ceased speaking in parables, this was a shock

---

[1] Ivor H. Jones, *The Matthean Parables: A Literary and Historical Commentary* (Leiden: E. J. Brill, 1995), 56–68.

[2] Norman Perrin, *Jesus and the Language of the Kingdom: Symbol and Metaphor in the New Testament Interpretation* (Minneapolis: Fortress Press, 1976), 56.

1

to his listeners: "Lo, now speakest thou plainly, and speakest no proverb" (Jn 16.29).

In the synoptic Gospels, the term *parabolē* (parable) is not limited to the strict definition of "parable" we have given above. The word can mean the following: a proverb or maxim (Lk 4.24, 6.39), a metaphor (Mk 3.23; Lk 5.36), a moral lesson (Lk 14.7), an aphorism (Mt 9.12; Mk 2.17; Lk 5.31), and so on.[3] For example, Jesus uses the term *parabolē* (parable) when referring to his own words, "Physician, heal thyself" (Lk 4.23). But, as we see in the KJV, the word is translated as "proverb," which more correctly defines what this expression is: a proverb or maxim, not a full-fledged parable.

The Gospels contain more than thirty full parables, that is, stories with one or several characters (or images) that contain a specific moral lesson (or lessons). If we add to this Jesus' short similes expressed in metaphorical language, similar to the parable in the manner of expression, then the total number exceeds sixty.[4]

Before we begin interpreting the parables of Jesus, we will first examine the history of the genre in the tradition of the Old Testament. Then we will try to answer the question: why did Jesus teach using parables? Finally, we will examine various ways of classifying parables: 1) by the place and time they were spoken, 2) by their content, 3) by their length, or by using other criteria. We will also direct our attention to the structure of the parable, its use of imagery, and its poetic elements. The final section of this chapter will be dedicated to various methods of interpretation, both ancient and modern.

[3]Cf. G. Haufe, "Παραβολη," *Exegetical Dictionary of the New Testament*, 3 vols, ed. Horst Balz and Gerhard Schneider (Grand Rapids, MI: Eerdmans, 1990–1993), 3:12–16, at 15.
[4]Scholars vary in their opinion on the total number of parables: Adolf Jülicher, *Die Gleichnisreden Jesu*, 2 vols (Freiburg: J. C. B. Mohr [Paul Siebeck], 1888–89), counts them as 53; C. H. Dodd, *The Parables of the Kingdom* (London: James Nisbet and Company, 1935), as 32; Joachim Jeremias, *The Parables of Jesus* (New York: Charles Scribner's Sons, 1972), as 41; Bernard Brandon Scott, *Hear Then the Parable*, rev. ed. (Minneapolis: Fortress Press, 1989), as 30; Arland J. Hultgren, *The Parables of Jesus: A Commentary* (Grand Rapids, MI: Wm. B. Eerdmans Publishing Co. 2002), as 38; Geza Vermes, *The Authentic Gospel of Jesus* (Oxford: Allen Lane, 2003), as 40; A. M. Hunter, *Interpreting the Parables* (Philadelphia: Westminster Press, 1961), as around 60; T. W. Manson, *The Teaching of Jesus: Studies of its Form and Content* (Cambridge: Cambridge University Press, 1967), 69, as 65.

1. Parables in the Old Testament

The only Old Testament analogue to the parables of Jesus is the instructive story that the prophet Nathan tells King David, after the latter took Bathsheba, the wife of Uriah, as his own wife, and ensured that Uriah would die by ordering him to an extremely dangerous area of an ongoing battle:

Prophet Nathan,
Mosaic, 12th century

> And the Lord sent Nathan unto David. And he came unto him, and said unto him, "There were two men in one city: the one rich, and the other poor. The rich man had exceeding many flocks and herds, but the poor man had nothing, save one little ewe lamb, which he had bought and nourished up; and it grew up together with him, and with his children; it did eat of his own food, and drank of his own cup, and lay in his bosom, and was unto him as a daughter. And there came a traveler unto the rich man, and he spared to take of his own flock and of his own herd, to dress for the wayfaring man that was come unto him, but took the poor man's lamb, and dressed it for the man that was come to him." And David's anger was greatly kindled against the man; and he said to Nathan, "As the Lord liveth, the man that hath done this thing shall surely die, and he shall restore the lamb fourfold, because he did this thing, and because he had no pity." And Nathan said to David, "Thou art the man" (2 Sam 12.1–7)

The Prophet Nathan accuses David,
Miniature, 10th century

In this case, what we see here is an allegory with several characters: a rich man, a traveler, a poor man, and the poor man's lamb. Three of the characters are metaphorical representations of actual people: the rich man is David, the sheep is Bathsheba, and the poor man is Uriah. Only the traveler, it would seem, has no real-world analogue. The one to whom the story is addressed is called to understand in this parable the seriousness of the sin he committed himself. But this does not happen. Then, the storyteller himself has to briefly and sharply interpret the parable, leaving only one possible interpretation for a single character in the story. The rest of the characters receive their interpretation in the light of that revelation.

An important aspect of the parable is the reason that it is spoken in the first place: the hearer is supposed to understand the main character to refer to himself, and to apply the lessons of the tale to his own life's situation. "The purpose of the parables is not merely to entertain, as may be the case with other folk stories. Their purpose is far more important. It is to bring about in the hearer a change of mind—or better, a change of heart—perhaps to move the hearer to conversion."[5] The parable of Nathan achieved its goal, though not immediately.

---

2. Why did Jesus speak in Parables?

As we turn to the parables of Jesus, we must first admit that, among all of Jesus' teachings, they are the most difficult to interpret. Even for his own contemporaries, they were mostly incomprehensible, a fact underlined by his disciples' repeated requests for clarification of individual parables (see Mt 13.35, 15.15). The same truth is reflected by the question that the disciples asked after Jesus told the parable of the sower. In the Gospel according to Matthew, the question is related in the following manner:

> And the disciples came, and said unto him, "Why speakest thou unto them in parables?" He answered and said unto them, "Because it is

[5]Madeleine I. Boucher, *The Parables* (Wilmington, DE: Michael Glazier, Inc., 1981), 16

given unto you to know the mysteries of the kingdom of heaven, but to them it is not given. For whosoever hath, to him shall be given, and he shall have more abundance; but whosoever hath not, from him shall be taken away even that he hath. Therefore speak I to them in parables, because they seeing see not; and hearing they hear not, neither do they understand. And in them is fulfilled the prophecy of Isaiah, which saith, 'By hearing ye shall hear, and shall not understand; and seeing ye shall see, and shall not perceive. For this people's heart is waxed gross, and their ears are dull of hearing, and their eyes they have closed; lest at any time they should see with their eyes and hear with their ears, and should understand with their heart, and should be converted, and I should heal them.'" (Mt 13.10–15)

As Jesus' answer indicates, he recognized the incomprehensibility of his own parables, and still he spoke them. As for the ignorance of his listeners, he explained it by quoting a prophecy of Isaiah, referring them to his own contemporaries. In Isaiah, these words had a very specific context that must be considered: they are part of his own retelling of his call to the prophetic ministry. This account begins with a description of a vision that Isaiah was found worthy of "in the year that king Uzziah died." Isaiah saw the Lord, sitting on a throne and surrounded by seraphim who exclaimed, "Holy, holy, holy is the Lord of hosts: the whole earth is full of his glory." These exclamations made the doorposts shake, and the house was filled with the smoke of incense. In terror, Isaiah exclaimed, "Woe is me! For I am undone; because I am a man of unclean lips, and I dwell in the midst of a people of unclean lips: for mine eyes have seen the king, the Lord of hosts." One of the seraphim flew up to the prophet, holding in his hands tongs with a hot coal. He touched the lips of the prophet with that coal and said, "Lo, this hath touched thy lips; and thine iniquity is taken away, and thy sin purged." Afterward, the prophet heard the voice of the Lord, who said, "Whom shall I send, and who will go for us?" Isaiah answered, "Here am I; send me." At that moment the words of Jesus to his disciples sounded in the lips of God: "Go, and tell this people, 'Hear ye indeed—but understand not; and see ye indeed, but perceive not.' Make the heart of this people fat,

The Prophet Isaiah,
Fresco, 14th century

and make their ears heavy, and shut their eyes; lest they see with their eyes, and hear with their ears, and understand with their heart, and convert, and be healed" (Isaiah 6.1–10).

Thus Jesus makes a direct connection between the situation in which Isaiah found himself when God sent him to preach to the Israelite nation, and his own mission. He admits that these people will only accept what he has to say with difficulty (*bareōs*), because they have closed their own eyes, that is, they have closed off all access inside themselves for the acceptance of the good news, brought to them by Jesus. First of all, the citation from Isaiah refers to those people who did not accept Jesus' teaching—that is, the spiritual leaders of the nation of Israel, the priests, scribes, and Pharisees. But this quote more or less refers even to the simple people who wanted to hear Jesus, those who came to Jesus without evil intentions or any desires to trip him up or catch him in a blasphemy. Their spiritual state did not allow them to fully understand the truths that he had to offer them. This is why Jesus uses a special form of address, which is formulated to help the people better absorb his truth.

What is the purpose, then, of the parable form itself? Is it to aid understanding or hinder it? At first glance, it would seem that Jesus, as a wise teacher, should take pains to aid the understanding of those he has come to teach.

Nevertheless, the causal relationship between hearing and understanding is differently expressed in the Gospel according to Matthew and the two other synoptics. In Matthew, as we have seen, Jesus' words are given in the following form: "Therefore speak I to them in parables, because they seeing see not . . ." In Mark's rendition, Jesus' words sound slightly different: "Unto you it is given to know the mystery of the kingdom of God, but unto them that are without, all these things are done in parables, that seeing they may see, and not perceive; and hearing they may hear, and not understand; lest at any time they should be converted, and their sins should be forgiven them" (Mk 4.11–12). Luke's version (Lk 8.10) is essentially the same.

In the original text of Mark and Luke's Gospels, instead of Matthew's *"dia touto . . . hoti"* (because . . . therefore), we have a different conjunction *"hina"* (so that). This conjunction gives the text a different meaning.

Scholars have argued about the meaning of this conjunction (*hina*) in this passage throughout the twentieth century.[6] Some believe it is a bad translation from Aramaic that changed the original meaning.[7] Others have argued against this.[8] Some have interpreted the meaning of the conjunction as referring to the goal, not the consequences of action.[9] A group of scholars argue that, in trying to explain the phenomenon of the parables' incomprehensibility, Mark created his own "theory of hardening" and put it into the mouth of Jesus, who in fact said nothing of the sort, considering his own parables to be understandable.[10]

All attempts to soften the apparent harshness of Jesus' words, or at least the form they are given in Mark and Luke, were connected first of all with a fear that a too-strict interpretation of this translation might lead to an understanding in line with Calvin's doctrine of predestination. According to this teaching, some people have been predestined for salvation, and some for perdition.[11] Those who are not predestined for salvation cannot possibly understand the meanings of the parables.

But a literal reading of this passage in the Gospel according to Mark in no way necessitates a Calvinist interpretation. On the contrary, it

[6]Nigel Turner, *Grammatical Insights into the New Testament* (London: T&T Clark International, 2004), 47–50.

[7]Manson, *The Teaching of Jesus*, 75–80.

[8]Matthew Black, *An Aramaic Approach to the Gospels and Acts*, 2nd ed. (Oxford: Clarendon Press, 1957), 153–58.

[9]C. H. Peisker, "Konsekutives *hina* in Markus 4:12," *Zeitschrift für die neutestamentliche Wissenschaft* 59 (1968): 126–27; Bruce Chilton, *A Galilean Rabbi and His Bible: Jesus' Own Interpretation of Isaiah* (London: SPCK, 1984), 93–94.

[10]Charles E. Carlston, *The Parables of the Triple Tradition* (Minneapolis: Fortress Press, 2007), 97–109.

[11]John Calvin, *Institutes of the Christian Religion* 3.21, trans. Henry Beveridge (London: Arnold Hatfield for Bonham Norton, 1599; electronic edition: Bellingham, WA: Logos Bible Software, 1997).

St Mark the Evangelist,
Miniature, 778–820.

resonates with Jesus' words in the Gospel of John: "For judgment I am come into this world, that they which see not might see, and that they which see might be made blind" (Jn 9.39). Here, the conjunction "*hina*" means "so that." In this instance, the conjunction establishes a causal relationship between Jesus' coming into the world and the result of his preaching. And it turns out that this result was not so much the illumination of those who before did not see, but rather the blinding of those who considered themselves to have sight already. But this does not mean that either the former or the latter were predestined for salvation or perdition. On the contrary, it is a result of the fact that some listen to the preaching and some do not, that some come to Jesus with faith, seeking spiritual illumination, while others, like the scribes and Pharisees, simply stick their fingers in their ears and shut their eyes.

These words are part of a dialogue between Jesus and the Jews, which takes place after he gave sight to a man blind from birth. The miracle itself, as described by John, vividly illustrates that double action that Jesus provoked in his listeners. Those who came to him with faith received illumination; those who came with doubt in their heart not only did not become illumined, but on the contrary only demonstrated their blindness to a greater extent. To the question "are we blind also?" Jesus answered, "If ye were blind, ye should have no sin. But now ye say, 'We see.' Therefore your sin remaineth" (Jn 9.40–41). Here the term used twice, *hamartia*, receives its proper translation as "sin," though in Classical Greek the word often meant "mistake" or "missing the mark." Thus, people's inability to see what should be obvious to them, to understand the meaning of words addressed to them, is a result of *sin*.

Sin leads to spiritual blindness and deafness. Teachers need special training if they are to instruct those who are physically blind or deaf. Special methods have been developed to better instruct both those who cannot see and those who cannot hear. The same is also true of those who instruct the spiritually blind and deaf. Teachers need a specific approach or format to better pass on their instruction. For Jesus, that was the parable.

But if teachers of the physically blind and deaf employ methods that make learning easier, in Jesus' case, the situation was slightly different. Returning to the meaning of his words, as they are rendered in Mark and Luke, we can ascertain that he speaks the parables *not* to make it easier for his listeners to understand his teachings. In fact, it seems that the opposite is true: he seems to make understanding more difficult for his listeners.

One of the already-offered explanations for this paradoxical aspect of Jesus' preaching, which attracted the attention of his own disciples several times, comes from the assumption that Jesus spoke in parables for the sake of his own safety:

> 'If you have ears, then hear'; if too many understand too well, the prophet's liberty of movement, and perhaps life, may be cut short. Jesus knew his kingdom-announcement was subversive. It would be drastically unwelcome, for different reasons, to the Romans, to Herod, and also to zealous Jews and their leaders, whether official or not. He must therefore speak in parables, 'so that they may look and look but never see'. It was the only safe course. Only those in the know must be allowed to glimpse what Jesus believed was going on. These stories would get past the censor—for the moment. There would come a time for more open revelation.[12]

We cannot in all seriousness accept such an interpretation, which simply ignores the obvious fact that the parables were not some kind of transitional or temporary form of Jesus' preaching. After all, he uttered them from the first days of his public ministry in Galilee until the very last days before his arrest, days that he spent in Jerusalem. All teachings that were not uttered in the form of parables were always given in parallel with parables, and not only in the concluding part of his ministry. This is made obvious by the Sermon on the Mount, which Matthew ascribes to the beginning of his ministry, and the numerous public conversations that

[12]N. T. Wright, *Jesus and the Victory of God* (Minneapolis: Fortress Press, 1997), 237.

St John Chrysostom,
Fresco, 1191

Jesus had with the Jews, as recounted in the Gospel of John. If Jesus was afraid to speak directly not only to sympathetic hearers but also to his opponents, then the vast majority of his words directed at the Jews (as recorded in the Gospels) would simply be absent.

The other explanation of Jesus' choice to speak in parables rests upon the fact that the very person of Jesus, his miracles and his preaching, provoked two extremely different reactions in his listeners. Some were strengthened in faith, while others were repulsed and angered. As scholars underline, many of Jesus' listeners "understood the call of the parable perfectly well, but were not ready to follow it."[13] Even the enemies of Christ accepted his parables on a cognitive level.[14] As proof of this, such scholars note the Pharisees' reaction when Jesus spoke the parable of the wicked tenants of the vineyard: "they sought to lay hold on him, but feared the people, for they knew that he had spoken the parable against them" (Mk 12.12).

A simple but convincing answer to the question of why Jesus spoke in parables is given by John Chrysostom: Jesus "continues in the metaphor to make the discourse more emphatic,"[15] and he used metaphorical imagery because he was speaking of exalted realities.[16] The same author has a different explanation as well: "Therefore neither at the beginning did he so discourse to them, but with much plainness; but because they perverted themselves, thenceforth he speaks in parables."[17]

---

[13]H. J. Klauck, *Allegorie und Allegorese in synoptischen Gleichnistexten* (Münster: Aschendorff, 1978), 251.

[14]Craig Blomberg, *Interpreting the Parables*, 2nd ed. (Downer's Grove, IL: IVP Academic, 2012), 42–43.

[15]John Chrysostom, *Homilies on the Gospel of John* 59.3 (NPNF[1] 14:214).

[16]Ibid. (NPNF[1] 14:215).

[17]John Chrysostom, *Homilies on the Gospel of Matthew* 45.1 (NPNF[1] 10:285).

Let us pay attention to the fact that when the disciples heard the first parable of Jesus, they did not ask for its interpretation. They instead asked, "Why speakest thou unto them in parables?" (Mt 13.10). Only after they received an answer, and with it an interpretation, did they dare ask a question referring to a different parable: "Declare unto us the parable of the tares of the field" (Mt 13.36). At first, they were not so much interested in the interpretation of the parable as in the reason why the Teacher had decided to use such a form of instruction. Their interest in the meaning of the parable is secondary. It must also be noted that the evangelists, in the vast majority of cases, do not mention even the slightest interest on the part of the disciples when it comes to interpretations of parables. One may even come to the conclusion that, having received an explanation of the first two, they were not interested in the content of the rest. In any case, if they did receive the Teacher's interpretations, they did not consider it necessary to pass them on to their descendants. Thus, the majority of parables remain unexplained in the Gospels themselves.

All scholarly debates concerning the interpretation of parables in the nineteenth and twentieth centuries centered exclusively on the question of their importance, content, and meaning. But this preoccupation with meaning, which is typical of modern man, was evidently less characteristic of Jesus' original listeners, who for the most part were simple peasants in Galilee, gathered in large numbers to hear him speak. It is possible that they were much less interested in the content of his preaching than in his person and in the miracles that he performed, or even the tone of his speech alone, which was so different from the style of the scribes and Pharisees (Mt 7.29). As Stephen Wright mentions, many of those who gathered to hear Jesus had never met him before, and were curious about this man that everyone was talking about. As they listened to him, it is possible the question they asked themselves was not "What does he mean?" but rather "What is going on?"[18]

Even in our days, when someone discusses a famous television personality (we apologize for a comparison that may seem inappropriate), people more often talk about what they wore or how they talked, than about the

---

[18]Stephen I. Wright, *Jesus the Storyteller* (London: SPCK, 2014), 95–96.

actual content of what they said. A person's image, his acting on stage or in front of a camera, has no less meaning for viewers than what he wants to convey. This is especially true of situations when someone sees a celebrity for the first time, either on screen or in person. The psychological effect of encountering a brilliant personality often leads to a state where words fail entirely: the image, the personality makes a much more vivid impression than words.

You can see something similar if you observe some people when they first encounter the Gospel. Having never encountered Jesus and his good news, at first, there is much that they do not understand. The Gospel plunges them into a world of images that are very distant from modern realities. The structure of the language is unfamiliar. On the one hand, it seems very simple, but on the other hand, it is rather difficult to understand. And yet, they continue to read, braving the difficulties of abstruse images and concepts, because in the words of Jesus, in his parables, they sense the presence of the One who spoke them. This sense of Christ's living presence is often the most striking impression that someone experiences when he or she first reads the Gospels. Questions about the meaning of this or that event, speech, or parable come later, during a second or third reading.

The parable genre shares elements of both prose and poetry. As a rule, the telling is in prose, but the figurative structure, language, laconic form of presentation, and axioms and sayings used repeatedly ("whoever has ears to hear, let him hear," etc.)—these are elements common to verse, giving each parable a poetic hue. Consequently, the way people listen to parables is similar to how they read poetry. As a rule, readers do not search for moral lessons in poems. Much more important are the images, the sounds, the rhythm, the play of words, or other techniques of poetic mastery.

Jesus often did turn to his listeners with direct instruction, even using the imperative (the Sermon on the Mount is a good example). In parables, however, he used a different method of delivery, which left a great deal more space for imagination, fantasy, and personal creative interpretation. In the parables of Jesus, we see not only a teacher of morality, but a poet who envelops his thoughts in flexible and multifunctional poetic forms, which presuppose a multi-layered reception by means of the heart more than the head.

Let us also not forget a simple fact. Though we might encounter parables primarily in their written form, which we then read, study, and analyze, Jesus' listeners heard his living word, with all its characteristic dynamism, typical of the spoken word and of interpersonal dialogue.[19] It is inevitable that as soon as parables are bound by the page, they lose those elements that the listeners would have caught, including the intonation of the Storyteller, his gestures, the emotional content of his delivery, the expression of his face and eyes.[20] Further, some aspects of his native speech would have been lost in translation from Aramaic to Greek,[21] and the same is true in every subsequent translation from Greek to other languages.

Nevertheless, in spite of the fact that in some sense every parable of Jesus that we read today in our own language is a reconstruction of what he said originally to his listeners, we still hear his living voice in the written text of these parables. And the written text resurrects before our eyes the image of the One who not only brought mankind the good news of the kingdom of God, but had the power to invest that news in vivid and memorable imagery.[22]

The parable is a bearer of important theological truths, and these truths are expressed not through precise definitions, but through metaphor:

> Jesus was a *metaphorical* theologian. That is, his primary method of creating meaning was through metaphor, simile, parable and dramatic action rather than through logic and reasoning. He created meaning like a dramatist and a poet rather than like a philosopher.... A metaphor communicates in ways that rational arguments cannot.... A metaphor, however, is *not* an illustration of an idea; it is a mode of theological discourse. The metaphor does more than explain meaning, it creates meaning. *A parable is an extended metaphor* and as such it

[19]John R. Donahue, *The Gospel in Parable* (Minneapolis: Fortress Press, 1988), 3.

[20]Richard Lischer, *Reading the Parables* (Louisville, KY: Westminster John Knox Press, 2014), 7–8.

[21]Jeremias, *Parables*, 25–26.

[22]David Wenham, *The Parables of Jesus* (Downers Growe, IL: InterVarsity Press, 1989), 13.

is *not a delivery system for an idea* but a house in which the reader/listener is invited to take up residence.[23]

The parable has a certain similarity to a fable or fairy tale. Like the fable, it is built on metaphor, and in some cases ends with a direct indication of how the metaphor relates to reality. Like a fairy tale, the parable does not pretend to be realistic and can contain various fantastical details or even end earlier than the listener might like. Having listened to a fable or a fairy tale, children will sometimes ask, "What happens next?" Adults might think this an inappropriate question, even a comical one, but this is only because they understand the rules of the genre.

The parable genre also has its own rules. One of these is that not all the details of the telling have equal significance and not every detail requires interpretation. John Chrysostom wrote that one should not pay attention to everything in a given parable.[24] A modern scholar writes: "Parable and reality are not connected with equal signs. Parables are not direct pictures of reality and do not claim to portray life as it should be. They only partially map the realities they seek to reveal. . . . We will never understand the parables unless we are willing to focus on the function of analogy."[25]

In other words, in every parable there are details that have functional importance, but there can be elements that have no metaphorical function at all. Any questions regarding the meaning of this or that detail that is not important for the meaning of the parable are thus, in effect, as inappropriate as a child's question about the continuation of a fairy tale that has already ended.

We believe that the key to answering the question of why Jesus chose the form of the parable as the most important means of transmitting his teaching should be sought in juxtaposing his parables with his miracles. The connection between Jesus' words and actions are obvious. Moreover,

---

[23]Kenneth E. Bailey, *Jesus through Middle Eastern Eyes* (London: SPCK, 2008), 279–80. Cf. also Kenneth E. Bailey, *Finding the Lost: Cultural Keys to Luke 15* (St Louis, MO: Concordia Publishing House, 1992), 15–22.

[24]John Chrysostom, *Homilies on Matthew* 64.3 (NPNF[1] 10:393–94).

[25]Klyne R. Snodgrass, *Stories with Intent: A Comprehensive Guide to the Parables of Jesus*, 2nd ed. (Grand Rapids, MI: William B. Eerdmans Publishing Co., 2018).

the majority of his actions as written down by the evangelists are miracles. We can say that the miracle was the most important means for Jesus' expressing himself *through action* as the Son of God, sent into the world by the Father. In just the same way, the parable was the most important means by which the Son of God expressed himself *through word*, transmitting to his listeners the good news that he was sent to announce.

People did not react to Jesus' miracles passively. Very often, as Jesus performed the miracle, he not only insisted on the faith of the one being healed, but even made faith the one condition for performing the miracle. Often a healing, though it was Jesus' action, needed to be accompanied by concrete actions on the part of the one being healed as well. For example, Jesus said, "Stretch forth thine hand" (Mt 12.13; Mk 3.5; Lk 6.19), "Arise, take up thy bed, and go unto thine house" (Mt 9.6; Mk 2.11; Lk 5.24). On the other hand, his miracles also inspired a *reaction* in those who were irritated and repulsed by his entire ministry. The miracle, in this case, is a challenge for both sides—the former through their active cooperation received healing, while the latter through their active opposition received eternal damnation.

In the same way, each parable is also a challenge to the listeners. A parable is a "realistic fiction,"[26] an earthly story with heavenly meaning,[27] "a genre that is designed to surprise, challenge, shake up, or indict."[28] As with many other texts of the Holy Scriptures, parables simultaneously "inspire and challenge; they both comfort and accuse. They are a two-edged sword."[29]

Though narrative in form, the parable is allegorical in content.[30] Its purpose is to transform the listener from a passive recipient of the good news into an active disciple of the One who brought the good news. It requires the personal, intellectual, and spiritual endeavors of those who

---

[26]John S. Kloppenborg, *The Tenants in the Vineyard* (Tübingen: Mohr Siebeck, 2010), 51.

[27]Peter Rhea Jones, *The Teaching of the Parables* (Nashville, TN: Baptist Sunday School Board, 1984), 131.

[28]Amy-Jill Levine, *Short Stories by Jesus* (New York: HarperOne, 2014) 3–4.

[29]Jan Lambrecht, S. J., *Out of the Treasure* (Leuven: Peeters Press, 1991), 195.

[30]Mark L. Bailey, "Guidelines for Interpreting Jesus' Parables," *Bibliotheca Sacra* 155:617 (1998): 29–38, at 30.

listen, personal labor to parse out its meaning, and only then it provokes the active working of the mind.[31] Every person must accept the parable in his own way. It seems that this is exactly why Jesus spoke in parables in the first place.

Jesus' choice to use parables as the primary mode of transmitting the good news he wanted to announce to the world is also connected with the inherent potential of this genre, which differentiates it from realistic narrative forms. In the Old Testament, God spoke with his people in the language of command, expressed in a strictly imperative mood, often accompanied with threats of punishments for disobedience. But in the New Testament, God speaks with his people in a different language. He no longer commands, respecting the free choice of every individual person. A contemporary Orthodox theologian wrote the following:

> The parable genre has the ability to encompass a wide swath of listeners, from simple fishermen to philosophers, subtle in thought. Every one of these can find something consonant with his own interests in a parable, and so the parable must have several layers of interpretation. The same words can transmit different degrees of truth. . . . In parables . . . the truth is not imposed. . . . Parables are the only means of reaching that profoundly personal depth of human consciousness that accepts neither coercion nor compulsion. . . . The living, never-ending dialogue of every parable with human consciousness allows it to move from a static form of communication to a dynamic, living cooperation through the characteristically unique aspect of its genre—a fluidity of interpretation that avoids direct and static meaning.[32]

Every parable offers a personal reading. Its meaning reveals itself to individual people based on their own life's circumstances, based on their life's unique context. Moreover, the meaning of the parable can be revealed

---

[31]C. H. Dodd, *The Parables of the Kingdom*, 16.

[32]Nikolai Sakharov, "Kratkii obzor metodiki sovremennogo tolkovaniya pritchei Khristovykh v sinopticheskikh Evangeliyakh" [A brief review of the methodology for the modern interpretation of the parables of Christ in the Synoptic Gospels], *Sbornik trudoe kafedry bibleistiki MDA* [Proceedings of the department of biblical studies of the Moscow Academy of Sciences] 1 (2013): 187–222, at 199, 207–209.

differently in each subsequent reading. This is true of individual people and entire generations. Based on the different levels of his own spiritual development, a person may understand the meaning of each parable differently. Entire groups of people may interpret their significance in a way based on their cultural context, the specific challenges of their time, and many other factors that affect interpretation.

It is exactly this fact that gives parables their unique quality of never growing old. Though they were initially addressed to a specific group of people, who lived in a specific historical period, the parables of Jesus remain significant for all subsequent generations. Every new age finds new approaches to the parables, new methods of interpretation. But everywhere and in all times, a universal principle remains constant: when attempting to understand the meaning of the parable, the reader or listener, willingly or unwillingly, applies its story to his own life's situation, just as King David should have done after the prophet Nathan told him the story of the sheep.

Jesus himself applied the historically specific words of Isaiah to those who listened to his parables. John the evangelist also quotes Isaiah when speaking of the reactions of Jesus' opponents to his miracles:

> But though he had done so many miracles before them, yet they believed not on him, that the saying of Isaiah the prophet might be fulfilled, which he spake, "Lord, who hath believed our report? And to whom hath the arm of the Lord been revealed?" Therefore they could not believe, because that Isaiah said again, "He hath blinded their eyes, and hardened their heart, that they should not see with their eyes, nor understand with their heart, and be converted, and I should heal them." These things said Isaiah, when he saw his glory, and spake of him. (Jn 12.37–41)

This passage gives additional confirmation of the close connection not only between Jesus' miracles and parables, but also between his listeners' reactions to both.

In their content, form, style, and action, parables are similar to prophecies. Many prophecies were predictions of coming events; parables are

The Evangelist Matthew and an Angel, Rembrandt, 1661

also. Prophets used the rich language of imagery, symbolism, and metaphor; parables use a similar language. Prophecies were intended to last for many centuries, their primary purpose lay in the fact that they would be fulfilled at some point, but fulfilled not necessarily only once, but many times, differently in different times. The Gospels are filled with references to prophecies that were fulfilled during the life and ministry of Jesus. Parables are also intended for a long life, for centuries in fact, and they also were fulfilled, that is, they proved their significance and relevance in different stages of humanity's history, as well as in the fates of individual people.

Every time a reader or listener sees himself in one of the characters of a parable, or his life's situation in the events of the story, or his own problem of communion with God or man in the problem described in the parable, the parable is, in effect, fulfilled like a prophecy. Every time a particular nation or generation act in a way that leads to consequences that are specifically described in a parable, that parable is fulfilled.

Jesus' own disciples saw his speaking in parables as a fulfillment of Old Testament prophecies. Jesus' teaching from the boat—the first collection of parables in the Gospel of Matthew—concludes with these words: "All these things spake Jesus unto the multitudes in parables; and without a parable spake he not unto them, that it might be fulfilled which was spoken by the prophet, saying, 'I will open my mouth in parables; I will utter things which have been kept secret [*kekrymmena*] from the foundation [*apo kataboles*] of the world'" (Mt 13.34–35). These words are a paraphrase of the second verse of Psalm 77 (LXX). In the Septuagint, the first half of the verse corresponds exactly with Matthew's version, and the second half is close in meaning: "I will open my mouth in parables; I will utter dark sayings [*problēmata*, lit. 'guesses' or 'riddles'] of old [*ap' archēs*]."

Every parable was simultaneously a riddle to be guessed and a problem to be worked out for the disciples. Parables remain so to this day for all who try to understand their meaning. The results of this process will depend greatly on the hermeneutical method used to explain the parable. Throughout history, there have been many such hermeneutic keys to unlock meaning. And still, every person must seek his own key, his own approach to the parable. We will speak more about this later in the section dedicated to the interpretation of parables.

3. The Parables of Jesus: Classification

The parables of Jesus that appear in the synoptic Gospels can be classified in various ways, including 1) by their length, 2) by their presence in one, two, or three of the Gospels, 3) by the presence or absence of interpretation within the text, 4) by the time and place of the parable's telling, 5) by its content.

Classification by Length

Some parables are lengthy stories in which several characters take part in events that unfold over a period of time. Among these we have the parable of the prodigal son (Lk 15.11–32). In this parable, we have three main characters (the father, the younger son, the elder son), and the action takes place over the course of many years (the story begins with a description of the youth of the younger son, his departure into a distant country, his time there, his return, and his reconciliation with his father). In the parable of the rich man and Lazarus (Lk 16.19–31), there are two characters, as well as some side characters (the dogs, the angels in heaven, the five brothers of the rich man mentioned in passing). The action begins on earth, and ends in the world beyond the grave. These parables are like visual compositions with different events occurring at different times but depicted together, such as can often be found in an icon.

On the opposite side of the spectrum, we have parables that last a single sentence and have a single image: the woman who puts leaven in

Origen

dough (Mt 13.33), the merchant who finds a precious pearl (Mt 13.45–36), the net cast into the sea (Mt 13.47–48). But even in these short parables, there are additional images that serve as foils to the main image (for example, the riches that the merchant must barter off to purchase the pearl, the fish caught by the net that are then sorted by quality). Such parables remind one of a picture with a single subject, in the center of which there is one character that is performing a particular action.

Such a classification by length was attempted even in the early Church. When examining the parables that Jesus spoke from the boat (Mt 13.1–33), Origen wrote that only the first two (the parables of the sower and of the tares) can be properly considered parables, since the next two that follow are not parables, but similes (*ou parabolas all' homoioseis*). Origen makes this distinction between a parable as a fully-fledged story and a simile as a short metaphorical saying, intended to direct the gaze to the kingdom of heaven, based on Jesus' own words: "Whereunto shall we liken (*homoiōsōmen*) the kingdom of God? Or with what comparison (*en tini parabolē*) shall we compare it?" (Mk 4.30). According to Origen, this makes it clear that there is a distinction between a simile and a parable. At the same time, Origen also admits that "simile" may be a generic term, while "parable" may be a more specific concept.

Classification by Inclusion in One, Two, or Three Synoptic Gospels

Each of the three synoptic evangelists used his own collection of parables, and each intersects only partially with the collections of the others. The following chart shows how all the parables are distributed throughout the three synoptic Gospels:

Parables	Matthew	Mark	Luke
Parables in Three Gospels			
The sower	13.1–9	4.1–9	8.4–8
The mustard seed	13.31–32	4.30–34	13.18–19
The wicked tenants	21.33–46	12.1–12	20.9–18
Parables in Two Gospels			
The houses on rock and sand	7.24–29		6.6–11
The leaven	13.33–35		13.20–21
The lost sheep	18.12–14		15.3–7
The wise steward	24.45–51		12.41–48
Parables in One Gospel			
The children in the street	7.31–35		
The wheat and the tares	13.24–30		
The treasure in a field	13.44		
The pearl of great price	13.45–46		
The net	13.47–50		
The unmerciful servant	18.23–35		
The laborers in the vineyard	20.1–16		
The two sons	21.28–32		
The wedding feast	21.28–32		
The ten virgins	25.1–13		
The talents and the minas	25.14–30		
The sowing and growth		4.26–27	
Awaiting the master of the house		13.32–37	
The two debtors			7.36–50
The good Samaritan			10.25–37
The friend at midnight			11.5–13
The rich fool			12.13–21
The watchful servants			12.35–40
The barren fig tree			13.6–9
The wedding feast			14.15–24

The tower builder	14.28–30
The king preparing for war	14.31–32
The lost coin	15.8–10
The prodigal son	15.11–32
The unjust steward	16.1–13
The rich man and Lazarus	16.19–31
The unprofitable servants	17.7–10
The persistent widow	18.1–8
The publican and Pharisee	18.9–14
The talents and minas	19.11–27

As this chart makes clear, the greatest number of parables is found in Matthew and Luke.

Sometimes parables are appended to a larger narrative, and sometimes they are given as separate blocks. For example, chapter thirteen of the Gospel of Matthew has a series of seven parables. Of them, two contain the most detailed interpretation given by Jesus himself, after his disciples' request. One, less expansive, includes an interpretation, and four of the shortest are left without any interpretation in the text. We find a similar series in chapter four of the Gospel of Mark. Luke also has several series of parables, included in chapters fifteen, sixteen, and eighteen.

The inclusion of the same parable in more than one synoptic Gospel is usually explained in the following ways: 1) the evangelists are telling the same parable that they both took from a single source (either oral or written), or from various versions of a single primary source, 2) Jesus repeated his parables in different situations, sometimes verbatim, sometimes with some important divergences. As one scholar notes, "It is important to realize that Jesus told his parables many times. It is impossible to imagine that an itinerant teacher like Jesus would use good stories like the prodigal son or the good Samaritan only once."[33] Or as another scholar says, "The fact that Jesus was an itinerant prophet meant, clearly, that he went from village to village, saying substantially the same things wherever he went. Local

[33]Marcus Borg, *Jesus: Uncovering the Life, Teachings, and Relevance of a Religious Revolutionary* (San Francisco: HarperSanFrancisco, 2006).

variations would no doubt abound. Novelty would spring up in response to a new situation, or a sharp question or challenge. But the historical likelihood—and it is very likely indeed—is that if he told a parable once he told it dozens of times, probably with minor variations."[34]

In certain cases, it seems obvious enough that it is the same parable recounted in several different Gospels (for example, the parable of the sower and the mustard seed, present in all three synoptic Gospels). But in other cases it seems more likely that we are encountering two different parables with a similar story structure, told by Jesus in two different situations and contexts (for example, the parable of the wedding feast in Matthew 22.1–14 and the parable of those called to the wedding in Luke 14.15–24, or the parable of the talents in Matthew 25.14–30 and the parable of the ten minas in Luke 19.11–27). As we examine individual parables that are included in more than one Gospel, we will indicate the various degrees of similarity they share.

Classification Based on the Presence or Absence of Interpretation in the Text

All the parables of Jesus can be conditionally divided into two major categories: those that he himself interpreted, and those that remain without his personal interpretation. Those parables that Jesus himself explained in answer to his disciples' request give us a hermeneutic key to understanding all other parables, because they show us how various symbols and images correspond to reality in his own understanding. This does not mean, however, that all the parables can be interpreted with the same template. What it does mean is that Jesus did not leave his disciples and followers in complete ignorance concerning the proper manner of understanding and interpreting his parables. His own interpretations contain hints for other interpreters, and his personal method of interpretation should be taken as foundational for everyone, whether a priest in church or a scholar at his desk, who desires to approach as close as possible to the meaning that Jesus himself placed in his parables.

[34]Wright, *Jesus and the Victory of God*, 170.

In contemporary New Testament scholarship, the leading point of view is that the interpretations of parables contained within the text of the synoptic Gospels belong not to Jesus, but to some subsequent editor of the text. It was these imaginary editors who decided to give an allegorical tone to the interpretation of the parables, which then became widespread in the early Church. According to this point of view, Jesus never interpreted his own parables because such an interpretation would have contradicted his own original intention to hide the meaning of the parables in a series of images and metaphors. To create a parable and then to immediately interpret it, they argue, is the same as devising a crossword, then immediately publishing the answers in the same page of the newspaper or magazine where it was printed. This point of view was widely supported in the twentieth-century vanguard of New Testament scholarship.[35]

Scholars who prefer the method of formal analysis (including Bultmann), considered it necessary to first place every utterance of Jesus into a specific category or genre (parable, proverb, story, etc.), and subsequently to assign to each genre a specially designed procedural template. Moreover, such scholars considered it necessary first to determine the *Sitz im Leben* of each parable (literally, "place in life")—that is, that specific life situation in which the early Church may have found this parable useful. If the life situation was found to be applicable to Jesus' own life and time, then the meaning of the parable could be ascribed directly to him (in cases where he himself interpreted the parable). Moreover, it was assumed that the received text of the parable in any case was the work of later editors, even if they shared Jesus' interpretive hermeneutic.[36]

For such scholars, one of the criteria for the authenticity of Jesus' interpretations was the closeness of the style of each particular parable to Semitic language and thought processes. These scholars thought that the lack of such closeness reduced the likelihood that a saying ascribed to Jesus could actually have come from him. Such an approach even led them

---

[35]Cf. Jeremias, *Parables*, 77–79, 81–85; Scott, *Hear Then*, 343–52; Robert Walter Funk, Bernard Brandon Scott, and James R. Butts, *The Parables of Jesus* (Sonoma, CA: Polebridge Press, 1988), 59, 65.

[36]Cf. Blomberg, *Interpreting the Parables*, 83–86.

to ascribe the interpretation of the parable of the sower (Mt 4.13–20) to a later editor, while the parable itself was ascribed to Jesus.[37]

We reject this point of view for at least two reasons.

First of all, such a view is based on the assumption that the text of the Gospel itself is not authentic, that the direct speech of Jesus as written down by the evangelists could in fact be ascribed to the evangelists themselves. Such an approach makes meaningless any attempt to interpret the text of the Gospel as it has come down to us, proposing instead to muse on its hypothetical prototype. Any attempts to single out the authentic center of such a text through first disassembling and fragmenting it are highly arbitrary and prone to bias. Either the text must be examined in the form in which we receive it (without ignoring possible variants in manuscripts), or the scholar will not be able to avoid a vicious circle of guesses and assumptions concerning the possible inauthenticity of each part of the text, and each saying of Jesus. At that point, one no longer studies the text, but some kind of invented prototype of the text.

Second, this point of view is contrary to the character of the interaction between Jesus and his disciples as described in the pages of the Gospels. Jesus chose the twelve apostles as a special group of intimate people to whom he revealed what remained hidden to others. He constantly reminded them of their special calling, including the already quoted passage: "It is given unto you to know the mysteries of the kingdom of heaven, but to them it is not given" (Mt 13.11); "Unto you it is given to know the mystery of the kingdom of God, but unto them that are without, all these things are done in parables" (Mk 4.11). The logical consequence of any rejection of the authenticity of Jesus' own interpretations must be also a rejection of the authenticity of the words here quoted, as well as the entire manner of interaction between Jesus and his disciples, which is so clearly reflected in the Gospel. This interaction was built on an opposition between "you and them," between "you and those outside." Within this given opposition, the disciples find themselves in a privileged position. They receive the answers to the crossword puzzle

---

[37]Jeremias, *Parables*, 77–79.

St John Chrysostom,
Mosaic, 9th century

from the Writer himself, because they would not have been able to figure it out themselves.

If Jesus, when he delivered the parables, had as his primary goal the concealment of their meaning, that does not mean that this intention extended to all of his listeners without exception. What was given to some ("those outside") in a hidden or veiled manner, for others (the disciples) could have been given in a more obvious fashion. One style of speech does not contradict the other, just as the reason for speaking in parables in the first place does not contradict the point that the listeners' reactions could be wildly divergent, from a sincere desire to understand them and plumb the depths of their meaning to a complete rejection and a desire to put their fingers in their ears and shut their eyes, lest they hear and see. Jesus himself predicted this wide range of reactions when he told his apostles that they were given to know the mysteries of the kingdom of God, while others were not.

He accompanied his own words with an aphorism that he also used in other situations: "For whosoever hath, to him shall be given, and he shall have more abundance, but whosoever hath not, from him shall be taken away even what he hath" (Mt 13.12, 25.29; Mk 4.25; Lk 8.18, 19.26). This aphorism should be understood not as an indication that God is unfair for giving something to one and taking it away from another, but rather as an explanation of how different people react to the actions of God. John Chrysostom explains:

> And although the saying be full of much obscurity, yet it indicates unspeakable justice. For what he says is like this: When any one has forwardness and zeal, there shall be given unto him all things on God's part also: but if he be void of these, and contribute not his own share, neither are God's gifts bestowed. For even what he seems to have, so he says, shall be taken away from him; God not so much taking it away, as counting him unworthy of his gifts. This we also do; when we see

any one listening carelessly, and when with much entreaty we cannot persuade him to attend, it remains for us to be silent. For if we are still to go on, his carelessness is aggravated. But him that is striving to learn, we lead on, and pour in much.[38]

Classification according to the Time and Place of the Parable's Telling

If we read the synoptic Gospels, we can conclude that Jesus spoke the parables during the entirety of his public ministry. Based on the time and place of the telling, we can divide Jesus' parables into three groups: those told in Galilee in the early days of his ministry, those told on the way to Jerusalem, and those told in Jerusalem not long before his suffering and death. These latter parables differ significantly from the former not only in theme, but also in their general tone.

In the Galilean parables, most of the stories are light, joyful, positive, filled with inspiring images: the sower generously sows his seeds not even thinking about what sort of soil they would land on (Mt 13.3–5); an entire tree grows from a tiny mustard seed, and birds come to take shelter in its branches (Mt 13.31–32); a man finds a treasure in a field and from the joy of finding it alone sells everything to buy that field (Mt 13.44); a merchant finds a pearl of great price (Mt 13.45); a man throws a seed into the earth, and it first grows a blade, then an ear, then the full grain in the ear, then finally the fruit (Mk 4.26–29); a man goes out to find his lost sheep, and, finding it, rejoices over it more than the ninety-nine he never lost (Mt 18.13); a good Samaritan finds a person who was attacked by robbers, tends his wounds, takes him to an inn, and pays the innkeeper for his keeping (Lk 10.33–35); a generous master opens his home for the poor, halt, maimed, and blind (Lk 14.21); a woman who lost her coin finds it, and then gathers her neighbors and says, "Rejoice with me, I have found my lost coin!" (Lk 15.8–9); a merciful father joyfully meets his prodigal son after that son's long journey through foreign lands, and even orders a feast in his honor with singing and merrymaking (Lk 15.20–25).

---

[38]John Chrysostom, *Homilies on the Gospel of Matthew* 45.1 (NPNF[1] 10:285).

The closer he came to Jerusalem, the more the tone of Jesus' parables changed, and became more and more filled with darker imagery and
themes of punishment, revenge, and judgment: the unmerciful rich man
who finds himself in hell begs Abraham to send him Lazarus with a bit
of water to cool his burning tongue, then asks him at least to be sent to
his brothers, who remained alive, but all of his requests were denied (Lk
16.22–31); a slave who received a single mina from his master kept it in a
handkerchief, and for this reason he was deprived of all he had, while he
is forced to watch as the enemies of the master are beaten in front of him
(Lk 19.20–27).

In the parables and teachings given in the temple of Jerusalem, the
theme of reprisal and judgment become dominant: the man who comes
to the feast in the wrong clothing is thrown into a pit outside, where there
is weeping and gnashing of teeth (Mt 22.11–14); the wicked tenants kill
at first the servants of their master, then his son, and finally the master
himself comes and kills the workers (Mt 21.35–41; Mk 12.1–9; Lk 20.9–16);
the doors are shut in the faces of the foolish virgins, and though they try
to get in, the master of the wedding feast rejects them (Mt 25.10–12); the
Son of Man finally divides the sheep from the goats and sends the latter
into eternal suffering (Mt 25.32–36).

The tone of the parables changes gradually—there is no sharp transition from major to minor keys, but gradual developments of the theme,
which generally fits the overall dynamics of the Gospels themselves. Each
of the four Gospels follows a similar dramatic arc. All four begin with joy
and triumph (whether they begin with the birth of Jesus as in Matthew
and Luke, the account of the baptism of Jesus and the beginning of his
ministry as in Mark, or John's exalted and hymn-like announcement that
the Word of God appeared in the world as light, which the darkness could
not comprehend). After this beginning a middle section follows, in which
we see a developing story of the battle of evil against good, especially the
continual battles of the scribes and Pharisees against Jesus. This struggle
led to Jesus' apparent defeat, his trial, and his suffering and death on the
cross. But in the final act of the drama, the defeat unexpectedly becomes
a victory: death is defeated by resurrection.

The southern
steps of the
Temple Mount,
Jerusalem

There are no parables in the beginning chapters of the Gospels, neither are there any in the account of Jesus' passion and the resurrection. In the central part of the three synoptic Gospels, however, the parables take center stage, along with the miracles, and their own thematic tone develops along with the dramatic arc of the narrative of the Gospel, inexorably leading the reader to the tragic final act of the conflict between Jesus and the Jews.

By place and time, the parables are divided in the following manner in the synoptic Gospels:

Parables	Matthew	Mark	Luke
Parables told in Galilee			
The houses on rock and sand	7.24–29		6.6–11
The children in the street			7.31–35
The wheat and the tares	13.24–30		
The sower	13.1–9	4.1–9	8.4–8
The mustard seed	13.31–32	4.30–34	13.18–19
The leaven	13.33–35		13.20–21
The treasure in a field	13.44		
The pearl of great price	13.45–46		
The net	13.47–50		
The sowing and growth		4.26–27	
The two debtors			7.36–50

Classification by content

Classifying the parables by their content is the most difficult task for the scholar. A. Hultgren, who wrote one of the most recent studies of the parables, divides them thematically into the following categories:

1) Parables concerning divine revelation
2) Parables concerning virtuous behavior
3) Parables concerning wisdom
4) Parables concerning the life in God
5) Parables concerning the final judgment
6) Allegorical parables
7) Parables of the kingdom[39]

Other scholars limit their categories to smaller numbers (such as four).[40] Among the most common thematic categories, the following are frequently used:

1) Parables of the kingdom of God
2) Parables of God and his relationship to man
3) Parables of human relations and interactions
4) Parables of the Messiah and the chosen people
5) Parables of life after death

In some ways, all the parables can be assigned to more than one category, and sometimes several simultaneously. At the same time, any attempts to classify parables by their content are prone to criticism because only the shortest parables have a single image and, consequently, a single theme. There are parables with two or three main themes. There are parables with a single major theme, but several minor ones. Consequently, Craig Blomberg offers the following categories:

1) Simple parables with three major themes

---

[39]Hultgren, *Parables*, 20–423.

[40]Hunter, *Interpreting the Parables*, 42–91; Madeleine I. Boucher, *The Parables*, 69–160; Robert H. Stein, *An Introduction to the Parables of Jesus* (Philadelphia: The Westminster Press, 1981), 82–145.

2) Complex parables with three major themes

3) Parables with two major themes

4) Parables with a single major theme[41]

Such a way of classifying the parables is extremely limited, however, since different scholars determine the number of themes differently. In a single parable, one scholar might see only a single theme, while another might see two or more.

---

4. The Parables of Jesus: Primary Structural Elements

The first structural element of parables is the image. Every parable must contain within itself at least one primary image, around which the secondary images gather. In the four parables that Jesus spoke from the boat, as recounted in the Gospel of Matthew (13.1–33), the primary images are seeds in the first two parables, the mustard seed in the third, and the leaven in the fourth. Surrounding the image of the seed in the first parable, we find the secondary images of the sower, four kinds of soil, birds, and thorns. In the second, we find the man who planted the seed in the earth, his enemy who planted tares among the wheat, the plants, the fruits, the slaves, the shearers, the reapers, and the granaries. In the third, the secondary images of the sower, the tree, and birds that hide in the tree are all dependent on the primary image. In the fourth parable, the secondary role is filled by the images of the woman who put the leaven into the flour and the rising dough.

With that said, it is not always easy to determine which image is primary and which is secondary. Who is more important in the parable of the sower—the sower himself or the seed? If we follow Jesus' own interpretation, the main image is the seed, since it symbolizes the word of God, while

---

[41]Blomberg, *Interpreting the Parables*, 197–406.

the four kinds of soil symbolize different people's reactions to the word. If we examine the parable through a christological lens, however (that is, with reference to the activity and ministry of Jesus himself), then doubtless the image of the sower is more important. If the sower is indeed God who "maketh his sun rise on the evil and on the good, and sendeth rain on the just and on the unjust" (Mt 5.45), then the central image is again the sower who generously casts his seed without prejudice regarding the kind of soil it falls into. Thus, the importance of the images can depend a great deal on the interpretation and the point of view with which one examines any particular parable or image.

The Evangelist Luke,
Miniature, 1609

In some parables, there are obviously two or even three primary images. Thus, in the parable of the prodigal son, there are three (Lk 15.11–32): the father, the elder brother, and the younger brother. In the parables of the rich man and Lazarus (Lk 16.19–31), the unjust judge and the persistent widow (Lk 18.1–8), the publican and the Pharisee (Lk 18.9–14), there are two. In the parable of the two sons (Mt 21.28–32), in spite of the presence of the father, the main characters are the sons; the father is there only to fill a secondary role. In the parable of the ten virgins (Mt 25:1–13), we see two main images, both of them collective: the five wise and the five foolish virgins. As for the bridegroom, he is either a secondary character or a primary character, depending on the emphasis of the interpretation, whether the point of the parable is considered primarily as the difference between the two types of virgins or as the reaction of the bridegroom to the actions of the virgins.

Parables that have a single primary image usually develop that image in great detail. The mustard seed, for example, turns not into some generic tree, but into a tree with branches that become a shelter for birds (Mt 13.32). The leaven is not simply placed into dough, but into "three measures of wheat" (Mt 13.33). The treasure is not found just anywhere, but rather it is hidden in a field; that is, one cannot find it unless one buys

The Bosom of Abraham,
Miniature, 1397

the whole field, and to buy the field, one must part with all one's possessions (Mt 13.44). Having cast the seed upon the ground, the man does not simply continue with his work; rather, he "should sleep, and rise night and day, and the seed should spring and grow up, he knoweth not how." Then the land does not simply produce the fruit, but it "bringeth forth fruit of herself; first the blade, then the ear, after that the full corn in the ear" (Mk 4.27–28). The king who goes to war does not simply do a risk assessment; he must sit down with his counselors to determine "whether he be able with ten thousand to meet him that cometh against him with twenty thousand" (Lk 14.31–32), and if he is not strong enough, he must send an embassy to his adversary to sue for peace.

Parables with two main images often use contrast to play the two images against each other. For example, the publican is opposed to the Pharisee, the poor man to the rich, the son who fulfilled his father's will to the one who did not, the wise virgins to the foolish, the merciful king to the merciless slave (Mt 18.23–30).

This principle of contrasting two opposed images is most appropriate in situations where the Teller wishes to surprise his listeners. Thus, for example, in the parable of the rich man and Lazarus, Jesus first describes the rich man in vivid detail, using all possible earthly goods to describe his life of luxury; then he spares no details in describing the poor man who lies in rags at the gates of the rich man. Such a situation would have been easily recognizable to Jesus' listeners; in fact, it is possible that Jesus had a specific model in mind when describing these two men. The ultimate fate of both is unknown to the listeners, however, and here is where they are to be greatly surprised. It turns out it is not the rich man who comes to the bosom of Abraham, but Lazarus; it is revealed that the rich man's sufferings in hell are implacable, and no miracle can save his brothers who refuse to listen to Moses and the prophets (Lk 16.19–31).

In parables with three or more characters, tension (or cooperation or antagonism) sometimes arises between one character and each of the others separately. In the parable of the talents (Mt 25.14–30), the lord first requires an account from the slave who acquired ten talents after receiving five. He ends by demanding an account of the slave who received only one talent, and here a conflict arises between master and slave.

Sometimes various characters enter the central relationship, as in the parable of the prodigal son (Lk 15.11–32). This parable has several storylines: the first, and most important, is the relationship of the father with the younger son, while the second is the way the older son relates to his father. In the process, we learn about the relationship between the elder and younger brothers as well. Tension arises between the younger son and the father, but also between the elder son and the father, as well as between the two brothers, the elder of whom does not even want to see the younger.

All the images used by Jesus in his parables are taken from everyday life and encompass various areas of human activity. He tells of kings and subjects, masters and slaves, rich men and paupers, parents and children, creditors and debtors, sowers and reapers, fishermen and their catch, the shepherd with his sheep. Different forms of currency are mentioned (talents, minas, drachmas), various kinds of plants and grains (fig trees, wheat, tares, and thorns), various animals (sheep, goats, swine), birds, and fish. The most significant images are taken from the realities of the Galilean village; more rarely, he uses images from city life.[42]

Using images familiar to his listeners, Jesus taught them to raise their minds from earthly realities to the reality that he called the Kingdom of Heaven or the Kingdom of God. For him, the presence of that reality in earthly life is evident—it invisibly fills human life, relationships, even objects and phenomena, giving meaning and justification to every aspect of human life.

For his listeners, however, this reality is far from evident. Their minds are chained to earthly objects in their original earthly meaning. Even the disciples are unable to understand fully the metaphorical language

[42]Scott, *Hear Then*, 79.

St Nikolai (Velimirovich)
of Zhicha and South
Canaan, PA

of Jesus. He calls them to avoid the leaven of the Pharisees, but they can only think of the fact that they forgot to bring bread (Mk 8.15–16). Sometimes he even spoke to his own disciples with the same words that he usually reserved for those outside: "Perceive ye not yet, neither understand? Have ye your heart yet hardened? Having eyes, see ye not? Having ears, hear ye not? And do ye not remember?" (Mk 8.17–18).

When considering why Jesus used images from the world of nature and human life, St Nikolai (Velimirovich) wrote:

Once a person has been inserted into this world, it is as though he is plunged into the sea of God's wisdom, expressed in the parables. But whoever looks at this wisdom with the eyes only, sees nothing except for the clothing that covers it. He sees the outer clothing of nature, but the spirit and the heart of nature he does not see. He hears and listens to nature, but all he can understand is nonsense voices, but nothing of meaning. It is not possible to see to the heart of nature with the eye, nor to understand its meaning with the ears. Spirit reveals spirit. Love senses love. . . . The world is a rich treasure trove of instructive parables, and whoever accepts it in this fashion and uses it thus will neither fall nor be ashamed. Even our Lord Jesus Christ himself used parables often in his instruction of people, that is, he used images from nature, from objects and events of this world. And often he used the simplest things and events to show just how nourishing is the seed and how profound the content in all of nature. . . . Christ, as though on purpose, chooses from this world the most mundane things to reveal to people the mystery of eternal life. After all, what can be more mundane than salt, leaven, a mustard seed, the sun, birds, grass, and the lilies of the field, the wheat and tares, the stones and sand? . . . For centuries, people looked at mundane realities similar to those described in the parables of the sower and the seed, of the wheat and the tares, of the talents, of the prodigal son, of the evil workers in the vineyard, but to none of them did the thought even occur that under the branches, so to speak, of these realities hides a seed that is so nourishing for the spirit of man. Only after the Lord himself spoke these parables and interpreted their meaning and showed them the seed did they begin to understand.[43]

The key to understanding the parables is faith. Again, this provides yet more similarity between the parable and the miracle. For all those whose heart is hard, who cannot see with their eyes nor hear with their ears, the meaning of the parable remains hidden. As the miracles of Jesus did not convince the scribes and Pharisees of the truth of his teaching, so also his teaching, expressed in parables, did not convince them that he is the Messiah, sent from God. But all who witnessed Jesus' miracles and heard his parables with faith came to an understanding of his messianic calling.

One of the most characteristic aspects of Jesus' speech was that he spoke "as one having authority, and not as the scribes" (Mt 7.29). Another no less characteristic aspect of his teaching was his ability to speak simply of complicated realities, to clothe truths difficult for the mind in simple images. Thus one may say that, in a sense, the parables at the same time both complicated and simplified understanding.

Some of Jesus' utterances, which were not simplified in the form of parables, seemed so beyond the generally accepted realities of earthly life that his listeners reacted in confusion and even anger, even those closest to him. For example, when Jesus said it would be easier for a camel to pass through the eye of a needle than for a rich man to enter the Kingdom of Heaven, his disciples "were exceedingly amazed, saying, 'Who then can be saved?'" (Mt 19.25). His words about divorce disturbed his listeners: "If the case of the man be so with his wife, it is not good to marry" (Mt 19.10). The Sermon on the Mount, with its direct calls to spiritual perfection may seem even today to be an impossible ideal, having nothing to do with real life. As for the reactions of the scribes and Pharisees to Jesus' teaching, it

---

[43]Nikolai (Velimirovich), *Tvoreniya* [Collected works], vol. 2 (Moscow, 2010), 325–27. Translated by DNK.

was sharply negative from the very beginning of his ministry until its end, growing ever more intense as time went by.

Parables did not give rise to such extreme reactions, because they gave more space in the soul and mind of the listeners (even the scribes and Pharisees) for self-reflection and analysis. As for those who were open to Jesus' preaching from the very beginning, whose hearts were like fruitful soil (Mt 13.8), every parable became a road sign to the Kingdom of Heaven, even if that kingdom was hidden behind images of earthly things.

It should be said that Jesus frequently used humor and irony in his parables as well.[44] There is a layer of subtle humor in the parable of the children playing in the streets (Mt 11.16–17). The hero of the parable of the unjust steward is a grotesque caricature, a swindler whose actions are described with a certain amount of sarcasm (Lk 16.1–8). There is also a humorous undertone in the descriptions of such characters as the judge in the parable of the persistent widow (Lk 18.2–5), or the man who did not want to get up from bed in the middle of the night to open the door for his friend (Lk 11.7). This man's actions must have "brought discreet smiles to all who heard the story because it was so true to life. Everyone was eager to hear how the story ended."[45]

A similar smile might have been inspired by the rich man who talked thus with himself: "What shall I do, because I have no room to bestow my fruits? . . . This will I do: I will pull down my barns, and build greater, and there will I bestow all my fruits and my goods. And I will say to my soul, 'Soul, thou hast much goods laid up for many years; take thine ease, eat, drink, and be merry'" (Lk 12.17–19).

Yet that smile would have immediately faded as the listeners heard the rest of the story, that is, God's words to the rich man, which appear suddenly in the story and completely change its tone.

[44]Richard Q. Ford, *The Parables of Jesus: Recovering the Art of Listening* (Minneapolis: Augsburg Fortress, 1997), 124–26.

[45]Simon J. Kistemaker, *The Parables: Understanding the Stories Jesus Told* (Grand Rapids, MI: Baker Academic, 2002), 149.

5. The Parables of Jesus: Methods of Interpretation

Those who listened to Jesus were people who lived in the same land, spoke the same language, were surrounded by the same objects, were familiar with the same holy books that he constantly cited. At the very least, the external aspects of the parables should have been completely understandable to them. Nevertheless, every person understood the internal content of the parables in his own way, or did not understand it at all. Judging by the words that we quoted in the previous section, Jesus himself did not intend that the instructions given in each parable would be universally and immediately understandable.

A metaphorical approach to interpreting the parables was offered by Jesus himself in those parables that he explained in detail for his disciples. In the parable of the sower, every detail is given an allegorical meaning. The sower is God or Jesus himself; the seed is the word of God; the birds are the devil; the stony ground is fruitlessness and inconstancy; the thorns are the cares of the world and riches; the good soil is a person's ability not only to hear and understand the word, but to bring forth fruit as well (Mt 13.19–23; Mk 4.14–20; Lk 8.11–15). In the parable of the tares, every detail is likewise given a clear metaphorical interpretation: "He that soweth the good seed is the Son of Man; the field is the world; the good seed are the children of the kingdom; but the tares are the children of the wicked one; the enemy that sowed them is the devil; the harvest is the end of the world; and the reapers are the angels" (Mt 13.37–39).

If interpreting Jesus' parables was no easy task even for his contemporaries, then the difficulty only becomes greater with each passing generation. The farther any generation is from the temporal and cultural context of Jesus' own life and times, the more variegated and allegorical the interpretations become. Even in the second century, Irenaeus of Lyons wrote that the parables allow for many possible interpretations.[46] As for the parable of the workers in the vineyard, Irenaeus himself interpreted it thus:

> Also by the parable of the workmen who were sent into the vineyard at different periods of the day, one and the same God is declared as having called some in the beginning, when the world was first created; but others afterwards, and others during the intermediate period, others after a long lapse of time, and others again in the end of time; so that there are many workmen in their generations, but only one householder who calls them together. For there is but one vineyard, since there is also but one righteousness, and one dispensator, for there is one Spirit of God who arranges all things; and in like manner is there one hire, for they all received a penny each man, having [stamped upon it] the royal image and superscription, the knowledge of the Son of God which is immortality. And therefore he began by giving the hire to those [who were engaged] last, because in the last times, when the Lord was revealed he presented himself to all [as their reward].[47]

In the third century, Origen (not without the influence of Philo of Alexandria) laid the foundation for a tradition of allegorical interpretation of the Gospel.[48] With reference to the parables, this tradition of interpretation held that it was possible to explain allegorically every single image, every single detail. If in Jesus' own interpretation of his parables a single image had a single meaning, in the allegorical tradition, a single image could have multiple meanings.

For example, when speaking of the treasure found in the field (Mt 13.44), Origen first insists that "the field, indeed, seems to me according to these things to be the Scripture, which was planted with what is manifest in the words of the history, and the law, and the prophets, and the rest of the thoughts," and the treasure hidden in the field is "the thoughts concealed

[46]Irenaeus, *Against Heresies* 2.27.3 (ANF 1:399).

[47]Irenaeus, *Against Heresies* 4.36.7 (ANF 1:518).

[48]See volume one of this work, Metropolitan Hilarion Alfeyev, *Jesus Christ, His Life and Teaching*, vol. 1, *The Beginning of the Gospel* (Yonkers, NY: St Vladimir's Seminary Press, 2018), 153–56.

and lying under that which is manifest, of wisdom hidden in a mystery." Later Origen says that the field can also signify Christ, and the treasure can be that which is hidden in Christ, for in him, according to Paul, "are hid all the treasures of wisdom and knowledge" (Col 2.3). A certain person who comes to the field "finds the treasure of wisdom whether in Christ or in the Scriptures. For, going round to visit the field and searching the Scriptures and seeking to understand the Christ, he finds the treasure in it; and, having found it, he hides it, thinking it is not without danger to reveal to everybody the secret meanings of the Scriptures." The purchase of the field is then interpreted as the Gentiles' acquisition of what had previously belonged to the Jews, for "when the man taught by Christ has bought the field . . . [it] is taken away from them and given to a nation bringing forth the fruits thereof (Mt 21.43), to him who in faith has bought the field, as the fruit of his having sold all that he had."[49]

In the fourth to fifth centuries, the allegorical method of interpreting the parables, many of which are clearly allegories in and of themselves, began to dominate in Christian exegesis. In this period, the tradition of allegorical interpretation continued in the writings of the Fathers of the Church in both West and East, but their respective schools of interpretation differed not only in the allegorical meaning offered, but in how much allegorical meaning was extracted from each parable.

The most allegorical interpretations were typical of the so-called Alexandrian school, represented by such fathers as Cyril of Alexandria (fifth century) and later Maximus the Confessor (seventh century), as well as other Byzantine authors who interpreted the Scriptures in a similar style.

Representatives of the so-called Antiochene school of interpretation showed a markedly more muted enthusiasm for allegory. The most famous of these, John Chrysostom, tried first of all to distill the most important moral lesson from each parable, and only drew upon allegory as an ancillary, helpful element, and even then not always. According to Chrysostom himself, it is not necessary to explain everything literally in a parable, but

---

[49]Origen, *Commentary on Matthew* 10.5–6 (ANF 9:416).

having come to understand the main point, it is best to pay attention to that and not delve any deeper into other possible interpretations.[50]

Chrysostom was no fan of excessive allegory in Origen's style; nevertheless, he was not opposed in principle to the allegorical method in and of itself. When it seemed justified to him, he also used allegorical interpretation.

As for Western fathers, many of them were interested in allegorical interpretation, including Ambrose of Milan, Hilary of Poitiers, and especially Augustine, who took many specific details from the interpretive tradition of Origen.[51]

Throughout the centuries, Christian commentators paid special attention to two major aspects of the interpretation of parables: the moral and the theological. In each parable, they examined a call to a particular virtue, such as mercy or compassion (e.g., the parable of the good Samaritan), concern for the poor (e.g., the parable of the rich man and Lazarus), constancy in prayer (e.g., the parable of the persistent widow), preparation for the dread judgment and the encounter with God (e.g., the parable of the ten virgins). In these same parables, they also examined warnings against vices that are the polar opposites of the already-examined virtues (indifference, inattention to the poor, inconstancy in prayer, lack of preparedness for death and judgment). In many parables, they examined implicit indications of God's attributes, such as his mercy to sinners (e.g., the parable of the prodigal son), his ability to forgive (e.g., the parable of the master and the debtor), his openness to people who are not part of the chosen people of God (e.g., the parable of those called to the feast).

In our own times, the interpretation of parables is the prerogative of two kinds of people: clergy of various Christian communities and scholars specializing in New Testament studies. Most passages read in services throughout the year include parables, and so preachers must again and again return to the interpretation of the parables, even when the content

[50]John Chrysostom, *Homilies on Matthew* 64 (NPNF[1] 10:280). Concerning Origen's interpretation, cf. Warren S. Kissinger, *The Parables of Jesus: A History of Interpretation and Bibliography* (Metuchen, NJ: Scarecrow Press, 1979), 12–18. Concerning the allegorical method, cf. Henri Crouzel, *Origène* (Paris: Lethielleux, 1985), 91–120.

[51]Concerning Augustine's interpretation of parables, cf. Kissinger, *Parables*, 18–27.

*St Augustine
teaches in Rome,*
Bennozzo
Gozzoli,
1464–1465

of a parable is well known to the congregation, or at least to those who have attended regularly and have heard the same texts read repeatedly over the course of many years. Such interpretations, as a rule, focus on theological or moral lessons. In addition, the preacher usually sets himself a goal to make the parable relevant to a contemporary listener, to bring out some key idea that, in his view, most answers the spiritual needs of his own parishioners.

As for the scholars of the New Testament, they have different goals entirely. For the last two centuries, many of them have been obsessed with the search for the "historical Jesus" and his *kerygma*, that is, his original teaching, and this has spilled over into their study of the parables. As a result, many scholars have rejected allegorical readings of the parables outright, not being interested in discerning any theological meaning that might connect the content of the parable with the life of the Christian community. In addition, they have developed various new methods of interpretation, each of which has its strengths and weaknesses.

The turning point in the history of scholarly research into the parables is generally considered to be the two-volume examination by the German scholar A. Jülicher, which was published in 1888–89 and marked a radical break from the Church's own interpretive tradition. Jülicher rejected even the possibility of an allegorical reading of parables, as well as the need to interpret them in the first place. According to him, the content of the parable is limited entirely to its literal meaning. Coming from an Aristotelian understanding of the difference between simile and metaphor,[52] Jülicher considered the parables to be elaborate similes through which the Lord told simple moral truths. As opposed to metaphors, such similes need no interpretation or any search for deeper or figurative meaning: it is enough only to know the historical context in which the parables were spoken.[53]

Jülicher's book came out in a time when the search for the "historical Jesus" led to the creation of an entire series of literary portraits of Jesus as a humanist, a preacher of "universal human values" and simple moral truths (among the scholars perpetuating this new image of Jesus were Schleiermacher, Hegel, Strauss, Renan, and Leo Tolstoy). In accordance with the spirit of the times, Jülicher gives a single simple meaning for each parable, which results in "bland generalizations in keeping with the old liberal view of the kingdom of God as being ushered in through the efforts of Christians. For example, the parable of the talents (Mt 25.14–30) commended faithfulness with everything entrusted to a person. The story of the unjust steward (Lk 16.1–13) encouraged the prudent use of the present to ensure a happy future. And the example of the rich man and Lazarus (Lk 16.19–31) illustrated the need to avoid a life of wanton wealth and pleasure."[54]

Jülicher's book inspired a flurry of criticism almost immediately after publication. The scholar was rebuked, in part, for analyzing Jesus' parables in the light of ancient Greek rhetoric, without fully appreciating the Hebrew tradition of allegorical interpretation. The English scholar William Sanday, one of the first to react to Jülicher's work, criticized him also for his desire to do away with allegory at any cost, for his interpretation of the parables

---

[52]See Aristotle, *Poetics* 1407a.—*Ed.*
[53]Jülicher, *Gleichnisreden* 1:169–171.
[54]Blomberg, *Interpreting the Parables*, 36–37.

out of the context of the Gospels, for an amateurish reference to the text, and for his inattention to the realities of the manuscript tradition.[55]

The narrow moralism of Jülicher and the fact that he transformed Jesus into an "apostle of progress,"[56] was further subjected to the criticism of Joachim Jeremias, who noted that Jesus was neither a simple preacher of progress, nor a "teacher of wisdom who inculcates moral precepts and a simplified theology by means of striking metaphors and stories."[57] A half-century after the publication of Jülicher's book, the attempt to make Jesus into a simple Jewish moralist-teacher was sharply attacked by the American scholar of parables Charles William Frederick Smith: "No one would crucify a teacher who told pleasant stories to enforce prudential morality."[58]

In spite of their own criticism of Jülicher's work, the most significant scholars of parables who wrote in the middle of the twentieth century—Dodd and Jeremias—followed him in rejecting the allegorical method of interpretation. They both saw the parables of Jesus as first of all belonging to the historical context of their telling, and they were willing to interpret them also in the light of Jesus' teaching concerning the kingdom of God. The former saw in Jesus' teachings a kind of "realized eschatology," while the latter saw his teaching as "eschatology in the process of being realized." As followers of the "redaction criticism,"[59] Dodd and Jeremias considered it possible to separate the allegorical overlay of the subsequent tradition of the Church from the presumed authentic core of Jesus' parables.

According to Dodd, to understand the meaning of the parables, it was first necessary to study the context in which they were spoken, to imagine the reaction of all those who heard them for the first time. The primary goal of the interpreter, he believed, was to find the proper context of the parable within the specific situation described in the Gospel, and from that to extract the proper meaning that would have been intended for those in

---

[55]William Sanday, *Essays in Biblical Criticism and Exegesis* (Sheffield: Sheffield University Press, 2001), 140, 147, 154.

[56]Jülicher, *Gleichnisreden*, 2:483.

[57]Jeremias, *Parables*, 19.

[58]Charles William Frederick Smith, *The Jesus of the Parables* (Philadelphia: The Westminster Press, 1948), 17.

[59]For more on this method, see Alfeyev, *Jesus Christ: His Life and Teaching*, 1:41–42.

that given situation. It is only a secondary task of the interpreter to consider the meaning of the parable for his own contemporaries.[60]

Dodd, following Jülicher, considered parables to be similes, though he did admit the possibility that the simile might be expanded into a more detailed narrative. He believed that in all types of parables "we have nothing but the elaboration of a single comparison, all the details being designed to set the situation or series of events in the clearest possible light, so as to catch the imagination." According to Dodd, "the typical parable, whether it be a simple metaphor, or a more elaborate similitude, or a full-length story, presents one single point of comparison. The details are not intended to have independent significance."[61]

Jeremias, for his part, insisted that "the parable is not an allegory, but a story drawn from life." In the father of the parable of the prodigal son, he saw not God, but an earthly father figure.[62] Nevertheless, he did admit the possibility that an earthly father could be an image of the heavenly Father and that the parable, in the final analysis, "describes with touching simplicity what God is like, his goodness, his grace, his boundless mercy, his abounding love."[63]

Subsequent scholarly works on the parables of Jesus developed several approaches, in some ways diametrically opposed to each other, in some ways complementary. Structural analysis of parables, which ignores their possible allegorical reading as well as the historical context of their telling, focused scholars' attention primarily on the internal structural elements of the parables or their various thematic elements or motifs, and how they acted in concert or opposition to each other. Such an analysis, which is based on a presupposition that the meaning of the text can be established in the collaboration between text and reader, assumed the possibility of a wide spectrum of meanings that depend entirely on the reader in each parable.[64]

---

[60]V. D. Doerksen, "The Interpretation of the Parables," *Grace Journal* 11 (Spring 1970): 3–20, at 11.

[61]Dodd, *Parables*, 7.

[62]Jeremias, *Parables*, 128.

[63]Ibid., 131.

[64]To read a survey of these new literary and hermeneutic methods of interpretations, see Blomberg, *Interpreting the Parables*, 151–96.

A significant amount of attention in modern scholarship is dedicated to the separation of "tradition" from "redaction," that is, separating whatever Jesus originally said from what the evangelists or even later editors might have added on their own. Very often the parables and other speeches ascribed to Jesus are rejected by such scholars as inauthentic, not belonging to Jesus at all, but to some hypothetical early Christian communities that ostensibly invented them and placed them in Jesus' mouth. To find their desired results, these scholars often start by tearing this or that parable out of its historical context entirely and putting it into another historical context that they themselves invented. Moreover, they then ignore the interpretations that appear in the very text of the Gospel, as well as those belonging to subsequent church tradition. Instead, they offer new interpretations that are based on apocrypha or simply on various inventions.

The American Biblical scholar Craig Evans convincingly criticizes all such so-called scholarship in his book *Fabricating Jesus: How Modern Scholars Distort the Gospels,* which is dedicated to debunking various pseudo-discoveries in modern New Testament scholarship. Writing about the tendency of certain scholars to examine the words of Jesus outside the narrative context given by the authors of the Gospels, Evans had this to say:

> The contexts found in the Gospels themselves, we are told, reflect early Christian beliefs and interests, not the actual contexts of the historical Jesus. What does this mean? . . . Some scholars assume that if there is a continuity between something attributed to Jesus and what the early church came to believe and emphasize, then Jesus' saying may not have originated with him but with the early church. . . . The problem with this approach is that Jesus becomes, as it were, a talking head—a "laconic sage" who uses terse, almost unfeeling language. Jesus begins to sound like a philosopher whose utterances are truisms and maxims. We are told that the contexts of Jesus' sayings supplied by the Evangelists are artificial, secondary, and misleading. At best, so goes the argument, we can only make educated guesses. And skeptical scholars are quick

to make educated guesses. Although almost two millennia removed, these scholars somehow think they are able to locate the original, non-Gospel contexts, and sometimes they just happen to be different from the contexts of the Gospels. . . . The net result is that Jesus' sayings lose what ancient context they have and become, in effect, skeletal sayings, sayings on which scholars may hang any likeness of Jesus they wish to fabricate. Without a context the free-floating sayings can mean virtually anything the interpreter wants to make of them.[65]

In our examination of the parables, we will mostly ignore this approach of New Testament scholarship, since the primary criterion for the decision to separate tradition from redaction is always based on the personal taste and opinions of the individual scholar. From our perspective, such an approach to the text of the Gospel has run its course and has been, for the most part, completely discredited, without having offered any solid results to the field of New Testament studies. A survey of the opinions of different scholars concerning the authenticity of any parable, or even some fragmentary portion of a parable, distracts from the content of the parable itself, and in no way aids our understanding of it. Our presumptive trust in the text of the Gospel itself, which we took as foundational in our examination of the life and teaching of Jesus, allows no such deconstruction of the Gospel text with the purpose of finding some fragment that may or may not shine a light on the "historical Jesus."

All the words of Jesus that are included in the canonical Gospels we assume to be authentic. Further, the words ascribed to Jesus in the non-canonical, apocryphal, or Gnostic literature, we reject as spurious. Among these, in part, are the parables that are included in the apocryphal "Gospel of Thomas,"[66] which scholars frequently examine together with the parables from Matthew, Mark, and Luke. Four parables in the "Gospel of Thomas" have no parallel in any canonical literature. One of them has

---

[65]Craig A. Evans, *Fabricating Jesus: How Modern Scholars Distort the Gospels* (Downers Grove, IL: InterVarsity Press, 2006), 123–24.

[66]The "Gospel of Thomas" is a literary work dated to the end of the first century or the beginning of the second. Fragments of this Greek text have been known since 1897, and a complete Coptic translation was found in 1945.

some superficial similarity to the parable of the net in Matthew,[67] while the three others have no similarity at all to the canonical parables.[68] They differ radically in content from the parables of the Gospels. The other ten parables from the "Gospel of Thomas" are nothing other than shortened or distorted versions of the parables from the synoptic Gospels.[69]

Scholarly interest in the "Gospel of Thomas" is largely founded on the brevity of the adages found in it. Scholars, taking for granted the notion that Jesus spoke in short, lapidary formulas that were later expanded and augmented by the authors of the four canonical Gospels, gave special attention to the "Gospel of Thomas" as a manuscript that might give them an opportunity to pontificate on the utterances of the so-called "historical Jesus,"[70] to shed light on the original, authentic words of Christ. The search for the so-called "Q source," which continued for most of the twentieth century, has often led scholars of the "Gospel of Thomas" to insist that this text was the closest to what they would have hoped to find in the "Q source."[71]

In fact, the "Gospel of Thomas" is actually nothing more than a cycle of Gnostic variations on the canonical text of the Gospel.[72] Because of this fact, we do not believe it proper even to consider the parables in this pseudo-Gospel in the same sentence as the parables from the canonical Gospels. Not only will referring to this manuscript not help us interpret the parables of Jesus, but it may even make their meaning more difficult to extract by giving them various Gnostic overtones that do not exist in the original text.

In recent decades, it has become popular in New Testament scholarship to place the parables within the context of an existing Jewish literary

[67] *Gospel of Thomas* 8.

[68] Ibid., 24, 101, and 102.

[69] For more on these parables, cf. Hultgren, *Parables*, 430–49.

[70] Mark Goodacre, *Thomas and the Gospels: The Making of an Apocryphal Text* (Grand Rapids, MI: Eerdmans Publishing Company, 2012), 1.

[71] Concerning the "Q source," see Alfeyev, *Jesus Christ: His Life and Teaching*, 1:61–63.

[72] Concerning the "Gospel of Thomas" as a Gnostic manuscript, see Hippolytus of Rome (3rd century) in his *Refutation of All Heresies* 5.2 (ANF 5:50), as well as Origen's *Homilies on Luke* 1.2 (Origen, *Homilies on Luke, Fragments on Luke*, trans. Joseph T. Lienhard, FOC 94 [Washington: The Catholic University of America Press, 1996], 5–6).

Hillel, Knesset menorah, Jerusalem

tradition, examining them in comparison with the parables of the rabbis.[73] Yet of the many rabbinical parables that have reached us, only one is ascribed to Hillel, who was a contemporary of Jesus, and even this parable's authenticity is not universally acknowledged.[74] Two more parables are ascribed to the schools of Hillel and another of Jesus' contemporaries, Rabbi Shammai.[75] All other rabbinic parables belong to a later period (there are around two thousand of them), dated to the third to fourth centuries and subsequent historical periods.[76] This point alone is enough, in our estimation, to consider these parables unable to shed much light on the parables of Christ.

Moreover, the parables of the rabbis often have as their goal the interpretation of a specific text of Holy Scripture. The parables of Jesus, on the contrary, are not at all directly connected to any texts of Hebrew Scripture. They are independent, short narratives that themselves require interpretation.

Finally, the so-called "parables" of the rabbis often include stories from the lives of famous rabbis that have no actual connection to the parable genre if one defines it strictly, as we have. As a rule, these are various curious stories that are more like anecdotes than parables. For example, in one of these "parables," Rabbi Eliezer was riding on a donkey and met a man with a very unpleasant and ugly face, who greeted him with the words: "Peace to you, teacher." Instead of an answer, the rabbi

[73]Cf. Brad H. Young, *Jesus and His Jewish Parables: Rediscovering the Roots of Jesus' Teaching* (New York: Paulist Press, 1989), 236–81; Vermes, *The Authentic Gospel*, 115–16; Brad H. Young, *Jesus the Jewish Theologian* (Grand Rapids, MI: Baker Academic, 1993), 129–94. Brad H. Young, *The Parables: Jewish Tradition and Christian Interpretation* (Grand Rapids, MI: Baker Academic, 2012), 3–38.

[74]Robert M. Johnston and Harvey K. McArthur, *They Also Taught in Parables: Rabbinic Parables from the First Centuries of the Christian Era* (Grand Rapids, MI: Zondervan, 1990), 90, 107.

[75]Ibid., 80.

[76]Craig A. Evans, *Jesus and His Contemporaries* (Leiden: E. J. Brill, 1990).

said, "*Raka!*[77] How frightening you are. Are all the people of your village that ugly?" The passerby then answered, "I do not know, but you should go and say to the Creator who made me: how horrible is the vessel that you made." Having heard this, the rabbi realized that he had sinned, came down from the donkey, fell to the ground before the man and asked his forgiveness.[78]

What similarity exists between this anecdote and the parables of Jesus? Practically nothing, except for the word "*raka*," which we do find in the Sermon on the Mount, but in a completely different context. In fact, the actions of this rabbi are exactly the kind of human interaction that Jesus sharply rebuked:

> But I say unto you, that whosoever is angry with his brother without a cause shall be in danger of the judgment, and whosoever shall say to his brother, "*Raka*," shall be in danger of the council; but whosoever shall say, "Thou fool," shall be in danger of hell fire. (Mt 5.22)

The parables of the rabbis and other such anecdotes from their lives can be of interest in the study of the thinking and actions of those whom Jesus criticized: the scribes and Pharisees. Another subject of scholarly inquiry is the question of what sort of influence *Christianity* had on such parables and anecdotes. If we speak of some influence of the rabbinic tradition on Jesus, the texts that have survived simply give no reason to suggest that such an influence existed. We can only guess that Jesus was not the inventor of the parable genre, but used an existing manner of telling stories, filling it with new content.[79] But even if we were to make such an educated guess, the only sources that could provide answers to this question are dated much later than the Gospels.

Ever since the 1960s, a tendency has arisen in modern scholarship that is much more tolerant of the ancient, long-lasting tradition of allegorical interpretation of the parables.[80] In spite of the continuing arguments concerning

---

[77]"Empty man" in Aramaic.

[78]Quoted in Young, *The Parables*, 9.

[79]Craig A. Evans, *Jesus and His Contemporaries*, 266.

[80]L. W. Barnard, "To Allegorize or Not to Allegorize?" *Studia Theologica* 36 (1982): 1–10, at 10; Nikolai Sakharov, "Kratkii Obzor," 197.

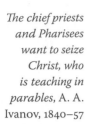

*The chief priests
and Pharisees
want to seize
Christ, who
is teaching in
parables*, A. A.
Ivanov, 1840–57

terminology such as "allegory" or "metaphor," more and more scholars have come to the conclusion that a figurative meaning (in some form) always exists in the parables of Jesus, or at least in a majority of them.

Not one of the methods of interpretation that scholars have offered from the late nineteenth to the early twenty-first century can be accepted as universal or applicable to all the parables of Jesus, or even to a majority of them. Each of these methods has its advantages and limitations. We believe that even the desire to develop a single method to interpret all the parables is misguided and doomed to failure. There is not, nor can there be, a universal method of interpreting narratives that were originally spoken in a way that assumed many different and variegated interpretations.

By using the many existing methods and by developing new ones, each interpreter of the parables may bring his own contribution to the treasure house of the interpretive tradition. This may mean that at times the allegorical method is appropriate, or at other times a moral lesson should be distilled, or again in a different case it may be helpful to consider the original historical context to benefit a contemporary audience. Sometimes a theological reading is called for, sometimes a literary analysis is helpful, or perhaps a comparative analysis of different versions of the same parable, especially if it appears in two or three Gospels. All these methods are justified, as long as they help the reader or the listener to find the meaning that is appropriate for his own level.

Chapter 2

TEACHING IN PARABLES

It is appropriate to begin our study of Jesus' parables with the third of Jesus' five long sermons that appear in the Gospel according to Matthew (Mt 13.3–52). This sermon includes four parables that Jesus spoke from a boat: the parable of the sower, the parable of the tares, the parable of the mustard seed, and the parable of the leaven. After these, he spoke three more parables inside a house on the same day: the parable of the treasure hidden in the field, the parable of the merchant who found the pearl of great price, and the parable of the net.

The parables of the sower and the mustard seed are also found in Mark and Luke (Mk 4.1–9 and 30–34; Lk 8.4–8 and 13.18–19) and the parable of the leaven is also found in Luke (Lk 13.20–21). Of the seven included in this sermon, three (the sower, the tares, and the net) include interpretations that Jesus himself gave to his disciples.

All seven parables of the thirteenth chapter of Matthew make up a single chain: though each has its own importance, it is simultaneously part of a larger narrative arc. To this same narrative arc, we may add the parable of the seed in the earth, which Mark included in his rendition of the sermon on the boat (Mk 4.26–29). In conclusion, then, we have a collection of eight parables that were told in a single day.

Why do Matthew and Mark differ in the number and kind of parables included in the sermon on the boat? The answer to this could be found here: "And with many such parables spake he the word unto them, as they were able to hear it. But without a parable spake he not unto them, and when they were alone, he expounded all things to his disciples" (Mk 4.33–34).

Jesus preaches at the lake of Gennesaret, Gustave Doré, 1860s

These words make clear that Jesus told more parables than Mark included in his account of the Gospel. He has three, Matthew has four, but only two of them match; counted together, we have five distinct parables spoken from the boat. In fact, there may have been far more than five, since Mark spoke of "many such parables." Furthermore, the expression "as they were able to hear it" indicates that the sermon was quite long, and the Gospels evidently recorded only certain sections of it.

Both Matthew and Mark introduce the sermon on the boat with a vivid description that allows the reader to see the event as in a painting. A scholar who specializes in the Gospel according to Mark, Joel Marcus, notes that in the beginning of Mark 4, the reader's attention is directed first to Jesus, then to the crowd, then back again to Jesus three times:

> And he began again to teach by the sea side:
> And there was gathered unto him a great multitude,
> So that he entered into a ship, and sat in the sea;
> And the whole multitude was by the sea on the land.
> And he taught them many things by parables,
> And said unto them in his doctrine, "Hearken!" (Mark 4.1–3)

This transfer of the readers' attention from Jesus to his listeners is like a camera in a documentary panning back and forth from the narrator to the audience.[1]

In the Gospel according to Matthew, we see a similar picture: as he left his house, Jesus sat on the banks of the lake. Then a great multitude gathered before him, so that he was forced to enter a boat (Mt 13.1–2). Only Matthew and Mark note that Jesus taught the people from the boat; Luke says nothing about either a boat or the sea (Lk 8.4). In Matthew, these listeners are *ochloi polloi* ("large crowds"), in Luke they are *ochlou pollou* ("a

---

[1]Joel Marcus, *Mark 1–8: A New Translation with Introduction and Commentary* (New Haven: Yale University Press, 2000), 293–94.

The sermon from the boat, A. A. Ivanov, 1840–1857

large crowd"), and in Mark they are *ochlos pleistos* ("an even larger crowd" than the one he mentioned before). In Matthew, Jesus "spake many things unto them in parables," in Mark, "he taught them many things by parables," and in Luke he "spake by a parable." The use of the plural in Matthew and Mark indicates that the reader of the Gospel will be offered a series of parables; as for Luke, only a single parable is offered, and the rest follow only after a break.

Mark's indication of an even larger crowd connects the account of the sermon on the boat with two previous episodes. In one of them, many people followed Jesus from Galilee, Judea, Jerusalem, Idumea, and from beyond Jordan, and even from the areas surrounding Tyre and Sidon. Jesus told his disciples "that a small ship should wait on him because of the multitude, lest they should throng him." Later Mark explains that "as many as had plagues . . . pressed upon him for to touch him . . . for he had healed many." As for demoniacs, they fell before him, crying out "Thou art the Son of God" (Mk 3.7–11). In the next scene, Jesus appears to be teaching in a house where it was so crowded that the disciples "could not so much as eat bread" (Mk 3.20). This picture of a huge crowd surrounding Jesus from all sides, constantly following him, the spectacle of people throwing themselves at him to be healed, the loud cries of demoniacs—all this contrasts strongly with the situation at the beginning of the sermon on the boat.

In the Gospel according to Luke, there is another occasion when Jesus taught from a boat (Lk 5.3). Evidently, Jesus used this way of speaking to the people more than once. In a time when artificial amplification of sound was impossible, the only opportunity for a large group of people to hear a sermon was to create suitable conditions for sound to travel well. For example, Jesus sometimes climbed a hill, while his listeners remained at a lower elevation to hear him better (Mt 5.1). Sound travels well over the surface of water, and it would have helped many more people hear what Jesus had to say.

1. The Sower

The parable of the sower is the first parable of Jesus recorded in the Gospel according to Mark. It is also the first full-fledged parable in Matthew and Luke, if we discount the parables of the house built on the rock and the house built on sand, which is part of the Sermon on the Mount (in Luke, the Sermon on the Plain), and the parable of the children in the street, which is included in a section about John the Baptist. The presence of the parable of the sower in all three synoptic Gospels and the importance of its place in all three accounts makes it the perfect parable to begin our analysis.

Matthew's version (Mt 13.3–9) is practically identical to Mark's (Mk 4.3–9). The version in Luke (Lk 8.5–8) is somewhat shorter. Here we offer Mark's version:

> Behold, there went out a sower to sow. And it came to pass, as he sowed, some fell by the way side, and the fowls of the air came and devoured it up. And some fell on stony ground, where it had not much earth; and immediately it sprang up, because it had no depth of earth. But when the sun was up, it was scorched; and because it had no root, it withered away. And some fell among thorns, and the thorns grew up, and choked it, and it yielded no fruit. And other fell on good ground,

and did yield fruit that sprang up and increased, and brought forth, some thirty, and some sixty, and some an hundred. And he said unto them, "He that hath ears to hear, let him hear." (Mk 4.3–9)

There are several insignificant differences between the evangelists in the way they describe the fate of the seed sown on the road. In Matthew and Mark, they are eaten by birds, while in Luke "it was trodden down, and the fowls of the air devoured it." The seed that fell on stony ground grew up quickly in Matthew and Mark, because the earth had no depth to it, and then it withered when the sun came up, for it "had no root." But in Luke, the seed "withered away, because it lacked moisture." The seed that fell on fruitful ground brought forth "some thirty, and some sixty, and some an hundred," while in Luke, it "bare fruit an hundredfold."

To understand the context of the parable, we must recall the significance of such essential objects as soil, seed, and tares (or weeds) for Jesus' listeners. This is not always obvious to a modern reader, and because of this the parable may seem like an abstract narrative in which the storyteller uses primarily abstract images, distant from everyday realities. Few city-dwellers of our time have ever seen a sower casting seed in a real field. The sowing of seed and the reaping of harvests long ago became mechanized processes, and even the modern mechanized version is known only to those who actively pursue agriculture as a way of life. City dwellers know anything about the labor of the sower only through literary examples or the paintings of such artists as Van Gogh.

The word "earth" (*'erets*), for an Israelite, was sacred. In spite of the difficult political situation of the time, Jews of Jesus' age continued to live in their own land, that is, the land promised by God to Abraham and his descendants (Gen 12.1–7). In earlier times, the Hebrews had won this land, with some difficulty, by seizing it from other nations, and they returned to it only after a long sojourn in Egypt and another forty years of wandering in the wilderness; finally, they returned to it a second time after the Babylonian captivity. This was the land of their fathers, their birthright (Gen 31.3, 48.21), to which the Hebrews were extremely attached. They knew that the master of their land was God himself; they were only wanderers

The Sower, Vincent van Gogh, 1888

who settled there (Lev 25.23). They remembered that agriculture was man's original calling (Gen 2.5, 15). They also knew that there was a direct connection between obedience to God and how the land would react to human labor:

> Wherefore ye shall do my statutes, and keep my judgments, and do them; and ye shall dwell in the land in safety. And the land shall yield her fruit, and ye shall eat your fill, and dwell therein in safety. . . . And if ye will not yet for all this hearken unto me, then I will punish you seven times more for your sins. And I will break the pride of your power; and I will make your heaven as iron, and your earth as brass, and your strength shall be spent in vain, for your land shall not yield her increase, neither shall the trees of the land yield their fruits. . . . And when I have broken the staff of your bread, ten women shall bake your bread in one oven, and they shall deliver you your bread again by weight: and ye shall eat, and not be satisfied. (Leviticus 25.18–19; 26.18–20, 26)

The word "seed" is found only in Luke's version; in Matthew and Mark, the seed itself is not mentioned, though its presence is assumed. The word "seed" (Hebrew *zera'*, Greek *sperma*) also had a profound symbolic significance. On the one hand, the seed is the beginning of the process of generation and increase in the plant world (Gen 1.12). On the other hand, the word "seed" also refers to a specific descendant of a person (Gen 4.23, 21.12–13; cf. Gal 3.16) and his descendants in general (Gen 22.17–18). The people of Israel is a holy "seed," which should never be mixed with the seed of foreigners (1 Esd 9.2). In second temple Judaism, the image of seed sometimes indicated the remnant that would return to the promised land after the end of their captivity.[2] In the Psalms, this return is described in images of sowing and harvest: "Turn back our captivity, O Lord, as the streams in the south. They that sow in tears shall reap in joy. They went forth and wept as they cast their seeds, but they shall return with rejoicing, bringing their sheaves" (Ps 125.4–6). Thus, seed is simultaneously a symbol of life, one's descendants, and the entire nation of Israel.

Thorns (Hebrew *qots*, Greek *akanthai*) first appear in Genesis, in God's words to Adam after his fall: "Cursed is the ground for thy sake; in sorrow shalt thou eat of it all the days of thy life; thorns also and thistles shall it bring forth to thee, and thou shalt eat the herb of the field" (Gen 3.17–18). In the Bible, thorns appear together with other symbols of suffering (its sharp edges are painful), disillusionment (it grows where no one planted it), and fruitless labor (it grows instead of the plants that man needs for nourishment).

When reading this parable, it is important to remember that Jesus used concepts that would have been quotidian, as well as religiously significant, for his listeners. If the everyday meaning of these concepts was obvious for all, the symbolism behind their mundane appearance would be revealed differently for each.

Not by accident do all three accounts end in the same formula: "He that hath ears to hear, let him hear!" This formula is used at the end of Luke's account of the parable of the sower, but in Matthew it comes after the interpretation of the parable of the tares (Mt 13.43). This same phrase occurs often in Jesus' direct speech (Mt 11.15, 25.30; Mk 4.23, 7.16; Lk 14.35). This phrase was one of Jesus' characteristic rhetorical devices, and it had several possible meanings depending on context. He used it to finish his

[2]Wright, *Jesus and the Victory of God*, 232–33.

parables, as well as their interpretation. Sometimes he used it outside the context of parables, but always at the end of a speech, in order to underline the importance of what he said. This phrase would have been spoken in a louder inflection than the rest of the speech (indicated by the preceding word "cried" in Mt 25.30 and Lk 8.8). In modern translations, this exalted character of the phrase is accentuated by the use of an exclamation point.

But what does the phrase mean? Evidently, it refers to what was spoken just previously, and it makes it clear that only those who "have ears" can fully understand the meaning and content of the preaching of Jesus. In contrast, Jesus said that his opponents "hear indeed, but understand not; and see indeed, but perceive not." Following the prophet Isaiah, he said that they "make their ears heavy, and shut their eyes" (Is 6.9–10; Mt 13.13–15). These words follow immediately after the parable of the sower and are a direct interpretation of the phrase we already mentioned. They are part of the episode we discussed above, in which the disciples asked Jesus to explain the meaning of the parable of the sower, and in answer Jesus pointed out their privileged position on the "inside," as opposed to "those outside," and for this reason they are given to know the mysteries of the kingdom of God.

In all three synoptic Gospels, this event is followed by Jesus' own interpretation of the parable. In Matthew and Luke, this interpretation is slightly shorter than Mark's version, but their general content and terminology are essentially the same:

> The sower soweth the word. And these are they by the way side, where the word is sown; but when they have heard, Satan cometh immediately, and taketh away the word that was sown in their hearts. And these are they likewise which are sown on stony ground: who, when they have heard the word, immediately receive it with gladness, and have no root in themselves, and so endure but for a time. Afterward, when affliction or persecution ariseth for the word's sake, immediately they are offended. And these are they which are sown among thorns: such as hear the word, and the cares of this world, and the deceitfulness

of riches, and the lusts of other things entering in, choke the word, and it becometh unfruitful. And these are they which are sown on good ground: such as hear the word, and receive it, and bring forth fruit, some thirtyfold, some sixty, and some an hundred. (Mk 4.14–20)

Who is the sower in the parable? Jesus does not mention this in his interpretation, which begins with the seed instead. Evidently, he assumes that the disciples already know. But when he interpreted the parable of the tares, which is thematically connected with the parable of the sower, Jesus openly said that "He that soweth the good seed is the Son of Man" (Mt 13.37). By analogy, we can apply the same interpretation to the parable of the sower: in it, Jesus speaks of himself and his teaching and how this teaching was accepted differently by different people. Thus, the parable of the sower becomes a kind of prelude for all the other parables of Jesus. It is not by accident that he told this parable before the other parables and the rest of the sermon on the boat.

What is the word that the sower sows? In Mark, this word is not qualified in any way. But in Matthew the sower sows "the word of the kingdom" (Mt 13.19), while in Luke, "the seed is the word of God" (Lk 8.11). Evidently, what Jesus has in mind is his own preaching. The expression "the word of the kingdom" refers to the challenge with which he began his preaching: "Repent, for the kingdom of heaven is at hand" (Mt 4.17). He also refers to the content of many parables, which begin with the phrase "Whereunto shall we liken the kingdom of God? Or with what comparison shall we compare it?" (Mk 4.30), or to the answers to these questions: "The kingdom of heaven is like to a grain of mustard seed," "the kingdom of heaven is like unto leaven," "the kingdom of heaven is like unto a treasure hid in a field," "the kingdom of heaven is like unto a merchant," "the kingdom of heaven is like unto a net" (Mt 13.31, 33, 44, 45, 47). The development of the theme of the kingdom of heaven or the kingdom of God, according to the synoptic Gospels, is the most important content of Jesus' preaching, from the first days of his public ministry.

This preaching is the same word of God given to the prophets, a direct continuation of God's revelation in the Old Testament. Jesus' listeners were doubtless familiar with the words of Isaiah:

> "For my thoughts are not your thoughts, neither are your ways my ways," saith the Lord. "For as the heavens are higher than the earth, so are my ways higher than your ways, and my thoughts than your thoughts. For as the rain cometh down, and the snow from heaven, and returneth not thither, but watereth the earth, and maketh it bring forth and bud, that it may give seed to the sower, and bread to the eater, so shall my word be that goeth forth out of my mouth: it shall not return unto me void, but it shall accomplish that which I please, and it shall prosper in the thing whereto I sent it." (Isaiah 55.8–11)

In this passage, the image of the sower is missing, but the image of the seed, the soil, and most importantly the word of God coming from the lips of God are all present. In the Christian exegetical tradition, this "word" is firmly connected to the Word (*Logos*) in the prologue to the Gospel of John (Jn 1.1–5), that is, with the Son of God who was in the beginning with God and who came to earth in the flesh—Jesus Christ. This Word does not return to God "void," but accomplishes the will of the Father who sent him into the world: "For I came down from heaven, not to do mine own will, but the will of him that sent me" (Jn 6.38).

The theme of the calling that sounds so vividly in Isaiah becomes a leitmotif of Jesus' preaching: he spoke of himself as one called into the world by the Father, and he spoke of the Father as the one who sent him. This theme is fully developed in the parable of the sower:

> "There went out a sower to sow." What a simple, and yet what a trium-phant beginning! It means: the time for harvest has come, the winter and the snow has prepared the earth, the lands have been plowed, the spring has come, and the sower went out to sow. . . . The human race, after thousands of years of torture and suffering, wandering and moan-ing, has been plowed and prepared to accept the divine seed of the life-bearing teaching; the prophets plowed the soil of human souls, and

Christ shone forth like spring after the long freeze of winter, and like the sower he has come out to sow. The prophets were the ploughmen; he—the sower. If the prophets sowed a few seeds here and there, they were still not their own seeds, but those taken from God. But Christ came out to sow his own seed. . . . The sower came out, but from where did he come, and where was he going? The Son of God came from the eternal bosom of his Father . . . he assumed human flesh to serve human beings as a human being. . . . The souls of human beings are his field. . . . From his eternal abode did he come and he came to his field to sow his own seed.[3]

And so, in the parable of the sower, Jesus spoke of himself. This makes the parable similar to the many other parables and teachings in which Jesus directed the attention of the listener to his own person or his own work. Such a style of preaching seemed unusual to his listeners, a fact especially evident in the Gospel according to John, where Jesus constantly spoke of himself to the Jews, irritating them more and more. The formula "I am" in this Gospel occurs even more often than "the kingdom of heaven is like unto . . ." in the other three (see Jn 6.35, 41, 51; 8.58; 10.9, 11, 14; 11.25; 14.6; 15.1, 5). Such a frequent repetition of this expression, together with appended images of the bread of life, the door of the sheep, the Good Shepherd, the grapevine, the way, the truth, the life, and the resurrection show vividly that all of Jesus' preaching was first and foremost a revelation of his own person.

The fact that the preaching of Jesus was focused on his own person is explained by his unique role as the Son of God, sent by the Father, who came to tell the will of God to all mankind in a special way—not in the manner of the prophets. The prophets were merely links of transmission between God and people. Jesus, on the other hand, was God incarnate, and as he spoke with people himself, he spoke also in the name of God the Father. This is why he directed his listeners' attention not to various separate aspects of his teaching, nor to his teaching in general, but rather to himself, the source of the teaching.

[3]Nikolai (Velimirovich), *Tvoreniya*, 2:327–28. Translated by DNK.

The Prophet Esdras,
Miniature, 8th century

There are a few parallels to the parable of the sower in the Second Book of Esdras. In this book, God speaks to Esdras in the following words:

> "For as the husbandman soweth much seed upon the ground, and planteth many trees, and yet the thing that is sown good in his season, cometh not up, neither doth all that is planted take root, even so is it of them that are sown in the world, they shall not all be saved." I answered then, and said, "If I have found grace, let me speak. Like as the husbandman's seed perisheth, if it come not up, and receive not the rain in due season, or if there come too much rain and corrupt it, even so perisheth man also which is formed with thy hands, and is called thine own image, because thou art like unto him, for whose sake thou hast made all things, and likened him unto the husbandman's seed." (2 Esd 8.41–44)

In another dialogue, God appears in the form of a sower, and his law in the form of the sowing:

> For behold I sow my law in you, and it shall bring fruit in you, and ye shall be honored in it forever. But our fathers which received the law, kept it not, and observed not thy ordinances, and though the fruit of thy law did not perish, neither could it, for it was thine, yet they that received it perished, because they kept not the thing that was sown in them. For we that have received the law perish by sin, and our heart also which received it. Notwithstanding the law perisheth not, but remaineth in his force. (2 Esd 9.31–33, 36–37)

We will not address the question of whether or not Jesus knew the Second Book of Esdras.[4] Even if he knew it or only the text upon which it

---

[4] 2 Esdras is part of the Old Testament apocrypha that exists only in translation in Latin, Syriac, Ethiopian, Arabic, and Armenian Bibles. Part of this text (chapters 1–2 and 14–16) may have been written after Christ, while the main part (chapters 3–13) was written before Christ.

is based, we can hardly speak of his use of the seed and sowing as a sort of literary allusion. Jesus was not an academic scholar who gathered his knowledge of life from books. He knew the sacred Scriptures of the Old Testament very well, and many of the images he used have direct parallels in Scripture. Yet no less important for him were direct observations from the lives of simple Galilean peasants. When he spoke of sowers, soil, seeds, and the growth of plants, he was alluding not to literary sources, but to what was happening before his eyes and what was well known to every person, not because of book knowledge, but because of personal observation.

The image of the sower is often connected with messianic and eschatological expectations, which were characteristic of Jesus' contemporaries. In all three synoptic Gospels, Jesus underlines the messianic character of the parable when he provides an explanation in his conversation with the disciples: "It is given unto you to know the mysteries of the kingdom of heaven" (Mt 13.11; Mk 4.11; Lk 8.10). In Matthew, this commentary is more expansive than in Mark: "Blessed are your eyes, for they see, and your ears, for they hear. For verily I say unto you, that many prophets and righteous men have desired to see those things which ye see, and have not seen them, and to hear those things which ye hear, and have not heard them" (Mt 13.16–17). In Luke, Jesus speaks similar words, but in a different place (Lk 10.23–24). This commentary presents Jesus' words and actions as the direct fulfillment of the expectation of the Old Testament prophets. In this context, the image of the sower is especially apt.

The seed sown by the sower falls on different kinds of soil. Jesus himself divides his listeners into four categories. The reactions of the first three categories of people differ from each other only in terms of cause, not in terms of effect—none of these people bears any fruit. Only those in the fourth group bring forth fruit.

We have no indication that Jesus knew of it. Clement of Alexandria, in his *Stromata*, referred to 2 Esdras. [This book is called "2 Esdras" in many English Bibles, but it is included as 3 Esdras in the appendix of the Slavonic Bible (it was also included in the appendix of the Clementine Vulgate and in the "Apocrypha" section of the King James Version and subsequent English versions that followed this pattern); sometimes scholars refer to it as 4 Esdras/Ezra or Latin Esdras/Ezra.—*Ed.*]

*The devil
tempts Jesus
in the desert,*
Miniature,
12th century

The first category includes all those from whom the enemy steals the word. When Matthew recorded Jesus' words, he named the enemy "the wicked one," while Mark calls him Satan, and Luke refers to him as the devil. These three terms indicate the same person in biblical history, who constantly—beginning with the first pages of the book of Genesis—opposes the will of God (Gen 3.1–5). Acting within the bounds set by God himself (see Job 1.6–12, 2.1–6), he nevertheless always tries to break out of those bounds and to enter the fray directly against God.

The devil is a tempter. All three synoptic Gospels include an account of the devil's temptation of Jesus in the desert before he began his public ministry (Mt 4.1–11; Mk 1.12–13; Lk 4.1–13). The subsequent accounts in the Gospels, which include many cases of demons being cast out of the possessed, show the reader a picture of constant warfare between Jesus and the demonic powers, at whose head stands the devil.

In his teachings, Jesus often spoke of this figure, calling him an enemy, or the devil, or the wicked one, or Satan, but he always speaks of himself as stronger: "When a strong man armed keepeth his palace, his goods are in peace, but when a stronger than he shall come upon him, and overcome him, he taketh from him all his armor wherein he trusted, and divideth his spoils" (Lk 11.21–22). The evil one is a dangerous enemy, and this is why the disciples are called to beseech God to deliver them from him (Mt 6.13).

In the parable of the sower, the devil's action is the first reason that a person might fail to respond to the word of God. The Gospel of Matthew describes this using the verb *harpazō* ("to steal," "to take away"), while Mark and Luke use the verb *airō* ("to take," "to take away"). God gives man his word as a gift, but the devil steals in upon the person to take this gift away from him. The lightning speed with which the devil steals the seed of the word of God is symbolized by the image of the bird that flies down to the seed and quickly picks it up to eat it.

The second category includes those who willingly answer the call of the word and accept it with joy, but have no roots and thus are inconstant. As soon as sorrows or persecution for the sake of the word come, they stumble. This is how Mark presents them. In Matthew's version, the same image is given in the singular, not the plural. In Luke, the people who belong to this group "for a while believe, and in time of temptation fall away" (Lk 8.13). The difference between the version in Matthew and Mark on the one hand, and that in Luke on the other, is due to the use of the same expression, translated in two different ways: the word *proskairos* in Matthew is a modifier that means "inconstant" (Mark simply renders the same idea but in plural), while Luke's *pros kairon* is written as two distinct words and means "during the passage of a certain amount of time."

The term "temptation" in Luke may indicate a connection between the first two groups of people, since the tempter, as a rule, is the devil. In Matthew and Mark, the expression "persecution . . . because of the word" indicates the future persecution of Christians. This reference to persecutions is one of the factors that lead many scholars, beginning with Jülicher, to ascribe the interpretation of this parable to the time of the early Church, rather than ascribing it to Christ himself.[5]

Yet Jesus frequently warned his disciples that they should expect persecutions, including in the Sermon on the Mount (Mt 5.10–12), as well as in his admonition to the twelve after he chose them (Mt 10.16–23, 28), and the teaching he delivered two days before the final Passover (Mt 24.9). If all

---

[5]Jülicher, *Gleichnisreden*, 524–38; Dodd, *Parables*, 145.

these mentions of coming persecutions are later additions, then a significant portion of Jesus' direct speech in the synoptic Gospels would prove to
be falsified, a later counterfeit. We reject such an interpretation because it
contradicts the fundamental principle of our approach to the Gospels.

The meaning of the word "seed" is key to understanding this text. The
lack of seed becomes the reason for falling away (in Luke) or the temptation to fall away (in Matthew and Mark) for those who belong to this
category. Evidently, we must take the "seed" to mean faith, since faith is
opposed to falling away in Luke's version.

It is also possible that the image of the plant that grows very quickly,
lacking good roots, indicates religiosity of two types: an external and
superficial devoutness on the one hand, and a deep and internal one on
the other. External religiosity presupposes a person's readiness to fulfill
a certain number of spiritual and moral rules and rituals without deeply
understanding their meaning (the earth into which the seed has fallen, in
Matthew and Mark, lacks depth). Internal devotion, on the contrary, may
be invisible to the external viewer, like a seed in the ground, but such com-
mitment is capable of giving a person the strength to overcome persecution, temptation, and testing.

The verb "will be offended" (*skandalizontai*, or "will stumble"; lit. "will
be scandalized"), applied to the people in this group, comes from the word
"offense" (*skandalon*, or "stumbling block"; lit. "scandal"), which in early
Christian tradition had a rich depth of meaning. On the one hand, offense
is that which must be firmly rejected:

> And if thy right eye offend thee, pluck it out, and cast it from thee: for
> it is profitable for thee that one of thy members should perish, and
> not that thy whole body should be cast into hell. And if thy right hand
> offend thee, cut it off, and cast it from thee: for it is profitable for thee
> that one of thy members should perish, and not that thy whole body
> should be cast into hell. (Mt 5.29–39)

On the other hand, the very activity of Jesus can also become a temptation: "Blessed is he, whosoever shall not be offended in me" (Mt 11.6).
The Apostle Paul directly says that the crucified Christ is "unto the Jews a

stumbling block [*skandalon*; 'offense,' 'scandal'], and unto the Greeks foolishness" (1 Cor 1.23).

It is in this context that we should understand the warning in the parable of the sower: those who accept only the external aspects of Jesus' word, only the beautiful outer aspect, but fail to understand its inner depth, will stumble and may fall away at some point in their life when external circumstances (sorrows, persecutions, and temptations) suddenly attack them.

The third group of people in the parable are those for whom, according to Matthew and Mark's version, "the care of this word, and the deceitfulness of riches, choke [*sympnigei*] the word, and [they become] unfruitful [*akarpos*]" (Mt 13.22). According to Luke, these people "when they have heard, go forth, and are choked with cares and riches and pleasures of this life, and bring no fruit to perfection" (Lk 8.14). These words should be understood within the general context of Jesus' teaching concerning cares, riches, and earthly pleasures.

The theme of riches appears constantly in Jesus' teaching, where it always has a negative connotation. After meeting the rich young ruler, Jesus exclaims, "How hardly shall they that have riches enter into the kingdom of God!" The disciples are horrified by these words, but he only repeats: "Children, how hard is it for them that trust in riches to enter into the kingdom of God" (Mk 10.23–24). In the Sermon on the Mount, Jesus said, "Ye cannot serve God and mammon" (Mt 6.24). In the Sermon on the Plain, he turns to the rich men with a stern rebuke: "Woe unto you that are rich! For ye have received your consolation" (Lk 6.24). The theme of riches and poverty is central to the parable of the rich man and Lazarus, in which the rich man dies and finds himself in hell (Lk 16.23).

It is typical that in Matthew and Mark's versions, Jesus speaks of "the deceitfulness of riches." The word *apatē* in classical Greek indicates deceit, falsehood, disillusionment, and unfulfilled hope. The falseness of earthly gain is underlined by the parable of the rich man who gathered such a harvest that he did not have enough space to store all his grain, and so he said to himself, "Soul, thou hast much goods laid up for many years; take thine ease, eat drink, and be merry" (Lk 12.19). Jesus calls such a man a fool.

The term "cares" also has a negative connotation in Jesus' teaching. An entire section of the Sermon on the Mount is dedicated to his admonition not to care for clothing, food, and drink, nor even to worry about tomorrow. As an example, he offers the birds of the air and the lilies of the field, for whom God himself cares. Instead of earthly cares, he offers "The kingdom of God and his righteousness." Jesus calls his followers to seek this kingdom first and foremost, and if they do, then all they need in this life will take care of itself (Mt 6.25–34). In the parable of the sower, the symbol of earthly cares is thorns (*akanthai*), a prickly plant that grows quickly and chokes the stalk of grain.

Thus Jesus offers three primary reasons why the word of God might remain unfruitful in some people: 1) the activity of the devil, 2) the inconstancy of the people themselves and the lack of any rootedness, 3) the riches and cares of this world (according to Luke, this also includes the pleasures of this life).

In opposition to these three categories of people, a fourth is now offered—those who not only hear the word but understand it and bring forth fruit (according to Matthew), who accept and bring forth fruit (according to Mark), who keep the word in a good and pure heart and bring forth fruit in patience (according to Luke). The common theme in all three versions is the verb *karpophoreō* (lit. "to bring forth fruit"). This verb indicates the positive result hoped for by the laboring sower.

The heart, which is mentioned in Luke's version, is modified by two adjectives: *kalē kai agathē* (lit. "beautiful and good"). Commentators often highlight the fact that these two terms were used in Greek philosophy to indicate the ideal combination of physical beauty and high moral qualities in a human beauty.[6] But this is unlikely to be anything other than a coincidence, especially considering that the original words were spoken in Aramaic.

One should not look for an allegorical meaning of the thirty-, sixty-, and one-hundred-fold harvest. In this case, the numbers are most likely symbols of the relative amount of fruit brought forth by the word of God

---

[6]Joseph A. Fitzmyer, *The Gospel According to Luke, I–IX* (Garden City, NY: Doubleday, 1981), 714.

in those who accept it with faith. They may also indicate various levels of spiritual perfection achieved by those who have believed and accepted the word. This is how John Chrysostom understands it:

> For being full of love for man, he marked out not one only way, nor did he say, "Unless one bring an hundred, he is an outcast"; but he that brings forth sixty is saved also, and not he only, but also the producer of thirty. And this he said, making out salvation to be easy. . . . "Art thou unable to strip thyself of thy possession? Give of thy substance. Canst thou not bear that burden? Share thy goods with Christ."[7]

In spite of the inevitable consequence that part of the seeds will perish, in the final analysis the action of the sower does achieve its goal: the seed that has fallen on good soil brings forth abundant fruit. What does this mean for Jesus and his mission? The same thing that he expresses in another place with the formula: "many are called, but few are chosen" (Mt 20.16, 22.14; Lk 14.24). It is inevitable that his mission prove successful, yet not everyone will be able to share in the fruits of victory, but only those who have come to believe in him and followed him.

When he gave the parable of the sower, Jesus spoke first of all about himself and his contemporaries—those who listened to his teaching and responded to it in different ways. If we are to examine this parable together with a series of other parables in which the assumed subject is the nation of Israel and its response to Jesus' preaching in general (these include the parable of the wicked tenants in Mt 21.35–41; Mk 12.1–9; Lk 20.9–16), then we can say that the fruitful soil assumes *not* the nation of Israel at all, but all the nations that eventually came to believe in Jesus. This is how the parable was understood by the early Church. Justin Martyr cites the parable of the sower when he speaks of Israel's rejection of the Messiah, insisting on the need for Christians to preach in the hopes of finding good soil.[8] Here he is speaking of the lands beyond Israel, and of ministry to those who are not members of the Hebrew nation.

---

[7]John Chrysostom, *Homilies on the Gospel of St Matthew* 45.2–3 (NPNF[1] 10:286).
[8]Justin Martyr, *Dialogue of Justin, Philosopher and Martyr, with Trypho, a Jew* 125 (ANF 1:262).

Though it has a direct connection to the history of Israel, this parable also has a universal meaning. The sowing that Jesus began during his earthly ministry was continued by his disciples after his death and resurrection, and subsequently by later generations of Christian teachers. The word of God did not always fall on good soil. But wherever it did, the harvest was great indeed. Entire nations were illumined by the light of the faith in the Gospels, thanks to the preaching of sowers of the word who labored to spread the message of the Gospel, who did not know whether their labor would bring any fruit at all, and, if so, what kind.

The parables of Jesus are fulfilled in the history of many nations. The Russian land for many centuries was that good soil into which the seed of the word of God fell and brought forth an abundant fruit of saints—pious princes, bishops, monks, martyrs, and fools for Christ. This land was called Holy Rus', because the idea of sanctity so deeply penetrated the consciousness of the Russian person that it seemed as if he ceased to even think of himself without Christ and his Church. But when persecutions came, the situation changed radically. Millions of people stood on the path of martyrdom, but some rejected their faith in Christ. These were those with no roots, as Jesus said. While the times were good, they believed, but when persecutions came, they were tempted and fell away.

Similar parallels can be drawn in the history of many other nations. But in contrast to the situation described in the parable, the same land can, in different historical periods, be either good or bad soil, and the seed, though falling on the same soil, can during different historical periods either be eaten by birds or choked by thorns, while at other times, in spite of all factors to the contrary, it might bring forth fruit a hundredfold.

The same can equally be said about individual people. The soul of a single human being, during different times in his life, can be represented as good soil or rocky soil, and the seed that falls into his heart can sometimes bring forth an abundant harvest, but at other times it may be choked with the thorns of cares or instead may be stolen away by the devil.

There is an essential difference between the situation represented in the parable and real life. Soil tends to be either fruitful or rocky by its nature. The quality of the soil does not depend on the soil itself. As for people, the

The Sower,
Vincent van
Gogh, 1888

situation is quite different. No man can *by nature* be incapable of responding to the word of God. As Chrysostom said,

> it being impossible for the rock to become earth, or the wayside not to be a wayside, or the thorns, thorns; but in the things that have reason it is not so. There is such a thing as the rock changing, and becoming rich land; and the wayside being no longer trampled on, nor lying open to all that pass by, but that it may be a fertile field; and the thorns may be destroyed, and the seed enjoy full security. For had it been impossible, this Sower would not have sown. And if the change did not take place in all, this is no fault of the Sower, but of them who are unwilling to be changed.[9]

God created every person capable of accepting his word into his heart, and the heart of every person in his natural, first-created form is always good soil. No human being exists who would by nature be excluded from the influence of God and his good news. Nevertheless, people do react differently to this good news. These different reactions become the reason why in some people God's good news brings forth fruit a hundredfold,

[9]John Chrysostom, *Homilies on the Gospel of St Matthew* 44.5 (NPNF[1] 10:281–82).

but sixty in another, and thirty in another, and in some, it brings forth no fruit at all.

2. The Parable of the Wheat and the Tares

The parable of the wheat and the tares follows immediately after the parable of the sower. There are many similarities between them. First of all, they both use similar imagery: seeds, a sower, the field (soil), and plants that grow from the seed. In the parable of the sower, Jesus did not specify what kind of seed was sown, but it is obvious from the context that he is speaking of wheat. This becomes evident in the parable of the tares, where the "good seed" is equated with wheat (Mt 13.24–25).

Wheat was the primary seed crop in Israel, since bread was made from it, and bread was the primary food source in Israel (cf. Gen 18.5, 31.54, 37.25). If in our time people usually eat something together with a bit of bread, in ancient Israel people ate bread, along with a small portion of something else (Gen 25.34). The word "bread" was essentially synonymous with "food" (Gen 3.19, 42.5–7). The entire epic story of Joseph and his brothers centers on the theme of bread.

The discussion of what followed what—the sowing after the plowing or the other way around—likely has nothing to do with the meaning of the parable of the sower and the parable of the tares. This was a subject introduced by Jeremias, who insisted that according to contemporary findings, in first-century Palestine, the land was not plowed before the sowing, but afterward. This meant that the sower had to walk on unplowed ground, chaotically throwing seeds about.[10] Other scholars argue against this, insisting that the land was plowed first.[11] But in our days, interest in this

---

[10]Jeremias, *Parables*, 11–12.

[11]K. D. White, "The Parable of the Sower," *Journal of Theological Studies* 15 (1964): 300–307. Jeremias' rebuttal can be found in Joachim Jeremias, "Palästinakundliches zum Gleichnis vom Säemann (Mark 4:3–8)," *New Testament Studies* 13 (1966–1967): 48–53.

debate has largely died down, since neither position gives us a particularly useful key to understanding the meaning of these parables.

The parable of the tares uses a group of images similar to those in the parable of the sower, but the focal point of the parable is entirely different, leading the listener's attention to a different theme:

The Parable of the Wheat and Tares, Domenico Fetti, 1622

> Another parable put he forth unto them, saying, "The kingdom of heaven is likened unto a man which sowed good seed in his field, but while men slept, his enemy came and sowed tares among the wheat, and went his way. But when the blade was sprung up, and brought forth fruit, then appeared the tares also. So the servants of the householder came and said unto him, 'Sir, didst not thou sow good seed in thy field? From whence then hath it tares?' He said unto them, 'An enemy hath done this.' The servants said unto him, 'Wilt thou then that we go and gather them up?' But he said, 'Nay, lest while ye gather up the tares, ye root up also the wheat with them. Let both grow together until the harvest, and in the time of harvest I will say to the reapers, "Gather ye together first the tares, and bind them in bundles to burn them, but gather the wheat into my barn."'" (Mt 13.24–30)

We saw only one sower in the parable of the sower, but here we see two sowers sowing in the same field. In the first parable, the sower cast only good seeds with the hopes of a rich harvest, but here both wheat and tares (or weeds) are sown. The image of the evil seed is also found in Second Esdras: "The evil is sown, but the destruction thereof is not yet come. If therefore that which is sown be not turned upside down, and if the place where the evil is sown pass not away, then cannot it come that is sown with good" (2 Esd 4.28–29). But as we mentioned before, it is very unlikely that Jesus' parables possess a literary dependence on this book.

The differences between the parables of the sower and of the tares are not limited solely to the ones mentioned above. If in the first parable the

The Sower of Tares, Sir John E. Millais, 19th century

sower is the main character, here we find new secondary characters: the enemy, the servants of the householder, the reapers. In the first parable the seed, once sown on good ground, grows and brings forth much fruit, but here the wheat grows at the same time as the tares. Finally, in the parable of the sower the harvest is only assumed, but here it is the culmination of the story.

The difference between these two parables becomes even more obvious when we compare their interpretations. In the Gospel according to Matthew, the interpretation of this parable does not follow immediately after the parable, but after the telling of four parables in a row, which in his version make up the sermon in the boat. As a result, the parables of the mustard seed and the leaven are situated between the telling of the parable and its interpretation, which Matthew renders as follows:

> Then Jesus sent the multitude away, and went into the house, and his disciples came unto him, saying, "Declare unto us the parable of the tares of the field." He answered and said unto them, "He that soweth the good seed is the Son of Man; the field is the world; the good seed are the children of the kingdom; but the tares are the children of the wicked one; the enemy that sowed them is the devil; the harvest is the end of the world; and the reapers are the angels. As therefore the tares are gathered and burned in the fire; so shall it be in the end of this world. The Son of Man shall send forth his angels, and they shall gather out of his kingdom all things that offend, and them which do iniquity, and shall cast them into a furnace of fire: there shall be wailing and gnashing of teeth. Then shall the righteous shine forth as the sun in the kingdom of their Father. He who hath ears to hear, let him hear." (Mt 13.36–43)

The entire plot of the parable of the sower is told from the point of view of the earthly history of mankind. But the central theme of the parable of

The Haystacks,
Vincent van
Gogh, 1888

the tares is the end of this age and the judgment that Jesus spoke of many times in other places, including in his final instruction to the disciples before the Last Supper (Mt 25.31–46). One of the connections between the two interpretations is the expression "this age," indicating earthly life in general. In the mouth of Jesus, this expression generally has a negative connotation. Thus, for example, in the parable of the unjust steward, the sons of the light are opposed to the sons of "this age" (Lk 16.8).

Another point of connection is the figure of the devil. In the parable of the sower, he steals the seed of the word of God from people, while in the parable of the tares, he sows his own seed at the same time that the Son of Man sows good seed. In both parables, the Son of Man is at the center of our attention; both parables focus on his mission. In the first, the devil plays a rather insignificant part, for his activity extends only to a certain portion of the people to whom Jesus has come to preach. In the second, the devil steals into the very center of the action, effectively enacting a "parallel mission" in the same field, among the same people to whom the Son of Man preaches. Moreover, in both cases the actions of the devil are short-lived. In the first, he enters into someone else's field to steal from it; in the second, also like a thief in the night, he comes while people sleep to sow his own seed, then he leaves.

Adam and Eve,
Albrecht Dürer, 1507

The parable of the tares concerns the battle between God and the devil, between good and evil, a battle that rages throughout this age, but it will end in the age to come. This battle continues throughout the course of the history of the Gospel. Here, it is told in a short and laconic form.

The symbol of good in the parable is the wheat, while the tares (*zizania*), which are plants that also belong to the grain family, are a symbol of evil. The word *zizania* in Greek corresponds to the Latin *lolium*. In Virgil, the term was used to indicate weeds that can hinder a good harvest.[12] In the Gospel text, the word primarily indicates a variant of this plant, whose scientific name is *lolium temulentum* (literally "a weed that makes one drunk"). It usually grows in the same land as wheat, and it even looks like wheat superficially, but it contains certain substances that can be poisonous for human beings (resulting in dizziness, sleepiness, and even convulsions).

The external similarity between these two plants forces us to recognize that evil is always a counterfeit of the good, and that the devil always mimics God. In the Old Testament, the devil seems to imitate God, taking upon himself the role of an interpreter of the commandments. God tells Adam: "Of every tree of the garden thou mayest freely eat, but of the tree of the knowledge of good and evil, thou shalt not eat of it; for in the day that thou eatest thereof thou shalt surely die" (Gen 2.16–17). Eve retells this commandment to the devil, but he answers: "Ye shall not surely die. For God doth know that in the day ye eat thereof, then your eyes shall be opened, and ye shall be as gods, knowing good and evil" (Gen 3.4–5). In the mouth of the devil, evil masks itself as good, just as the tares mask themselves as wheat.

In Jesus' own interpretation, all the details of the parable are interpreted allegorically except for one: nothing is said concerning the servants of the householder. We can only guess that the householder is the Son of Man, and the servants are the apostles. They were disturbed that the

[12]Virgil, *The Georgics* 1.69.

mission of Jesus was not crowned with immediate success, that the devil walked alongside him in this world, stealing the word from people, that many completely rejected his preaching. They even asked permission to call down fire from heaven to destroy those in Samaria who would not accept Jesus. Jesus, however, called them to patience, saying: "Ye know not what manner of spirit ye are of" (Lk 9.55). Let us remember that in Luke the interpretation of the parable of the sower ends with an indication that those "on the good ground are they, which in an honest and good heart . . . bring forth fruit with patience" (Lk 8.15).

The Harvest,
A. Venetsianov, 1820

According to Jesus, the field is the world. This indicates the universal character of his mission. What he says and does refers not only to Israel, but to the whole world. He may have insisted in the beginning of his public ministry that he was sent only "to the lost sheep of the house of Israel" (Mt 10.6), but the closer he came to his final hour, the more often he reminded his listeners that the Gospel must be preached "in the whole world" (Mt 26.13). His final command to his disciples, according to Mark, took this form: "Go ye into all the world, and preach the Gospel to every creature" (Mk 16.15). In Matthew's Gospel, the risen Jesus commanded his disciples to go and teach "all nations" (Mt 28.19). The parable of the tares belongs to the early stage of his public ministry, yet even at this moment Jesus predicted that his preaching would be heard in the entire world.

Who are the sons of the kingdom and the sons of the evil one? In his conversation with the Jews in Capernaum, Jesus called the nation of Israel the sons of the kingdom, but he predicted that these sons would be cast out into the outer darkness, while "many shall come from the east and the west, and shall sit down with Abraham, and Isaac, and Jacob, in the kingdom of heaven" (Mt 8.11). The context of that conversation gives no doubt as to the meaning of Jesus' words: the representatives of Israel are the sons of the kingdom by birth and calling, but not by the way they responded to that call. After Israel failed to meet God's expectations, the sons of the

The Harvest,
Peter Bruegel
the Elder

kingdom became determined not by birth, but by faith. In the parable of
the tares, the sons of the kingdom are those who have come to believe in
Jesus because of his word (Jn 4.41). In another place, Jesus calls them sons
of light (Lk 16.8).

As for the sons of the evil one, they are the opponents of Jesus, that is,
the scribes and Pharisees, along with all whom they managed to convince
of their righteousness. Jesus addressed harsh words to them:

> Ye are of your father the devil, and the lusts of your father ye will do.
> He was a murderer from the beginning, and abode not in the truth,
> because there is no truth in him. When he speaketh a lie, he speaketh
> of his own: for he is a liar, and the father of it. . . . He that is of God
> heareth God's words; ye therefore hear them not, because ye are not
> of God. (John 8.44, 47)

The Jews answered by alleging that Jesus had an evil spirit (Jn 8.48).
Jesus often conducted similar dialogues—which were often very revealing
and sharp in their tone—in parallel with a parable, in which he proclaimed
the same truth, but in a less harsh manner, using the figurative language
of story.

The image of the harvest, which dominates in the final act of the parable, had already become associated with the judgment of God in the Old Testament:

> Let the heathen be wakened, and come up to the valley of Jehoshaphat, for there will I sit to judge all the heathen round about. Put ye in the sickle, for the harvest is ripe. Come, get you down, for the press is full, the fats overflow, for their wickedness is great. Multitudes, multitudes in the valley of decision: for the day of the Lord is near in the valley of decision. The sun and the moon shall be darkened, and the stars shall withdraw their shining. (Joel 3.12–15)

In this text of the Prophet Joel, however, God's judgment is primarily seen as judgment over the enemies of Israel and the restoration of the glory and power of the Israelite kingdom (Joel 3.19–20). In Jesus' preaching, the judgment is something completely different—it is the universal judgment that awaits the whole world at the end of the age. The harvest, then, is a symbol of the end of the world, after which comes the separation of the righteous from those who commit iniquity.

Jesus frequently reminded his disciples of the nearness of this event, using the image of the harvest among others. In Samaria, he said to them, "Lift up your eyes, and look on the fields; for they are white already to harvest. And he that reapeth receiveth wages, and gathereth fruit unto life eternal, that both he that soweth and he that reapeth may rejoice together" (Jn 4.35–36). In his final instruction to the disciples before the Last Supper, when he spoke of his second coming and the dread judgment, Jesus developed the same images that appear first in the parable of the tares. He directly alludes to the final harvest as described by the Prophet Joel:

> Immediately after the tribulation of those days shall the sun be darkened, and the moon shall not give her light, and the stars shall fall from heaven, and the powers of the heavens shall be shaken. And then shall appear the sign of the Son of Man in heaven, and then shall all the tribes of the earth mourn, and they shall see the Son of Man coming in the

clouds of heaven with power and great glory. And he shall send his angels with a great sound of a trumpet, and they shall gather together his elect from the four winds, from one end of heaven to the other. (Mt 24.29–31)

In this depiction of the final judgment, the Son of Man sits "upon the throne of his glory . . . and all the holy angels with him." All nations will gather before him, and he will separate them "as a shepherd divideth his sheep from the goats." Those on the left Jesus calls "they" (*autoi*) or "those" (*houtoi*), while those on the right he calls "the righteous" (*dikaioi*). As in the parable of the tares, the story ends with the blessedness of the righteous: "And these shall go away into everlasting punishment, but the righteous into life eternal" (Mt 25.31–46).

The idea of the separation of the righteous from the others is a central theme of Jesus' teaching concerning the dread judgment, and it appears as central in all parables that refer to the theme of the final judgment, including the parable of the tares, the parable of the net, "which, when it was full, they drew to shore, and sat down, and gathered the good into vessels, but cast the bad away" (Mt 13.48), and the parable of the ten virgins, five of whom are allowed to enter the marriage feast, but five are not (Mt 25.1–13).

The parable of the tares begins a series of six parables that in the Gospel according to Matthew begin with the words: "The kingdom of heaven is likened unto . . ." or "Again, the kingdom of heaven is like unto . . ." (Mt 13.24, 31, 44, 45, 47). The first and final parable of this sequence (the tares and the net) are dedicated to the theme of the dread judgment. The other four parables—the mustard seed, the leaven, the treasure hidden in the field, the merchant who finds a pearl of great price—are not concerned with the theme of judgment, but they further reveal the understanding of the "kingdom of heaven" as it refers to the earthly life of man. This accords with the double meaning that the terms "kingdom of heaven" and "kingdom of God" had in Jesus' preaching, indicating simultaneously the judgment after death and the spiritual reality that, like the tree that comes from the mustard seed, develops during the course of earthly existence.

The Harvest,
A. A. Plastov,
1945

In the writings of the holy fathers, both in the East and West, the parable of the tares is interpreted in light of the life of the Church after the death and resurrection of Jesus. John Chrysostom notes that false prophets come after true prophets, and false apostles after true apostles, the antichrist after Christ. Thus heretics follow their father the devil in sowing seed on a field already sown with good seed:

> Many of the prelates, I mean, bringing into the churches wicked men, disguised heresiarchs, gave great facility to the laying of that kind of snare. For the devil needs not even to take any trouble, when he has once planted them among us. After this he [Jesus] points out the thing to be superfluous too, not hurtful only; in that, after the land has been tilled, and there is no need of anything, then this enemy sows again; as the heretics also do, who for no other cause than vainglory inject their proper venom. And not by this only, but by what follows likewise, he depicts exactly all their acting. For, "When the blade was sprung up," says he, "and brought forth fruit, then appeared the tares also"; which kind of thing these men also do. For at the beginning they disguise themselves; but when they have gained much confidence, and

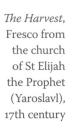

The Harvest,
Fresco from
the church
of St Elijah
the Prophet
(Yaroslavl),
17th century

someone imparts to them the teaching of the word, then they pour
out their poison.[13]

Augustine also interprets the parable of the tares with reference to the
life of the Church, but he interprets the image of the tares more broadly.
In this image he also understands all those who on earth are members the
Church, but who will not enter the kingdom of heaven:

> Ye see tares among the wheat, ye see evil Christians among the good;
> and ye wish to root up the evil ones; be quiet, it is not the time of
> harvest. That time will come, may it only find you wheat! Why do
> ye vex yourselves? Why bear impatiently the mixture of the evil with
> the good? In the field they may be with you, but they will not be so in
> the barn. Now ye know that those three places mentioned yesterday
> where the seed did not grow, "the way side," "the stony ground," and
> "the thorny places," are the same as these "tares." They received only a
> different name under a different similitude. For when similitudes are
> used, or the literal meaning of a term is not expressed, not the truth but
> a similitude of the truth is conveyed by them. I see that but few have
> understood my meaning; yet it is for the benefit of all that I speak. In
> things visible, a way side is a way side, stony ground is stony ground,
> thorny places are thorny places; they are simply what they are, because

[13]John Chrysostom, *Homilies on Matthew* 46.1 (NPNF[1] 10:288).

the names are used in their literal sense. But in parables and similitudes one thing may be called by many names; therefore there is nothing inconsistent in my telling you that that "way side," that "stony ground," those "thorny places," are bad Christians, and that they too are the "tares."[14]

These interpretations are only two of numerous examples of how the content of the parable has been developed and interpreted within the context of a specific historical time period. Both texts come from the late fourth to early fifth centuries. For the Church, this was an age of war against heresies—at first Arianism, which rejected the divinity of Jesus Christ, then a whole series of subsequent heresies. Secular authorities often got involved in this battle, sometimes on the side of the Church, sometimes on the side of its opponents. Chrysostom saw in the parable of the tares a concrete indication that heretics should not be killed.[15] In his time, such an interpretation held great significance, because the civil authorities could use the sword not only against its own enemies, but also against the enemies of the Church. Chrysostom argues against this in detail:

And this he said, to hinder wars from arising, and blood and slaughter. For it is not right to put a heretic to death, since an implacable war would be brought into the world. By these two reasons then he restrains them; one, that the wheat be not hurt; another, that punishment will surely overtake them, if incurably diseased. Wherefore, if you would have them punished, yet without harm to the wheat, I bid you wait for the proper season. But what means, "lest ye root up the wheat with them?" Either he means this: if you are to take up arms, and to kill the heretics, many of the saints also must needs be overthrown with them; or that of the very tares it is likely that many may change and become wheat. If therefore ye root them up beforehand, ye injure that which is to become wheat, slaying some, in whom there is yet room for change and improvement. He does not therefore forbid our checking heretics, and stopping their mouths, and taking away their freedom of speech, and

[14]Augustine, Sermon 23.1–2 (NPNF[1] 6:334).
[15]John Chrysostom, *Homilies on Matthew* 46.1 (NPNF[1] 10:288).

Galileo Galilei, Justus
Sustermans, 1636

Monument to Giordano
Bruno in Rome on the
Campo de' Fiori, the place
of his execution

breaking up their assemblies and confederacies,
but our killing and slaying them.[16]

In the history of the Western Christendom,
there was a long period when groups of Christians—with the help of civil authorities—systematically eradicated all whom they deemed heretics and
witches, and sometimes merely those who thought
or believed differently. Officially, these executions
were matters of state, but such criminal proceed-
ings were initiated by the so-called Inquisition,
which actively worked in many European countries
from the thirteenth to the seventeenth centuries.
Among the most famous victims of the Inquisition was Giordano Bruno, who was burned alive in
1600, and Galileo Galilei, who was imprisoned in
1633 (among his crimes was the "heresy of heliocen-
trism," the idea that the Earth orbits the Sun).

The actions of the Inquisition were proof of the
radical deviation of the medieval Catholic Church
from the teachings expressed in the Gospel. Even
to this day, the "pyres of the Inquisition" are often
cast in the teeth of Christians by those who make
no distinctions between the Church of the East and
Christianity in the West. In the Christian East, executions of heretics were
extremely rare. One example is the burning alive of several people accused
of the Judaizing heresy in Moscow in 1504. In this case, those who were
on the side of such extreme measure against heresies included certain
prominent members of the clergy, even though, as with the Inquisition,
the execution was officially performed by the civil authority.

Let us turn away from this short historical digression to modern times.
What can the parable of the tares say to a person of the twenty-first century?
First of all, it speaks much of the patience of God. Often people ask the same

[16]Ibid.

question again and again: Why does God not punish
sinners, criminals, villains? Why does God allow evil
to persist, why does he allow the evil to live among
the good and perpetrate their crimes in their midst?
The answer is found not in God's alleged inability to
see evil or his permissiveness, but rather in God's
patience. Even in the Old Testament, God spoke
through the lips of the prophet: "I have no pleasure
in the death of the wicked, but that the wicked turn
from his way and live" (Ezek 33.11). In the New Testament, the Apostle Paul insists that God "will have
all men to be saved, and to come unto the knowledge of the truth" (1 Tim 2.4). These words show that
God's patience endures and he never loses hope that
the sinner, while he lives, will repent.

The Apostle Paul, Icon
painted by St Andrei
Rublev, *c.* 1410

As is well known, some of those who lived in the first generation of
Jesus' followers assumed that the promise of the end of the age and the
second coming would occur during their own lives. They expected the
second coming any day, and were surprised that it had not come yet. To
answer these expectations and confusion, the Apostle Peter offered the
following response: "The Lord is not slack concerning his promise, as some
men count slackness; but is longsuffering to us-ward, not willing that any
should perish, but that all should come to repentance" (2 Pet 3.9). God's
longsuffering, according to the apostle, should be considered salvation (2
Pet 3.15), since it gives an opportunity to the unrepentant to come to repentance, for the evil to turn to good, for the tares to transform into wheat.

In any case, man should never assume the role of judge, or dare to
determine who belongs to the wheat, and who to the tares, since the final
judgment belongs to God alone. In God's eyes, the righteous man may
end up being someone whom everyone treated with contempt. Lazarus
from the parable, the thief on the cross, the sinful woman who anointed
Jesus' feet, and the publicans and sinful women with whom Jesus broke
bread—all these images appear frequently in the Gospel story, reminding
us that "God hath chosen the foolish things of the world to confound the

Pharisees, James
Jacques Joseph
Tissot, 1886

wise, and God hath chosen the weak things of the world to confound the things which are mighty, and base things of the world, and things which are despised, hath God chosen, yea, and things which are not, to bring to nought things that are" (1 Cor 1.27–28). Only God knows the deepest secrets of man, and so it is only in his power to separate the wheat from the tares. But even he refrains from doing this until the dread judgment, leaving both good and bad to grow until the harvest.

One of the characteristic aspects of the Pharisee's religiosity was the idea that the righteous must be separated from sinners. Even the word "Pharisee," as is well known, means "one who is set apart." The Pharisees sincerely thanked God for *not* being like "other people" (Lk 18.11). The Essene community of Qumran had a similar sense of self. Among the community of Jesus' disciples, however, everything is quite different. In it, sinners sit together with the righteous, and God's longsuffering allows the tares to grow with the wheat. Finally, the parable of the tares reminds us that the devil works at the same time as God, that evil exists on earth together with good. Evil and good are closely intertwined in this world, like the ears of the wheat and the tares, which even intertwine on the root level.[17] Because

[17] Aleksandr Shargunov, *Evangelie dnya* [The Gospel of the day] vol. 1–2 (Moscow: 2008), 303.

of their external similarity, it is sometimes difficult to tell which plant is which.[18] It is even more difficult, while weeding out the one, to avoid harming the other. In the parable of the sower, Jesus speaks of people, like seeds, who have been sown among thorns. They quickly grow, but the thorns choke them, as it were. In the parable of the tares, he paints a different picture. The wheat grows in the midst of tares, but the tares will not choke it. Man is called to battle against evil, to fight for his own spiritual survival, uprooting the seeds of evil not in the people surrounding him, but first and foremost in himself.

3. The Seed in the Ground

In the Gospel according to Mark, the sermon on the boat includes three parables. Of these, two are included in Matthew's version: the parable of the sower and the parable of the mustard seed. Mark places a third parable between them, which is not found in the other synoptic Gospels:

> And he said, "So is the kingdom of God, as if a man should cast seed into the ground, and should sleep, and rise night and day, and the seed should spring and grow up, he knoweth not how. For the earth bringeth forth fruit of herself: first the blade, then the ear, after that the full corn in the ear. But when the fruit is brought forth, immediately he putteth in the sickle, because the harvest is come." (Mk 4.26–29)

This parable is connected with the parables of the sower, the seed, and the wheat and tares in the Gospel of Matthew, as well as with the parable of the mustard seed, which is included in the sermon on the boat in both Matthew and Mark's Gospels. All four parables use the image of the seed, the connective tissue among the four stories. In each of them, however, the image has a different thematic focus.

---

[18]Justin (Popovich), *Tolkovanie na evangelie ot Matfeya* [Commentary on the Gospel of Matthew], *Sobranie tvorenii* [Collected works], vol. 5 (Moscow: Palomnik, 2014), 5–466, at 304.

Wheat, Contemporary photograph

Some scholars suggest that Mark's parable of the seed in the earth was the foundational story for Matthew's subsequent elaboration, which became two parables: the sower and the tares.[19] The reason for this is the common elements between the two: a man, seeds, ears of wheat, plant growth, bearing fruit, and the harvest. Similar processes are examined: a man sows seed and sleeps while the seed grows; when the stalk of wheat brings fruit, he sends out reapers. These externally similar elements are, however, where the similarities end. The two parables have two different plotlines; consequently, they require two different interpretations. Using a similar set of images, Jesus created two different stories, just as a tailor can make two completely different suits out of the same material.

The central theme of the parable of the seed in the ground is found in the adjective *automatē*, which is used as an adverb and is translated "of herself" (or "by itself"). In the New Testament, this adjective is only used in this specific way twice: the second time is found in Acts, in the account of Peter, who, when leaving prison together with an angel, went through the gate that opened to them of its own accord (cf. Acts 12.10). In the parable, after the man throws the seed into the ground, everything occurs by itself: the seed grows and develops thanks to the fruitfulness of the earth.

This expression "the earth bringeth forth fruit of herself" is an allusion to the third day of creation in Genesis:

> And God said, "Let the earth bring forth grass, the herb yielding seed, and the fruit tree yielding fruit after his kind, whose seed is in itself, upon the earth." And it was so. And the earth brought forth grass, and herb yielding seed after his kind, and the tree yielding fruit, whose seed was in itself, after his kind. And God saw that it was good. (Gen 1.11–12)

---

[19]Jülicher, *Gleichnisreden*, 562–63; Manson, *The Teaching of Jesus*, 222–23; T. W. Manson, *The Sayings of Jesus* (London: SCM Press, 1964), 192.

The Third Day of Creation, Julius Schnorr von Carolsfeld, 1860

If the heavens, the earth, the light, and the firmament in the midst of the waters were created immediately at God's command (Gen 1.1–10), the creation of plant life is given to the earth itself. From this moment, the earth contains within itself a creative potential that is realized in several stages: first, the soil accepts into itself various forms of seeds; then, feeding them with its nourishment, it allows them to grow and turn into plants and trees; finally, these plants and trees bring forth fruit. This word "fruit" indicates the final stage of a long process that seems to happen by itself. In reality, of course, it is not an automatic process at all, because behind this seemingly automatic process is the power that God gave to the earth.

An additional connection to Genesis can be found in the expression "And should sleep, and rise night and day." This expression should be understood in the sense that man sleeps at night, and gets up during the day. The order of words here corresponds to the biblical understanding that the day begins with the evening of the previous day. Sleep is not, therefore, the end of a day of sunlight, but rather that which precedes it. Such a perspective is also reflected in Genesis: "And the evening and the morning were the first day" (Gen 1.5). There may also be another hidden allusion to Genesis

Christ and the Pharisees, Ernst Zimmerman, 19th century

in that it echoes the fact that God "resteth on the seventh day from all his work which he had made" (Gen 2.2).

If the central portion of this parable is dedicated to the description of the process of growth, in the margins of the story (in the beginning and end) we see the figure of a man who orchestrates the whole process. He initiates it, having thrown the seed into the ground, and he also gathers the harvest. Who is this person? If we use the same allegorical structure that we find in the parables of the sower and tares, this person can by analogy be the Son of Man. He throws the seeds of his teaching into the soil of men's heart: having fallen into their hearts, it invisibly begins to grow and develop.

Here it is appropriate to recall Jesus' conversation with the Pharisees concerning the kingdom of God: "And when he was demanded of the Pharisees, when the kingdom of God should come, he answered them and said, 'The kingdom of God cometh not with observation; neither shall they say, "Lo here!" Or, "Lo there!" For behold, the kingdom of God is within you'" (Lk 17.20–21). This dialogue reflects the vast difference between Jesus' understanding of the kingdom of God and his listeners' assumptions about it. They believed that it would come in the future, and that they should expect and prepare for it. Moreover, they believed that it would be a local authority in a specific geographical location—Israel, naturally. But Jesus spoke of a kingdom that had already come and that they should not expect or seek it somewhere else. The kingdom of God "is come unto you" he insisted (Mt 12.28), meaning that this kingdom was on earth at that moment in history, not that it would come in some distant future.

The kingdom of God is a concept that refers to man's interior world, to his spiritual life, to his heart. But it is not a static reality: the kingdom of God does not come with observation; it invisibly grows within man. Note that Jesus, according to Mark, did not compare this kingdom to a seed, nor to the earth, nor to the plant, nor to the fruit. The kingdom of God is not like any of these images, but rather, it is like all the images put together, in their interaction. The final result is the growth of the seed into a fruit-bearing plant. But the most important accent in the parable is found not in the result, but in the process, not in the goal, but in the progress toward it.

The parable does not include a single indication that the plant needs to be cultivated. This could perhaps invite the following interpretation: man does not need to labor to acquire the fruits of the kingdom of God within him that God expects of him. God has already done all the work himself, and man can simply sleep, get up, and go to sleep again. Such an interpretation, of course, does not fit the general tone of Jesus' preaching, which called all to active cooperation with God. Thus, for example, we have the following stark call: "From the days of John the Baptist until now the kingdom of heaven suffereth violence, and the violent take it by force" (Mt 11.12).

Even though it is not clear in this specific parable, from the general context of Jesus' preaching, it is evident that he does not expect mankind to passively imbibe his teaching, then wait for it to bring fruit within them automatically. In his preaching, the word "fruit" always refers to the result of man's own labors. In the Sermon on the Mount, Jesus echoes John the Baptist: "every tree that bringeth not forth good fruit is hewn down, and cast into the fire" (Mt 7.19). If the tree had to bring forth its own fruit, without any efforts from the man who tends it, then the Sermon on the Mount would have been unnecessary, nor would any of Jesus' moral teachings have any weight, for they all call his listeners to concrete action.

Since the evangelist did not offer a specific interpretation of this parable, we can postulate several layers of meaning for it, as do both ancient and modern commentators. At the same time, we acknowledge the fact that these readings do not exhaust all possible meanings. This parable can be interpreted with reference to Jesus' mission on earth through the preaching of the apostles and their successors, to the revelation of divine truth in the history of mankind, to the spiritual life of an individual human being, and to the final judgment and the retribution after death.

With reference to Jesus' ministry, the parable can mean that the goal for which he came to earth will be achieved regardless of external circumstances and of people's cooperation or antagonism. If he sowed the seeds of truth on the earth, they will inevitably grow, and nothing will restrain the growth of the kingdom, though sometimes the growth may seem to be invisible.[20] The final stage of his mission will be the dread judgment, when he will send the reapers down to earth to gather the harvest.

As for the spread of the Gospel through the preaching of the apostles, the parable can also mean that in spite of all external antagonism, this good news will still spread, no matter what. The power of the soil, in this case, becomes an image of the divine power that acts through the preaching of the apostles. Writing to the Corinthians, the Apostle Paul told them not to pay attention to the one from whom they heard the good news. God himself stands behind the actions of every individual apostle, whoever he may be:

> Who then is Paul, and who is Apollos, but ministers by whom ye believed, even as the Lord gave to every man? I have planted, Apollos watered, but God gave the increase. So then neither is he that planteth anything, neither he that watereth, but God that giveth the increase. Now he that planteth and he that watereth are one, and every man shall receive his own reward according to his own labor. For we are laborers together [synergoi] with God. Ye are God's husbandry; ye are God's building. (1 Corinthians 3.5–9)

---

[20]Blomberg, *Interpreting the Parables*, 283.

We should note that when Paul spoke of the growth of the Church as the kingdom of God on earth, he was using the same images that Jesus used in the parable of the seed in the ground. When he stresses that God himself increases the growth of the seed, he speaks of himself and the other apostles as fellow-laborers [or "coworkers," "cooperators"—*synergoi*] with God. The call to such cooperation is something that fills Jesus' preaching, especially in his specific instructions to the apostles.

Ancient commentators see in this parable an intimation of the gradual development of divine truth within the history of mankind from the Old Testament prophets to the preaching of Christ and his disciples. Moreover, the Old Testament is often seen as a kind of childhood, while the coming of Christ and his ministry are humanity's youth, and the subsequent life of the Church is adulthood (cf. Gal 3.23–25, 4.1–7):

> First comes the grain, and from the grain arises the shoot, and from
> the shoot struggles out the shrub; thereafter boughs and leaves gather
> strength, and the whole that we call a tree expands; then follows the
> swelling of the germen, and from the germen bursts the flower, and
> from the flower the fruit opens: that fruit itself, rude for a while, and
> unshapely, little by little, keeping the straight course of its develop-
> ment, is trained to the mellowness of its flavor. So, too, righteous-
> ness—for the God of righteousness and of creation is the same—was
> first in a rudimentary state, having a natural fear of God; from that
> stage it advanced, through the Law and the prophets, to infancy; from
> that stage it passed, through the Gospel, to the fervor of youth: now,
> through the Paraclete, it is settling into maturity.[21]

Finally, the parable is interpreted with reference to the spiritual life of each individual person. In this case, it shows us how righteousness and a virtuous life gradually bear fruit in a person, which he may not even notice at first:

> For surely to produce the blade is to have still the tenderness of a good
> beginning. Indeed the blade reaches the ear when virtue conceived

---

[21]Tertullian, *On the Veiling of Virgins* 1 (ANF 4:27–28).

The Prophet Joel,
Michelangelo, 1508–12

in the spirit burgeons in the growth of a good deed. Truly it brings forth the full corn in the ear when virtue grows so much that it can assume the nature of a strong and perfect deed, and when it has produced its fruit, immediately He puts in the sickle because it is the time of harvest.[22]

The fact that this parable of the seed points to God's judgment after human history is made obvious by the presence of images of reaping and harvest. We have already spoken of these images, which first appear in the book of the prophet Joel (Joel 3.12–15), in our examination of the parable of the wheat and the tares.

The variety of possible interpretations should not distract us from the obvious fact that this parable—like the parables of the sower and wheat and tares—has a Christocentric focus. Along with these two, this parable speaks of Jesus and his mission on earth. This mission was preceded by the preaching of the prophets and John the Baptist, and it would continue with the preaching of the apostles and their descendants, even to the final judgment, when God will finally gather all the fruits of all the seeds he has sown on earth. Thus, in a few lines, the entire history of Christianity is described.

4. The Mustard Seed

The parable of the mustard seed continues the series of parables in which the primary image is a seed. This parable is found in all three synoptic Gospels. In Matthew and Mark it concludes the sermon on the boat, while in Luke it is found on its own. Here is the version according to Matthew:

[22]Gregory the Great, *Homilies on Ezekiel* 2.3.5; Saint Gregory the Great, *Homilies on the Book of the Prophet Ezekiel*, trans. Theodosia Tomkinson (Etna, CA: Center for Traditionalist Orthodox Studies, 2008), 296.

Another parable put he forth unto them, saying, "The kingdom of heaven is like to a grain of mustard seed, which a man took, and sowed in his field, which indeed is the least of all seeds, but when it is grown, it is the greatest among herbs, and becometh a tree, so that the birds of the air come and lodge in the branches thereof." (Mt 13.31–32)

In Mark's version the parable begins with a question as the premise, after which the story itself is told. Moreover, in Mark's version, there is no man; the entire process is described as though it occurred without human interference:

The Parable of the Mustard Seed, Icon, 20th century.

And he said, "Whereunto shall we liken the kingdom of God? Or with what comparison shall we compare it? It is like a grain of mustard seed, which, when it is sown in the earth, is less than all the seeds that be in the earth. But when it is sown, it groweth up, and becometh greater than all herbs, and shooteth out great branches, so that the fowls of the air may lodge under the shadow of it." (Mk 4.31–32)

Luke's version (Lk 13.18–19) has similarities to both of the others. As with Mark's version, it begins with a question. As with Matthew's, there is a man present. But unlike the other two, Luke's version has no mention of the mustard seed being the smallest seed of all. If in Matthew, the man sows the mustard seed in his field, and in Mark, it is sown into the earth, in Luke's version, the man plants it in his own garden. In Luke's version, the process of the seed's growth and its transformation into a tree is described the most laconically and schematically.

The mustard seed is indeed quite small, about one millimeter in diameter. From it, an annual herbaceous plant grows, the seeds of which contain mustard oil. The Greek name of this plant (*sinapi*) comes from the word *sinos* ("hurt," or "lesion") and *opsis* ("vision"). This combination is based on the fact that if mustard oil gets in the eyes, it causes tears. In Palestine, this plant can grow up to three meters tall. In all three synoptic Gospels, this plant is called a tree; moreover, both Matthew and Mark use the term *lachanon* (literally "vegetable"). The combination of these two words probably refers to the fact that although this plant is not a tree, it can grow to be as tall as a real tree.

In Jesus' preaching, the mustard seed is usually used as a synonym for something very small, insignificant, unnoticeable. The expression "faith as a grain of mustard seed" (Mt 17.20) indicates very little faith indeed. In this parable, however, the tiny seed becomes a great tree. "The mystery of the Kingdom resides in the paradoxical polarity between its embryonic state of little importance and its developed state of universal majesty."[23] Another scholar notes, "The kingdom of God is both coming and present, both rushing in imminently and already at work drawing the world into the future . . ." The parable of the seed therefore reflects "a tension between the two modalities of the kingdom."[24]

The image of the tree in which birds can perch is found in the prophets:

> Thus saith the Lord God, "I will also take of the highest branch of the high cedar, and will set it; I will crop off from the top of his young twigs a tender one, and will plant it upon an high mountain and eminent. In the mountain of the height of Israel will I plant it, and it shall bring forth boughs, and bear fruit, and be a goodly cedar, and under it shall dwell all fowl of every wing; in the shadow of the branches thereof shall they dwell." (Ezek 17.22–23)

> Therefore his height was exalted above all the trees of the field, and his boughs were multiplied, and his branches became long because of the multitude of waters, when he shot forth. All the fowls of heaven made their nests in his boughs, and under his branches did all the beasts of the field bring forth their young, and under his shadow dwelt all great nations. (Ezek 31.5–6)

[23]Werner H. Kelber, *The Kingdom in Mark: A New Place and a New Time* (Philadelphia: Fortress Press, 1974), 40.

[24]James G. Williams, *Gospel against Parable: Mark's Language of Mystery* (Sheffield: Almond Press, 1985), 134.

*The Parable
of the Mustard
Seed,*
Jan Leychen,
1791–1826

The tree grew, and was strong, and the height thereof reached unto heaven, and the sight thereof to the end of all the earth. The leaves thereof were fair, and the fruit thereof much, and in it was meat for all; the beasts of the field had shadow under it, and the fowls of the heaven dwelt in the boughs thereof, and all flesh was fed of it. (Dan 4.10–11)

Nevertheless, one should not exaggerate the importance of such literary parallels, since Jesus most likely used the image of birds living on tree branches because he drew upon the natural life surrounding him, not because he had read it in a particular text. Once more, it bears repetition that although Jesus knew Scripture very well, he did not refer to it as to a direct source for quotations. His preaching was not "bookish"—it was addressed to simple people, and for the most part he used images and symbols from daily life, not written works.

What does this parable say? First of all, again, it speaks of the preaching of Jesus, his mission, which began very humbly, but would soon spread over the entire earth. A man, surrounded by a small group of people, preached and performed miracles for a little more than three years. After his death, there were only about one hundred and twenty people left who considered themselves to be members of his community (Acts 1.15). The exponential growth of the Church began with Pentecost (Acts 2.41), and by the fourth century many millions reckoned themselves followers of Jesus. In our own time, the total number of Christians in the world is more than two billion. If to these we add the Christians who lived during the past two millennia from the death of Jesus, we can truly speak of a geometric progression, in which the beginning and end points are so far apart that the comparison between the size of the mustard seed and the tree that comes from it are not nearly proportional.

Did Jesus foresee such growth? Naturally he did, since he spoke of it often with his disciples. In his own time, this was not only far from obvious, but completely unlikely, in the same way that old, childless Abraham must have thought God's promise of descendants "as the dust of the earth" (Gen 13.16) to be unlikely. Nevertheless, the prophecy of the massive growth of believers began to come true even in the first generation of Christian converts.

What was the reason for this unprecedented growth? Was it only Jesus' teaching? The Gospels answer this question with Jesus' own words, spoken not long before his last Passover: "Verily, verily, I say unto you, except a corn of wheat fall into the ground and die, it abideth alone. But if it die, it bringeth forth much fruit" (Jn 12.24). Though in this parable we are examining a mustard seed, not a "corn of wheat," the meaning is the same. Any seed must die first before it can grow and bring forth fruit. For Jesus, who knew that he came into the world to give his life for the sake of the world (Jn 10.17), the image of the seed was always closely connected with the theme of death and resurrection.

It is possible that the words about the grain of wheat from John's Gospel contain a key to understanding all the synoptic parables that are thematically connected to seeds. In all these parables, Jesus speaks of seeds and growth. But in the general context of Jesus' mission, the path between seed and fruit had to pass through death. This coming death, which Jesus foreknew from the beginning, gives his words a different tone than those of any other preacher at any other time on earth.

It is no surprise, then, that in the early Church the image of the seed is frequently associated with martyrdom. Tertullian's words concerning the

blood of martyrs being the seed of the Church are
very well known.[25] St Ambrose of Milan adds:

> The grain is, admittedly, very simple and ordi-
> nary. But grind it, and you will see what vigour it
> has. So, too, faith appears at first to be simple and
> ordinary, but if crushed by its enemies it spreads
> everywhere the virtue and grace it contains, and its
> pungent odour fills all those who hear or read it.
> Our martyrs, Felix, Nabor, and Victor were a grain
> of mustard seed. They guarded within their hearts
> the perfume of the faith. . . . The Lord himself is a
> grain of mustard seed. . . . He chose to be crushed
> and ground so that we might say, "We are the good
> fragrance of Christ before God." (2 Cor 2.15)[26]

The Church of the Holy
Spirit within the Monastery
of the Holy Spirit, Vilnius

The three martyrs who are here mentioned suffered in the beginning of
the fourth century. Later, their remains were transferred to Milan, where
Ambrose served as bishop. The Church has always stressed the importance of the feat of martyrdom. Liturgies were served on the tombs of
martyrs, and churches were built over their remains. In many cities, the
relics of martyrs became focal points for thousands of pilgrims. It was
quite frequent for a martyric death to be the seed that led to the growth of
Christianity in a particular city or country.

The author of this book had the honor of living in the Monastery of the
Holy Spirit in Vilnius for two years. In the cathedral church of this monastery lie the incorrupt relics of the martyrs Antony, John, and Eustratius,
who served at the court of Prince Olgerd and were martyred in 1347. It
was their martyrdom that began the spread of Christianity in Lithuania.
Prince Olgerd, who ordered their martyrdom, returned to Christianity
later and before his death took monastic vows. All his twelve sons were

---

[25]Tertullian, *The Apology* 50.13 (ANF 3:55).

[26]Ambrose of Milan, *Commentary on Luke* 7.178–79, in *Commentary of Saint Ambrose
on the Gospel according to Saint Luke*, trans. Íde M. Ní Rian, (Dublin: Halcyon Press, 2001),
247–48.

The Holy New Martyrs and Confessors of Russia, Icon, 20th century

Christians. Two or three generations after Olgerd, Lithuania became a Christian country.

There are many similar cases in the histories of various nations. The means for the spread of Christianity over the centuries is no less paradoxical than the Christian faith itself. It would seem that massive exterminations of the followers of Christ, such as in Soviet Russia in the 1920s and 1930s, should lead to a weakening of the faith and the destruction of the Church. And for a short period of time, it might seem that this did indeed happen. But after the suffering and death, resurrection inevitably followed, and millions of new believers replaced the thousands who were tortured and killed.

That this occurred at every new stage of Christianity's spread only confirms Jesus' words to his disciples: the internal power of his teaching is like the potential within a seed that falls into the good soil of human hearts. The good soil, together with the soil's intrinsic potential power, produces a plant that brings forth fruit a hundredfold. This seed cannot even be choked by sowing tares right next to it. This seed gives increase and brings fruit in and of itself, thanks to the potential imbued within it at the beginning. This seed, which is externally insignificant and unobtrusive, grows into a great tree, in whose branches birds can find shelter.

The White Savior, Icon, Kizhi, 16th century

What Jesus brought to this earth cannot be reduced to something as simple as a "teaching." His preaching, of course, has an unconditional and absolute character for Christians, but the meaning of his coming to earth is not limited by the dogmas of the teaching itself. The Church that he established is the place in which he continues to be present and continues to fulfill his mission. But this mission on earth is not even limited by the creation of the Church. Being God himself, he is greater and wider than his teaching, and even his own Church. According to the words of the Apostle Paul, "in him dwelleth all the fullness of the Godhead bodily" (Col 2.9).

That which Jesus brought to people is best expressed with a concept that he used very often: the kingdom of heaven. As it turns out, it is wider and greater than any "teaching," than any "church," "religion," or any other such concept.

The kingdom of heaven is not subject to definition, since it is greater than any definition. In Jesus' teachings, it reveals itself through a series of similes that form the backbone of his parables. In Jesus' ministry, it is revealed first of all through his suffering, death, and resurrection. In the final analysis, the kingdom of heaven is identical to Jesus himself, who is "the way, the truth, and the life" (Jn 14.6).

Man can come into contact with this kingdom of heaven both through the teaching of Jesus and through the Church, even without being torn away from his daily life. Jesus does not pull people out of the world; like the wheat among the tares, Christians remain in this world awaiting the coming harvest. To join this kingdom, neither the sower, nor the reaper, nor the fisherman needs to reject his profession. All they must do is learn to see within daily life that dimension that Jesus reveals and that he indicates by the strange, mysterious phrase: "the kingdom of heaven."

5. The Leaven in the Meal

In the Gospel according to Matthew, the sermon on the boat ends with the parable of the leaven in the meal. This short parable follows immediately after the parable of the mustard seed.

> Another parable spake he unto them: "The kingdom of heaven is like unto leaven, which a woman took, and hid in three measures of meal, till the whole was leavened." (Mt 13.33)

In the Gospel according to Luke, these same two parables are given in the same order. In Luke, the parable is preceded by a question: "Whereunto shall I liken the kingdom of God?" (Lk 13.20)

Because in both Gospel accounts these two parables happen one after the other, and because of the apparent thematic similarity of both, they are frequently interpreted together. John Chrysostom, speaking of the image of the mustard seed, wrote,

> Thus he meant to set forth the most decisive sign of its greatness. Even so then shall it be with respect to the Gospel too, says he. Yea, for his disciples were weakest of all, and least of all; but nevertheless, because of the great power that was in them, it has been unfolded in every part of the world. After this he adds the leaven to this similitude. . . . For as

this converts the large quantity of meal into its own quality, even so shall
you convert the whole world. . . . As therefore the leaven then leavens
the lump when it comes close to the meal, and not simply close, but so
as to be actually mixed with it (for he said not, "put," simply, but "hid");
so also ye, when you cleave to your enemies, and are made one with
them, then shall you get the better of them. And as the leaven, though
it be buried, yet is not destroyed, but little by little transmutes all into
its own condition; of like sort will the event be here also, with respect
to the Gospel. . . . And marvel not, if discoursing about the kingdom,
he made mention of a little seed and of leaven; for he was discoursing
with men inexperienced and ignorant, and such as needed to be led on
by those means. For so simple were they, that even after all this, they
required a good deal of explanation. . . . For great is the power of the
Gospel, and that which has been once leavened, becomes leaven again
for what remains. And as a spark, when it has caught in timber, makes
what has been burnt up already increase the flame, and so proceeds to
the rest; even so the Gospel likewise. But he said not fire, but leaven.
Why might this be? Because in that case the whole effect is not of the
fire, but partly of the timber too that is kindled, but in this the leaven
does the whole work by itself. Now if twelve men leavened the whole
world, imagine how great our baseness, in that when we being so many
are not able to amend them that remain—we, who ought to be enough
for ten thousand worlds, and to become leaven to them.[27]

In contemporary scholarship, the parables of the mustard seed and the
leaven are also often interpreted together, since they have the same meaning.[28] The similarity is also underlined in cases when, like Chrysostom, the
parable is interpreted with reference to the growth of Christianity. But can
we limit the meaning of the parable to this theme alone? And can we really
be limited to interpreting the images of the mustard seed and the leaven
as having the same meaning?

---

[27]John Chrysostom, *Homilies on Matthew* 46.2–3 (NPNF[1] 10:289–90).
[28]Cf. Blomberg, *Interpreting the Parables*, 391–95.

The leaven is a microscopic substance that is added to food for a specific purpose. Yeast is added to make bread rise and to change its taste. In the Old Testament, leaven was given a special, religious significance. It was connected first of all with the prohibition of eating anything leavened during the weeklong celebration of Passover. In the Law of Moses, the penalty for breaking this commandment was death:

> Seven days shall ye eat unleavened bread, even the first day ye shall put away leaven out of your houses: for whosoever eateth leavened bread from the first day until the seventh day, that soul shall be cut off from Israel. And ye shall observe the feast of unleavened bread; for in this selfsame day have I brought your armies out of the land of Egypt; therefore shall ye observe this day in your generations by an ordinance forever. In the first month, on the fourteenth day of the month at even, ye shall eat unleavened bread, until the twenty-first day of the month at even. Seven days shall there be no leaven found in your houses, for whosoever eateth that which is leavened, even that soul shall be cut off from the congregation of Israel, whether he be a stranger, or born in the land. Ye shall eat nothing leavened; in all your habitations shall ye eat unleavened bread. (Ex 12.15, 17–20)

The original reason for this prohibition in Jewish tradition is an object of speculation among scholars to this day, as is the theological significance for removing leaven from the home for an entire week. According to one explanation, leaven was a symbol of sin. According to another interpretation, the destruction of all old leaven was a symbol of renewal that must occur every year. This kind of interpretive tradition is reflected in the words of the Apostle Paul:

> Know ye not that a little leaven leaveneth the whole lump? Purge out therefore the old leaven, that ye may be a new lump, as ye are unleavened. For even Christ our Passover is sacrificed for us, therefore let us keep the feast, not with old leaven, neither with the leaven of malice and wickedness; but with the unleavened bread of sincerity and truth. (1 Cor 5.6–8)

Baked bread and
grains of wheat

St Paul's words about the leaven of malice and wickedness resonate with Jesus' words about the leaven of the Pharisees, which is hypocrisy (Lk 12.1). In Matthew and Mark, an entire dialogue between Jesus and his disciples is dedicated to this leaven:

> And when his disciples were come to the other side, they had forgotten to take bread. Then Jesus said unto them, "Take heed and beware of the leaven of the Pharisees and of the Sadducees." And they reasoned among themselves, saying, "It is because we have taken no bread." Which when Jesus perceived, he said unto them, "O ye of little faith, why reason ye among yourselves, because ye have brought no bread? Do ye not yet understand, neither remember the five loaves of the five thousand, and how many baskets ye took up? Neither the seven loaves of the four thousand, and how many baskets ye took up? How is it that ye do not understand that I spake it not to you concerning bread, that ye should beware of the leaven of the Pharisees and of the Sadducees?" Then understood they how that he bade them not beware of the leaven of bread, but of the doctrine of the Pharisees and of the Sadducees. (Mt 16.5–12)

In this case, the leaven symbolizes an element that, having spread itself through the entire teaching of the Pharisees and Sadducees, made it powerless to reveal the path to the kingdom of heaven. This element is what Jesus calls hypocrisy.

In this parable, the image of the leaven possesses a more positive significance. Before us we see an example of how the same image can have different meanings depending on what reality it is called to represent.

The image of the woman who prepares bread could only evoke positive associations for Jesus' listeners. Most of them would have been men. When they would come home, their wives would greet them with warm, freshly-baked bread. The women who were among Jesus' listeners would have recognized themselves in the image of the woman. So both the men and the women would have understood the literal meaning of his words very well. As for the figurative meaning, each of them would have understood it differently.

If we return to the comparison between the parables of the mustard seed and the leaven, we must note the differences in the superficial elements of the images. The image of the seed is taken from agricultural life, which was primarily the domain of men (in Matthew and Luke, it is a man that casts the seed into the ground), while the image of the leaven is from the daily life of the home, which was primarily the domain of women. The seed begins to grow within the earth, then breaks out into the open and turns into a plant, but the ground does not change during that process. As for the leaven, it remains inside the dough, not coming out in any way, but it transforms the nature, the taste, and the smell of the dough.

Even this simple comparison of the external aspects of the images forces us to think about whether or not they were intended to reflect the same internal thematic meaning. As we have seen, the image of the leaven seems to perform a different function than the image of the seed. It points to the same reality of the kingdom of heaven, but it reveals it in a different way.

The image of the leaven seems more thematically similar to the images that we encounter in the Sermon on the Mount than to the mustard seed: the salt of the earth and the light of the world (Mt 5.13–14). Not incidentally, in Mark's version of the sermon on the boat, we find words that are similar to the Sermon on the Mount: "And he said unto them, 'Is a candle brought to be put under a bushel, or under a bed? and not to be set on a candlestick?'" (Mk 4.21) Evidently, Jesus expressed the same idea in both the Sermon on the Mount and the sermon on the boat, and this idea is different from the main theme of the parable of the mustard seed.

The images of salt, light, and candles, as it seems to us, have the same thematic significance (or meaning). They are intended to indicate the *qualitative effect* of the presence of Jesus' followers on the world. Salt, when it is found in food, gives it flavor. A candle fills with light the room in which it is placed. Yeast in dough makes the loaf rise. Christians are called to fulfill the same function in the world that the salt fulfills in food, the light in a room, and the leaven in meal.

Continuing this analogy, we may also say that the relationship between candle and room, salt and food, and leaven and meal is the relationship between two foreign elements. They do not belong to the same category, but provide an additional quality that is lacking in the original state. In the same way, the followers of Jesus, living in the world, are strangers to the world. They are in the world, but not of the world (Jn 17.14–18).

If we examine the parable of the leaven in relation to the spiritual life or the internal world of an individual person, then here too we find differences from the parable of the mustard seed. There, the main focus of the story is the difference in size between the seed and the tree. But in this parable, the focus is not so much on a quantitative difference, but on a *qualitative one:* the presence of the kingdom of God in the soul of a person qualitatively changes his entire life, giving it a taste and fullness that it did not have before. As St Justin (Popovich) wrote,

> The action of the leaven is like the action of Christ's teaching. Just as the leaven gradually fills up the entire loaf until it changes its taste completely, so the theanthropic teaching of the Savior gradually fills the soul, the body, and the heart of a person, until it overwhelms even the smallest part of his essence.[29]

It must also be noted that the parable indicates a very precise quantity of flour: three measures. The term *saton* (measure) in Greek indicates a standard measure of solids, equaling approximately one and a half Roman modes, or around thirteen liters. In other words, a measure is not a handful

---

[29]Justin (Popovich), *Tolkovanie na Evangelie ot Matfeya,* 305–6. Translated by DNK.

The Parable of the Leaven, illustrated by Jan Leychen, 1791–1825

of flour, but most like a full and heavy bag of flour. Three measures of flour is about forty liters. In other words, this was enough to bake bread for more than one hundred people.[30] We should not picture a loaf of bread for dinner, but a large amount of bread for a feast with many guests present. Therefore, it is appropriate to recall the image of the wedding feast that symbolizes God's generosity (Mt 22.1–14). We can also recall Jesus' words: "Good measure, pressed down, and shaken together, and running over, shall men give into your bosom" (Lk 6.38).

Sometimes the three measures of wheat are interpreted allegorically to indicate the three aspects of the human person (spirit, soul, and body)[31] or three categories of people (for examples, Greeks, Jews, and Samaritans).[32] But this excessive allegorizing tends to lead away from the meaning of the parable, instead of leading one toward its understanding. Further, it is unlikely that we can learn any lesson by conflating the three measures of leaven in Matthew with the three measures of meal that Sarah makes for the three wanderers (Gen 18.6). More likely, the number three in this case

[30]Cf. Barclay Newman and Philip Stein, *A Handbook on the Gospel of Matthew* (New York: United Bible Societies, 1988), 402; Blomberg, *Interpreting the Parables,* 394.

[31]Cf. Jerome, *Commentary on the Gospel of Matthew* 2.13.33 (CCSL 77:109; St Jerome, *Commentary on Matthew,* trans. Thomas P. Scheck [Washington: The Catholic University of America Press, 2008], 159–60).

[32]Theodore of Mopsuestia, *Fragments* 74.1–11 (TU 61:121).

is used to underline the contrast between the large quantity of loaves that the woman is planning on baking and the tiny amount of leaven needed for that amount of flour.

6. The Treasure Hidden in the Field and the Pearl of Great Price

In the Gospel of Matthew, the parable of the leaven concludes the series of parables spoken from the boat. According to this Gospel, Jesus then dismissed the people and entered a house. There his disciples approach him, asking for an interpretation of the parable of the wheat and tares. He explains its meaning, and after that he adds another three parables: the treasure hidden in the field, the pearl of great price, and the net.

Why were these parables addressed to the disciples, not the people? Is there, in fact, any essential difference between the parables he addressed to the people and the parables he spoke to the small circle of his disciples?

Those scholars who follow various deconstructive tendencies suggest that the parable first existed as a collection of tales without any given context regarding the place of their telling or the identity of the audience (an example of such a collection is the apocryphal Gospel of Thomas). Jeremias even suggests that some parables that were initially spoken to a large audience were later recontextualized for a narrower audience when the Gospels were written.[33] This occurred, according to Jeremias, in those cases when the parable lost its original "place in life" (*Sitz im Leben*) and was used by the Church for the purposes of the community's general edification.[34]

Such propositions, however, are extremely hypothetical in nature, since they are not based on any indications contained in the Gospel text

[33]Jeremias, *Parables*, 47–48.
[34]Ibid., 43.

itself, and so they can hardly be expected to answer the question we asked above. If we simply follow the Gospel text, Jesus sometimes told parables in the presence of the disciples alone, and sometimes before all the people, including the Pharisees.

Thus, for example, in the Gospel of Luke, we find a series of parables, some of which are addressed to the people (Lk 14.25–35), some to the Pharisees (Lk 15.2–32), and some to the disciples (Lk 16.1–13). But when Jesus addresses parables to his disciples, Luke does mention that "the Pharisees also . . . heard all these things" (Lk 16.14). Jesus continues to address different audiences: "He said unto them . . ." that is, the Pharisees (16.15), "then said he unto the disciples" (17.1), "and when he was demanded of the Pharisees . . . he answered them" (17.20), "and he spake a parable unto them to this end" (18.1), "and he spake this parable unto certain which trusted in themselves that they were righteous . . ." (18.9).

Sometimes the choice of a specific audience is entirely obvious. For example, it is natural that the parable of the publican and the Pharisee (Lk 18.9–14) be directed at the Pharisees. Yet in other cases, the reason for the choice of audience is less obvious. This is true of the parables of the treasure in the field, the pearl, and the net. Though they were addressed to the disciples alone, their context and general focus do not seem to differ radically from those parables that were told from the boat to the entire gathered mass of people.

Nevertheless, if we leave aside all scholarly hypotheses and simply focus on the fact that the parables were spoken in the contexts given by the evangelists, then we cannot fail to come to the conclusion that the choice of audience was not accidental. It seems obvious that the passage from public preaching to discussion with a small group of disciples would also be reflected in some kind of narrative shift in the parables themselves. Let us examine this point in more detail.

The six parables that follow in sequence in Matthew 13, beginning with the parable of the wheat and tares, all have the same beginning, which indicates that the parables reveal the nature of the kingdom of heaven. Moreover, the first four parables all refer to the public ministry of Jesus in some way. The parable of the sower speaks of his mission and its fruits;

the parable of the wheat and tares speaks of how the devil tries to effect his own "parallel mission" among the same people to whom Jesus ministers; the parable of the mustard seed concerns the abundant nature of the fruits of the seeds that Jesus sows; the parable of the leaven reveals how the kingdom of heaven, which Jesus brought to earth, qualitatively transforms the world, filling its life with new content and meaning.

The two parables that follow—the treasure and the pearl—speak of the worth of that same kingdom of heaven and elucidate the lengths to which a person will go to acquire it. This image would not have meant much to the majority of those who came to hear Jesus preach from the boat, since none of them had yet sacrificed anything for the sake of the kingdom of heaven and Jesus himself. But the disciples had already forsaken all and followed him (Lk 5.11). They could not fail to ask themselves the questions that finally Peter asked aloud on behalf of all the disciples: "Behold, we have forsaken all, and followed thee: what shall we have therefore?" (Mt 19.27) This was a group of people that Jesus took away from their everyday life, separated from their relatives, teaching them an unfamiliar way of life and with no promise, for all that, of anything other than suffering, persecution, hatred, and misunderstanding (Mt 10.16–23). Naturally, they needed some moral support, which Jesus offered them, at least in part, through these parables of the treasure and the pearl.

These two parables are so similar in structure and content that it is easier to examine them together. They both occur only in the Gospel according to Matthew:

> Again, the kingdom of heaven is like unto treasure hid in a field, the which when a man hath found, he hideth, and for joy thereof goeth and selleth all that he hath, and buyeth that field. Again, the kingdom of heaven is like unto a merchant man, seeking goodly pearls, who, when he had found one pearl of great price, went and sold all that he had, and bought it. (Mt 13.44–46)

The similarity of both is seen, first of all, in the external structure and in their shared imagery. The treasure and the pearl are images that are close in meaning and significance. In both parables, someone finds something

The Parable of the Pearl, Jan Lcychcn, 1791–1826

unexpected. Also in both, the person must sell everything he has to acquire the thing he finds. One difference arises: in order to acquire the treasure, the man must buy the entire field, while the pearl is bought as a single object without any additional burden. Another difference can be found in the joy and the concealment of the finding in the first parable, while in the second there is neither one nor the other. Finally, a third difference is that the kingdom of heaven is likened to the sale in one parable, while it is likened to the merchant in the other. But this last difference is only a reflection of Jesus' peculiarity of telling parables: it is not always the case that the object links exactly with its likeness; oftentimes the likeness refers to the situation at large, not to a specific element of the story.

The tradition of burying treasure into the ground was widely practiced in ancient times. In an age when people had no ability to put their valuables into a safe at home or a safety deposit box in a bank, it was often just as difficult a task to preserve a treasure as it was to bury it. The slave who received a single talent from his master found no better use for it than to bury it in the ground, thinking that this would at least keep the master's silver safe. When the master returned after a long absence, the slave returned the silver intact (Mt 25.25).

Treasures were buried underground if a city or a country was at risk of invasion. Josephus described the consequences of the sack of Jerusalem, noting especially:

> Yet was there no small quantity of the riches that had been in that city still found among its ruins, a great deal of which the Romans dug up; but the greatest part was discovered by those who were captives, and so they carried it away; I mean the gold and the silver, and the rest of that most precious furniture which the Jews had, and which the owners had treasured up underground, against the uncertain fortunes of war.[35]

The Parable of the Pearl,
Domenico Fetti, 17th century

Even to this day, archeological digs in places where large and prosperous cities once stood uncover not only artifacts of various cultural strata, but also many precious objects that were buried significantly deeper. This is true not only of tombs but also of other underground chambers that were dug for the purposes of protection.

Thus, in the first parable, the man finds a treasure hidden in a field. The Greek word *thēsauros,* a generic term to indicate various kinds of precious objects and artifacts, is used to indicate this treasure. In classical Greek, this term often meant "buried treasure." In the Septuagint, it is most often used to indicate the treasures of God's house, that is, the silver and gold vessels kept in the temple of Jerusalem, as well as the treasure of the king's house (1 Kg 14.26; 2 Kg 24.13), which were various precious things that belonged to the rulers of Israel.

Why did the man have to hide the treasure as soon as he found it? Because the price of a field with a treasure buried within it would have become so expensive that he would not have been able to buy it. He had enough money to buy only the field; in order to purchase the treasure within it, he would have had to have significantly more. Moreover, the

[35]Josephus, *Wars of the Jews* 7.5.2; Josephus, *The Works of Josephus*, trans. William Whiston (Peabody, MA: Hendrickson Publishers, 1987 [repr.]), 756.

The Parable of the Pearl,
Stained glass window in the
parish church of Hagley (UK)

hiding of the treasure, according to specialists in the history of ancient Israel, was a crime and could have led to his punishment. However, as Blomberg notes, the question of the ethical nature of the man's action has absolutely no relevance to the point of this parable. We are dealing with a simile, a symbol, not a discussion on the importance of laws concerning the ownership of land.[36]

What was this man doing in someone else's field? How did he end up there in the first place? Some scholars think that Jesus is speaking of a hired agricultural worker on a rich landowner's farm.[37] Others make the plausible assertion that a hired worker would hardly have enough personal means to buy the land he was hired to work on.[38] Neither interpretation does anything to illuminate the meaning of the parable.

Some ancient commentators saw a special, hidden meaning in the fact that the treasure was buried in the field. Origen, the master of allegorical interpretations, considered it necessary to examine the field and the treasure as separate symbols.[39] We have already examined his particular interpretation of this parable, which is founded on his understanding that the field symbolizes the literal meaning of the Scriptures, while the treasure is the hidden, allegorical meaning of Scripture.

The key moment in the parable, however, is not the difference between the treasure and the field, but the fact that the treasure is an unexpected find: the man finds it in a place where he never expected to find it. Is there a figurative meaning in the unexpectedness of this find? It seems to be the case. The kingdom of heaven is here imagined as something that is hidden from human gaze, something concealed so deep that it is not found

[36]Blomberg, *Interpreting the Parables*, 381–85.
[37]Jeremias, *Parables*, 198.
[38]Hultgren, *Parables*, 411.
[39]Origen, *Commentary on the Gospel of Matthew* 10.5 (ANF 9:416).

easily or quickly. Thus it can become an unexpected discovery that is not intended to be handed out to everyone immediately. The discovery of the kingdom of heaven is accompanied by joy, but it is not necessary to share that joy with just anyone, lest that which was so unexpectedly found be quickly lost.

The pearl in the next parable is an equally unexpected discovery. The word used to indicate the pearl is *margaritēs*, which we also find in the Sermon on the Mount in the words: "Give not that which is holy unto the dogs, neither cast ye your pearls before swine, lest they trample them under their feet, and turn again and rend you" (Mt 7.6). In the Old Testament, pearls symbolized the most

The Parable of the Pearl, Sir John E Millais, 19th century

precious thing that a person can own (Prov 8.11, 31.10). Pearls were difficult to acquire, and the pearl trade was an extremely profitable business.[40]

Objects made from pearl are a special kind of precious material, because pearls are neither crystal nor stone; they are formed in the sea, inside mollusks. In ancient times, it was believed that lightning strikes formed pearls inside shells,[41] but the real reason for their formation is the presence of a foreign body inside the shell, such as a small stone or a grain of sand. Layers of mother of pearl slowly aggregate around this foreign body in concentric spheres. Individual pearls can differ in price by orders of magnitude. When appraising a pearl, one of the criteria of assessment is the size of the pearl. Other factors include the form, the color, and the amount of sparkle.

The most expensive pearl ever was sold for 11.8 million dollars in 2011. This pearl, which weighs 55.95 carats, was found in the middle of the sixteenth century, and was worn in the royal regalia of several Spanish queens (you can see the pearl in portraits done by Velasquez). The last owner

[40]See Metropolitan Hilarion Alfeyev, *Jesus Christ, His Life and Teaching*, vol. 2: *The Sermon on the Mount* (Yonkers, NY: St Vladimir's Seminary Press, 2019), 342–43.

[41]Isaac the Syrian, *Homily* 34.4 (CSCO 554:136; Isaac of Nineveh [Isaac the Syrian], 'The Second Part,' Chapters IV–XLI, trans. Sebastian Brock, Corpus Scriptorum Christianorum Orientalium 555 [Leuven: Peeters, 1995], 148).

La Peregrina, the most
expensive pearl ever sold
at auction

of the pearl before its record-breaking sale was the actress Elizabeth Taylor.

For a professional merchant of pearls, finding a pearl of such price (for this is the kind of pearl we are discussing) would have been incredibly lucky. It was indeed worth it to sell everything to acquire such a pearl.

The meaning of both of these parables can be expressed in a single idea. Jesus underlines that the kingdom of heaven is more precious than any earthly gain. It is an absolute treasure, while all earthly precious things are relative. For its sake, a person may indeed sell everything he has or reject everything he already owns. In the most radical form, this call is expressed in Jesus' words to his disciples: "Everyone that hath forsaken houses, or brethren, or sisters, or father, or mother, or wife, or children, or lands, for my name's sake, shall receive an hundredfold, and shall inherit everlasting life" (Mt 19.29) He says something similar to this when he answered the rich young man's question about what was needed to inherit eternal life: "If thou wilt be perfect, go and sell that thou hast, and give to the poor, and thou shalt have treasure in heaven; and come and follow me" (Mt 19.21).

We see that for Jesus there was not a great difference between parable and reality. What we hear him speak in parable form, which is symbolic in nature and allows for multiple interpretations, in other situations he offers as direct calls to action that could be immediately answered positively or negatively. The disciples answered "yes," the rich young man answered "no."

If we speak of secondary topics, there are certain specific differences between the two parables. In the first, the kingdom of heaven is presented as an unexpected discovery, while in the second, it is the result of a search. The merchant is seeking good pearls, and finally he finds one that is worth selling everything else to acquire. The man who bought the field, it seems, was not seeking anything in particular. He unexpectedly stumbled upon the kingdom of heaven, finding it as a treasure buried in someone else's field.

This difference may indicate that people find the kingdom of heaven by different paths. Some seek it and find it, which literally corresponds to Jesus' words from the Sermon on the Mount: "Ask, and it shall be given you; seek, and ye shall find; knock, and it shall be opened unto you: for every one that asketh receiveth; and he that seeketh findeth; and to him that knocketh it shall be opened" (Mt 7.7–8). For some others, it is as though the kingdom overtakes them while they are looking for something else entirely.

The mention of joy as the most important reason why the man sells everything he has and acquires the field with the treasure may indicate the emotional component of the discovery of the kingdom of heaven. Finding the kingdom is not reduced to a rational process of becoming confirmed in some specific point of view. The kingdom is not a worldview or a way of thinking. When the kingdom of heaven appears in someone's life, he reacts with his whole essence, including the heart. The joy of finding the kingdom is similar to that all-encompassing emotion that is described in these words: "Thou shalt love the Lord they God with all thy heart, and with all thy soul, and with all thy mind, and with all thy strength" (Mk 12.30). No single component of human nature should be excluded from one's love for God and his presence.

In the second parable, the merchant's actions may be interpreted as calculating. He sells everything and buys the pearl not out of a sense of joy, but because he believes that the worth of the pearl more than outweighs its cost. But such an interpretation contradicts the overall tone of the narrative, which is largely determined by the tone of the previous parable. If the emotional element of joy is not explicitly central to the story of the merchant, that does not mean that it is entirely absent. Selling everything that one has for the sake of a single pearl, in any case, is a rare and risky action. After all, the merchant does not sell all his pearls to buy a single pearl of great price; he sells everything he has, including, naturally, his own house. Like Jesus, the merchant becomes homeless, leaving nothing for himself on this earth other than the pearl he acquired.

Christ Pantocrator enthroned,
Icon, 16th century

The parables of the treasure and the pearl underline a theme that appears in many other parables and teachings of Jesus. The kingdom of heaven is not a moral teaching or a certain kind of spirituality or religiosity. The kingdom of heaven is Jesus himself. We once again return to a point that we believe to be central to understanding all his parables. There is not, and cannot be, any other treasure in the life of man that would supersede Jesus in importance and significance. He is the absolute and most precious treasure, since Jesus is God himself, God as he revealed himself to mankind.

7. The Net

The series of parables that began in the boat and continued in the house ends with the parable of the net, one of a small number of parables that was interpreted by the author himself. More than that, the telling of the parable ends with a dialogue between Jesus and his disciples that summarizes the entire series of parables:

> "Again, the kingdom of heaven is like unto a net, that was cast into the sea, and gathered of every kind, which, when it was full, they drew to shore, and sat down, and gathered the good into vessels, but cast the bad away. So shall it be at the end of the world: the angels shall come forth, and sever the wicked from among the just, and shall cast them into the furnace of fire; there shall be wailing and gnashing of teeth." Jesus saith unto them, "Have ye understood all these things?" They say unto him, "Yea, Lord." Then said he unto them, "Therefore every scribe which is instructed unto the kingdom of heaven is like unto a man that is an householder, which bringeth forth out of his treasure things new and old." (Mt 13.47–52)

This entire passage is unique to the Gospel of Matthew and is not found in any other Gospel. It can be divided into three sections: the parable, its interpretation, and the dialogue with the disciples. The parable itself, in turn, can also be divided into three parts: first the process of catching fish is described, then the process of pulling the net to the shore, then the sorting of the fish.

Jesus purposely chose this series of images to conclude the entire teaching that he began in a fishing boat in front of the crowd but completed in a house, surrounded by his disciples. The process of fishing was known to them in every detail. At least four of them—those whom he called before the rest—were professional fishermen: Peter, Andrew, James, and John (Mt 4.18–22; Mk 1.16–20).

Three of the four—Peter, James, and John—were highlighted by the Gospel accounts as the group of disciples closest to Jesus. Their calling was accompanied by one of Jesus' first miracles: after they had fished all night and not caught a single fish, Jesus commanded them to throw their nets into the water. "And when they had this done, they enclosed a great multitude of fishes, and their net broke." It was at this moment that Peter first realized who Jesus was, while James and John were filled with fear at the miracle. Jesus told Peter: "Fear not; from henceforth thou shalt catch men." As a result of this miracle, "they forsook all, and followed him" (Lk 5.1–11).

The three parables spoken by Jesus in the house could not have been more appropriate for the disciples' situation. Only recently they abandoned everything to follow him, and so they could have easily seen themselves in the main characters of the first two parables. As for the images of the net and the fish from the third parable, on the one hand they fit very well into a fisherman's view of life, while on the other hand, they also go to the heart of their new calling. They would all become fishers of men.

Jesus wanted to convey the essence of his good news to his disciples in the most recognizable imagery. This is made clear by the use of the word "having sat" (*kathisantes*), which in no way is connected with the process of the angels separating the good from the evil: nowhere does it say that the angels will perform this action seated. But fishermen sorted fish while

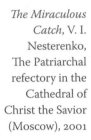

The Miraculous Catch, V. I. Nesterenko, The Patriarchal refectory in the Cathedral of Christ the Savior (Moscow), 2001

sitting, and thanks to this detail, the image that Jesus uses is vivid in the imagination of the disciples. Jesus preferred not to use abstract concepts, but rather concrete, visual images.

The link between the miracle that accompanies the calling of the first disciples and the parable of the net illustrates a general point scholars make concerning the connection between Jesus' miracles and his parables: in the Gospels, the parables play the same role as the miracles.[42] This in no way diminishes the importance of the miracles as real events that occurred in life. It only witnesses to the fact that there was an intimate connection between what Jesus said and what he did. Through both miracles and parables, he expressed the same truth that he announced at the beginning of his public ministry: "the kingdom of heaven is at hand" (Mt 4.17).

The main part of the parable of the net concerns the final judgment. In this sense, it is similar to the parable of the wheat and the tares. The instruction in the house begins with the disciples' question concerning the meaning of the parable of the tares. Jesus patiently interprets all the images he used in the parable, the main point of which was the separation of the righteous from all others at the final judgment. He concludes his interpretation thus: "The Son of Man shall send forth his angels, and they shall gather out of his kingdom all things that offend, and them which do

[42]Craig Blomberg, "The Miracles as Parables," in *Gospel Perspectives*, vol. 6: *The Miracles of Jesus* (Sheffield: Sheffield Academic Press, 1986): 327–59, at 327–28.

The Dread Judgment, Triptych, detail, Fra Beato Angelico, 1450

iniquity, and shall cast them into a furnace of fire: there shall be wailing and gnashing of teeth" (Mt 13.41–42). In the parable of the net, we hear the same words: "And shall cast them into the furnace of fire: there shall be wailing and gnashing of teeth" (Mt 13.50). These two interpretations form a thematic arc that connects the beginning and the end of his teaching in the house.

The two parables differ in their imagery. In the first, since Jesus speaks to the crowd, he uses images that are familiar to farmers. In the second, since he speaks to his disciples, he uses imagery associated with fishing. However, the meaning of both is the same. Both speak of the final reality that will conclude human life: the dread judgment.

There is also a link between the disciples' request that began the explanations that Jesus gave in the house and his question that concludes the instruction ("Have ye understood all these things?"). As an experienced teacher, Jesus first explicates the portion of his teaching to the crowd that the disciples did not understand, and then offers them examples from their own experiences to cement their understanding, and finally he asks them if they understood his words. In the same way that textbooks often conclude each section with a series of questions for students, Jesus asks this final question at the end. The question is not yet a test that assumes comprehensive knowledge of the subject; the test will be the rest of their lives. While they are still at the beginning of their journey, the teacher must merely be assured that they understand him.

Their affirmative answer most likely did not refer to all the parables. It likely refers to the parables that Jesus interpreted himself: the sower, the tares, and the net. Evidently, Jesus repeated these parables in different contexts: this is shown by the fact that some of them appear in Luke's account at a different point in his ministry. Nevertheless, this first time—when Jesus began speaking in parables to the people from the boat, then continued with his disciples in the house—would have impressed itself on their memory profoundly. Otherwise, the parables would not have survived in the form they took in Matthew and Mark's Gospels, that is, in the form of a complete, continuous narrative, not individual stories uttered at different times and in different places.

The instruction given in these parables concludes with a phrase that stands apart, as though not connected with the preceding events. This is the saying concerning a scribe who is like a householder who takes both new and old things out of his treasure house. In effect, it is a miniature parable, since it is built on a simile.

Concluding a long sermon with a short parable is a characteristic device for Jesus. In the Sermon on the Mount, the parable of the house on the rock and the house on the sand (Mt 7.24–27) becomes the epilogue for the entire sermon. Moreover, this epilogue not only summarizes the main point of the sermon, but also explicates how the sermon can be applied directly to life. The most important theme of the parable of the houses built on rock and sand is the idea that it is not enough to listen to Jesus' words. It is far more important to fulfill them in action. Similar devices are used in formal rhetoric: having finished his speech, the orator does not so much summarize as bring his audience's attention to the practical application of his words.

In its structure, the conclusion of both sermons is quite similar: "Therefore whosoever heareth these sayings of mine, and doeth them, I will liken him unto a wise man, which built his house upon a rock . . ." (Mt 7.24); "Therefore every scribe which is instructed unto the kingdom of heaven is like unto a man that is an householder, which bringeth forth out of his treasure things new and old" (Mt 13.52). In both cases, Jesus uses the adjective *homoios* ("like," or "similar"), which is the foundational principle of any parable that uses simile. Unlike the Sermon on the Mount, however, a sermon given in parables is an entire series of similes.

Thus the words concerning the scribe act as a kind of epilogue. Yet they move the attention of the listener from what he spoke of before to a theme that seems new and unexpected. Where did the scribe come from? Jesus first spoke to the crowd, then to his disciples, but he concludes with a mention of a certain scribe who is instructed in the kingdom of heaven. Who is this scribe? It seems that none of the disciples was such a scribe.

The word "scribe" (*grammateus*) nearly always has a negative connotation in the Gospels. For the evangelists, the scribe is one who has assimilated a certain number of prescriptions of the Mosaic law, but does not live in accordance with this law, someone who is well-read, who knows many passages of Scripture by heart, but who cannot correctly interpret them. More often than not, the term "scribe" is used together with the term "Pharisee." In Matthew 23, the expression "woe unto you, scribes and Pharisees, hypocrites" (Mt 23.13–15, 23, 25, 27) is a kind of refrain.

The Jewish scribes, mentioned in the Gospels, were for the most part Jesus' opponents. Together with the chief priests, the Pharisees, and the elders, they participated in the conspiracy that led to his execution. Nevertheless, in two separate cases, the term "scribe" has a positive connotation in Jesus' speech. The first is the present parable. The second is found in words spoken to the Jews: "Behold, I send unto you prophets, and wise men, and scribes, and some of them ye shall kill and crucify, and some of them shall ye scourge in your synagogues, and persecute them from city to city" (Mt 23.34). Unexpectedly, in this case the scribes are not included in the list together with the Pharisees and hypocrites, whom Jesus constantly accuses, but in the noble company of the prophets and wise men sent by God to the people of Israel.[43]

[43]Some scholars believe that Matthew highly valued the profession of the scribe and was himself a scribe. Cf. A. M. Gale, *Redefining Ancient Borders: The Jewish Scribal Framework of Matthew's Gospel* (New York: T & T Clark International, 2005), 105–11; D. E. Orton, *The Understanding Scribe: Matthew and the Apocalyptic Ideal* (London: T & T Clark, 1989), 165–76. From our point of view, there are not sufficient grounds for such an assertion.

The Evangelist Matthew, Icon, 14th century

These words appear in a longer address to the people and the disciples: "The scribes and Pharisees sit in Moses' seat: all therefore whatsoever they bid you observe, that observe and do; but do not ye after their works: for they say, and do not" (Mt 23.2–3). Here Jesus accuses the scribes and Pharisees not for some aspect of their teaching, but rather for their behavior, especially for their tendency to see only parts of the Law that have secondary importance, while ignoring the most important parts of the Law. They assiduously fulfill various rules, but they cast off the internal meaning of those actions, requiring people only to practice various external actions that they themselves do not follow.

As for the scribe who is instructed in the kingdom of heaven, we must understand this to be someone who accepted Jesus' teachings and joined the company of his disciples. We know that other than the apostles and other public disciples, Jesus also had secret disciples among the Jerusalem elite. One of these was Nicodemus, who is mentioned only in the Gospel of John (Jn 3.1–2, 19.39), and Joseph of Arimathea, who appears in all four Gospels. The latter at least is literally a scribe who has been instructed in the kingdom of heaven.

Joseph of Arimathea, Fresco, Novgorod the Great, 14th century

Was Jesus then speaking of Joseph or anyone else in particular or did he have in mind no specific man? This we simply do not know. The expression "that which is new and old," however, likely refers to a theme that is especially fully developed in the Gospel of Matthew: the theme of the relationship between the New and Old Covenants, between the teaching of Jesus and the Law of Moses. This theme dominates in the Sermon on the Mount; it is a leitmotif in many other sermons and sayings of Jesus.

In one of these, he speaks of new wine that should not be poured into old wineskins (Mt 9.17; Mk 2.22; Lk 5.37). The new wine, all interpreters both ancient and modern agree, symbolizes the teaching of Jesus, while the old wineskins are those old forms that come from the law of Moses, but have become too narrow for the new teaching.

The form of the expression itself, that is, the similarity of the scribe to the householder who brings out both new and old treasures from his treasure house, evidently mirrors the simile of the old and new wineskins. According to John Chrysostom, the scribe in this case represents the worth of the Old Testament:

Do you see how so far from excluding the Old Testament, he even commends it, and speaks publicly in favor of it, calling it a treasure? So that as many as are ignorant of the divine Scriptures cannot be householders, such as neither have of themselves, nor receive of others, but neglect their own case, perishing with famine. And not these only, but the heretics too, are excluded from this blessing. For they bring not forth things new and old. For they have not the old things, wherefore neither have they the new, even as they who have not the new, neither have they the old, but are deprived of both. For these are bound up and interwoven one with another.[44]

Naturally, any teaching given in parable form would have been surprising to listeners because of its newness. The form itself was unusual, and no less unusual was the content that hid behind the similes and comparisons and images from everyday life, as well as behind that mystical, constantly repeated phrase: "the kingdom of heaven."

Jesus recognized the newness of his teaching, but at the same time, he did not tire of underlining his teachings' continuity with the works of the prophets. The Old Testament, with its strictness, wisdom, and depth, was precious to Jesus. He saw his own teaching as an addition to the treasure house in which the prophets, wise men, and scribes of Israel had also added their spiritual riches.

This continuity was brilliantly captured by the Apostle Paul, who insisted, on the one hand, that the mission of Jesus was a direct continuation of the mission of the Old Testament prophets (Heb 1.1–2), and on the other hand that in Jesus himself "are hid all the treasures of wisdom and knowledge" (Col 2.3). Paul traced a straight line of inheritance from the prophets not only to Jesus, but also to his apostles, underlining that the Church he founded is built "upon the foundation of the apostles and prophets, Jesus Christ himself being the chief corner stone" (Eph 2.20).

---

[44]John Chrysostom, *Homilies on the Gospel of Matthew* 47.4 (NPNF[1] 10:294).

*St John
Chrysostom*,
Icon, detail.
14th century

Chapter 3

OTHER GALILEAN PARABLES

In the previous chapter, we examined eight parables that were told, according to the Gospels of Matthew and Mark, in the course of a single day. In this chapter, we will examine four more Galilean parables: the children in the street, the two debtors, the lost sheep, and the unmerciful servant.

1. The Children in the Street

The short parable of the children in the street in the Gospels of Matthew and Luke refers to the period of Jesus' ministry when John the Baptist was already imprisoned, but had not yet been beheaded. Jesus told this parable when he was visited by two disciples of the Baptist, who had sent them to Jesus to ask the question: "Art thou he that should come, or do we look for another?" (Mt 11.2) Without directly answering the question, Jesus asked the disciples of John to tell him what they saw and heard with their own eyes and ears: "The blind receive their sight, and the lame walk, the lepers are cleansed, and the deaf hear, the dead are raised up, and the poor have the Gospel preached to them" (Mt 11.5–6).

After these disciples of John leave, Jesus turned to the crowd and spoke of the importance of John the Baptist (Mt 11.7–13; Lk 7.24–28): "If ye will receive it, this is Elijah, which was for to come" (Mt 11.14). In Matthew's account, the transition from this teaching to the parable occurs through

John the Baptist, Icon,
14th century

this phrase: "He that hath ears to hear, let him hear" (Mt 11.5). In Luke's version, there is another phrase added in transition: "And all the people that heard him, and the publicans, justified God, being baptized with the baptism of John. But the Pharisees and lawyers rejected the counsel of God against themselves, being not baptized by him" (Lk 7.29–30).[1]

Since it is part of a larger teaching about John the Baptist, the parable finishes with a commentary in which Jesus connects his own mission to John's:

But whereunto shall I liken this generation? It is like unto children sitting in the markets, and calling unto their fellows, and saying, "We have piped unto you, and ye have not danced; we have mourned unto you, and ye have not lamented." For John came neither eating nor drinking, and they say, "He hath a devil." The Son of Man came eating and drinking, and they say, "Behold a man gluttonous, and a winebibber, a friend of publicans and sinners." But wisdom is justified by her children. (Mt 11.16–19)

There are no major textual differences between Matthew's and Luke's versions. In Luke (Lk 7.31–35), the beginning of the parable is slightly differently worded: "whereunto shall I liken *the men* of this generation? And to what are they like? They are like unto children . . ." In critical editions, the ending of the parable differs in Matthew: "But wisdom is justified by her actions" (or "deeds," "works"; *ergōn*).[2] Ancient commentators worked from editions that had the ending found in Luke.[3] It is possible that "her

[1] In some manuscripts of the Gospel according to Luke, the parable is further preceded by the words "Then the Lord said." In modern critical editions of the New Testament, this phrase is lacking. Cf. Kurt Aland, *Synopsis Quattuor Evangeliorum* (Stuttgart: Deutsche Bibelgesellschaft, 1985), 152.

[2] Ibid., 152.

[3] Cf. John Chrysostom, *Homilies on the Gospel of Matthew* 37.5–6 (NPNF[1] 10:247); Hilary of Poitiers, *Commentary on the Gospel according to Matthew* 11.9 (SC 254:262); Hilary of Poitiers, *Commentary on Matthew*, trans. D.H. Williams, FOC 125 (Washington: The Catholic University of America Press, 2012), 134.

children" is the original text that was changed in certain manuscripts of the Gospel of Matthew because of the influence of the words "the works of Christ" (Mt 11.2).[4]

The expression *genea tautē*, which is usually translated as "this generation," has a firmly negative connotation in Jesus' words. He calls his contemporaries' generation evil, adulterous, and sinful (Mt 12.39; Mk 8.38; Lk 11.29).

In spite of the brevity of this parable, it provides many difficulties for interpretation:

> The interpretation of the parable has been contested for centuries. . . . The first problem is to understand the figure of the children sitting in the marketplace and crying out to one another. Are they two groups, one of which wants to play wedding, the other, funeral, but cannot agree? . . . Or is it rather that the children are two groups, one of which proposes to play first at wedding, then at funeral, but cannot get the other group, sulky and capricious, to go along with either proposal?[5]

> The picture is not entirely clear and has been interpreted as depicting two groups proposing alternate games, "wedding" and "funeral," or one group proposing the two different games to their recalcitrant companions who refuse to join either. . . . The parable itself can be read both ways, but the verses appended require the latter approach. The interpretation clearly allegorizes the parable in light of Jesus' festive ministry contrasted with John the Baptist's more somber preaching. The one group of children then actually fills both contrasting roles and the other group, standing for the unresponsive Jews, acts as the judge between them.[6]

In this case, we agree more with those who hold that one of the two groups of children (the active group) plays both games, while the other group (the passive one) refuses to play either game. But we must also point

---

[4]M. J. Suggs, *Wisdom, Christology and Law in Matthew's Gospel* (Cambridge, MA: Harvard University Press, 1970), 33.

[5]Fitzmeyer, *The Gospel according to Luke I-IX* (New York: Doubleday, 1981), 678.

[6]Blomberg, *Interpreting the Parables*, 263.

to something that modern commentators often miss: the text says nearly nothing about the funeral or wedding game; second, the actions described by the children occur in the past tense (we played, we sang, you did not dance, you did not weep). The existence of a funeral or wedding game is nothing more than a guess, while the parable is actually talking about the reaction of one group of children to the music of another group, not to their actions or their game.

The verb *auleō*, translated as "to play on a pipe," comes from the word *aulos*, an ancient woodwind instrument used in Greece. Analogous instruments existed in ancient Israel, used in dances and in ritual mourning (see Mt 9.23). The verb *thrēnō* means "to sing a funeral song," "to groan," "to weep loudly." From this, we get the word *thrēnos:* "cry" or "weeping."

Both musical terms symbolize the sound of a human voice. These two different moods expressed by musical instruments correspond to two types of preaching: that of John the Baptist and that of Jesus. Both called their listeners to repent, using the same formula (Mt 3.2, 4.17). But this call was colored differently in the way each one employed it. The way of life of each of these preachers also provided additional overtones to the general tone of their ministry, something that Jesus himself makes clear in his own interpretation of the parable.

As for the question of who is symbolized by each group of children, scholars do not agree here either. Some believe that the active group of children rebuke John the Baptist and Jesus both: the former for his absences at wedding feasts due to his extreme asceticism, the latter for his lack of participation in mourning, for he always feasted.[7] Others (the majority) believe that the active group of children symbolize both John and Jesus, while the passive children are the Jews.

The literal meaning of the answer to the question "to what shall I liken this generation" forces us to suppose that this generation is likened to the group of children who played musical instruments and sang sad songs. Yet there are many reasons to consider that in fact this generation is likened to the other group of children—those who do not react to any music, joyful or sad.

[7] R. C. Tannehill, *Luke* (Nashville, TN: Abingdon, 1996), 133.

It is possible that here we encounter a particularity of Jesus' speech patterns, which we mentioned before when we examined the parables of the treasure in the field and the pearl of great price. That is, the likeness or simile does not always refer to that concrete element of the narrative picture that it seems to point to at first. In the series of parables that we examined in the previous chapter, the kingdom of heaven is likened to, in series, a man who sowed good seed, a mustard seed, leaven, a treasure hidden in a field, and a merchant who seeks good pearls. In two cases of five, however, the likeness does not refer to the indicated character: in the parable of the tares, it is not the man, but the seed that is the image of the kingdom of heaven. And in the parable of the pearl, it is not the merchant, but the pearl that symbolizes the kingdom of heaven.

With this in mind, we can confirm, together with ancient commentators, that Jesus and John the Baptist are symbolized by the active, not the passive children. Moreover, those who play on the pipe represent Christ, while those who sing a sad song symbolize John the Baptist. This is the interpretation given by John Chrysostom:

> Now what he says is like this: We have come each of us an opposite way, I and John . . . Mark, for instance, the whole race of man, how it is astonished at the wonder of men's fasting, and at this hard and self-denying life. For this reason it had been so ordered, that John should be thus brought up from his earliest youth, so that hereby (among other things) his sayings might obtain credit. But wherefore, it may be asked, did not he himself [i.e., Jesus] choose that way? In the first place he did also himself proceed by it, when he fasted the forty days. . . . Nevertheless he did also in another mode accomplish this same object. . . . Leaving therefore John to be illustrious by his fasting, he himself came the opposite way, both coming unto publicans' tables, and eating and drinking. . . . The fault is not then theirs who were not believed, but they are to be blamed who did not believe. . . . Therefore also he says, "We have piped unto you, and you have not danced"; that is, "I have exhibited the freer kind of life, and you obeyed not"; and, "We have mourned, and you have not lamented"; that is, "John followed the

St Jerome,
Caravaggio, 1606

rugged and grave life, and you took no heed." And he says not, he this, I that, but the purpose of both being one, although their modes of life were opposite, for this cause he speaks of their doings as common.[8]

St Jerome underlines that the children who sit in the markets are compared with the Jewish people within the parable itself. God sent preachers to them, but since they did not want to listen, not only did they say as much, but they screamed it at the top of their lungs. The two kinds of preaching are as follows: an admonition to virtue and a call to repentance. The Jews disdained this double path to salvation, having accepted neither John nor the Son of Man.[9]

Cyril of Alexandria, for his part, wrote that John the Baptist, having preached a baptism of repentance, showed himself to be a model for those who should weep, while the Lord, having preached the kingdom of heaven, showed in himself the same joy and illumination that he promised to his disciples in the form of unlimited joy and a life without sorrows. The pipe, in Cyril's words, symbolizes the sweetness of the kingdom of heaven, while the tears symbolize the suffering in Gehenna.[10]

[8]John Chrysostom, *Homilies on the Gospel of Matthew* 37.5 (NPNF[1] 10:247).
[9]Jerome, *Commentary on the Gospel of Matthew* 2.11.16 (CCSL 77:82–83).
[10]Cyril of Alexandria, *Commentary on the Gospel of Matthew* 142–44 (TU 61:198–99).

The expression "wisdom is justified by her children" is understood differently by various commentators. The phrase could be understood in the sense that people will always find justification for their actions, for their lack of desire to hear the voice of the preacher. If this is the case, the word "wisdom" is used ironically. Chrysostom sees in these words a continuation of Jesus' accusation of the Jews: "though ye be not persuaded, yet with me after this ye cannot find fault."[11]

On the other hand, the word "wisdom" can be interpreted positively as well. Jerome understands wisdom to represent the providence and teaching of God, while the children he believes to be the apostles, to whom the Father revealed what he hid from the wise and from those who consider themselves wise.[12] Hilary of Poitiers believes that the words "wisdom is justified" were spoken by Jesus concerning himself, for he himself is Wisdom, not by action, but by nature.[13]

Commentators who identify Jesus with Wisdom itself base their assertion on early Christian tradition, which itself harks back to the words of the Apostle Paul, who called Jesus "the power of God and the wisdom of God" (1 Cor 1.24). Such an identification is strengthened not only by the personification of wisdom in the Old Testament, but also by the mention of her children (Prov 8.32) and her sons (Sir 4.12).

2. The Two Debtors

In Luke, the parable of the two debtors is part of the account of the sinful woman who anoints Jesus' feet after she enters the house where Jesus is dining with a Pharisee. In Luke's account, this episode takes place during Jesus' Galilean ministry. There is a similar episode in the Gospels of Matthew and Mark, but there the event occurs in the final days of Jesus' earthly life, and it occurs in Bethany, near Jerusalem, in the house of a certain

[11]John Chrysostom, *Homilies on the Gospel of Matthew* 37.5 (NPNF[1] 10:247).
[12]Jerome, *Commentary on the Gospel of Matthew* 2.11.16 (CCSL 77:83).
[13]Hilary of Poitiers, *Commentary on the Gospel of Matthew* 11.9 (SC 254:262; FOC 134–35).

Simon the leper (Mt 26.6–7; Mk 14.3). There is yet another similar episode in the Gospel of John. There also, the event also occurs in Bethany, but in the house of Lazarus, and it is Mary, the sister of Lazarus, who anoints Jesus' feet (Jn 12.1–8).

Was this the same event, or was it two or even three different events? Scholars offer different answers. There are, in fact, four major versions: 1) All the evangelists are describing the same event, but only the details differ.[14] 2) The synoptic Gospels all describe one event, while John describes a different event.[15] 3) One event is described by Luke, another by Matthew, Mark, and John.[16] 4) There are three different events—the first is described by Luke, the second by Matthew and Mark, the third by John.[17]

We consider the third version to be the most likely. A detailed explanation of this position falls outside the scope of this book, since we are focusing here on the parables of Jesus, and the parable occurs in only one of the four accounts (in Luke). We will merely point out the most obvious divergences from the other evangelists in Luke's account:

1) Luke's episode occurs in Galilee, not in Bethany.

2) It occurs early in Jesus' public ministry.

3) The woman anoints not the head of Jesus (as in Matthew and Mark), but his feet (as in John).

4) The event occurs in the house of Simon the Pharisee, not Simon the leper (as it does in Matthew and Mark).

5) The woman is called sinful (the other evangelists do not mention this detail).

6) She washes the feet of Jesus with her tears and wipes them with her hair (this detail is not present in the other evangelists).

---

[14]Among these scholars is Charles Dodd, who believes that the variations in the account arose in the oral tradition. Cf. Dodd, *Historical Tradition,* 162–73.

[15]Chrysostom is of this opinion; see John Chrysostom, *Homilies on the Gospel of Matthew* 80.1 (NPNF[1] 10:480).

[16]Augustine was of this opinion; see Augustine, *On the Harmony of the Gospels* 2.79 (NPNF[1] 6:173–74).

[17]Origen believed this was so; see Origen *Commentary on the Gospel of Matthew* 77 (GCS 38[2]:181–82).

7) Neither the disciples at large (Matthew) nor Judas in particular (John) react negatively to her actions, but the Pharisee does.

8) The episode contains an exchange between Jesus and the Pharisee (which is absent in the other Gospels).

9) There is no conversation between Jesus and his disciples.

10) There is no reference to this woman's action as a preparation for Jesus' burial.

11) At the end of the account, Jesus turns directly to the woman (which he does not do in the other accounts); this even occurs twice.

Christ in the Home of Simon the Pharisee, Anonymous master of the French school, 15th century

Since Luke's account has some significant divergences from the other three evangelists, and since it alone includes the parable that interests us here, we will examine this account in isolation from the analogous accounts in the three other Gospels. The account must be examined in its entirety, since the parable is a major part of the whole:

> And one of the Pharisees desired him that he would eat with him. And he went into the Pharisee's house, and sat down to meat. And, behold, a woman in the city, which was a sinner, when she knew that Jesus sat at meat in the Pharisee's house, brought an alabaster box of ointment, and stood at his feet behind him weeping, and began to wash his feet with tears, and did wipe them with the hairs of her head, and kissed his feet, and anointed them with the ointment. Now when the Pharisee which had bidden him saw it, he spake within himself, saying, "This man, if he were a prophet, would have known who and what manner of woman this is that toucheth him, for she is a sinner." And Jesus answering said unto him, "Simon, I have somewhat to say unto thee." And he saith, "Master, say on." "There was a certain creditor which had two debtors: the one owed five hundred pence, and the other fifty. And

when they had nothing to pay, he frankly forgave them both. Tell me therefore, which of them will love him most?" Simon answered and said, "I suppose that he, to whom he forgave most." And he said unto him, "Thou hast rightly judged." And he turned to the woman, and said unto Simon, "Seest thou this woman? I entered into thine house, thou gavest me no water for my feet, but she hath washed my feet with tears, and wiped them with the hairs of her head. Thou gavest me no kiss, but this woman since the time I came in hath not ceased to kiss my feet. My head with oil thou didst not anoint, but this woman hath anointed my feet with ointment. Wherefore I say unto thee, her sins, which are many, are forgiven; for she loved much. But to whom little is forgiven, the same loveth little." And he said unto her, "Thy sins are forgiven." And they that sat at meat with him began to say within themselves, "Who is this that forgiveth sins also?" And he said to the woman, "Thy faith hath saved thee; go in peace." (Lk 7.36–50)

This story can be divided into four parts: the account of the woman and of the Pharisee's initial response to her actions; the dialogue that contains the parable of the two debtors; the interpretation of the parable in the form of an exchange with Simon; the words addressed to the woman and the reaction of those in attendance.

The host of the meal is at first given a generic characterization: "one of the Pharisees." The name of the Pharisee only appears later, when Jesus addresses him directly. Throughout the Gospels, the Pharisees openly opposed Jesus. The fact that he accepted an invitation from one of them to dine with him testifies to Jesus' readiness to speak with any person, including his opponents. Though he sharply rebuked the Pharisees as a group or a party, calling them hypocrites, blind guides, fools and blind, a generation of vipers (Mt 23.13–33), Jesus never extended these epithets to every individual member of any group without exception. Moreover, the episode described by Luke occurred during an early period of Jesus' ministry, before his conflict with the Pharisees entered its final, and most intense, stage.

The woman who anointed Jesus' feet with myrrh is twice called a sinful woman in Luke's account (*hamartolos*). This term, when referring to a woman, could only mean that she was a prostitute, since the term refers to her manner of life in general, and no other manner of living could have been so generally named. This is how most ancient commentators understood the word "sinful" in this particular case. Amphilochius of Iconium (fourth century), wrote:

> But the Pharisees murmured that he eats with sinners, not understanding this. . . . For he himself—who had joined Zacchaeus the tax collector to the rational flock of the apostles—snatched the sinful prostitute, a worker of countless evils, from the devil like a lamb, and restored her to the fold unharmed. . . . He eats with the Pharisees and does not cast off the tax collectors, he accepts the Samaritan woman and deems worthy the word of the Canaanite woman, and yields the hem of his garment to the woman with the issue of blood, and was not ashamed.[18]

As we said before, only in Luke's account does the woman wash Jesus' feet with her tears and kiss them. This detail gives the entire account a special emotional resonance that cannot fail to be reflected in how we hear the parable of the two debtors.

The parable itself is remarkable for its brevity, which contrasts with many other parables from the Gospel of Luke. There is neither a fleshed-out narrative, nor a large group of characters. The image of two debtors will also be used in the parable of the unmerciful servant (Mt 18.23–35), but there the image plays a different role. These two parables show us an example of how the same image, placed in various contexts, can be used for different purposes.

The first debtor owes a significant sum of money, corresponding to five hundred days' wages for a day laborer. The second man owes a debt ten times smaller, yet this second sum is not merely symbolic. The creditor forgives both debts, and this ends the narrative portion of the parable. What follows is its interpretation, which directly applies to the situation at hand. Jesus' direct address to the Pharisee as the prototype of one of the

---

[18]Amphilocius of Iconium, *Homily 4: On the Sinful Woman* (PG 39:69; trans. Ed.).

characters in the parable, which allows him no room to interpret the parable in his own way, echoes how Nathan spoke to King David: "Thou art the man" (2 Sam 12.7). But while Nathan came to David to accuse him of a deadly sin, here we have a different situation: Jesus comes to the house of the Pharisee and reacts not so much to his behavior as to his way of thinking.

This way of thinking is what Jesus rebuked in his diatribe against the Pharisees, and the later we get in his public ministry, the more strident the rebuke becomes. The Pharisees perceived righteousness and holiness to be first and foremost the outward fulfillment of a certain number of external rules, which in their eyes raised them above normal people, separating them from the rabble. Their posture toward sinners was disdain, especially toward publicans and prostitutes, who in their eyes were living symbols of sin (and, it must be said, they had reasons to believe so).

It is unclear how the woman, who was a well-known prostitute, ended up inside the house of a Pharisee. Naturally, she had not been invited. We can only guess that she was among those who followed Jesus, and walked in together with other people who accompanied him, both men and women. She could not have presumed to have a place at the table, and so she sat at the feet of the Teacher while he ate and spoke with the host.

From Jesus' own words, other details become evident as well: the host, having invited Jesus into his home, did not show him the usual marks of respect. He did not offer him water to wash his feet, he did not pour any oil on his head, and he did not even greet him with the traditional kiss. The woman, on the contrary, not only anointed the feet of Jesus with myrrh, but repeatedly kissed them, which was a sign of intense love, sincere emotion, and profound repentance.

Love and forgiveness—these are the main themes of the parable. From Jesus' words, it is not entirely clear what comes first and what second. On the one hand, it seems that forgiveness comes as a consequence of love, yet it also seems clear that love is the consequence of forgiveness. Jesus said of the woman that her sins are forgiven "for she loved much." As for the Pharisee, these words refer directly to him: "to whom little is forgiven, the same loveth little." The mutual dependence of love and forgiveness is

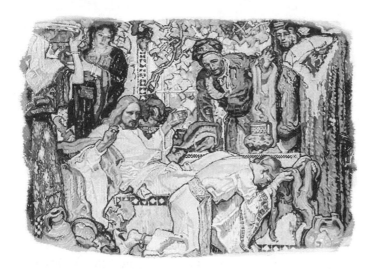

*Mary anoints
Jesus*, Cornwell,
1931

so strong that both can be true: love can be both a source and a product
of forgiveness; likewise, forgiveness can precede love, but it can follow it
as well.

The Pharisee's actions show that his encounter with Jesus produced no
internal transformation. We do not know why he invited Jesus into his house
in the first place. It is possible that he was curious to speak to a teacher of
whom he had heard many things. It is possible that like other Pharisees and
scribes, he wanted to test him, and catch him in a blasphemy. Whatever
the case may be, the Gospel narrative suggests that nothing changed in this
Pharisee's life. He accepted Jesus into his home as one among many guests
who visited his house, he showed Jesus poor hospitality, and evidently let
him go without learning much from his encounter.

As for the sinful woman, on the contrary, the encounter with Jesus produced a complete internal transformation. Everything she does shows vividly that she answered the call that often sounded upon Jesus' lips: "Repent,
for the kingdom of heaven is at hand." It is unlikely that she asked herself
the question, "What sort of kingdom of heaven is this man preaching?"
With her feminine intuition, which had not been dulled despite her sinful
way of life, she sensed the presence within him of that new dimension of
life that was often revealed in his preaching and through his person. Her
repentance was sincere and profound; it indicated a complete change of

her way of thinking and living. We do not know anything about her subsequent fate, but it is somewhat presupposed.

As the episode continues, we see Jesus' attention gradually move from the host of the meal to the woman who sat at his feet. In the beginning, reclining at the Pharisee's table, he spoke only with the host. At some point, he turned to the woman, but continued speaking with the Pharisee. Finally, he turned directly to the woman and repeated the words that he uttered in other situations: "Thy sins be forgiven thee" (Mt 9.2; Mk 2.5; Lk 5.20).

These words always angered the Pharisees. But if in other cases Jesus reacted to the annoyance of the surrounding people and explained his actions, in this case, he ignores them. It is as though he fails to notice anyone and continues to speak only to the woman, saying another phrase that many whom he healed also heard from him: "Thy faith hath saved thee" (Mt 9.22; Mk 5.34, 10.52; Lk 8.48, 17.19, 18.42).

The parable of the two debtors is similar in meaning to another parable that Jesus spoke later: the parable of the publican and the Pharisee (Lk 18.9–14). There, the Pharisee is opposed to a publican (a tax collector)— another representative of the most despised class of people. It is typical also that the Pharisee will not be altogether condemned; all that Jesus will say is that the publican walked out of the temple "justified more than the other." Likewise, in the parable of the two debtors, the one whose forgiven debt is larger loves his creditor more than the one whose debt is smaller, yet it is not said that the other debtor did not love the creditor at all.

In the final analysis, the parable of the two debtors speaks of God's readiness to accept any person: a sinner as well as someone who considers himself righteous. He allows the former and the latter both to begin their life with a clean slate.[19] With that said, the one who is forgiven more may be more capable of faith, repentance, and improvement than the one who is forgiven less.

The classical example of such repentance and radical inner and outer transformation is Mary of Egypt (5th century). According to her *Life*, Mary was a prostitute from a young age and led a dissolute life for many years.

---

[19]Blomberg, *Interpreting the Parables*, 198.

Once, she traveled to Jerusalem for the feast of the Exaltation of the Cross. In Jerusalem, she wanted to visit the Church of the Holy Sepulcher, but some mysterious force prevented her from entering the church. Recognizing her own sinfulness, Mary immediately left the world, went to the desert, and spent forty-seven years in the strictest asceticism and constant prayer. The only person who saw her after this point was a monk named Zosimas, and it was he who told the world of her labors. Toward the end of her life, Mary achieved such a level of holiness that during prayer she levitated, she could walk on water, and she knew the entire text of Scripture by heart, though she had never read it.

The *Life* of St Mary of Egypt, written down in the sixth century by Sophronius of Jerusalem, was extremely popular in the Christian East for many centuries. To this day, it is read in its entirety during the services of the fifth Thursday of Lent in Orthodox churches.

3. The Lost Sheep

The other two parables that we are examining in this chapter are found in the Gospel according to Matthew. The first—the parable of the lost sheep—has both a prologue and epilogue that act as an interpretation.

The prologue to the parable is the account of how the disciples approached Jesus to ask who is greatest in the kingdom of heaven. In answer, Jesus, called a child to himself, set the child in the midst of the disciples and said,

> Verily I say unto you, except ye be converted, and become as little children, ye shall not enter into the kingdom of heaven. Whosoever therefore shall humble himself as this little child, the same is greatest in the kingdom of heaven. And whoso shall receive one such little child in my name receiveth me. But whoso shall offend one of these little ones which believe in me, it were better for him that a millstone were hanged about his neck, and that he were drowned in the depth of the

The Twelve Apostles,
Icon, 20th century

sea. Woe unto the world because of offenses! For it must needs be that offenses come, but woe to that man by whom the offense cometh! Wherefore if thy hand or thy foot offend thee, cut them off, and cast them from thee: it is better for thee to enter into life halt or maimed, rather than having two hands or two feet to be cast into everlasting fire. And if thine eye offend thee, pluck it out, and cast it from thee: it is better for thee to enter into life with one eye, rather than having two eyes to be cast into hell fire. Take heed that ye despise not one of these little ones; for I say unto you, that in heaven their angels do always behold the face of my Father which is in heaven. For the Son of Man is come to save that which was lost. (Mt 18.3–11)

Arguments about primacy often arose in the community of Jesus' disciples. Such arguments are typical for any group of people who gather around a single teacher, but who are all accepted by him with equal status. In such a group, as a rule, one or several people naturally emerge as leaders, depending on their capabilities, character traits, and singleness of purpose. In other cases, the teacher himself may give preference to one or several of the group. Among the twelve, the obvious leader was Peter; furthermore, a group of three disciples were especially preferred, which included John and James the sons of Zebedee, in addition to Peter.

These arguments concerning primacy that arose among the disciples referred first of all to their relationship to the Teacher. Mark tells us that they were walking on the road and discussing who was greatest among them (Mk 9.34). When he heard them argue, Jesus said to them: "If any man desire to be first, the same shall be last of all, and servant of all" (Mk 9.35). After he said this, he called the child to himself, and then spoke the words that Matthew recorded.

The same situation appears in Luke: "And there was also a strife among them, which of them should be accounted the greatest" (Lk 22.24). In

Luke's telling, the answer to the disciples' question is as follows:

> The kings of the Gentiles exercise lordship over them; and they that exercise authority upon them are called benefactors. But ye shall not be so; but he that is greatest among you, let him be as the younger; and he that is chief, as he that doth serve. For which is greater, he that sitteth at meat, or he that serveth? Is not he that sitteth at meat? But I am among you as he that serveth. (Lk 22.25–27)

Jesus Washes His Disciples' Feet, Pskov Icon, 16th century

In John's Gospel, the answer to the same question is expressed in action: Jesus washes the disciples' feet at the Last Supper (Jn 13.2–12); he then reinforces this teaching: "If I then, your Lord and Master, have washed your feet, ye also ought to wash one another's feet" (Jn 13.14).

Of the four evangelists, only Matthew mentions that the argument of the disciples concerned primacy not in terms of earthly rewards, but in the kingdom of heaven that Jesus spoke of so often to them. From his own words, they knew that in this kingdom a certain hierarchy would exist: some would be greater than others (Mt 11.11). But they did not know what that meant exactly or how it would reflect their own personal situation.

It is possible that these arguments concerning primacy were inspired, whether they knew it or not, by the situation that was supposed to arise after the coming of the promised kingdom. It was not by accident that James and John approached Jesus with the request to sit at his right and left hand in his glory (Mk 10.37). Matthew adds an analogous request, but spoken by the mother of those two brothers (Mt 20.20–21). It is possible that Matthew wanted to soften the negative impression created in the readers of Mark's version. Neither can we exclude the possibility that his version of the disciples' question about primacy (who is greater in the kingdom of heaven?) was an attempt to soften and ennoble the subject of the argument as it was related by the other evangelists (who is greater?).

Whatever the case may be, in Jesus' conversation with his disciples as it occurs in Matthew's version, he states that the criteria for determining the importance of people in the kingdom of heaven are opposed to earthly criteria for determining rank. This theme is constant in Jesus' preaching; it arises many times in different situations. The Beatitudes in the Sermon on the Mount (Mt 5.3–12) are an expansion of this theme. The truly blessed, that is, the truly fortunate are not those whom the world considers to be fortunate (the rich, the happy, the proud, the successful), but those who by earthly standards have not succeeded at all (the poor in spirit, the weeping, the meek, those who hunger and thirst after righteousness, the persecuted). The true victor is not he who properly avenges an insult, but he who, having been slapped on the cheek, offers the other to be slapped as well (Mt 5.38–39). Many parables speak about the same thing: he who is justified is not the righteous yet proud Pharisee, but the humble though sinful publican (Lk 18.9–14). He who finds salvation is not the rich man who rejoiced every day of his life, but the poor man Lazarus (Lk 16.19–31). The true neighbor is not the priest or Levite, but the good Samaritan (Lk 10.18–37).

In the situation we are presently discussing, Jesus offers the example of a child, for the child corresponds to the criteria of the Beatitudes much more than an adult. He is humble, meek, inoffensive, pure of heart; he weeps when others make fun of him; he is not capable of answering evil for evil. Jesus calls his disciples to humble themselves like a child. It is this quality that is one of the most important and unique characteristics of the disciple of Jesus. The list of Beatitudes begins with humility (Mk 5.3).

Later, Jesus begins a new theme: that of offenses. They "must come" not because God wills them to, but because in a world where good and evil are closely intertwined, offenses, like tares, grow in the same field as the wheat. Nevertheless, the responsibility for spreading these offenses belongs to specific people—evil does not exist as something abstract, but is always personified. A disciple of Jesus must firmly oppose all offenses, even if that means being ready to part with a member of his own body.

This same metaphor is used in the Sermon on the Mount, immediately after Jesus says, "Whosoever looketh on a woman to lust after her hath committed adultery with her already in his heart" (Mt 5.28). The woman is not a temptation to man in and of herself: her attraction to him is natural (Gen 3.16), just as his attraction to her is as well. But as soon as this attraction becomes the object of sinful desire, willingly or unwillingly, by her will or by the will of the man, it becomes a temptation. The one "by whom offenses come" is anyone who exploits the basest instincts, such as those who profit off the female body (pimps, owners of brothels, and anyone who is involved in the commodification of lust and sin). Jesus has very harsh things to say to such people. It would be better for them and for those around them, if they decided to hang a millstone on their neck and to drown in the depths of the sea.

From the theme of offenses (i.e., temptations), Jesus continues by admonishing his disciples not to despise those who, like children, seem to be insignificant or small in the world's estimation. Then he continues on to his description of the Son of Man, who came to seek and save what was lost, words that are the direct introduction to the parable of the lost sheep. In Matthew's version, the parable was written thus:

> How think ye? If a man have an hundred sheep, and one of them be gone astray, doth he not leave the ninety and nine, and goeth into the mountains, and seeketh that which is gone astray? And if so be that he find it, verily I say unto you, he rejoiceth more for that sheep, than for the ninety and nine which went not astray. Even so it is not the will of your Father which is in heaven, that one of these little ones should perish. (Mt 18.12–14)

Luke's version of this parable is preceded by his description of all the publicans and sinners approaching Jesus to hear him. The Pharisees and scribes, seeing this, complained, "This man receiveth sinners, and eateth with them" (Lk 15.2). In answer, Jesus turns to the Pharisees and scribes and tells them the parable of the lost sheep.

The parable is quite close to Matthew's version, but with certain differences. First of all, the man leaves ninety-nine sheep not in the mountains, but in the desert. Second, having found the lost sheep, he not only rejoices at finding it, he "layeth it on his shoulders," and having come back home, he calls together all his friends, and says to them: "Rejoice with me, for I have found my sheep which was lost." The end of Luke's version also differs from Matthew's: "I say unto you, that likewise joy shall be in heaven over one sinner that repenteth, more than over ninety and nine just persons, which need no repentance" (Lk 15.5–7).

And so, we have two versions of the same story with a slightly different thematic focus in each.[20] In Matthew's version, the sheep symbolizes one of these "little ones"—in Luke's version, the lost sinner. For the purposes of interpretation, this difference can be quite significant, were it not for Matthew's concluding observation that the Son of Man has come to seek and save those who are lost. These words are hardly a reference to children, since one cannot call them lost. Rather, these words more likely refer to people who are invisible, humble, humiliated, and marginalized, that is, those who occupy the lowest steps of the social hierarchy. The child who was placed before the disciples plays a similar role to the main character of a parable. His presence should be understood not literally, but metaphorically, intended to help the listener focus on a new set of coordinates, where all that is small and insignificant in the world's estimation becomes great and important in the kingdom of heaven.

This parable can also be interpreted as a symbol of the passage from the Old to the New Testaments. In the Old Testament, God dealt with a nation, with a collective, with society. The entire moral structure of the Old Testament was based on the understanding that the wholeness of the nation was of utmost importance, even if that meant the need to sacrifice certain individuals, that is, those who broke the law or in some other ways did not fit into the social order. In the New Testament, God turns from the collective to the individual, from the ninety-nine sheep, which symbolize a healthy flock (i.e., human society) to a single sheep, and further, one that is lost, that is, an individual person who has found himself, for whatever reason, outside the flock. In the Old Testament, a person who was guilty of a serious sin was eliminated for the preservation of the spiritual health

[20]A. Puig i Tàrrech, "Interpreting the Parables of Jesus, a Test Case: The Parable of the Lost Sheep," *Gospel Images of Jesus Christ in Church Tradition and in Biblical Scholarship*, ed. Christos Karakolis, Karl-Wilhelm Niebuhr and Sviatoslav Rogalsky (Tübingen: Mohr-Siebeck, 2012): 253–89, at 261.

of the entire society (see Lev 24.13–21). In the New Testament, the sinner is seen as someone who is lost. God personally turns to him and goes to find him, in the same way that he sought fallen Adam in Eden, speaking to him directly (Gen 3.9).

The Good Shepherd,
Mosaic, 20th century

God's relationship with the sinner is the central theme of this parable. If sin, temptation, and evil deserve condemnation in and of themselves, that does not mean that every sinner, everyone that is tempted, every evildoer must likewise be condemned. Sin, in this parable, is interpreted as a deviation from the proper path. Man sins because he has lost his way, has strayed from the flock, has become lost. He should be not condemned, but pitied. God does not forget man, even if man forgets God. He continues to remember him and does not simply wait for him to return, but he goes out to find him.

In this parable, as in a drop of water, we find a reflection of the entire history of God's relationship with the human race, a relationship described in the pages of the Bible. Even in the Old Testament, God was presented as the Shepherd of the nation of Israel (Gen 49.24; Ps 79.2). Like a shepherd, God cares not only for the nation at large, but for every individual person who hopes in him:

> The Lord is my shepherd; I shall not want; he has made me to dwell in a place of green pasture. He has nourished me beside the water of rest; he has restored my soul. He has guided me into paths of righteousness for his Name's sake. Yea, though I walk in the midst of the shadow of death, I will fear no evil, for thou art with me. Thy rod and thy staff, they have comforted me. (Ps 22.1–4)

The relationship between the ancient Israelites and their sheep was caring and gentle. This is vividly displayed in the prophet Nathan's parable of the sheep whom a poor man "bought and nourished up; and it grew up together with him, and with his children; it did eat of his own food, and drank of his own cup, and lay in his bosom, and was unto him as a daughter" (2 Sam 12.3). With the same gentleness does God care for his people: "He shall feed his flock like a shepherd; he shall gather the lambs with his arm, and carry them in his bosom" (Is 40.11).

God's gentle, loving relationship with man was revealed in the fact that he sent his only-begotten Son into the world. He became the Shepherd for all the sheep who are lost and scattered, who have perished. Mark and Matthew tell of Jesus' reaction to the crowds who came to him in the following words: "When he saw the multitudes, he was moved with compassion on them, because they fainted, and were scattered abroad, as sheep having no shepherd" (Mt 9.36; Mk 6.34). John includes an entire discourse in which Jesus speaks of himself as the Good Shepherd (Jn 10.11, 14–15).

In the present parable, however, the focus is not on Jesus' role as shepherd for the whole flock of the lost sheep of the house of Israel (Mt 10.6, 15.24), but on his individual relationship with a single one of these lost sheep. For him, every single person has absolute and indisputable value. The related words *planē* ("wandering") and *apoleia* ("perdition"), which are both used in the texts we have quoted, speak of various degrees of separation from God. The first might indicate a temporary error, the second a permanent loss. Yet God considers no wandering or perdition to be without the possibility of return. Even for one who has died, there is hope for resurrection.

Jesus' attitude to sinners shocked those who considered themselves to be righteous—the Pharisees and scribes. Jesus told them, "The publicans and the harlots go into the kingdom of God before you" (Mt 21.31). When they brought him a woman caught in the act of adultery, he did not condemn her (Jn 8.10–11). He also did not condemn the sinful woman who came to him with an alabaster vessel filled with oil of myrrh (Lk 7.37–39). Jesus saw every sinner not with the eye of the Pharisees but with the eyes of God, who extends a gaze of love, gentleness, and fellow suffering, like a shepherd who has lost his favorite sheep.

In addition to the passages from the Old Testament we have already noted, in which God is described as a caring shepherd, there is a text that seems like a direct parallel to the parable of the lost sheep. This is found in the book of Ezekiel:

For thus saith the Lord God, "Behold, I, even I, will both search my sheep, and seek them out. As a shepherd seeketh out his flock in the day that he is among his sheep that are scattered, so will I seek out my sheep, and will deliver them out of all places where they have been scattered in the cloudy and dark day. And I will bring them out from the people, and gather them from the countries, and will bring them to their own land, and feed them upon the mountains of Israel by the rivers, and in all the inhabited places of the country. I will feed them in a good pasture, and upon the high mountains of Israel shall their fold be; there shall they lie in a good fold, and in a fat pasture shall they feed upon the mountains of Israel. I will feed my flock, and I will cause them to lie down," saith the Lord God. "I will seek that which was lost, and bring again that which was driven away, and will bind up that which was broken, and will strengthen that which was sick; but I will destroy the fat and the strong; I will feed them with judgment." (Ezek 34.11–16)

The similarity with the parable is evident. Both passages describe God's care not only for the flock in general, but for each sheep individually. Both passages speak of lost sheep that the shepherd seeks out and returns to the flock. Yet the general tone of the prophecy differs significantly from Jesus' parable. The main point of the prophecy is to accuse the shepherds of the nation of Israel, who "feed themselves . . . but feed not the flock. . . . [T]he diseased [they] have not strengthened, neither have [they] healed that which was sick, neither have [they] bound up that which was broken . . . neither have [they] sought that which was lost." As a result, the sheep have been left without a shepherd, wandering about and getting lost in the hills, "and none did search or seek after them" (Ezek 34.2–6). In Jesus' parable, this accusatory tone is completely absent.

Ezekiel's promise that God himself will become the shepherd is a prophecy that is fulfilled in the person of Jesus, who is the Good Shepherd of the lost sheep. In the parable he tells, however, he provides no criterion by which the shepherd will separate the sheep that deserve healing and care from those who will receive judgment. In the parable of the lost sheep, only

Christt the
Good Shepherd,
Mosaic,
5th century

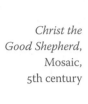

the first category of sheep is considered, symbolized by the lost sheep. All others are left to the ninety-nine who are not lost.

So who is meant by the others? And why is there more rejoicing in heaven over a single sinner who repents than over ninety-nine righteous people? Does righteousness not have its own worth? Do only repentant sinners have value in God's eyes? What about those who did not fall into sin? Are they worthless and will they be abandoned in the deserts or the mountains?

All such questions are appropriate only if we examine the parable outside the context in which it was told. According to Luke, the context was the polemic between Jesus and the Pharisees. Within this specific context we can determine the meaning of an important detail of the parable: the shepherd does not simply leave to seek the lost sheep. Before he does this, he leaves the ninety-nine who are not lost. This means that those who are not lost and the righteous in this case are the Pharisees and scribes. The word "righteous" is used here in the same negative sense that Jesus used when speaking of the purported righteousness of the Pharisees and scribes in the Sermon on the Mount (Mt 5.20). Their righteousness is external, affected, and therefore worthless in the sight of God. God turns aside from such righteousness; in fact, he abhors it (Is 1.10–15). Without any vacillation, he will leave behind this entire group of people who are righteous only in their own estimation,[21] in order to find those who, according to them, are unworthy of either attention or care.

[21] Cf. Jones, *Teaching,* 172.

The Good Shepherd, Fresco, 19th century

The fact that in this case the word "righteous" has a negative meaning, in contrast to the generally accepted opinion in scholarly literature,[22] is proven by these righteous "not having any need of repentance." The term "repentance" (*metanoia*) has a universal meaning in the New Testament, as it does in all subsequent Christian literature. Not only those who are universally acknowledged to be sinners require repentance; all the rest are in need of it also. If that were not so, Jesus would not have made the theme of his preaching the words of John the Baptist: "Repent, for the kingdom of heaven is at hand" (Mt 3.2, 4.17). These words referred to all his listeners, without exception; consequently, among them, from Jesus' point of view, there was not a single person who did not need repentance.

The theme of joy is present in both versions of the parable (Matthew and Luke). Matthew describes the shepherd's joy at finding the lost sheep in more laconic language; Luke depicts this more emotionally. Still, joy is always the reaction to the repentance that begins the sinner's return to the path of salvation.

---

[22]Cf. Blomberg, *Interpreting the Parables*, 216–17.

The Good Shepherd,
De Champaigne,
17th century

In contrast to the parable of the prodigal son (Lk 15.11–32), in the parable of the lost sheep the theme of repentance is not developed at all. There, repentance is described as the conscious action of a person who has decided to return to his father after many years in a far country, and the father is described as patiently awaiting his son's return. Here, on the contrary, the initiative is taken by the shepherd: he does not wait for the sheep to find the path back to the flock; he goes out to find it. The sheep does not return to him; he comes to it. In both cases, however, the account ends with man's encounter with God, an encounter that is shown as a source of joy not for the person, but for God. In the parable of the prodigal son, this joy is symbolized by the feast that the father announces in honor of his returned son, accompanied by singing and jubilation.

Repentance is a consequence of the conscious decision man makes in favor of God. Yet this choice is not always the result of the spiritual efforts of the man alone. Very often repentance itself occurs thanks to something that in the language of Christian theology is called prevenient grace—God's action that opens in the person the space necessary for internal transformation. Such a change occurred with people who met Jesus during the course of their earthly lives: the publican Levi (Lk 5.27–32), the publican Zaccheus (Lk 19.1–9), the sinful woman (Lk 7.36–50). In these, as in many other cases:

> [Repentance] comes about . . . as a response to prevenient grace. . . . Where grace is demonstrated, and when the one in need of repentance is not taken by the throat but is set free in the safety and space that grace affords, repentance has a chance. . . . It is a response, but it is above all a gift that is granted by God himself.[23]

[23]Hultgren, *Parables*, 62.

The concluding words of the parable in the Gospel of Matthew possess profound theological meaning: "It is not the will of your Father which is in heaven, that one of these little ones should perish." They contradict, first of all, the widespread assumption that everything happens according to God's will: both good and evil, both the salvation and the perdition of people. Second, they contradict the soteriology that initially was formulated by Augustine, and later was cast in a much harsher form by Luther and Calvin, the leaders of Protestantism. We have already mentioned this teaching, which in

The Good Shepherd,
Muriglio, 1660

short insists that some people are predestined for salvation, and others for damnation. According to Calvin, the mystery of God's will, which it pleased him to reveal to us, is witnessed by him in his own Word. Calvin claimed that among these mysteries was predestination, that God predestined some for salvation, and some for eternal damnation, that God does not create all men in the same state, but that some he creates for eternal life and some for eternal curse. God, Calvin claimed, chooses some according to his own mysterious designs, and rejects all others.[24]

This teaching was one of many attempts in history to reconcile the idea of God's omnipotence with the fact that evil acts in the world, that some people purposefully oppose God's will, that some inherit eternal blessedness, and others are condemned to eternal suffering. If this is so, then it is God's will—this is what Calvin's followers insist. But such an idea radically contradicts the Gospel's words that it is *not* God's will that even one human being be lost. Like a good shepherd, God will always go out to seek the lost sheep and will always rejoice when he finds it.

The parable of the lost sheep was a popular theme in early Christian art. Beginning in the second century, both painted and sculpted works of art depicted Christ as a beardless youth with an uncovered head, carrying a sheep on his shoulders. In the same century we find the fresco of the Good Shepherd in the Roman catacombs of Callixtus and Domitilla. In

[24]Calvin, *Institutes of the Christian Religion* 3.21.

The Good Shepherd,
Sculpture, Rome,
AD 300–350

the beginning of the third century, Tertullian noted that he had seen similar paintings on chalices and lamps.[25]

To this same period belongs the famous statue of the Good Shepherd in the Lateran museum in the Vatican. The young shepherd with long hair, dressed in a short tunic with no sleeves, is depicted with a pack hanging from his right shoulder. The head of the shepherd is turned halfway toward the head of the sheep. He holds the front feet of the sheep in his left hand, the back feet with his right. The head of the sheep is also turned to the head of the shepherd. The curly hair of the shepherd naturally flows into the curls of the sheep's wool, which is intended to underline the harmonious oneness of the two figures, who have become part of a single composition.

This statue, as the other early depictions of Christ as the Good Shepherd, belongs to that period of Christian art when the theological justification for iconography had not been fully formulated, and Christians preferred allegorical depictions to more realistic ones. It seems that Christians did not pray before these images; they were merely intended to remind them of particular stories in the Gospels. The allegorical nature of the image of the Good Shepherd completely corresponds to the allegorical interpretation of the parable of the lost sheep, since it points to Jesus as the Savior of the world who cares for every person, including those who have been rejected, humiliated, and insulted, who have strayed from the flock, who have become lost on the way.

[25]Tertullian, *On Modesty* 10.12 (CCSL 2:1301; ANF 4:85)

4. The Unmerciful Servant

The parable of the unmerciful servant also has a prologue and epilogue. The prologue is a conversation between Jesus and Peter, which appears only in Matthew: "Then came Peter to him and said, 'Lord how oft shall my brother sin against me, and I forgive him? Till seven times?' Jesus saith unto him, 'I say not unto thee until seven times, but until seventy times seven'" (Mt 18.21–22).

In later Rabbinic literature, including the Babylonian Talmud, there is an admonition to forgive a sinner three times, but not to forgive him a fourth time.[26] It is possible that this admonition reflects an earlier teaching that would have been known in Jesus' time, which Peter knew, so that when he asked about forgiving seven times, he intended it as more than double the patience required.[27] But Jesus had nothing to do with Talmudic casuistry and legalistic pedagogy. He gives Peter a symbolic number that means there can be no limit to one's forgiveness of others' sins, "not setting a number here, but what is infinite and perpetual and forever. For even as ten thousand times signifies often, so here too. . . . So that he has not limited the forgiveness by a number, but has declared that it is to be perpetual and forever."[28]

Judging by context, this conversation took place in the presence of the other disciples, since the parable ends with an instruction not only for Peter, but for all the apostles. It is also not out of the realm of possibility that the whole event occurred before other witnesses as well:

> Therefore is the kingdom of heaven likened unto a certain king, which
> would take account of his servants. And when he had begun to reckon,

[26]Babylonian Talmud, Tractate Yomah; Michael L. Rodkinson, trans., *The Babylonian Talmud: Original Text, Edited, Corrected, Formulated, and Translated into English*, vol. 6a (Boston: The Talmud Society, 1918), 137, 139. In the the first instance, this particular admonition is ascribed to Jose ben R. Jehuda, a Palestinian rabbi of the second century, while the second instance is attributed to Jose ben Hanina, a Palestinian rabbi of the third century.

[27]Leon Morris, *The Gospel according to Matthew* (Grand Rapids, MI: William B. Eerdmans Publishing Company, 1992), 471.

[28]John Chrysostom, *Homilies on the Gospel of Matthew* 61.1 (NPNF[1] 10:345).

The Parable of the Unmerciful Debtor, Sir John E. Millais, 19th century

one was brought unto him, which owed him ten thousand talents. But forasmuch as he had not to pay, his lord commanded him to be sold, and his wife, and children, and all that he had, and payment to be made. The servant therefore fell down, and worshipped him, saying, "Lord, have patience with me, and I will pay thee all." Then the lord of that servant was moved with compassion, and loosed him, and forgave him the debt. But the same servant went out, and found one of his fellow servants, which owed him an hundred pence; and he laid hands on him, and took him by the throat, saying, "Pay me what thou owest." And his fellow servant fell down at his feet, and besought him, saying, "Have patience with me, and I will pay thee all." And he would not, but went and cast him into prison, till he should pay the debt. So when his fellow servants saw what was done, they were very sorry, and came and told unto their lord all that was done. Then his lord, after that he had called him, said unto him, "O thou wicked servant, I forgave thee all that debt, because thou desiredst me. Shouldest not thou also have had compassion on thy fellow servant, even as I had pity on thee?" And his lord was wroth, and delivered him to the tormentors, till he should pay all that was due unto him. So likewise shall my heavenly Father do also unto you, if ye from your hearts forgive not everyone his brother their trespasses. (Mt 18.23–35)

The last phrase is an epilogue to the parable, which connects it to Peter's question. As in the parable of the lost sheep, the prologue and the epilogue help form a thematic arc that also provides an internal interpretation for the parable.

This parable is one of several instructions that Jesus gave concerning forgiveness. He spoke earlier about the need to forgive debtors in the Sermon on the Mount. In the prayer "Our Father," and in its interpretation,

God's forgiveness of man is directly dependent on whether or not a person is able to forgive his neighbors (Mt 6.12, 14–15).

The Apostle Peter,
Icon, 6th century

In Luke we find a situation analogous to Peter's question about forgiving seven times: "Take heed to yourselves: if thy brother trespass against thee, rebuke him; and if he repent, forgive him. And if he trespass against thee seven times in a day, and seven times in a day turn again to thee, saying, 'I repent,' thou shalt forgive him" (Lk 17.3–4). In Luke, these words are isolated from any larger context, neither fitting with the preceding section nor the subsequent one. They were not an answer to a question from Peter, and they were apparently uttered under different circumstances. The number seven here plays the same role as "seventy times seven" in Matthew. One must forgive a sinner as many times as he sins.

The difference between the words in Matthew and in Luke refers not so much to the number as to the theme of repentance. In the first case, Jesus speaks of forgiving a person whether or not he repents, in the second, Jesus speaks of forgiving a person who sins and repents. Matthew's account of Jesus' answer to Peter also lacks a reprimand. To be sure, in Matthew that theme appears slightly earlier in Jesus' words that one should admonish a sinning brother in secret first, then in the presence of one or two witnesses, and if he does not repent, then one should leave him to the judgment of the Church (Mt 18.15–17). Thus the thematic connection between Jesus' teaching on forgiveness in Matthew and Luke is quite evident, even if the focal point is slightly different.

Ultimately, the Gospel does not definitively answer the question, "Is repentance a condition of forgiveness or not?" In some cases, as in the passage from Luke, repentance is noted, while in other cases nothing is said about repentance at all. Judging by the fact that in the "Our Father" and its interpretation, which have universal significance, Jesus speaks of forgiving debtors with no reference to whether they are repentant, or whether they ask for forgiveness, we should take this model for behavior as an ideal to which every disciple of Jesus should strive. Forgiveness of those who ask for forgiveness is evidently a minimum that is absolutely necessary for all, or perhaps a first step on the path leading a person to acquire the ability to forgive absolutely all debtors.

In any case, this question has no direct bearing on the content of the parable of the unforgiving servant. In this parable, the servant's debtor falls to his feet and begs him to wait until he can pay off his debt. The servant himself had done the same thing before his own master just before. The most important point of the parable is not this detail, but the difference between the way the king reacted to his slave, and the way the slave reacted to his debtor. The parable does not answer the question of whether we must forgive only those who ask forgiveness. It draws a general picture built on the contrast between the behavior of the two debtors.

Scholars note that the situation described in the parable gives us a good sense of what it was like for the Hebrews to live under Roman rule.[29] The parable begins with the king deciding to call in his servants' debts. This is nothing other than a financial inspection, carried out by order of the highest local governmental authority. They bring a certain debtor who owes a massive amount of money to this king. Since the debtor has no way to pay his debt, the king orders that all his property be confiscated, including his wife and children.

This initial creditor of the parable is first called literally a "man king" ([*anthrōpō basilei*] since this expression is typically Semitic, most translations simply omit the word "man"). Later in the parable he is given the designation *kyrios*, which is translated "lord." This is the term that the Septuagint uses for God, especially when translating the holy name of God "Yahweh." In the New Testament, it is used both to refer to God the Father and Jesus.

The first and second debtors are described using the term *doulos* and *syndoulos*, meaning "slave" and "fellow slave," that is, the two debtors are

[29]William R. Herzog, *Parables as Subversive Speech: Jesus as Pedagogue of the Oppressed* (Louisville, KY: Westminster John Knox Press, 1994), 131–49; Luise Schottroff, *The Parables of Jesus* (Minneapolis: Ausburg Fortress, 2006), 196–204.

of equal social standing, and they most likely are slaves of the same master. The second slave, furthermore, can have other *syndouloi* (fellow slaves) who have compassion on him. Most of the story takes place within the society of the slaves of a single master, while the main theme of the parable is the interaction between the first slave and his master, as well as his interaction with one of his fellow slaves.

In the parables of Jesus, the term *doulos* occurs often, in both singular and plural forms. Slaves, or servants, are the main characters of twelve parables: the wheat and the tares, the unforgiving servant, the wicked tenants, the wedding feast, the wise slave, the expectations of the household, the slaves who do not sleep, those called to the feast, the talents, the prodigal son, the worthless slaves, the ten minas.[30] The term *doulos* also occurs in Jesus' speech outside parables, for example in these passages:

> The disciple is not above his master, nor the servant above his lord. It is enough for the disciple that he be as his master, and the servant as his lord. If they have called the master of the house Beelzebub, how much more shall they call them of his household? (Mt 10.24–25)

> But it shall not be so among you; but whosoever will be great among you, let him be your minister; and whosoever will be chief among you, let him be your servant. (Mt 20.26–27)

> Henceforth I call you not servants; for the servant knoweth not what his lord doeth. But I have called you friends, for all things that I have heard of my Father I have made known unto you. (Jn 15.15)

> Remember the word that I said unto you, "The servant is not greater than his lord." If they have persecuted me, they will also persecute you; if they have kept my saying, they will keep yours also. (Jn 15.20)

The time of Jesus' earthly life coincided with the greatest spread of slavery in the Roman period. If in the early days of the Roman republic there were comparatively few slaves, one of the results of the wars of conquest of the late Republic was a huge increase of the number of prisoners of war,

---

[30]This list is found in Hultgren, *Parables*, 437.

Roman mosaic,
a young woman
with two slaves
serving her

who were not killed but sold into slavery. The end of the Republic, which occurred in 27 BC in the reign of Octavian Augustus, caused the institution of slavery to develop further. The number of slaves in the territory of the Roman Empire of Jesus' time is counted differently by historians. It is considered possible that in Italy alone, there were two to three million slaves, and the ratio of slaves to freemen was 1 to 2 or 2 to 5.[31] Beyond Italy, however, including in Israel, the number of slaves was far smaller.

A slave was considered the property of his master, similar to land, real estate, or cattle. The authority of a master over his slave was absolute. A master could arbitrarily beat, maim, castrate, or even kill his slave. Marriage between slaves had no legal status: it was considered no more than cohabitation that could be ended by the master's will. Slaves were not the subjects, but the objects, of law. A certain improvement in the legal status of slaves began in the middle of the first century AD (including the *Lex Petronia de servis,* which is believed to date to AD 61).[32] In Jesus' time, such measures had not yet taken place. Only in the fourth century, during the reign of Constantine, was the punishment for the premeditated killing of a slave legally equated to the murder of a freeman, and this law only came

---

[31]M. I. Finley, *Ancient Slavery and Modern Ideology* (New York: The Viking Press, 1980), 80; P. A. Brunt, *Italian Manpower, 225 B.C.–A.D. 14* (London: Oxford University Press, 1971), 4, 121–24.

[32]M. von Albrecht, *Istoriya rimskoy literatury ot Andronika do Boeziya i ee eliyanie na posleduyushchie epokhi* [The history of Roman literature from Andronicus to Boethius and its influence on later eras] (Moscow: Greko-Latinskii Kabinet Y. A. Shichalina, 2004), 1320.

about under the direct influence of Christian morality on the legal system of the Roman Empire.

The status of the slaves in the parable reflects the status of slaves in the Roman Empire of Jesus' time. The fate of the slave was entirely in the hands of the master. To have mercy or to punish, to forgive a debt or not, to determine the nature of punishment—all this depended on the will of the master.

In this parable, when the king realized the size of the slave's debt, he commanded that the debtor himself be sold, as well as his wife, children, and holdings. When the debtor later refuses to forgive the debt of his fellow slave, he has the authority to put him into prison. How realistic are either of these scenarios?

Confiscation of property was a common legal practice in Roman law. Emperor Tiberius routinely filled the coffers of the state by confiscating individuals' property if they were accused of conspiracy or convicted of crimes. This confiscation could be total or partial. In some cases, the children of the condemned could keep part of the property. Laws concerning the amount, degree, and form of confiscation constantly changed in the Roman Empire. Hebrew law did not allow for the possibility of confiscating property, but in practice, such confiscation did occur.

As for the sale of a slave, his wife, and children to pay off a debt, such a punishment was not part of either Roman or Jewish law. Nevertheless, there are traces of such practices in the Old Testament. The Law of Moses only allowed one to be sold into slavery as a punishment for theft (Ex 22.3). Yet the Bible tells of a case when a creditor required that both sons of a debtor be sold to him to repay their father's debt, which he was unable to pay before he died (2 Kings 4.1). Further, during a time of famine, the Jews sold their own sons and daughters into slavery to feed themselves (Neh 5.5). Finally, some prophets use the metaphorical image of selling people into slavery to pay a debt (Is 50.1; Am 2.6).

It was forbidden by Jewish law to imprison someone because of an unpaid debt. Yet it was common practice in Roman law of the first century A D.[33] This practice is reflected in the words of the Sermon on the Mount:

[33]Hultgren, *Parables*, 27.

Ancient Greek amphora, one talent equaled the weight of a standard amphora filled with water

Agree with thine adversary quickly, while thou art in the way with him, lest at any time the adversary deliver thee to the judge, and the judge deliver thee to the officer, and thou be cast into prison. Verily I say unto thee, thou shalt by no means come out thence, till thou hast paid the uttermost farthing. (Mt 5.25–26)

Therefore, the story told in the parable is based, if not on actual written law, then at least on actual practical precedents. Nonetheless, it is not necessary to overemphasize the realism of the parable. The sum that Jesus gives for the first slave's debt to the king is intentionally hyperbolic. In the ancient Near East, ten thousand was the largest number used in counting, while a talent was the largest unit of currency; consequently, ten thousand talents is literally the largest sum of money that a person of that time could imagine.[34]

The term "talent" in the Greco-Roman world indicated a unit of weight, roughly equal to 100 lbs. By the first century AD, this term became a unit of currency, equal to six thousand denarii, which was the yearly wages of two thousand day-laborers.[35] Ten thousand talents was an astronomical sum, compared by some modern scholars to roughly four billion US dollars.[36] Only the noblest courtier, no lower in rank than a provincial governor, might even dream of lending such a sum to an emperor.[37] All the same, the number is not out of the realm of the possible. Carthage had to pay Rome ten thousand silver talents after Scipio Africanus' victory in the Second Punic War, and

[34]Barclay M. Newman and Philip C. Stine, *A Translator's Handbook on the Gospel of Matthew* (London, New York, Stuttgart: United Bible Societies, 1998), 595.

[35]Hultgren, *Parables*, 23, 274–75.

[36]Gerald O'Collins, *Jesus: A Portrait* (Maryknoll, NY: Orbis Books, 2008), 98.

[37]Jeremias, *Parables*, 210.

the payment was made in installments over the course of fifty years.[38] According to Flavius Josephus, the Syrian king Ptolemy the Lesser paid one thousand talents to Pompey to avoid the death penalty; from this payment, Pompey paid his army their wages.[39]

The sum that the first slave owed the king exceeded the debt owed to him by the second slave by five or six hundred thousand times over. This ratio is intended to illustrate the central point of the parable: every person is incalculably indebted to God. The astronomical sum of ten thousand talents symbolizes mankind's unpayable debt before God, which can be compared with no other debts that one person may owe another.

The very idea of a financial debt is used here metaphorically. The term used in Matthew 18.27—*daneion* ("debt")—is found in no other place of the New Testament. In Greek, this term is as a rule applied to indicate a loan of money. The prayer "Our Father" uses another word to demonstrate indebtedness—*opheilēmata*, and for the debtor, the related word *opheiletais*. In the parable, the debtor is called by the same term (literally "a debtor [*opheiletēs*] of ten thousand talents").

Both debtors use the same phrase to placate their creditors: "Have patience with me." Moreover, in critical editions of the New Testament, the first debtor's request is accompanied by a promise: "I will pay it all back," while the second says, "I will return it to you," without the word "all."[40] Just as the repayment of the first sum, considering its astronomical value, was unrealistic for the first debtor, so too was the repayment of the second debtor realistic, since he owed his fellow slave only one hundred denarii. The parallelism between the two actions of the two debtors is underlined by the fact that they both fall on their knees before their creditor. This pose, however, has a different meaning in front of a king and in front of a fellow slave.

The king does not simply agree to the first slave's request and delay the repayment of the debt. He "was moved with compassion, and loosed

[38]Livy, *The History of Rome* 30.37.5; *Livy with an English Translation in Fourteen Volumes*, vol. 8, Books 28–30, trans. Frank Gardner Moore, Loeb Classical Library, vol. 381 (Cambridge, MA: Harvard University Press, 1949), 507.
[39]Josephus, *The Antiquities of the Jews* 14.3.2; *Works of Josephus*, 368.
[40]Aland, *Synopsis*, 254.

him, and forgave him the debt." The verb *aphēken* ("forgave") indicates the full forgiveness of the debt without any consequences. This is the same verb used in the prayer "Our Father": "And forgive [*aphes*] us our debts [*opheilēmata*] as we forgive [*aphiemen*] our debtors [*opheiletais*]." In other words, the parable becomes a vivid illustration of the words that follow after "Our Father" and interpret it in the Sermon on the Mount: "For if ye forgive men their trespasses, your heavenly Father will also forgive you. But if ye forgive not men their trespasses, neither will your Father forgive your trespasses" (Mt 6.14–15).

The forgiveness that God gives a debtor is complete and total. God does not simply put off the payment of a debt nor does he simply write off part of a debt. He forgives the entire debt completely. And this occurs not because man has promised God to return what is owed (after all, this promise in the parable is not realistic). This happens because of God's mercy. The verb "moved with compassion" indicates a quality that is rarely found in earthly kings, but which in the Old Testament is stressed as one of the essential qualities of God (see Ex 34.6; Deut 4.31; 2 Chr 30.9; Neh 9.17; Ps 85.5, etc.). In the book of Exodus, God said,

> If thou lend money to any of my people that is poor by thee, thou shalt not be to him as an usurer [i.e., one who lends money at interest], neither shalt thou lay upon him usury. If thou at all take thy neighbor's raiment to pledge, thou shalt deliver it unto him by that the sun goeth down, for that is his covering only; it is his raiment for his skin. Wherein shall he sleep? And it shall come to pass, when he crieth unto me, that I will hear, for I am gracious. (Ex 22.25–27)

The limitless mercy of God strongly contrasts with the mercilessness of the slave, who thus becomes a kind of anti-God. He does not make any concessions: he does not offer any additional time to pay the debt, nor does he suggest a reduction of the debt. The actions of the slave could perhaps have been understandable if the massive debt he owed the king still remained. But this is not the case, and this is the story's central contrast: he had just been forgiven a massive debt when he encountered his fellow slave.

The first slave, in this parable, is thus shown not only as merciless to his own fellow slave, but also ungrateful to his king. The Old Testament constantly repeats the theme that every person must thank God for all his benefits. The entirety of Psalm 102 is dedicated to it:

> Bless the Lord, O my soul, and all that is within me, bless his holy Name.
> Bless the Lord, O my soul, and forget not all his benefits:
> who forgives all thine iniquities, who heals all thy diseases,
> who redeems thy life from corruption, who crowns thee with mercy and compassion,
> who satisfies thy desire with good things, so that thy youth shall be renewed like the eagle's.
> The Lord executes mercy and judgment for all them that are wronged.
> He made known his ways unto Moses, his will to the children of Israel.
> The Lord is compassionate and merciful, long-suffering and plenteous in mercy.
> His wrath will not endure until the end, neither will he be angry forever.
> He has not dealt with us according to our iniquities, nor rewarded us according to our sins.
> As high as heaven is above the earth, so the Lord has strengthened his mercy toward them that fear him.
> As far as the east is from the west, so far has he removed our iniquities from us.
> As a father has compassion on his children, so the Lord has compassion upon them that fear him. (Ps 102.1–13)

The figure of the king in this parable is similar to the description of God in Psalm 102. Like God, he is merciful, longsuffering, and generous; he does not requite the sinner according to his iniquity, but he forgives him all his sins. The call of the Psalmist to his own soul is resonant with the moral call that undergirds the entire parable: man must not forget the benefits

God bestows upon him. The slave in the parable does not answer this call, in no way expressing his gratitude to the king, either in word or deed. In this case, gratitude in words is not required, but gratitude in action should have been expressed by forgiving his fellow slave.

In what sense is man a debtor before God? This is not a rhetorical question if we consider that many people do not regard themselves as God's debtors at all. First of all, each receives the gift of life from God: there is not a single person who has appeared on this earth by his own choice. One's homeland, parents, health, abilities, and opportunities for self-realization—all this is part of that list of benefits that man receives from God without deserving any of it. In this sense, every person is a debtor before God merely because he appeared on this earth, received an education and formation, and was able to grow up and become an adult.

In this parable, forgiveness is stressed, that is, the main point is that God forgives every person his personal debt to him. This indebtedness grows with the person's own age: the more he sins, the greater the debt before God, who forgives him as often as that person sins and repents. But this rule is not automatic and infallible. If a person is ungrateful, if he does not emulate God in his mercy and does not forgive his own debtors, God will punish him in the end.

The parable reveals three of God's qualities: omnipotence, mercy, and justice. These qualities exist in him equally, and can be revealed in answer to any of man's actions. God has ultimate authority over man: if he desires to reckon with man, nothing can prevent him from doing so. But when man turns to him praying for forgiveness, he writes off all debts, no matter how massive they may seem. God denies forgiveness only when a person who has been forgiven by him does not forgive his own debtors in turn. Here we see God's justice manifested, a quality that in Scriptures is often expressed in terms of wrath. Thus, in the parable, the king becomes angry and hands the slave over to the torturers.

The term "torturers" metaphorically points to the eternal fate of unrepentant sinners, whom God will send "into hell, into the fire that never shall be quenched, where the worm dieth not, and the fire is not quenched" (Mk 9.43–44). In Jesus' sermons and parables, both the suffering of sinners

One of the first images of Jesus Christ with a nimbus, detail of a fresco in the Roman catacombs, 4th century

and the blessedness of the righteous is depicted as eternal (Mt 25.46). It may seem that the words of the parable "till he should pay all that was due unto him" contradict this reading. It is for this reason, based on this phrase, as well as the expression from the Sermon on the Mount ("Thou shalt by no means come out thence, till thou has paid the uttermost farthing," Mt 5.26) that the Catholic Church developed the doctrine of purgatory: an intermediate state between heaven and hell, where a sinner is subjected to sufferings that are temporal, impermanent.

In this parable, however, the term "till" (*heōs*), does not indicate any passage of time. The opposite is true: the limitless nature of the suffering completely accords with the astronomical size of the debt. Ten thousand talents is such a huge sum that no one person will ever be able to pay it off, even if all his holdings are sold, even if his wife and children are sold into slavery, even if he himself is given over to the torturers. This is how John Chrysostom understands the words "till he should pay all that was due unto him," that is, forever, because he would never be able to repay it.[41]

The most important point of the parable, however, is not the threat of eternal sufferings, which is present in many other parables, nor is it the teaching of God's mercy, but rather it is the call to forgive debtors. The theme of the limitless mercy of God ends up being ancillary. The most important challenge of the parable is found in its epilogue: "So likewise shall my heavenly Father do also unto you, if ye from your hearts forgive not everyone his brother their trespasses" (the words "their trespasses" are not found in some early manuscripts).[42] This epilogue dots all the I's, transferring the attention of the listener from the domain of financial debt into the domain of interpersonal relationships, where other laws must rule, dictated not by the principles of fairness and expediency, but by man's striving to emulate God in his mercy.

This is further underlined by the expression "from your hearts." The way that Jesus calls us to act is dictated not by rational considerations, but by that internal quality that is related to divine mercy. God's actions toward man are not subject to the laws of expediency or just retribution. On the contrary, God desires to forgive man, even if his sins are obvious to others (Lk 7.37–39). But Jesus also wants man to learn how to see his neighbor in the same way as God sees man: with love, sympathy, mercy, readiness to forgive any offense, no matter how serious it may be.

---

[41]John Chrysostom, *Homilies on the Gospel of Matthew* 61.4 (NPNF[1] 10:379).
[42]See *Novum Testamentum graece*, 28th rev. ed., Eberhard Nestle, Ewrin Nestle, Kurt Aland, et al., eds. (Stuttgart: Deutsche Bibelgesellschaft, 2012).

Chapter 4

PARABLES ON THE WAY TO JERUSALEM

In the previous chapters, we primarily examined the Gospel of Matthew. Now, we will mostly turn to the Gospel of Luke. The majority of the parables recorded in this Gospel were told by Jesus outside Galilee—on the way to Jerusalem. In general Luke dedicates less time to the Galilean period of Jesus' ministry than Mark and Matthew, instead devoting a large part of his account (Lk 9.51–19.27) to his description of Jesus' final journey to Jerusalem. According to Luke, Jesus told sixteen parables on the way. We will examine them all in this chapter, except for two: the parable of the wedding feast and the ten minas. These we will examine in chapter five, together with the parables that, according to Matthew and Mark, Jesus told in Jerusalem.

To conclude this chapter, we will examine the only parable that Matthew records on the way from Galilee to Jerusalem: the parable of the workers in the vineyard. Thus, we will examine fifteen parables: fourteen from the Gospel of Luke and one from the Gospel of Matthew.

1. The Good Samaritan

According to Luke, the good Samaritan is the first parable that Jesus told on the way to Jerusalem. This journey began with Jesus sending "messengers before his face; and they went, and entered into a village of the Samaritans, to make ready for him. And they did not receive him, because

*The Good
Samaritan,*
Van Gogh, 1890

his face was as though he would go to Jerusalem" (Lk 9.52–53). The path
from Galilee to Jerusalem passed through Samaria, but Luke says nothing
about how much time Jesus spent in Samaria on the way to Jerusalem. He
only mentions that after the Samaritans did not receive him in one village,
they "went to another village" (Lk 9.56), presumably also in Samaria.

Jesus had visited Samaria earlier, and this visit is vividly described in the
Gospel of John (Jn 4.4–42). That time Jesus was going from Judea to Galilee, but now he was traveling in the opposite direction. From the Gospel
of John, we also know that the "Jews have no dealings with the Samaritans"
(Jn 4.9). The enmity between Jews and Samaritans began with the events
described in the Second Book of Kings, when the northern ten tribes of

Israel were taken to Assyria after 722 BC, and the
king of Assyria relocated non-Israelites to Samaria.
These new inhabitants, while not abandoning their
old gods, also began to worship the God of Israel:
"They feared the Lord, and served their own gods,
after the manner of the nations whom they carried
away from thence" (2 Kg 17.24–33).

The syncretism of monotheism with polythe-
ism was characteristic of the Samaritans for many
generations (2 Kg 17.41). By the time of Jesus, the
Samaritans were primarily monotheistic: their

The Good Samaritan,
Rembrandt, 1633

temple on Mount Gerizim, built during the time of Alexander the Great,
was destroyed around 128 BC, yet they continued to regard it as a holy
mountain (Jn 4.20). The Jews treated the Samaritans antagonistically not
only because of their differences in faith, but also along ethnic lines: in the
Samaritans the pure blood of God's people was mixed with the blood of
foreign nations.

The parable of the good Samaritan was told soon after Jesus was turned
away from the Samaritan village. It is possible that he told it in the second
Samaritan village mentioned above, or perhaps on the road in Samaria, or
perhaps already in Judea after he had passed through Samaria. The event
that follows the parable describes how Jesus came to the house of Martha
and Mary (Lk 19.38–42), and this home was in Bethany, near Jerusalem (Jn
11.1). Finally, we cannot exclude the possibility that this parable was told in
the area beyond Jordan, since the main character of the parable is traveling
from Jerusalem to Jericho (Lk 10.30). In any case, Samaritans frequently
appear in the Gospel (Lk 17.16–19; Jn 4.4–42), and Jesus shows them good
will several times.[1]

The prologue of the parable recounts that a lawyer "stood up, and
tempted him, saying, 'Master, what shall I do to inherit eternal life?'" Jesus
answered his question with another question: "What is written in the law?
How readest thou?" And the lawyer answered, "Thou shalt love the Lord

---

[1]J. P. Meier, "The Historical Jesus and the Historical Samaritans: What can be Said?" *Biblica*
81 (2000): 202–232, at 231.

thy God with all thy heart, and with all thy soul, and with all thy strength, and with all thy mind, and thy neighbor as thyself." Jesus replied, "Thou hast answered right: this do, and thou shalt live" (Lk 10.25–28). In the parallel account in Matthew, Jesus himself quotes the Old Testament commandments to answer the lawyer (Mt 22.34–40). In Mark, this episode is given in greater detail than in either Matthew or Luke (Mk 12.28–34).

Yet only in Luke does this event have a continuation, when the lawyer, "willing to justify himself," asks another question: "And who is my neighbor?" This then becomes the reason for Jesus to tell the parable:

> "A certain man went down from Jerusalem to Jericho, and fell among thieves, which stripped him of his raiment, and wounded him, and departed, leaving him half dead. And by chance there came down a certain priest that way, and when he saw him, he passed by on the other side. And likewise a Levite, when he was at the place, came and looked on him, and passed by on the other side. But a certain Samaritan, as he journeyed, came where he was, and when he saw him, he had compassion on him, and went to him, and bound up his wounds, pouring in oil and wine, and set him on his own beast, and brought him to an inn, and took care of him. And on the morrow when he departed, he took out two pence, and gave them to the host, and said unto him, 'Take care of him, and whatsoever thou spendest more, when I come again, I will repay thee.' Which now of these three, thinkest thou, was neighbor unto him that fell among the thieves?" And he said, "He that showed mercy on him." Then said Jesus unto him, "Go, and do thou likewise." (Lk 10.30–37)

According some scholars,[2] certain details of the parable parallel events in the Second Book of Chronicles, which refers to the time of wars between the kingdoms of Israel and Judah. Here we read the account of how the sons of Israel took as prisoners of war twenty thousand Judeans and wanted to send them to Samaria, but the prophet Oded walked before the army that was going to Samaria and convinced the leaders to have mercy on the

[2]Cf. John Drury, *The Parables in the Gospels: History and Allegory* (London: Crossroad Publishing Company, 1985), 134–35.

The monastery of the temptation near Jericho

prisoners. As a result, some of the leaders, having listened to the words of the prophet, "with the spoil clothed all that were naked among them, and arrayed them, and shod them, and gave them to eat and to drink, and anointed them, and carried all the feeble of them upon asses, and brought them to Jericho, the city of palm trees, to their brethren; then they returned to Samaria" (2 Chr 28.8–15).

There are a fair number of parallel events in both passages. Both have to do with Samaria; in both cases Jericho is also mentioned; in both, mercy is shown to those who fell into calamity. The symbol of this mercy in both cases involves oil, which was frequently used for medicinal purposes to aid healing (wine was used to stop infection). The lawyer, being well-read in the Scriptures, could not fail to know the account from Chronicles. Perhaps Jesus wanted to remind him, through this parable, of past examples of noble behavior.

Jesus begins his parable with a description of a calamitous situation that befell a certain person traveling from Jerusalem to Jericho. This road passes through a deserted area. This was a dangerous road; it was even called the "Ascent of Blood" because of frequent attacks by robbers on travelers.[3]

It is possible that the priest who walked by did not approach the poor man because he feared that robbers were somewhere nearby. It is also

[3]J. Wilkinson, "The Way from Jerusalem to Jericho," *The Biblical Archaeologist* 38.1 (1975): 10–24, at 18–19.

The Good
Samaritan,
V. I. Surikov. 1874

possible that he thought the wounded man was already dead: the word *hēmithanēs* literally means "half-dead" and could be used to describe a person who lay without moving, in an unconscious state, visibly no different from a corpse. The priest, by law, was not allowed to touch a corpse, lest he be defiled (Lev 21.1–2). Some interpreters stress this desire to preserve ritual purity when describing the priest's actions.[4]

But such proscriptions did not extend to the Levites. Unlike the priest, the Levite did not simply walk past, he first approached and looked. Nevertheless, he did not help the suffering man, though the reasons for his neglect are not mentioned.

Priests and Levites were among the most honored members of the Israel's society. Both served at the temple in Jerusalem, and though Levites played a secondary role, they also belonged to the ranks of the servants of the Temple. Jesus did not choose these two representatives by chance. Like the scribes and Pharisees, they were considered models of behavior for all.

In this case, however, only the Samaritan shows proper behavior. His sympathy for the person who had been attacked by robbers is expressed by the verb *esplangchnisthē* ("had compassion"). This verb is often used

---

[4]Maurice Casey, *Jesus of Nazareth: An Independent Historian's Account of His Life and Teaching* (London: T&T Clark International, 2010), 302.

in the Gospels (Mt 9.36, 14.14, 15.32, 18.27, 20.34; Mk 1.41, 6.34, 8.2, 9.22; Lk 7.13, 10.33, 15.20), primarily when referring to Jesus himself. It comes from the word *splangchnon* ("inward parts," "womb," figuratively, "heart") and indicates mercy or compassion as an interior quality that is natural to a person and that makes him like God. Among the three main characters of the parable, only the Samaritan is shown to possess such an essential quality.

The Storyteller puts special emphasis on the actions of the good Samaritan: "This detailed concentration on the figure of the Samaritan portrays the nature of love for one's neighbor more eloquently than any abstract statement of principle could do."[5] Love for one's neighbor is manifest in action. It is expressed in a person's capacity to empathize with the one who is suffering, to enter into every detail of his calamitous situation and to use all that is within one's power to help him. Instead of trying to run away from the place as quickly as possible, as the priest and the Levite did, the Samaritan uses both his time and money to help his suffering neighbor. More importantly, he does it with heart.

Two denarii, the sum that the Samaritan paid to the innkeeper, would have been enough to feed a healthy man for an entire month.[6] In any case, the sum would have been more than enough to pay for a room and board for one to two weeks, as well as medicines for the poor man. Yet the Samaritan does not limit himself simply to leaving him at the inn. He promises the innkeeper to return to pay all extra expenses, should the two denarii not be enough.

The parable is a commentary on the Old Testament commandment quoted by the lawyer: "Love thy neighbor as thyself" (Lev 19.18). Moreover, the commentary expands beyond a simple answer to the question "Who is my neighbor?" Having asked this question, the lawyer evidently expected to receive a list of certain people, and, consequently, everyone else would not be considered his neighbor. Further, he may have hoped to receive an

---

[5]Stephen I. Wright, *Jesus the Storyteller* (Louisville, KY: Westminster John Knox Press, 2015), 107.

[6]Kenneth W. Harl, *Coinage in the Roman Economy, 300 BC to AD 700* (Baltimore, MD: The Johns Hopkins University Press, 1999), 277–78.

*The Good
Samaritan*,
Von Carolsfeld,
19th century
engraving

answer that stated whether one's neighbors were limited to the members of the tribes of Israel, or if one should include other people.

Yet the answer that he receives from Jesus completely altered the perspective from which one can even examine the original question: "Who is my neighbor?" From the parable, it becomes clear that one's neighbor is anyone who needs help: this is how one may formulate the lesson of the parable. But Jesus wants the lawyer to identify himself with the suffering man, not to look at the situation with an analytical eye from the outside, but from within. Therefore, instead of directly answering the question, he himself asks the lawyer who of the three—the priest, the Levite, or the Samaritan—was a neighbor to the man who became a victim of thieves. The lawyer perfectly understood the meaning of the question and of the parable, but he cannot bring himself to say the word "Samaritan" in a positive manner, and so he described him instead of naming him: "He that showed mercy on him."

The good Samaritan symbolizes Christ. Augustine mentioned that when Jesus answered the Jews' question: "Say we not well that thou art a Samaritan, and hast a devil?" (Jn 8.48), Jesus only rejects the second accusation, but not the first. Augustine goes on to explain that in the parable, the good Samaritan is Christ himself. He himself came to the wounded man, he showed him mercy, and acted as a neighbor to one whom he did not consider to be a stranger.[7]

Origen was the first to offer a more expansive allegorical interpretation of all the major elements of the parable. The man who fell prey to the thieves is Adam. Jerusalem is Eden, and Jericho is the world. The thieves are the evil powers; the priest is the law and the Levites are the prophets. The Samaritan is Christ. The wounds are disobedience, and the donkey is the body of the Lord.[8] The inn that accepts all who wish to enter is the Church, and the promise of

The Good Samaritan,
Nicolas Morot, 1880

the Samaritan to return is a symbol of the second coming of Christ.[9] We find a similar interpretation with even more details in Augustine.[10]

Such a detailed interpretation of every aspect of the parable may seem artificial and even distracting from the main point. But it draws upon the original message that lies at the heart of identifying the good Samaritan with Christ. Such an identification would hardly have occurred to the original listeners of the parable; in the tradition of the Church, however, this has become the foundational interpretation. The good Samaritan is the Son of God, who had mercy on stricken humanity, torn apart by passions, sins, and satanic influence. He came to fallen, suffering, and wounded mankind, he carried us on his shoulders. He brought us into the Church, where he arranged everything for our spiritual healing and the complete restoration of our original state. And then, he promised to come again, to make sure that humanity has healed completely.

---

[7]Augustine, *Homilies on the Gospel of John* 43.2 (PL 35:1707; NPNF[1] 7:240).

[8]In the sense that God, after taking on human flesh, bore upon himself the sins of all mankind (cf. 1 Pet 2.24).

[9]Origen, *Homilies on the Gospel of Luke* 34.3 (SC 87:402–404; FOC 94:138).

[10]Augustine, *Questions on the Gospels* 2.19 (CCSL 44B:62–63).

2. The Friend at Midnight and the Persistent Widow

The parable of the friend at midnight in the Gospel of Luke is part of a larger teaching dedicated to prayer. It begins thus: "As he was praying in a certain place, when he ceased, one of his disciples said unto him, 'Lord, teach us to pray, as John also taught his disciples'" (Lk 11.1). In answer, Jesus speaks the words of the prayer "Our Father" in a slightly shortened form, if compared to the version given during the Sermon on the Mount in the Gospel of Matthew (Mt 6.9–13).

In the Sermon on the Mount, after the "Our Father," Jesus teaches about the need to forgive debtors (Mt 6.14–15). A little later, Jesus returns to the theme of prayer and gives a teaching (Mt 7.7–11) that is nearly identical to Luke's addition to the parable of the friend at midnight, which follows the "Our Father":

> And he said unto them, "Which of you shall have a friend, and shall go unto him at midnight, and say unto him, 'Friend, lend me three loaves, for a friend of mine in his journey is come to me, and I have nothing to set before him?' And he from within shall answer and say, 'Trouble me not; the door is now shut, and my children are with me in bed; I cannot rise and give thee.' I say unto you, though he will not rise and give him, because he is his friend, yet because of his importunity he will rise and give him as many as he needeth. And I say unto you, ask, and it shall be given you; seek, and ye shall find; knock, and it shall be opened unto you. For every one that asketh receiveth; and he that seeketh findeth; and to him that knocketh it shall be opened. If a son shall ask bread of any of you that is a father, will he give him a stone? Or if he ask a fish, will he for a fish give him a serpent? Or if he shall ask an egg, will he offer him a scorpion? If ye then, being evil, know how to give good gifts

unto your children, how much more shall your heavenly Father give the Holy Spirit to them that ask him?" (Lk 11.5–13)

To understand the meaning of the parable, we must imagine the situation that it describes. In Palestinian villages and towns of Jesus' time, there were no shops. Every family independently prepared food for the day. Bread was the main staple. Every morning, people baked the amount of bread their entire family would need for that day. If they expected guests, they would bake bread separately, so that it would be fresh for the arrival of the guests. The same was true of other food for guests. Nothing was left for the following day, since tomorrow is supposed to take care of itself, for there are enough cares for today (see Mt 7.34). It would have been impossible to find bread in a village at night, except perhaps if you were to ask a friend with many children, who might have had a small amount left in reserve.

Naturally, there was no postal service or telephones to warn about an unexpected visit. If a person were coming home from a long journey and arrived in his village at a late hour, it would have been completely natural for him to knock on the door of his friend. By the laws of eastern hospitality, the friend was obliged not only to open the door, but also feed his friend and put him to sleep in his own house. A guest could come to his friend without warning, at any time of day or night, and he could expect not only food and lodging, but also to be received with joy. More than that, during the entire length of his stay in the house of a friend, he could expect to be treated like a member of the family; the life of the friend's family would in a significant way depend on his own needs and interests. These are the unwritten laws of hospitality that continue to be followed without demur in the East to this day.

In this parable, we encounter three main characters: a certain person, a guest who arrives unexpectedly, and a friend who lives in the same village. This friend, evidently, lives in a typical Palestinian house, which was not divided into rooms. Everyone (husband, wife, and children) slept in the same room, on a single bed, which would have been laid directly on the floor. The doors to the house were locked. To stand in the middle of

Christ preaches
to the apostles,
Fresco,
14th century

the night to open the door would mean waking up everyone in the house, to disturb one's nearest and dearest. Therefore, the first reaction of the awakened man would be to reject the request. But the persistent friend does not leave, and finally he receives what he asked for: not because of friendship, but because of his persistence.

The word "friend" (*philos*) occurs four times in the parable. It might even seem to be a parable about friendship, about the laws of hospitality and mutual aid. But this is not the case. The Storyteller designs this everyday situation in such a way that he introduces a new theme: persistence in prayer. And it turns out that everything he said about friendship has a symbolic meaning related to this theme. The main point of the parable becomes the persistence of a person, his annoyance and peskiness (the tern *anaideia* literally means "shamelessness"). This quality symbolizes that disposition with which a person must turn to God in prayer.

The teaching that follows the parable as an interpretation is nearly identical to a passage from the Sermon on the Mount. In our opinion, this proves that Jesus repeated his teachings more than once. Like a persistent friend, Jesus himself often and persistently repeated teachings to his disciples, so that they might better absorb their simple truths, including the admonition to pray always and not to despair (Lk 18.1).

Jesus dedicated another parable to this same theme. It is appropriate to examine it here, since it is similar in content to the parable of the friend at midnight:

> "There was in a city a judge, which feared not God, neither regarded man. And there was a widow in that city, and she came unto him, saying, 'Avenge me of mine adversary.' And he would not for a while, but afterward he said within himself, 'Though I fear not God, nor regard man, yet because this widow troubleth me, I will avenge her, lest by her continual coming she weary me.'" And the Lord said, "Hear what the unjust judge saith. And shall not God avenge his own elect, which cry day and night unto him, though he bear long with them? I tell you that he will avenge them speedily. Nevertheless when the Son of Man cometh, shall he find faith on the earth?" (Lk 18.2–8)

The plot of the parable of the friend at midnight seems to take place in a small village where everyone knows one another, where there would be no judges or courts or petitioners. Thus, this second parable must occur in a city, where all three would have been present. Unjust judges and lawyers who fear neither God nor men always were and always will be, just as there always were and always will be those who need their protection, though they may have a hard time drawing their professional interest. As a rule, such interest grows with the size of the expected fee.

In ancient Israel, widows belonged to the poorest social stratum. They did not receive a pension and did not have any regular source of income, since they did not work (women in general rarely worked for money). As a rule, widows were dependent upon relatives, were generally badly taken care of, and had no social safety net. The law of Moses forbade the oppression of orphans and widows (Ex 22.22), to judge foreigners, orphans, and widows unlawfully, or to take any clothing from a widow as financial security (Deut 24.17, 27.19). The law further prescribed that landowners must leave a portion of their harvest for foreigners, orphans, and widows (Deut 24.19–21), as well as a tithe of all the fruits of the land (Deut 26.12). Yet these rules were not always followed. Naturally, a judge could expect no payment from a widow, and those two mites (literally or figuratively) that she might have been able to pay (see Mk 12.42) were of no interest.

Nevertheless, a person who fears neither God nor man needs not only money, but also comfort. And the annoyance of the widow was a thorn in his side, since she could have come to his house, or met him in the street. The desire to get rid of her finally forces the judge to take her case with a single aim in mind: to prevent her bothering him ever again.

Both parables speak of the interpersonal relationship between man and God, and they illustrate the same general point: we must pray persistently, annoyingly, without stopping. But in what sense can we connect the image of a God who answers prayers with the three images that we find in these parables: the friend who did not want to get up from bed, but who got up because of the persistence of the man at his door, the father who would never give his son a stone instead of bread (or a serpent instead of fish or a scorpion instead of an egg), and the judge who feared neither God nor man? These images are rather *opposed* to the image of the Father as described by his Son. The didactic logic of both parables is built on a principle of evidence by contradiction: if even a sleeping friend will get up and open the door, then all the more so will God, who "neither slumber[s] nor sleep[s]" (Ps 120.4). If an earthly father will give his son what he asks for, then how much more will the heavenly Father "give good things to them that ask him?" (Mt 7.11). If even the unrighteous judge will take the case of the persistent widow, then all the more will God, who "is a righteous judge" (Ps 7.11) fulfill the request of those who pray to him.

In the Sermon on the Mount, Jesus counsels us not to say too much in prayer (Mt 6.7), but on the other hand, he calls us to constancy and persistence in prayer: "Ask, and it shall be given you; seek, and ye shall find; knock, and it shall be opened unto you" (Mt 7.7). How are we to understand this persistence? Does it mean that a person can convince God through long prayers or even force God to do what he wants, something that God otherwise would not have done? Such an understanding may seem consonant with the Old Testament's depiction of God, but it badly fits the image of God that is revealed in the New Testament.

In the New Testament, God himself is represented as the persistent friend of man: "Behold, I stand at the door, and knock: if any man hear my voice, and open the door, I will come in to him, and will sup with him, and he with me" (Rev 3.20). At the Last Supper, Jesus said, "He that hath my commandments, and keepeth them, he it is that loveth me; and he that loveth me shall be loved of my Father, and I will love him, and will manifest myself to him. . . . If a man love me, he will keep my words; and my Father will love him, and we will come unto him, and make our abode with him" (Jn 14.21, 23).

"Behold, I stand at the door," William Homan Hunt, 1856

God's insistent desire to come visit man, to knock on his door, to dine with him, to make an abode with him—this is a new aspect of the mutual relationship between God and man that is revealed in the ministry and preaching of Jesus. Jesus reveals to mankind God as friend, God who does not answer prayers because he is convinced by persistence, but because he is man's friend and gives him what he asks with love. Jesus moves the image of God's relationship with man from the juridical sphere (man sins, God punishes; man repents, God forgives; man asks, God gives) into the sphere of interpersonal, even familial relationship. The idea that God does not need man is foreign to the New Testament; on the contrary, God and man need each other, and prayer becomes the natural means of their conversation.

What we have said here in no way contradicts the obvious fact that in both parables one person comes to another with a specific request. The friend comes to his friend to ask for bread; the widow asks the judge to defend her from an adversary. If we were to project these images onto prayer, then we may be tempted to think that prayer is only necessary as a means to receive from God certain benefits that we need, to achieve specific goals with God's help. But the images of this parable should not be interpreted literally.

Naturally, man can pray to God for specific things. The prayer "Our Father," which preceded the parable of the friend at midnight, contains several petitions for specific needs. Yet the prayer has only a single petition that can be interpreted as referring to earthly needs: "Give us this day our daily bread." But even this petition has been interpreted in Christian tradition as indicating not only earthly food, but also "the bread which came down from heaven" (Jn 6.41). All the other petitions refer to the theme of the mutual relationship between God and man and to the realities of the spiritual life of man. This understanding is only strengthened by these words, which do refer to earthly needs: "for your Father knoweth what things ye have need of, before ye ask him" (Mt 6.8).

Everything we have already said means that man's earthly needs and cares can be one reason for prayer, but they should not constitute the majority of the content of prayer, because God knows about our needs even before we tell him of them. The most important content of prayer should be converse with God itself. If the result of our prayer is that God comes to us and makes his abode with us, then together with himself he will bring all other good things. The kingdom of God, to which man becomes assimilated through prayer, covers all earthly needs and cares. Jesus said, "Seek ye first the kingdom of God, and his righteousness, and all these things shall be added to you" (Mt 6.33). Earthly good things can be, so to speak, a free addition to prayer, but they should not be the goal of prayer.

The fact that prayer first of all assumes the realization of the kingdom of God is also attested to by the allusion to the second coming of Jesus, which—somewhat unexpectedly—ends the parable of the persistent widow: "Nevertheless, when the Son of Man cometh, shall he find faith on the earth?" (Lk 18.8). These words follow immediately after a remark about God's longsuffering. The theme of God's longsuffering, together with the reference to the second coming, could remind the reader of the eschatological expectations that filled the consciousness of Jesus' disciples during his life and after his resurrection. If we interpret these words about his second coming literally, we know that the disciples believed that the second coming was "near, even at the doors" (Mt 24.33), and the fact that it did not come, they ascribed to his longsuffering. This is what Peter meant when he wrote, "The Lord is not slack [*bradynei*] concerning his promise, as some men count slackness; but is longsuffering [*makrothymei*] to us-ward, not willing that any should perish, but that all should come to repentance" (2 Pet 3.9).

Jesus describes the final result of prayer in the following words: "If ye then, being evil, know how to give good gifts unto your children, how much more shall your heavenly Father give the Holy Spirit to them that ask him?" (Lk 11.13). In the parallel text from the Sermon on the Mount, he spoke of "good things" (Mt 7.11), but here Jesus speaks of the Holy Spirit. As a rule, commentators see this reference to the Holy Spirit as a redaction by Luke's own hand. But in this case, as in other places, when scholars try to find the editor's hand in a manuscript, thereby claiming to seek Jesus' "original" sayings and to separate them from a later adaptation, we are dealing with nothing other than speculation based on absolutely no textual evidence. Why would Jesus himself *not* refer to the Holy Spirit if in his conversation with the disciples at the Last Supper he speaks of the Spirit constantly and in great detail (Jn 14.16–17, 25–26; 15.26–27; 16.5–15)? Or was that conversation also an invention of the early Church?

In the Gospels, the Holy Spirit is mentioned many times: 12 times in Matthew, 6 in Mark, 17 or 18 in Luke, and around 15 in John. Some of these references are included in Jesus' direct speech, and we have no reason to think that this is the work of a later editor. In all three synoptic Gospels, Jesus insists that blasphemy against the Holy Spirit will not be forgiven (Mt 12.32; Mk 3.29; Lk 12.10), and he promises his disciples that the Holy Spirit will speak through them (Mt 10.20; Mk 13.11; Lk 12.12). At the Last Supper, Jesus promises to send the Holy Spirit to his disciples instead of himself (cf. Jn 16.7). After the resurrection, he breathed on them and said, "Receive ye the Holy Spirit" (Jn 20.22). His final commandment to the disciples speaks of the Spirit: "Go ye therefore, and teach all nations, baptizing them in the name of the Father, and of the Son, and of the Holy Spirit" (Mt 28.19). Thus it is clear that Jesus' teaching on the Holy Spirit is an integral part of his teaching about God and God's grace.

The experience of communion with the Holy Spirit is described in detail in the book of Acts, which records the descent of the Holy Spirit upon the apostles (Acts 2.1–4). Altogether, the book of Acts refers to the Holy Spirit 57 times. This experience is inextricably linked with prayer. It is prayer that becomes the channel through which the Holy Spirit is given to man. Persistent, sincere, constant, and heart-felt prayer, like the request of the persistent widow, opens to man the possibility of coming to know God, one in three Persons. In answer to his prayer, by the intercession of the Son of God, the Holy Spirit was sent to him (Jn 14.26, 16.7). This, then, is the most important fruit of prayer.

The teaching that follows the parable of the persistent widow ends with the following words: "Nevertheless, when the Son of Man cometh, shall he find faith on the earth?" (Lk 18.8). What is the faith that is meant here? Evidently, this is the faith that produces constant prayer. This is the prayer that the Apostle Paul described in his epistles: "Rejoice evermore. Pray without ceasing. In everything give thanks. . . . Quench not the Spirit" (1 Thess 5.16–19).

In the Eastern Christian tradition, the ideal of constant prayer finds full expression in the practice of the Jesus prayer—the constant repetition of a short prayer to Jesus. Its longest version is this: "Lord Jesus Christ, Son of God, have mercy on me, the sinner." Shorter versions also exist. The spread of this prayer is connected with the flourishing of monasticism in the fifth century. The first written reference to the Jesus prayer also belongs to this period, in the writings of Diadochus of Photiki, who wrote about the "constant invocation of the Lord Jesus."[11] According to Diadochus, the grace of God teaches the mind of an ascetic to utter the words "Lord Jesus Christ" (this is the form of the prayer offered by Diadochus) in the same way that a mother teaches her child to say "Father" until the child has the habit of repeating it even in sleep.[12]

From its origin in a monastic setting, the Jesus prayer became popular also among laypeople. Its simplicity and brevity, the possibility of saying it

---

[11]Diadochus of Photiki, *One Hundred Texts on Spiritual Knowledge and Discrimination* 85 (PG 65:1200; *The Philokalia: The Complete Text*, Compiled by St Nikodimos of the Holy Mountain and St Makarios of Corinth, trans. G. E. H. Palmer, Philip Sherrard, and Kallistos Ware, 4 vols [London: Faber and Faber, 1983–1999], 1:285).

[12]Diadochus of Photiki, *One Hundred Texts on Spiritual Knowledge and Discrimination* 61 (PG 65:1187; *Philokalia* 1:271).

in a way that no one would even notice, and most importantly, the power of the name of Jesus Christ, which has a potent spiritual effect on a person—all this helped the practice of the Jesus prayer spread into every strata of Byzantine society.

In Russia, this practice also found wide acceptance, a fact reflected in many literary works. One of these was a book published in 1881, usually called *The Way of the Pilgrim*, which tells of a simple peasant who decided to acquire the art of the Jesus prayer. The book vividly shows that the practice of the Jesus prayer was widespread not only among monks but also among laypeople even up until the beginning of the twentieth century. This practice is preserved within the Orthodox Church to the present day.

The classic words dedicated to the theme of constant prayer often turn to images of the persistent friend and widow:

> Faith gives wings to prayer, and without it we cannot fly up to Heaven. . . . Though the judge did not fear God, yet because a soul, widowed from him through sin and a fall, troubles him, he will avenge her of her adversary, the body, and of the spirits who make war upon her. . . . Do not say, after spending a long time at prayer, that nothing has been gained; for you have already gained something. And what higher good is there than to cling to the Lord and persevere in unceasing union with him?[13]

We should know that we stand in need of repentance throughout the twenty-four hours of the night and day. The meaning of the word *repentance*, as we have learned from the true means of its performance, is this: continual and intense supplication which by means of prayer filled with compunction draws nigh to God in order to seek forgiveness of past offenses, and entreaty for preservation from future ones.

For this reason our Lord fortified our infirmity by prayer, saying, "Awake, watch, and pray that ye enter not into temptation." (Mt 26.41)

---

[13]John Climacus, *The Ladder of Divine Ascent* 28.26, 28, 29; John Climacus, *The Ladder of Divine Ascent* (Boston: Holy Transfiguration Monastery, 2012), 237.

He strongly corroborates his word and induces us to become the more zealous by the parable of the friend who went to his friend in the middle of the night and asked him for bread, and he says, "Verily I say unto you, though he will not rise and give him because he is his friend, yet because of his importunity he will rise and give him as many as he needeth" (Lk 11.8).[14]

3. The Rich Fool

The next parable in Luke forms part of a teaching dedicated to the theme of riches. The event that led to its telling does not appear in the other synoptic Gospels. One of the people turned to Jesus with a request: "Master, speak to my brother, that he divide the inheritance with me." People often turned to the scribes and Pharisees with such requests, since such conflicts were resolved on the basis of the law of Moses. In this case, evidently, the man believed that Jesus' moral authority or his knowledge of the law would help him resolve this conflict with his brother. But Jesus refuses to grant the request, and answers, "Man, who made me a judge or a divider over you?" Without continuing this conversation, Jesus then turns to the disciples and the people that surrounded him, saying, "Take heed, and beware of covetousness: for a man's life consisteth not in the abundance of the things which he possesseth" (Lk 12.13–15). These words about riches accord exactly with Jesus' many other instructions concerning wealth.

The theme of riches is one of the most constant in the Gospels, beginning with the Sermon on the Mount (Mt 6.19–21, 24). The Gospel of Luke contains a stern warning to the rich who are sated and who like to laugh: "But woe unto you that are rich! For ye have received your consolation. Woe unto you that are full! For ye shall hunger. Woe unto you that laugh now! For ye shall mourn and weep" (Lk 6.24–25). This warning is a direct antithesis of the blessedness of those who are poor, hungry, and who weep, which is found in the same Gospel (Lk 6.20–21).

[14]Isaac the Syrian, Homily 70; *The Ascetical Homilies of Saint Isaac the Syrian* (Boston: Holy Transfiguration Monastery, 2011), 487.

*The Parable of
the Rich Fool,*
Rembrandt, 1627

The parable of the rich fool is one of several parables that refer to the
theme of riches:

> The ground of a certain rich man brought forth plentifully, and he
> thought within himself, saying, "What shall I do, because I have no
> room where to bestow my fruits?" And he said, "This will I do: I will pull
> down my barns, and build greater; and there will I bestow all my fruits
> and my goods. And I will say to my soul, 'Soul, thou hast much goods
> laid up for many years; take thine ease, eat, drink, and be merry.'" But
> God said unto him, "Thou fool, this night thy soul shall be required of
> thee. Then whose shall those things be, which thou hast provided?" So
> is he that layeth up treasure for himself, and is not rich toward God.
> (Lk 12.16–21)

Told, as it was, immediately after his warning about covetousness, this
parable is a vivid illustration of that passion. The literal meaning of the
word *pleonexia* is greed, avarice, love of gain. The character who embod-
ies this quality in the parable is a man who is exemplary in many ways.
He works, plans, gathers, and strives to preserve his property.[15] There is
nothing amoral in his behavior itself (if we do not believe, as some scholars

[15]Hultgren, *Parables*, 109.

do, that the rich man was consciously leeching off the local economy of the region,[16] or that by gathering the grain in his barn he was consciously creating a local shortage to raise the price of bread[17]). He is successful, careful, prudent, and he managed to gather enough goods to last him for many years.

The characteristic quality of this man is that he is described as completely isolated from human society. Nothing is said about a wife or children to whom he might leave his property, nor of friends with whom he might share it. He does not even bother to ask someone else's counsel. He asks himself. His plan is simple: I will break down the old and I will build new. I will put together everything that I have gathered. There can be no result other than what he said, not to himself, but to his own soul: "Take thine ease, eat, drink, and be merry." In his thoughts and plans for the future, this person in no way extends beyond his own ego. The entire circle of his acquaintances is limited to his own person.

So we see before us not merely a rich man; first and foremost, this is an egotist. The question that he asks himself—"What shall I do?"—is similar to the question of the rich young man: "What shall I do that I may inherit eternal life?" (Mk 10.17; Mt 19.16; Lk 10.25). However, the resonance of the question of the rich fool and the rich young ruler is only cursory. The young man, it seems, was sincerely bothered by the question of how he could inherit eternal life. He came to the Teacher to ask that question. The rich man in the parable cares nothing for eternal life. He does not go anywhere to seek counsel; he asks himself a question, which is more likely rhetorical than an actual question with any real meaning.

We cannot read the parable as Jesus' denunciation of financial success. It would be incorrect, based on the parable, to believe that a failed businessman is closer to the kingdom of heaven than a successful one, or that a lazy person is more precious in the sight of God than one who loves to work. The rich fool, who decided to lock up all his grain in a barn, is

[16]Luise Schottroff and Wolfgang Stegemann, *Jesus and the Hope for the Poor* (Maryknoll, NY: Orbis Books, 1986), 97.

[17]Mary Ann Beavis, "The Foolish Landowner (Luke 12:16b–20): The Parable of the Rich Fool," *Jesus and His Parables: Interpreting the Parables of Jesus Today*, ed. V. George Shillington (Edinburgh: T&T Clark Ltd., 1997), 55–68, at 64–65.

more like the slave who received a single talent and buried it in the ground, unlike the other slaves who, having received their talents, put them to use and increased them (Mt 25.14–30). In the parable of the talents, we do not see any praise of the rich man's good business sense, but neither do we see any praise of laziness or any condemnation of industriousness.

The teaching that follows the parable is nearly word for word a repetition of the Sermon on the Mount (Mt 6.25–34):

> Therefore I say unto you, take no thought for your life, what ye shall eat, neither for the body, what ye shall put on. The life is more than meat, and the body is more than raiment. Consider the ravens: for they neither sow nor reap, which neither have storehouse nor barn, and God feedeth them; how much more are ye better than the fowls? And which of you with taking thought can add to his stature one cubit? If ye then be not able to do that thing which is least, why take ye thought for the rest? Consider the lilies how they grow: they toil not, they spin not; and yet I say unto you, that Solomon in all his glory was not arrayed like one of these. If then God so clothe the grass, which is today in the field, and tomorrow is cast into the oven; how much more will he clothe you, O ye of little faith? And seek not ye what ye shall eat, or what ye shall drink, neither be ye of doubtful mind. For all these things do the nations of the world seek after; and your Father knoweth that ye have need of these things. But rather seek ye the kingdom of God, and all these things shall be added unto you. (Lk 12.22–31)

The expression "the nations of the world" is not present in the parallel text in the Sermon on the Mount. This phrase exactly characterizes the rich man from the parable. He is a man of the world. There is no vertical dimension in his life; he knows no other values than financial success:

> His behavior is an open challenge to everything that the word of God teaches. He walks a road directly opposed to everything we know of Christ's teaching. . . . Everything that we have, we have received as a loan. But all this belongs to the Lord God; we are only stewards over God's goods. As for the rich man, it did not even occur to him to share

with those who do not have anything. . . . He applies all his efforts solely to preserve everything for himself. He acts like a thief who steals from God. And he wants to hide his stolen goods in a safe place. It was sheer madness for him to ensure that these goods would last him many years, considering everything could have been destroyed in a fire over the course of a single hour. . . . The parable of the rich fool reminds us that this foolish world in which we live (if everything is determined by earthly success and all the wisdom of life is limited to how to achieve this success) stands on very shaky ground.[18]

In this parable, the word "soul" seems to be used in the same sense as in the Old Testament, including in the prophecy of Isaiah: "It shall even be as when an hungry man dreameth, and, behold, he eateth; but he awaketh, and his soul is empty: or as when a thirsty man dreameth, and behold, he drinketh; but he awaketh, and, behold, he is faint, and his soul hath appetite" (Is 29.8). Here a soul is described as suffering from hunger and thirst, not the body as it might have been expected. We find an analogous usage in Proverbs: "The full soul loatheth an honeycomb; but to the hungry soul every bitter thing is sweet" (Prov 27.7). Jesus' words "take no thought for your life [*psychē*, lit. 'soul'], what ye shall eat, or what ye shall drink" (Mt 6.25) follows the same traditional use of the word "soul."

The rich man of the parable is sure that these earthly good things will bring comfort and joy to his soul. Yet his soul is never satisfied with earthly riches, as the experience of millions has shown:

How can a soul eat and drink? The body, not the soul, eats and drinks what is gathered in the fields. And the rich man is thinking of the body when he speaks of the soul. His soul has become so identified with his body, has become so similar to it, that he only knows it by its name. It is impossible to show more clearly the pernicious triumph of the body over the soul. . . . The soul does not eat perishable food, but this is what he offers the soul. The soul mourns for its heavenly fatherland, where its true granaries and sources of water abide, but he keeps chaining

[18]Alexander Shargunov, *Evangelie dnya* [The Gospel of the day], 2 vols (Moscow: Sretensky Monastery, 2010), 2:72–73. Translated by DNK.

it to the earth, and then he has the audacity to promise that he will preserve the soul, chained as it is, for many years. The soul rejoices in God, but he does not even mention the name of God. The soul is filled with righteousness and mercy, but he does not even think of performing deeds of righteousness and mercy to the poor, the unhappy, and the wretched with his riches.[19]

One can be outwardly successful and rich, but inwardly miserable. No amount of acquisition can fill the abyss that yawns within him when a man gathers riches for himself "and is not rich toward God."

Earthly life may seem endless, but sooner or later the moment of truth comes, which is so vividly depicted in the parable. This can be the voice of God that suddenly intrudes in a person's life, or a tragic event that happens involving one of his loved ones. In such cases, what before seemed precious loses its worth in the blink of an eye. Finally, sickness, old age, and the approach of death can force a person to think of eternity.

In this parable, death comes to the rich man unexpectedly, as it often happens in real life. But the coming of death is preceded by the voice of God: this voice speaks to the same soul that the rich man had addressed with self-satisfaction and illusory contentment. And suddenly it becomes clear that his soul is about to be taken, and all that he gathered will remain behind. Life will end in a flash, and there will be nothing to hold on to.

God does not speak to the rich man by name. He calls him *aphrōn* ("fool")—the same word used in the Greek version of Psalm 13.1: "The fool has said in his heart, 'There is no God.'" The rich fool says the same thing to himself. It does not even occur to him to thank God for the bountiful harvest or to ask God's guidance in prayer to find out how best to use the harvest. In his life, God is absent: even if he formally acknowledges the existence of God, this in no way corresponds to his system of values, nor with his internal reality.

Psalm 13 continues much like the parable:

They are become corrupt and abominable in their ways; there is none that doeth good, no not one. The Lord looked down from heaven upon

[19]Nikolai (Velimirovich), *Tvoreniya*, 2:412–13. Translated by DNK.

the children of men, to see if there were any that understand and seek after God. They are all gone astray, they are altogether useless, there is none that doeth good, no not one. Shall not all the workers of iniquity know, who eat up my people as they eat bread? They have not called upon the Lord. There were they in great fear, where no fear was; for God is in the generation of the righteous. (Ps 13.1–5)

The parable says nothing about the rich man doing abominable works, but the words about doing nothing good and failing to call upon God certainly apply to him. As for the words that the rich man speaks to his own soul, they contrast sharply with a challenge from the book of Isaiah to give one's soul to the hungry:

Is it not to deal thy bread to the hungry, and that thou bring the poor that are cast out to thy house? When thou seest the naked, that thou cover him, and that thou hide not thyself from thine own flesh? Then shall thy light break forth as the morning, and thine health shall spring forth speedily, and thy righteousness shall go before thee; the glory of the Lord shall be thy reward. Then shalt thou call, and the Lord shall answer; thou shalt cry, and he shall say, "Here I am." If thou take away from the midst of thee the yoke, the putting forth of the finger, and speaking vanity, and if thou draw out thy soul to the hungry, and satisfy the afflicted soul; then shall thy light rise in obscurity, and thy darkness be as the noon day, and the Lord shall guide thee continually, and satisfy thy soul in drought, and make fat thy bones; and thou shalt be like a watered garden, and like a spring of water, whose waters fail not. (Is 58.7–11)

The Old Testament prophet views a person's spiritual calm as directly related to his ability to share bread with the hungry, and if needed, to give him even his own soul. This is what Jesus means when he speaks of "being rich toward God." Earthly riches are just as temporary and quickly passing as earthly life. Anyone who makes the acquisition of wealth the main purpose of life is a fool. Death will deprive him of these riches, and he will be able to take into eternity only those treasures that he managed to lay up in heaven while he was still upon earth. These treasures are the virtues that Isaiah lists, and the presence or absence of these becomes the most important criterion that determines one's final judgment at the second coming (Mt 25.31–46).

The rich man of the parable lives and acts as though neither God nor other people even exist. But he also ignores another reality—death. He closes his eyes to death and plans his life for many years into the future. Death comes unexpectedly, and he is unprepared for the encounter with this uninvited guest.

St John of the Ladder, Abbot of Sinai, Icon, 13th century

Christian ascetic tradition has developed a philosophy founded on the idea that remembrance of death is one of the fundamental values of the spiritual life. St John Climacus writes, "As of all foods, bread is the most essential, so the thought of death is the most necessary of all works."[20] According to St Symeon the New Theologian, whoever lives with the remembrance of death strains to know what will happen to him after his death and his passage from this life.[21] This idea radically differs from the modern world's relationship with death, which is founded on silence, avoidance, and pretending that death does not exist.

The Christian call to remember death is inspired not by a desire to poison one's earthly joys. If Christianity had forbidden joy, there would not be so many calls to rejoice in the pages of the New Testament (Mt 5.12, 28.9; Lk 10.20; 1 Pet 1.6, 4.13; Rom 12.15; 2 Cor 13.11; Phil 2.18, 3.1, 4.4; 1 Thess 5.16). Yet the joy that Christianity calls us to and that Jesus gives does not flow from the abundance of earthly riches. And this joy is not dimmed by the remembrance of death. On the contrary, it illumines a person's life with that special light that transforms the orientation of one's values.

---

[20]John Climacus, *The Ladder of Divine Ascent* 6.4 (HTM trans., p. 108).

[21]Symeon the New Theologian, *One Hundred Theological and Practical Chapters* 13 (SC 51bis:43; Symeon the New Theologian, *The Practical and Theological Chapters and the Three Theological Discourses,* trans. Paul McGuckin, Cistercian Studies 42 [Kalamazoo, MI: Cistercian Publications, 1982], 36).

St Symeon the New Theologian, Fresco, 20th century

The system of values that Jesus offers in the Gospels is directly contrary to the values of the rich fool. Jesus promises his disciples neither calm, nor riches, nor joys. On the contrary, he predicts that they will suffer, feel sorrow, and be deprived of earthly things. But in these sorrows, they can expect joy, not earthly joy that quickly fades, but the joy that "no man taketh from you" (Jn 16.22), which not even death can take away. The source of this joy is Jesus Christ himself—the Son of Man and the Son of God.

4. The Watchful Servants

In the Gospel according to Luke, the parable of the rich fool forms part of a larger teaching that Jesus gave on the way from Galilee to Jerusalem.

The next part of this instruction is dedicated to the theme of the kingdom of God. It begins with a passage we find only in Luke: "Fear not, little flock; for it is your Father's good pleasure to give you the kingdom" (Lk 12.32). These words, though spoken in the presence of a large crowd, are directed first of all to the disciples, as well as to all who will follow them in the future. The "little flock" is the Church, which began with a small group of people who became Jesus' disciples during his life. This group of people was given the greatest gift that anyone can receive: the kingdom of God. Here the kingdom is spoken of as an inheritance given after death, as well as a present reality and an experience that they can attain in earthly life.

What is necessary for a person to acquire the kingdom of God? Jesus answers in the following words: "Sell that ye have, and give alms; provide yourselves bags which wax not old, a treasure in the heavens that faileth not, where no thief approacheth, neither moth corrupteth. For where your treasure is, there will your heart be also" (Lk 12.33–34). These words partially overlap with the Sermon on the Mount (Mt 6.19–21), as well as with some of Jesus' other teachings, including the words he spoke to the rich young ruler (Mt 19.21; Mk 10.21; Lk 18.22).

Then Jesus begins to speak of his second coming. He will speak in more detail about this in Jerusalem before his arrest (Mt 24.4–51), but he already calls his disciples to spiritual vigilance on the way to the holy city:

> Let your loins be girded about, and your lights burning, and ye your-selves like unto men that wait for their lord, when he will return from the wedding, that when he cometh and knocketh, they may open unto him immediately. Blessed are those servants, whom the lord when he cometh shall find watching. Verily I say unto you, that he shall gird him-self, and make them to sit down to meat, and will come forth and serve them. And if he shall come in the second watch, or come in the third watch, and find them so, blessed are those servants. (Lk 12.35–38)

A girdle (or belt) was part of man's underwear used sometimes to travel, and sometimes in the performance of certain kinds of work. One could also gird the loins when going to an official audience with a local author-ity. In everyday life, girding one's loins was not considered necessary. For example, Peter did not wear a girdle when he caught fish with the other disciples. Before he jumped into the sea, he put on his girdle (Jn 21.7).

Girding the loins is a common metaphor in the Old Testament, which referred to readiness to begin a journey. It comes from the command to eat the Passover lamb, which the nation of Israel received from God before the Exodus from Egypt: "And thus shall ye eat it: with your loins girded, your shoes on your feet, and your staff in your hand; and ye shall eat it in haste: it is the Lord's Passover" (Ex 12.11). Girding the loins was necessary to walk swiftly or to run (1 Kgs 18.46; 2 Kgs 4.29). At the same time, in order to speak with God, a person had to gird his loins (Job 38.3, 40.2).

A lit lamp is another metaphor indicating vigilance in the middle of the night. Usually, all lamps were quenched at night. If a lamp remained lit, this meant that the inhabitants of the house were expecting someone's arrival. This is the image that undergirds the parable of the ten virgins, which is dedicated to the same theme and ends with the following words: "Watch

The Wise Servant, Jan Leychen, 1791, 1826

therefore, for ye know neither the day nor the hour wherein the Son of Man cometh" (Mt 25.13).

In the parable of the watchful servants, the master left to go to a wedding; this is another thematic similarity to the parable of the ten virgins. The wedding feast, as a rule, ends late at night or even early in the morning: the second watch of the night is the time between nine o'clock at night and midnight, and the third watch is the time from midnight to three o'clock in the morning. At this time, no one normally wears a girdle or keeps the lamps lit. The servants who await the return of their master are an exception to the rule. The watchful servants are called blessed twice: in the beginning and at the end of the parable. This expression is often found in the Gospels, including in the Sermon on the Mount (Mt 5.3–11) and in Luke's account of the Sermon on the Plain (Lk 6.20–22). Usually it indicates an inner, spiritual joy that is a consequence of fulfilling the will of God and receiving his blessing.

The most unusual aspect of the parable is the behavior of the master who finds his servants still awake. In defiance of all accepted norms and conventions, he, having returned tired from the wedding feast, seats his own slaves at table and begins to serve them. In another parable, Jesus will say, "But which of you, having a servant plowing or feeding cattle, will say unto him by and by, when he is come from the field, 'Go and sit down to meat?' And will not rather say unto him, 'Make ready wherewith I may sup, and gird thyself, and serve me, till I have eaten and drunken; and afterward thou shalt eat and drink'?" (Lk 17.7–8). These words describe the usual order of things in the society of Jesus' contemporaries. But the situation in the parable is far from ordinary: the master and his slaves seem to switch places, in the same way that Jesus, having taken off his outer garments during the Last Supper, girded himself and washed his disciples' feet (Jn 13.4–5).

This is proof that the parable vividly describes a christological dimension. The master is the Son of Man, who "came not to be ministered unto, but to minister, and to give his life a ransom for many" (Mt 20.28). He says to his disciples, "For whether is greater, he that sitteth at meat, or he that serveth? Is not he that sitteth at meat? But I am among you as he that serveth" (Lk 22.27). He expects his disciples to retain constant readiness, spiritual tension, vigilance; in return, he promises them the kingdom of heaven.

There is also an eschatological dimension to the parable. The dinner at which the master, having girded himself, will serve his own slaves, refers to the reality of the kingdom of God as life after death. It is there that the righteous will "sit down with Abraham, and Isaac, and Jacob" (Mt 8.11). In the Revelation of St John, this feast of the righteous in the kingdom of heaven is called the marriage supper of the Lamb (Rev 19.9).

This theme of spiritual vigilance continues in the passage after the parable, which includes two more parables:

> "And this know, that if the goodman of the house had known what hour the thief would come, he would have watched, and not have suffered his house to be broken through. Be ye therefore ready also: for the Son of Man cometh at an hour when ye think not." Then Peter said unto him, "Lord, speakest thou this parable unto us, or even to all?" And the Lord said, "Who then is that faithful and wise steward, whom his lord shall make ruler over his household, to give them their portion of meat in due season? Blessed is that servant, whom his lord when he cometh shall find so doing. Of a truth I say unto you, that he will make him ruler over all that he hath. But and if that servant say in

Jesus and His Disciples,
G. Tucco, 1886–1894

his heart, 'My lord delayeth his coming', and shall begin to beat the menservants and maidens, and to eat and drink, and to be drunken, the lord of that servant will come in a day when he looketh not for him, and at an hour when he is not aware, and will cut him in sunder, and will appoint him his portion with the unbelievers. And that servant, which knew his lord's will, and prepared not himself, neither did according to his will, shall be beaten with many stripes. But he that knew not, and did commit things worthy of stripes, shall be beaten with few stripes. For unto whomsoever much is given, of him shall be much required, and to whom men have committed much, of him they will ask the more." (Lk 12.39–48)

We find similar parables in the Gospel of Matthew (Mt 24.43–51). There, Jesus tells it not on the way to Jerusalem, but in Jerusalem itself. As with Luke's version, Matthew's parable can be summarized by the challenge: "Therefore be ye also ready: for in such an hour as ye think not the Son of Man cometh" (Mt 24.44). In Matthew, however, this challenge is immediately followed by the parable of the wise servant, while in Luke, the parable is preceded by a question raised by Peter: "Lord, speakest thou this parable unto us, or even to all?" As often happens, Jesus does not answer the question directly, and instead continues to teach, as though the question had not even been asked. From the content of the parable, the disciples must decide for themselves what the answer to the question is.

Matthew's version differs little from Luke's in terms of plot. Luke speaks of a faithful ruler of a household, and Matthew speaks of a faithful servant; he gives to the other servants not a measure of bread, but food; he beats not the servants and slave women, but his friends; the master convicts him to have the same fate not as the unfaithful, but as the hypocrites. In all other points, the two versions are virtually identical. Only the end of Luke's version contains a significant difference.

Before us we have two versions of the same parable, but the context of Jesus' telling is differently described in the two Gospels. The most natural way of explaining this difference, in our opinion, is that Jesus simply told the same parable in two different places—once on the way to Jerusalem and a second time in Jerusalem on the eve of his arrest.

It is possible that the Apostle Paul knew the version written by Luke. He writes in his First Epistle to the Corinthians:

> Let a man so account of us, as of the ministers of Christ, and stewards of the mysteries of God. Moreover it is required in stewards, that a man be found faithful. But with me it is a very small thing that I should be judged of you, or of man's judgment; yea, I judge not mine own self. For I know nothing by myself; yet am I not hereby justified; but he that judgeth me is the Lord. Therefore judge nothing before the time, until the Lord come, who both will bring to light the hidden things of darkness, and will make manifest the counsels of the hearts, and then shall every man have praise of God. (1 Cor 4.1–5)

The term "steward" here is a translation of the Greek word *oikonomos*, which is the same word that Luke uses for his faithful servant. In the early Church, the term had a specific theological connotation: it referred to the apostles, to priests, and in a broad sense to all members of the Christian community.[22] A related term, *oikonomia*, became associated with divine providence as expressed in the creation of the world and mankind, in the incarnation of the Son of God, and in the salvation of mankind through his death on the cross.

The Apostle Paul used the term "steward" to refer to himself as a servant of Christ. Moreover, he stressed that every steward must be faithful—this is where we might read an allusion to the parable. Yet the greatest similarity between Paul's words and the parable is their shared reference to the second coming of the Lord, who will "bring to light the hidden things of darkness."

---

[22]Ignatius of Antioch, *Epistle to Polycarp* 6 (SC 10:176; Ignatius of Antioch, *The Letters*, trans. Alistair Stewart, PPS 49 [Yonkers, NY: St Vladimir's Seminary Press, 2013], 102–105).

Here it is appropriate to remember Jesus' words from the same sermon that includes the parable of the wise servant: "For as the lightning cometh out of the east, and shineth even unto the west, so shall also the coming of the Son of Man be" (Mt 24.27). What remains hidden to many during earthly life will be brought to light, revealed, and found with utter clarity during the second coming. The second coming will be an experience of revelation and illumination, and it will occur "in a moment, in the twinkling of an eye" (1 Cor 15.52).

It is this suddenness of the second coming that is the major theme of the parable of the wise servant. The parable is not talking about the slave's desire to fulfil the will of his master; this desire is assumed. Rather, the point is the importance of the current moment, and that one should not put off one's answer to God's call.[23]

The parable is built on a different structure than many others, in which good is contrasted with evil, the wise with the foolish, the faithful with the unfaithful. Here the same person plays two roles: a positive and a negative one. Moreover, the positive role is ascribed to him from the very beginning ("blessed is that servant"), while the negative role is more a hypothetical possibility than a reality ("but and if that servant").

In Luke's version, the example of the faithful servant or steward has a positive connotation, while the behavior of the same slave in a situation when he begins to beat others and drink too much is explained as something added to his originally positive description. In Matthew's version, the situation is similar, except for an important distinction: in the second half of the parable, the slave is called evil ("but and if that evil servant shall say . . ."). This may cause us to think that the story was about an evil servant from the beginning. But this distinction should not be dwelt on too much, because all it shows is that Jesus' second telling of the parable changed from a major to a minor key, so to speak, which is fully consistent with the circumstances of the final days of Jesus' earthly life.

---

[23] Anna Wierzbicka, *What Did Jesus Mean?: Explaining the Sermon on the Mount and the Parables in Simple and Universal Human Concepts* (Oxford: Oxford University Press, 2001), 399.

The reward of the faithful steward is described with the words "he will make him ruler over all that he hath." These words may remind the reader of the story of Joseph, who was sold into slavery by his own brothers, taken to Egypt, where he became great and acquired the trust of Pharaoh, who "made him overseer over his house, and all that he had he put into his hand" (Gen 39.4). The fate of Joseph was a classic example of how a person, thanks to his own abilities and God's help, can rise up from the lowest rank of the social system to one of the very highest, to become the right hand of the ruler, and practically to possess the ruler's own power. In such a way, the fate of the faithful steward in the parable does not go beyond the realm of possibility.

In contrast, the punishment that awaits the evil servant is expressed in terms that are far from realistic. Having come unexpectedly, the master "will cut him in sunder," a verb (*dichotomeō*) that literally means "to chop in half." According to the Gospel of Matthew, this is the fate that awaits the hypocrites (*hypokritai*), a term Jesus usually used to describe the scribes and Pharisees. According to Luke, this is the lot of the unbelievers (*apistoi*): and this term can indicate both the pagans and those who did not come to believe in Christ.

The words that the servant says in his own heart are a literal translation from Greek meaning "my master tarries," and in Luke—"my master tarries in coming." Peter provides a commentary on this phrase that can be found in his second epistle, which we have quoted above: "The Lord is not slack concerning his promise, as some men count slackness; but is longsuffering toward us, not willing that any should perish, but that all should come to repentance" (2 Pet 3.9). The apostle, following his master, calls us to spiritual vigilance, to "account that the longsuffering of our Lord is salvation" (2 Pet 3.15).

The entire context of Jesus' teaching indicates that this parable belongs to the time between his first and second comings. Looking ahead to the future fates of his disciples and his Church, Jesus speaks of the division that arises not only between different nations, not only between different groups of people, but even within a single human being. In a previous parable he contrasted Israel with the new nation that will be found worthier than the chosen people, but now he shows how the same person can share the lot of the blessed (if he fulfills the will of God) or the lot of the unfaithful (if he thinks that God is absent or that his return is delayed).

The Apostle Paul wrote that "the word of God is living and powerful, and sharper than a two-edged sword, piercing even to the dividing asunder of soul and spirit, and of the joints and marrow, and is a discerner of the thoughts and intents of the heart" (Heb 4.12). This image reminds us of the man who is chopped in half. The faithful servant is precisely one who is faithful to the word of God, who answers its call and makes this incarnate in his own life. The unfaithful servant is he who does not want to listen to the word or to follow it. The two-edged sword of the word of God divides mankind into two parts: the sheep and the goats, those who will enter the kingdom of heaven and those who will inherit eternal suffering. But this same sword also divides a single person in half, if his life does not accord with the righteousness of God, if that person is not ready to reject the works of darkness and put on the armor of light (see Rom 13.12).

The evil servant forgot about his master, and in his absence began to act as though the master did not exist at all. The Old Testament describes evil and iniquity as direct results of a lack of belief in the existence of God and his presence among us: "The fool has said in his heart, 'There is no God.' They are become corrupt and abominable in their ways; there is none that doeth good, no not one" (Ps 13.1).

Jesus did not live at a time of mass unbelief. His contemporaries and fellow Jews believed in the existence of God. This did not prevent most Jewish people from failing to recognize Jesus as the promised Messiah, or from failing to answer his call to repentance. Nor did it prevent the religious and political elites of that time and place from openly opposing him and eventually orchestrating a criminal conviction under the Roman authority. His first coming divided the people of Israel into two unequal parts: those who believed in him, and those who remained indifferent to his preaching, or even those who openly opposed him. His second coming will permanently divide those who fulfilled the will of God (regardless of ethnicity and social status) from those who, like the evil servant, lived their lives as though God does not exist.

The entire history of mankind, after the crucifixion and resurrection of Jesus, all the way to the second coming of Christ, fits within that period of time symbolically indicated by the absence of the master from the house. This period has ended up being much longer than the first Christians expected. If during Jesus' time not a single fool would have dared to say aloud that God did not exist, then as the centuries passed, mankind became only more brazen in disavowing God's authority over his creatures.

The modern age has borne witness to many different attempts to dispel God as much as possible from human society. The philosopher-deists of the eighteenth to the nineteenth centuries devised a "model" of God that regarded him as a sort of abstract source of existence who created all natural laws, but afterward ceased to involve himself in the life of the world, giving people the opportunity to work out their own affairs without him. The next step was the materialism of the nineteenth to the twentieth centuries, which not only declared that God does not exist, but tried to prove this as a fact established by science. Even today, many still hold to this pseudo-scientific position, trying to link it to the *a priori* presence of moral norms in human societies.

Yet it is entirely clear that "without God, everything is permitted." This popular expression ascribed to Dostoyevsky[24] in fact has a long pre-history. In the third century, the Latin theologian Lactantius wrote, "For while they imagine that we are a care to no God, or that we are about to have no existence after death, they altogether give themselves to the indulgence of their passions; and . . . think that it is allowed them."[25] One of the heroes of *The Brothers Karamazov* said, "were mankind's belief in its immortality to be destroyed, not only love but also any living power to continue the

---

[24]This phrase is considered a summary of Ivan Karamazov's thought in *The Brothers Karamazov*. Many philosophers, including Jean-Paul Sartre, quote it as an actual, authentic representation of Dostoevsky's own views.

[25]Lactantius, *The Divine Institutes* 2.1 (ANF 7:40).

F. M. Dostoyevsky, 1879

life of the world would at once dry up in it. Not only that, but then nothing would be immoral any longer, everything would be permitted."[26]

Moral permissiveness is the direct result of lack of faith in God and immortality; if there is no God, there is no judgment, no life after death. Consequently, there is no retribution after death. Many contemporaries of Dostoyevsky believed in the possibility of building a "godless morality," one that would allow people a safe co-existence on earth without any reference to the kingdom of heaven or other "idealistic" values. But history shows us again and again that if morality fails to be founded on absolute values, it will always have a relative nature. Universal human values disappear, and every person creates for himself a system of values that fits his own desires.

Such developments in history cannot fail to influence the life of the Church as well. In the early Church, the expectation of the imminent second coming was intense. With time, however, the sense of its imminence began to be dulled; today, many of those who call themselves Christian believe the Church's teaching of the dread judgment is a mere relic of the deep past. For many, Christianity exists in a much-lightened version, one that does not require too much of people, one that is deprived of the original radicalism of Jesus' preaching.

The words that conclude Luke's version of the parable, it seems, soften this radical tone somewhat. The slave who knew the will of his master, but did not fulfill it, "shall be beaten with many stripes," but the slave who did not know as much "shall be beaten with few stripes." Here Jesus raises the possibility that some people may act in an evil way not through a conscious antagonism to God's will, but because of ignorance. And if the one who willingly opposed God can expect the most severe punishments (he will be

---

[26]Fyodor Dostoevsky, *The Brothers Karamazov*, trans. Richard Pevear and Larissa Volokhonsky (New York: Knopf Doubleday Publishing Group: 1991), 57.

chopped in half), then the one who sins in ignorance will still be punished, but not as severely.

In the Gospel according to Luke, the following words are added to the end of the parable: "For unto whomsoever much is given, of him shall be much required; and to whom men have committed much, of him they will ask the more." Jesus spoke these words to his disciples, reminding them of the moral responsibility that is laid upon them. At the final judgment, Christians will receive the strictest judgment. The Apostle Peter said as much: "For the time is come that judgment must begin at the house of God, and if it first begin at us, what shall the end be of them that obey not the Gospel of God? And if the righteous scarcely can be saved, where shall the ungodly and the sinner appear?" (1 Pet 4.17–18). The house of God is the Church—the community of Christians who have lived throughout human history. They will be judged by the word of God that all of them heard, though only some of them acted upon it.

5. The Barren Fig Tree

The short parable of the barren fig tree is part of the sermon that Jesus gave after he was told of the "Galileans, whose blood Pilate had mingled with their sacrifices" (Lk 13.1). No other historical record tells of this incident. Josephus, who wrote about the history of Pilate's interactions with the Jews and Galileans in great detail, does not mention it, though he does mention a different episode connected with a rebellion in Samaria:

> But the nation of the Samaritans did not escape without tumults. The man who excited them to it was one who thought lying a thing of little consequence, and who contrived everything so that the multitude might be pleased; so he bid them to get together upon Mount Gerizim, which is by them looked upon as the most holy of all mountains, and assured them, that when they were come thither, he would show them those sacred vessels which were laid under that place, because Moses

put them there. So they came thither armed, and thought the discourse
of the man probable; and as they abode at a certain village, which was
called Tirathaba, they got the rest together to them, and desired to go
up the mountain in a great multitude together; but Pilate prevented
their going up, by seizing upon the roads with a great band of horse-
men and footmen, who fell upon those that were gotten together in
the village; and when it came to an action, some of them they slew,
and others of them they put to flight, and took a great many alive, the
principal of which, and also the most potent of those that fled away,
Pilate ordered to be slain.[27]

Some scholars believe that the Gospel of Luke mentions this incident,
and the mention of the Galileans is a mistake. In that case, however, the
evangelist would be guilty not only of confusing Galileans with Samaritans, but he would be guilty also of an anachronism: Josephus records that
this incident happened after the death of Jesus Christ. It occurred in AD
35, and as a result, Pilate was called back to Rome. Moreover, Josephus
does not mention any sacrifices, which is a crucial point in the episode as
recounted by Luke.

There is one other historical event recounted by Josephus that scholars
believe could be a prototype for Luke's account. This event is recounted
before the crucifixion of Jesus Christ:

But Pilate undertook to bring a current of water to Jerusalem, and
did it with the sacred money, and derived the origin of the stream
from the distance of two hundred furlongs. However, the Jews were
not pleased with what had been done about this water; and many ten
thousands of the people got together, and made a clamor against him,
and insisted that he should leave off that design. Some of them also
used reproaches, and abused the man, as crowds of such people usually do. So he clothed a great number of his soldiers in their dress,
who carried daggers under their garments, and sent them to a place
where they might surround them. So he bid the Jews himself go away;

[27]Josephus, *The Antiquities of the Jews* 18.4.1; *Works of Josephus*, 482.

but they boldly casting reproaches upon him, he gave the soldiers that signal which had been beforehand agreed on; who laid upon them much greater blows than Pilate had commanded them, and equally punished those that were tumultuous, and those that were not; nor did they spare them in the least: and since the people were unarmed, and were caught by men prepared for what they were about, there were a great number of them slain by this means, and others of them ran away wounded. And thus an end was put to this sedition.[28]

The ruin of the tower of Siloam, David Martin, 1639–1721

This account, however, has even less in common with the mention of the event in Galilee that Luke records. It can be assumed that in a generally unstable situation of constant revolt in occupied territories, such incidents arose frequently, and the one that Luke mentions is one of many similar cases. The fact that Josephus does not mention it in no way proves that it did not happen. The image of Pilate in the Gospel—an especially cruel Roman prefect who was not squeamish about shedding blood and who had no sense of respect for what the Jews considered sacred—completely fits with his characterization in Josephus.

The expression "whose blood Pilate had mingled with their sacrifices" indicates that the episode in Luke occurred when the Galileans were offering sacrifices. The slaughter of sacrificial animals only happened in the temple of Jerusalem. Thus we have a situation involving a group of pilgrims from Galilee who came to Jerusalem to offer sacrifices; there, during the time of sacrifice, for whatever reason, they were killed by Pilate's soldiers. Their blood was then mingled with the blood of the sacrificial animals. Evidently, this incident occurred not long before Jesus was told of it: it was offered as breaking news.

Luke tells the reader nothing about who related this news to Jesus. Judging by context, it seems likely that they were eyewitnesses of the event,

[28]Josephus, *The Antiquities of the Jews* 18.3.2; *Works of Josephus*, 480.

or that they came from a place where they heard the news from eyewitnesses. Perhaps they were scribes or Pharisees who wanted to gauge Jesus' reaction to the news. They probably expected him to condemn Pilate's action, or to give some kind of explanation of the event based on generally-accepted assumptions concerning divine justice.

Jesus, however, gives no personal assessment of the prefect's actions. As for divine justice, he indicates that it cannot be measured by human understanding, which is generally built on the principles of just desserts. In fact, there is no direct connection between any concrete sin and this apparent retribution for sin.[29] Jesus expresses this thought as a question, and then passes to the main theme of his teaching. We remember that his preaching began with a call to repentance (Mt 4.17; Mk 1.15). The account of the sudden death of the Galileans becomes for a him a reason to call those who survived to repentance once again:

> And Jesus answering said unto them, "Suppose ye that these Galilaeans were sinners above all the Galilaeans, because they suffered such things? I tell you, nay; but, except ye repent, ye shall all likewise perish. Or those eighteen, upon whom the tower in Siloam fell, and slew them, think ye that they were sinners above all men that dwelt in Jerusalem? I tell you, nay; but, except ye repent, ye shall all likewise perish." (Lk 13.2–5)

The story of the fall of the tower of Siloam is another incident that no other historical source mentions. It is possible that this tower was part of a military fortification around Jerusalem, perhaps one of the towers built into the ancient walls of the city. According to Josephus, the city was surrounded by a triple wall. The oldest of these walls was difficult to overcome because of the surrounding pits and the hill on which it was built. It began on the north side of the so-called "Hippicus" tower and ended at the Western gallery of the temple. On the other side, it began at the same point, passing next to the pool of Siloam, ending at the Eastern gallery of the temple.[30]

---

[29]Xavier Léon-Dufour, *Life and Death in the New Testament: The Teachings of Jesus and Paul*, trans. Terrence Prendergast (San Francisco: Harper & Row, 1986), 7.

[30]Josephus, *The Wars of the Jews* 5.4.1–2; *Works of Josephus*, 703–704.

Evidently, one of the towers of this wall that was near the source and pool of Siloam, which is mentioned in the Gospel of John (Jn 9.7, 11), crumbled and fell, killing eighteen people. Again, this event probably happened not long before Jesus mentioned it.

Both events—the death of the Galileans and the death of the eighteen people in the collapse of the tower—become a reason for Jesus to remind his listeners to repent, because death lies in wait for everyone. Moreover, Jesus rejects the widespread idea that sudden death or death as the result of a tragic event is somehow a punishment for sins. He said that those who died were not more sinful that those who remained alive. Further, their death should become a warning for people who have not yet brought forth fruits of repentance.

This leads Jesus to tell a parable that at first might seem unconnected with the previous episode:

> A certain man had a fig tree planted in his vineyard, and he came and sought fruit thereon, and found none. Then said he unto the dresser of his vineyard, "Behold, these three years I come seeking fruit on this fig tree, and find none; cut it down; why cumbereth it the ground?" And he answering said unto him, "Lord, let it alone this year also, till I shall dig about it, and dung it. And if it bear fruit, well, and if not, then after that thou shalt cut it down." (Lk 13.6–9)

The connection between the parable and the preceding section is tangential. The Galileans remained alive only because God gave them time for repentance. God's longsuffering becomes the theme of the parable of the fruitless fig tree.

The custom of planting fig trees in a vineyard was widespread in the ancient world. Pliny, in his *Natural History,* wrote that the shadow cast by a fig tree is gentle, though broad, and so there can be no reason not to plant it in vineyards.[31] Fig trees were indeed generally cultivated with dung.[32]

---

[31]Pliny, *Natural History* 17.89; Pliny, *Natural History with an English Translation*, trans. H. Rackham, vol. 5, Loeb Classical Library 371 (Cambridge, MA: Harvard University Press, 1950), 63.

[32]Pliny, *Natural History* 17.256, p. 177.

The Parable of the Barren Fig Tree, Jan Leychen, 1791–1826

It was typical to hoe the roots of a fig tree in spring to help it produce better fruits.[33] These actions are exactly what the gardener offers to do when he suggests that the master give the tree another year.

As a rule, fig trees were planted in vineyards not so that they would produce figs, but to give the grapevine a place to grow. In this sense, scholars' questions about why the fig tree in the parable needed to be removed for being barren are not specious.[34] Yet such questions have no direct connection to the plot of the parable.

Some scholars see a link between the parable and the miracle of the withering fig tree, since in both cases the fig tree is barren (Mt 21.18–21; Mk 11.12–14, 20–24). One can also see a connection between the parable and the preaching of John the Baptist and Jesus: "every tree which bringeth not forth good fruit is hewn down, and cast into the fire" (Mt 3.10).

The lack of the good fruit of repentance in a person (Mt 3.8) can become a reason for punishment, such as the sudden death of the Galileans and those who were crushed by the ruined tower of Siloam. But God shows longsuffering; he does not chop down the barren fig tree, even after waiting for three years. He gives it another chance to grow for a full year.

As a rule, in such parables the character of a king or lord or master is a symbol for God himself. This parable is no exception. But in addition to the master, there is another character—the worker of the vineyard, who intercedes for the fig tree and promises to work to help the tree bear fruit next year. Who is this intercessor?

The Old Testament is filled with examples of people interceding before God for other people, asking God to show longsuffering. Abraham, for example, interceded for the inhabitants of Sodom: "Wilt thou also destroy the righteous with the wicked? . . . That be far from thee to do after this

---

[33]Pliny, *Natural History* 17.263, pp. 181–83.

[34]Charles W. Hedrick, *Many Things in Parables: Jesus and His Modern Critics* (Louisville, KY: Westminster John Knox Press, 2004), 86–87.

manner . . . that be far from thee! Shall not the Judge of all the earth do right?" (Gen 19.23, 25). He then asks if God will destroy Sodom if at least fifty, forty-five, forty, thirty, twenty, or ten righteous are found in the city. The dialogue sounds like an auction: Abraham gradually lowers the number of righteous, and in the end God promises not to destroy the city even for the sake of ten righteous men.

The type of divine justice presented here is different from the one offered by Jesus in the Gospel of Luke. Abraham's intercession is a direct result of his understanding that sudden death is a punishment for sins; therefore, the righteous must be spared. Jesus speaks of the opposite: the victims of violence or misfortune are no more sinful than those who remained alive. Divine justice acts differently from the way people imagine. God leaves alive not only the righteous, but sinners as well, to give them a chance to repent and change their way of life (just as he leaves the tares among the wheat until the time of harvest).

Another example of a mediator between God and man was Moses. When he was on Mount Sinai, the people made a golden calf and began to worship it. God said, "I have seen this people, and, behold, it is a stiff-necked people. Now therefore let me alone, that my wrath may wax hot against them, and that I may consume them; and I will make of thee a great nation" (Ex 32.9–10). But Moses spoke back to God, reminding him of the promises he gave to Abraham, Isaac, and Jacob. And God "repented of the evil which he thought to do unto his people" (Ex 32.14). Moses himself enacted justice, as he understood it, and the swords of the sons of Levi destroyed nearly three thousand people (Ex 32.25–28). After this, he returned to God and said, "Oh, this people have sinned a great sin, and have made them gods of gold. Yet now, if thou wilt, forgive their sin; and if not, blot me, I pray thee, out of thy book which thou hast written." But God remains unmoved: "Whosoever hath sinned against me, him will I blot out of my book" (Ex 32.31–33) And he struck down with plague those who worshiped the calf.

These Old Testament models of mediation between the people and God foreshadow that "advocate with the Father, Jesus Christ the righteous, and he is the propitiation for our sins, and not for ours only, but also for

St Isidore of Pelusium, Miniature from the Menologion of Basil II, 985

the sins of the whole world" (1 Jn 2.1–2). He, "because he continueth ever, hath an unchangeable priesthood. Wherefore he is able also to save them to the uttermost that come unto God by him, seeing he ever liveth to make intercession for them" (Heb 7.24–25). Like Moses, who asked to be blotted out of the book of life, Jesus offered his own life as sacrifice for mankind: "It is Christ that died, yea rather, that is risen again, who is even at the right hand of God, who also maketh intercession for us" (Rom 8.34).

This is how the ancient commentators understood the parable. According to Isidore of Pelusium, the master of the vineyard is God, the gardener is the Son of God, the vine is Israel or all mankind. The law and the prophets could not improve the people or force them to bring fruit. Only the Son of God with his teaching and suffering can bring them to repentance. If this does not happen, they will be cut off from the righteous in eternity.[35]

The words of the gardener to the master reveal the New Testament's understanding of Jesus Christ as intercessor before God not only for the chosen nation, but also for the whole world. Even if the longsuffering of God the Father has run out, the Son of God is ready to step into the breach as mediator between him and sinful mankind. This completely changes the Old Testament's understanding of divine justice. From this moment, even

---

[35]Isidore of Pelusium, *Letters* 1.312 (PG 78:364).

the barren fig tree has an intercessor in the good gardener who is ready to work on it and fertilize it, just to see if it will bear fruit.

Jesus' teaching breaks several stereotypes that were typical of Old Testament assumptions about how God and man's relationship is built:

1) For the sins of a single person or a group of people God can punish a large number of people or even a whole nation.

2) Sudden death catches sinners as a punishment for sins, while the righteous should be delivered from sudden death.

3) The death of innocent people placates God (as it was with the sons of Levi who shed the blood of their brothers according to Moses' command).

At the same time, the parable of the barren fig tree shows that God's longsuffering is not limitless. Sooner or later man must give an account of his deeds, of the fruits that he bore or failed to bear. The time during which these fruits are expected corresponds to the extra year given to the barren fig tree in the parable. If this year, in which the gardener will take special care of the tree, does not help the tree bear fruit, then it will be chopped down.

The further year granted to the fig tree symbolizes the entire period of time between the first and second comings of the Son of God. During this time, the Son of God will lead people to repentance through the Church he established on earth, showing mercy and longsuffering all the while:

Repentance is a surgical procedure that excises sin; it is a heavenly gift and a marvelous power that by grace defeats the consequence of the laws. For this reason, repentance does not deny the prostitute, it does not scare away the adulterer, it does not turn away the drunkard, it does not abominate the idol worshipper, it does not banish the reviler; it chases away neither the blasphemer nor the proud; rather, it changes all of them. . . . The purpose of God, who is longsuffering toward sinners, aims at two things propitious for salvation. He espouses them with the salvation from repentance and endows their descendants with the means to advance in virtue. To repeat this point: God is longsuffering, so, if the sinner repents, he will not withhold salvation even from his descendants. In other words, even if the one who sins falls unrepentant, he spares the root many times in order to safeguard the crops. Moreover, when the root falls into complete wickedness, God beneficently postpones the punishment, awaiting the salvation of those who repent.[36]

The longsuffering of God has no limits. With regard to mankind as a whole, it acts within the temporal limits of human history, and with reference to each person, it acts within the limits of his lifetime. Yet the final outcome of the life of each person depends not only on God. To a significant degree, it depends on the will and choice of man, on whether or not the person follows God and desires to fulfill his will and live by his commandments.

6. The Tower Builder and the King Preparing for War

Two short parables—of the tower builder and the king preparing for war—are found only in the Gospel according to Luke. They are part of a larger teaching that begins with a passage found in the other two synoptic Gospels, but they add an important element to that teaching. This follows immediately after the parable of the wedding supper (Lk 14.15–24), which was told in the home of a Pharisee on the way from Galilee to Jerusalem. Continuing this account, Luke writes the following:

> And there went great multitudes with him; and he turned, and said unto them, "If any man come to me, and hate not his father, and mother, and wife, and children, and brethren, and sisters, yea, and his own life also,

[36]John Chrysostom, *Homily 7, On Repentance and Compunction* 2.4; *St John Chrysostom on Repentance and Almsgiving*, trans. Gus George Christo, FOC 96 (Washington: Catholic University of America Press, 1988), 87.

he cannot be my disciple. And whosoever doth not bear his cross, and come after me, cannot be my disciple. For which of you, intending to build a tower, sitteth not down first, and counteth the cost, whether he have sufficient to finish it? Lest haply, after he hath laid the foundation, and is not able to finish it, all that behold it begin to mock him, saying, 'This man began to build, and was not able to finish.' Or what king, going to make war against another king, sitteth not down first, and consulteth whether he be able with ten thousand to meet him that cometh against him with twenty thousand? Or else, while the other is yet a great way off, he sendeth an ambassage, and desireth conditions of peace. So likewise, whosoever he be of you that forsaketh not all that he hath, he cannot be my disciple." (Lk 14.25–33)

The first part of the teaching—concerning the rejection of one's family and even life itself—corresponds to Jesus' answer to the disciples (according to all three synoptics), in response to Peter's question: "Behold, we have forsaken all, and followed thee; what shall we have therefore?" (Mt 19.27; Mk 10.28; Lk 18.28). In Matthew and Mark's versions, however, Jesus' answer refers to the need to leave home, brothers and sisters, father, mother, wife, and children, but in Luke's version Jesus calls his disciples to hate them.

We have already spoken about the hidden meaning of this term in the Gospels.[37] Jesus here speaks of absolute faithfulness to himself and to his mission, which requires complete rejection of any relational ties, but only if that is necessary. For example this is necessary when one's family actively hinders a disciple of Jesus from fulfilling his mission, like Jesus' own family, in the early stage of his public ministry, which hindered him in various ways, thinking "he is beside himself" (Mk 3.21).

Some people try to soften the radical nature of this saying, citing the particularities of the Hebrew tongue, in which the word "hate" can mean "to love less." Thus, for example, in one of the verses of the book of Genesis, it is said that Jacob loved Rachel more than Leah, and in the next verse, she is called "unloved" (Genesis 29.30–31). In the Septuagint, the word

[37]See Alfeyev, *Jesus Christ: His Life and Teaching,* 1:434–37.

Jacob and Rachel
at the Well,
L. Giordano,
1600

is rendered as *miseitai* ("hated"), the passive form of the verb *miseō* ("to hate"), which is the same verb used in the passage we are examining in Luke. Even in this softened form, however, Jesus' words contain a demand that is very difficult to fulfill and that assumes a complete self-rejection on the part of his disciples.

Jesus, doubtless, recognized the radicalism of this demand. Therefore, he considered it his duty to warn his disciples: before they can answer his call, they have to carefully examine themselves and gauge their strength. This call contrasts with that haste and readiness with which, it might seem, the disciples threw aside their usual pursuits, left behind their parents, and followed Christ.

Yet as we examine the account of Jesus calling the first disciples, we first notice that they probably already knew who he was at the moment of the call. So, in following him, they were not walking into the complete unknown.[38] Second, if they did leave their families behind, then it was only for a time, while they traveled with Jesus. If Peter had abandoned his family after he followed Christ, he would not have been able to receive him in his own house, to eat with him at table, and to give him a place to sleep.

---

[38]See Alfeyev, *Jesus Christ: His Life and Teaching,* 1:373–86.

Even years after the death and resurrection of Jesus, some of the apostles, including Peter, remained married (1 Cor 9.5).

This circumstance alone, since it refers to the closest disciples of Jesus, shows us that his words about rejecting family, or even hating them, cannot be interpreted as a universal, literal imperative. In the final analysis, all the apostles except for Judas gave their life to the service of the mission for which they were chosen by the Teacher. Almost all of them ended their lives as martyrs. By this, they proved that they had come, in Jesus' words, to hate their own lives.

The parables of the tower builder and the king preparing for war are often called twin parables, since they are both structured along the same lines, they follow each other in the text, and they are both intended to reveal the same theme using two parallel images. There is a similar series of images in one of the proverbs of Solomon:

> Through wisdom is an house builded, and by understanding it is established, and by knowledge shall the chambers be filled with all precious and pleasant riches. A wise man is strong; yea, a man of knowledge increaseth strength. For by wise counsel thou shalt make thy war, and in multitude of counsellors there is safety. (Prov 24.3–6)

In this passage, we also read about building and about war. Moreover, the connective tissue between both is wisdom.

In Luke, the parable of the tower builder begins with a question: "Who among you . . . ?" This rhetorical question is used in two other parables: the lost sheep (Mt 12.11, Lk 15.4) and the unprofitable servant (Lk 17.7). The point of this technique is to lead a listener into the story, to make him think: how would he have acted in place of the protagonist?

Moreover, in all three parables, we find wealthy characters: one of them is capable of building a tower with his own money, another has one hundred sheep, the third has a slave whom he does not consider it necessary to thank for his work. This is evidence of the fact that among Jesus' listeners there were people belonging to different social strata, including those who were wealthy. Jesus speaks to them also, not only to the poor of the city and country.

In the first parable, the tower is a stone fortification built on the man's own land. Such fortifications—whether circular or square—were built for different reasons: to contain the fruits of the harvest, to provide a resting place, or to guard part of one's territory. To build such a tower required a significant amount of money, and so failing to plan for the expense in advance could result in the person's becoming an object of ridicule if he started the project but was unable to finish it. This is the connotation of the verb *empaizō* ("to mock," "to ridicule," "to make fun of"). Among cultured people, where the preservation of honor is given special significance, such a fate for the builder could have been catastrophic.

In contrast, the situation in the second parable is fraught with much more dangerous consequences. In the first parable, the man is simply risking his honor; in the second, he risks his own life and the life of his soldiers. The situation described in the second parable is typical for the history of the Israelite nation as recorded in the Bible: wars with pagan kings make up nearly all the content of the historical books of the Old Testament.

In both cases, the parable's main character must not only anticipate risks, but he must also do this *seated*. We noticed a similar detail in the parable of the net that "when it was full, they drew to shore, and *sat down*, and gathered the good into vessels, but cast the bad away" (Mt 13.48). The image of a man who calculates possible risks while seated underlines the thoroughness required.

Excessive literalism in interpreting both these parables may lead to questions that are difficult to answer. For example, can a person accurately calculate in advance the risks involved in remaining in the community of Jesus' disciples? Can he truly weigh his strength and answer Jesus "yes" or "no" depending on whether or not he has the necessary resources? Is it even possible for an answer to God's own call to be a product of rational calculation? And how does such reckoning beforehand actually fit the general tone of Jesus' calls to follow him? Doesn't the disciple need more inspiration and ardor than cold calculation?

Inspiration, ardor, zeal—these were the qualities of the disciple closest to Jesus—Peter. Calculation, forethought, and advance planning were completely foreign to him. He acted spontaneously, impulsively, as did

The Entry of the Lord into Jerusalem, Miniature, 12th century

many of the other disciples, such as the Sons of Thunder—James and John. And it seems that Jesus never condemned them for this or challenged them to change their course of action, to become more calculating and cool-headed, to sit down before each action and seek counsel concerning its possible results.

Both parables should be read, first of all, as a warning. Jesus journeys on his way to Jerusalem, where he will be condemned to death. He feels this and knows this. And he also knows that his disciples can expect the same fate: he warned them of this many times. He wants them to make the final determination to follow him independently, with full responsibility, understanding what complete self-rejection and sacrifices will be required.

The words that conclude this teaching sound like a conviction: "So likewise, whosoever he be of you that forsaketh not all that he hath, he cannot be my disciple." Among those who heard these words were his disciples. As they approached Jerusalem, he considered it his responsibility to warn them of the cost of discipleship, to force them to ask themselves one more time: are they ready to walk with him all the way to the end of the road that he walks?

One example that shows a concrete application of both parables can be found in the choice that every person makes when he decides to dedicate

St John Cassian of Rome,
Icon, 15th century

his life to the service of the Church, whether as a cleric or a monk. Ancient church canons indicate that there is a minimum age for ordination to the priesthood. One must be at least twenty-five years old to be ordained a deacon, and at least thirty to be ordained a priest. A young man was given time to assess his strength and abilities, to calculate risks, to a certain extent. He must understand that if he accepts ordination outside the married state, he can never marry after becoming a cleric. If he is married, but becomes widowed or divorced, he cannot marry a second time. Service to the Church lays a whole series of other limitations on a man. It requires that all his interests, including his personal and family life, be secondary to the service of the Church.

Even stricter rules exist for the monk. He gives God an oath to abstain from marriage and family life, to be obedient to the ecclesiastical authorities, to reject his own will. Monasticism is a way of life that does not fit into a framework of "common sense." It requires spiritual efforts that transcend normal human abilities. Having taken monastic vows, a person burns all his bridges, because there is no way back, just as there is no possibility for a king, having begun a battle with an army of ten thousand, to sue for peace when he is being routed by an army twice as large and strong.

The golden age of monasticism was the fourth century. John Cassian, one of the founders of western monasticism, lived at this time. He offered an interpretation of the parable of the king preparing for war that refers directly to monastic vows:

> And thinking, according to that parable in the Gospel, that he who goes forth with ten thousand men against a king who comes with twenty thousand, cannot possibly fight, they should, while he is yet a great way off, ask for peace; that is, it is better for them not even to take the first step towards renunciation, rather than afterwards following it up coldly, to involve themselves in still greater dangers. For it is better

not to vow, than to vow and not pay. But finely is the one described as coming with ten thousand and the other with twenty. For the number of sins which attack us is far larger than that of the virtues which fight for us.[39]

In the ascetical literature of the fourth and following centuries, the monastic life is described as spiritual warfare that the ascetic wages "not against flesh and blood, but against principalities, against powers, against the rulers of the darkness of this world, against spiritual wickedness in high places" (Eph 6.12). In the rite of monastic tonsure, a person receives new clothing, and each item symbolizes armor. The symbolism of the monastic habit comes from the words of the Apostle Paul:

Wherefore take unto you the whole armor of God, that ye may be able to withstand in the evil day, and having done all, to stand. Stand therefore, having your loins girt about with truth, and having on the breastplate of righteousness, and your feet shod with the preparation of the Gospel of peace, above all, taking the shield of faith, wherewith ye shall be able to quench all the fiery darts of the wicked. And take the helmet of salvation, and the sword of the Spirit, which is the word of God. (Eph 6.13–17)

The words of the apostle, however, are not addressed only to monks; they are addressed to the whole Christian community.

The spiritual life of every Christian—not only the monk and the priest—is subject to the laws of warfare. In this war, we need sober judgment. No person should pick up a burden that he will not be able to carry later. This is the main point of the parables of the tower builder and the king preparing for war.

---

[39]John Cassian, *The Institutes of John Cassian* 7.15 (NPNF[2] 11:252–53).

7. The Lost Coin

We have already examined the parable of the lost sheep, focusing primarily on the account in Matthew. This parable exists also in Luke (Lk 15.4–7). In Matthew's version, the parable is part of a larger teaching given in Galilee. After finishing it, Jesus left Galilee and came to Judea (Mt 19.1). This journey, which Matthew covers in a single verse, takes ten chapters in Luke's account (Lk 9.51–19.27). On this journey, according to Luke, Jesus told the parable of the lost sheep, then he told three other parables: the lost coin, the prodigal son, and the unjust steward.

While reading the parables of Jesus, we cannot fail to notice that in most of them both the major and minor characters are men. For a patriarchal society, where the role of women was limited to the raising of children and the running of the household, this was natural. Men worked in the fields and vineyards, took money as loans and made repayment, received percentages and speculated on them, built houses, herded sheep, sold pearls, caught fish, built towers, and waged wars. In a word, men did the things that were worth speaking about in parables. The life of women rarely became the subject of public attention, and women in general were rarely talked or written about.

But there are four exceptions to this rule. In these four parables, women's work or women's daily lives are mentioned: the leaven (Mt 13.33–35; Lk 13.20–21), the ten virgins (Mt 25.1–13), the lost coin (Lk 15.8–10), and the persistent widow (Lk 18.1–8). Moreover, only in the parable of the lost coin does a woman symbolize God.[40]

Three of these parables are "twins" of other parables, in which the main character is a man: the parable of the leaven is twin to the parable of the mustard seed (Mt 13.31), the parable of the persistent widow is twin to the parable of the friend at midnight (Lk 11.5–8), and the parable of the lost coin is twin to the parable of the lost sheep. In each case, the "twins" are joined by the conjunction "or":

[40]Hultgren, *Parables*, 64.

Or what woman having ten pieces of silver, if she lose one piece, doth not light a candle, and sweep the house, and seek diligently till she find it? And when she hath found it, she calleth her friends and her neighbors together, saying, "Rejoice with me; for I have found the piece which I had lost." Likewise, I say unto you, there is joy in the presence of the angels of God over one sinner that repenteth. (Lk 15.8–10)

The Found Drachma,
John Everett Millais, 1865

The coin is a drachma (a "piece of silver"), a small silver coin of Greek origin that was widely used as currency in Judea. The weight of a drachma varied depending on the age or the place of origin. For example, the Attic drachma weighed 4.32 grams of silver, the Aegina drachma weighed 6.24. Two drachmas made up a didrachma (see Mt 17.24), four were a tetradrachma or a "stater" (Mt 17.27), one hundred drachmas (twenty-five staters) was a mina (Lk 19.13). One Attic talent was sixty minas, or six thousand drachmas, while the Corinthian talent was one hundred minas, or ten thousand drachmas. During Jesus' time, a drachma was about the same worth as a denarius, which was a coin that represented the day's wages of a day laborer.

The woman from the parable is sometimes described as "rather wealthy," since she has her own home and her own friends.[41] But this is a stretch. In the parable nothing is said about her having "her own house." She could have lost the drachma in a house where she lived together with her family. And the presence of friends does not mean she is wealthy: even in the poorest village, a poor woman would have friends and neighbors. A wealthy woman would not have thought that the loss of a single drachma was any kind of tragedy, nor that finding it was a source of such joy.

[41] Amy-Jill Levine, *Short Stories by Jesus: The Enigmatic Parables of a Controversial Rabbi* (New York: HarperOne, 2014), 42.

The Found Drachma,
Domenico Fetti, 1618–22

Evidently, this woman is far from wealthy. Other scholars even add details, e.g., that she is a young, unmarried woman, living in her parents' house, while the ten drachmas are her dowry, and the loss of even one drachma might put at risk her potential marriage.[42] It is possible that the drachma fell from her headdress (it was not uncommon for silver coins to be included in women's headdresses).[43]

To find the lost drachma, the woman lit a lamp (*lychnos*) and began to sweep the room. She looked for it carefully and patiently, until she found it, just as the man who lost his sheep had searched for it long and patiently. In both cases, the result of the search is successful, and both rejoice. In the second case, the woman does not rejoice more over the drachma she found than over the ones that were not lost, but the story does mention that she shared her joy with friends.

Jesus himself offers an interpretation of the parable: the woman represents God, and the lost drachma—a sinner. The finding of the coin is repentance, and the friends are the angels of God. From the parable itself we learn that God does not rejoice alone; he invites the angels to participate in his joy. The angels are his closest helpers; they always see his face (Mt 18.10), always do his will with regard to people, both in this life (Mt 1.20, 2.13, 19; Lk 1.11, 26, 2.9, 13) and after death (Lk 16.22). "Thus it will be at the end of the age. The angels will go out and separate the wicked from the righteous" (Mt 13.49), "and he will send out his angels with a trumpet blast, and they will gather his elect from the four winds, from one end of the heavens to the other" (Mt 24.31).

The image of the lamp from the parable is sometimes given an allegorical interpretation, e.g., symbolizing the divine light that illumines the depths of the human soul, with the drachma representing the image of God in man. Macarius of Egypt wrote,

[42]Jeremias, *Parables,* 133.
[43]S. Weir, "A Bridal Headdress from Southern Palestine," *Palestine Exploration Quarterly* 105 (1973): 101–109.

That woman who lost the piece of silver, first lighted the lamp, and then set the house in order, and thus, the house being set in order and the lamp lit, the piece of silver was found, buried in dirt and filth and earth. So now the soul cannot of itself find its own thoughts, and disengage them; but when the divine lamp is lit, it lights up the darkened house, and then the soul beholds its thoughts, how they lie buried in the filth and mire of sin. The sun rises, and then the soul beholds its loss, and begins to recall the thoughts that were mingled among the dirt and uncleanness. For indeed the soul lost her image when she transgressed the commandment.[44]

According to Symeon the New Theologian, the lamp is Christ himself. Speaking of people who "kept God's commandments unto death . . . [and] have sold their possessions, distributed them to the poor, and followed Christ through their patient endurance of temptations, and for love of God . . . have lost their souls in the world and found them again for eternal life," Symeon writes:

And finding their souls, they have found them in a light which is spiritual, and in this light they have seen *the light unapproachable*, God himself, according to that which stands written: *In thy light we shall see light*. How then is it possible for someone to find the soul that he has? Pay heed. Each person's soul is the silver coin which was lost, not by God, but by each of us, because he immersed himself in the darkness of sin; and Christ, who truly is light, has come and, in a way that only he knows, has met with those seeking him, and allowed them to see him. This is what it means for a man to find his soul: to see God, and in his light to become higher than all the visible created universe, and to have God as his shepherd and teacher.[45]

Thus we have the following series of symbols: the woman symbolizes God, the lamp represents the Son of God, the light of the lamp stands

[44]Macarius the Egyptian, *Fifty Spiritual Homilies* 11.4; *The Fifty Spiritual Homilies of St Macarius the Egyptian*, trans. A. J. Mason (London: SPCK, 1921), 81.
[45]Symeon the New Theologian, *Epistle* 1.455–70; *The Epistles of St Symeon the New Theologian*, ed. and trans. H. J. M. Turner (Oxford: Oxford University Press, 2009), 61.

for the divine light that illumines the darkness of sin. The finding of the drachma, consequently, symbolizes the restoration of the image of God in man through the activity of divine grace.

The interpretation of the drachma as the image of God became universally accepted in the tradition of the Eastern Christian Church, and it even entered into the hymnography of the Church. As for the lamp, in some cases it represents not Jesus, but John the Baptist, concerning whom Jesus said, "He was a burning and shining lamp, and for a while you were content to rejoice in his light" (Jn 5.35). This interpretation is reflected in the penitential canon of Andrew of Crete:

> I have discolored with the passions the first beauty of the image, O Savior. But seek me, as once thou didst seek the lost coin, and find me. (Great Canon, Ode Two, Fifth Thursday of Great Lent, slightly edited)

> O Savior, I am the coin marked with the King's likeness, which thou didst lose of old. But, O Word, light thy lamp, thy Forerunner, and seek and find again thine image. (Great Canon, Ode Six, Fifth Thursday of Great Lent, slightly edited)

8. The Prodigal Son

In the Gospel according to Luke, the parables of the lost sheep and lost coin lead to Jesus' most important parable regarding repentance and the love of God: the parable of the prodigal son.

We can say without exaggeration that the parable of the prodigal son is the most famous of all Jesus' parables. It represents one of the most powerful witnesses to the mercy of God in the Gospels and in all of world literature. Charles Dickens called this parable the greatest short story of all time.[46]

---

[46]John MacArthur, *A Tale of Two Sons: The Inside Story of a Father, His Sons and a Shocking Murder* (Nashville, TN: Thomas Nelson, 2008), 3.

The image of the merciful father and his suffering, lost son are given so many touching details that for centuries the parable became a source of inspiration for theologians, philosophers, writers, poets, and artists. The Russian composer Sergei Prokofieff wrote a ballet inspired by the plot of the parable, the Englishmen Arthur Sullivan and Benjamin Britten wrote an operetta and an opera, respectively. Rembrandt's famous painting *The Return of the Prodigal Son* is one of many in a long list of famous paintings inspired by this parable, along with notable examples of Rubens and Dürer. The plot of the parable served as Shakespeare's inspiration in writing of *The Merchant of Venice* and *Henry IV*.[47] Dostoyevsky used elements of the parable in many works, including the novels *A Raw Youth* (also known as *The Adolescent*), *Crime and Punishment,* and *Brothers Karamazov*.[48]

The Prodigal Son,
Hieronymus Bosch,
1491–1516

This parable is found only in the Gospel according to Luke and it is the third in a trilogy of parables that begin with the words: "Then drew near to him all the publicans and sinners for to hear him. And the Pharisees and scribes murmured, saying, 'This man receiveth sinners, and eateth with them'" (Lk 15.1–2). According to Luke, it was the Pharisees and scribes who are the main audience for the parable, though the disciples are present as well. Doubtless, there was also a crowd, among whom were publicans and sinners:

---

[47]Ibid.

[48]N. S. Izmestieva, "Ob odnom evangel'skom siuzhete u F. M. Dostoevskogo ('Vozbrashchenie bludnogo syna' v romane *Podrostok*)" [On a gospel story by F. M. Doestoevsky, "The return of the prodigal son," in the novel *A Raw Youth*], *Vestnik Udmurtskogo universiteta* [Bulletin of Udmurt University] 5 (2006): 35–46; V. I. Gabdullina, "'Bludnii syn' kak model' pobedenija: evangel'skii motiv v kontekste biografii i tvorchestva F. M. Dostoevskogo" ["'The Prodigal Son' as a model of behavior: a gospel motif in the context of the biography and works of F. M. Dostoevsky"], *Vestnik Tomskogo gosudarstvennogo pedagogicheskogo universiteta* [Bulletin of Tomsk pedagogical state university] 6 (2005): 16–22.

And he said, "A certain man had two sons, and the younger of them said to his father, 'Father, give me the portion of goods that falleth to me.' And he divided unto them his living. And not many days after the younger son gathered all together, and took his journey into a far country, and there wasted his substance with riotous living. And when he had spent all, there arose a mighty famine in that land, and he began to be in want. And he went and joined himself to a citizen of that country; and he sent him into his fields to feed swine. And he would fain have filled his belly with the husks that the swine did eat, and no man gave unto him. And when he came to himself, he said, 'How many hired servants of my father's have bread enough and to spare, and I perish with hunger! I will arise and go to my father, and will say unto him, "Father, I have sinned against heaven, and before thee, and am no more worthy to be called thy son. Make me as one of thy hired servants."' And he arose, and came to his father. But when he was yet a great way off, his father saw him, and had compassion, and ran, and fell on his neck, and kissed him. And the son said unto him, 'Father, I have sinned against heaven, and in thy sight, and am no more worthy to be called thy son.' But the father said to his servants, 'Bring forth the best robe, and put it on him; and put a ring on his hand, and shoes on his feet; and bring hither the fatted calf, and kill it; and let us eat, and be merry. For this my son was dead, and is alive again; he was lost, and is found.' And they began to be merry. Now his elder son was in the field, and as he came and drew nigh to the house, he heard music and dancing. And he called one of the servants, and asked what these things meant. And he said unto him, 'Thy brother is come, and thy father hath killed the fatted calf, because he hath received him safe and sound.' And he was angry, and would not go in. Therefore came his father out, and entreated him. And he answering said to his father, 'Lo, these many years do I serve thee, neither transgressed I at any time thy commandment, and yet thou never gavest me a kid, that I might make merry with my friends. But as soon as this thy son was come, which hath devoured thy living with harlots, thou hast killed for him the fatted calf.' And he said unto him, 'Son, thou art ever with me, and all that I have is thine. It was meet that we should make merry, and be glad: for this thy brother was dead, and is alive again; and was lost, and is found.'" (Lk 15.11–32)

The parable of the prodigal son is the longest of all Jesus' parables. It can be divided into three parts, corresponding to four main story arcs of the plot. The first part is the prologue: in it, the initial incident of the story is indicated, from which three different story arcs will develop, connected with three main characters in the parable. In the second part, the story concerns the younger son: how he leaves his father's house, his misadventures in a distant land, his repentance, and his return. The third part is dedicated to the reconciliation of father and son,

The Return of the Prodigal Son, Rembrandt, 1668

and here the figure of the father is central. In the fourth part, the third character of the parable appears—the elder son. His conflict with the father is described; here too, the figure of the father looms large yet again.

In some sense, the parable of the prodigal son is a summary of the entire Gospel. If one had to choose a single parable of all the ones Jesus told that would most completely encapsulate the general thrust of his good news to mankind, then this would be the parable to choose. If one had to choose a single image in the New Testament that best corresponds to what Jesus says about his Father, that would be the image of the father from the parable of the prodigal son. If one had to find a single symbol that best reflects Christianity's vision of man's relationship with God, that would be the prodigal son.

The plot of the parable reflects the most fundamental aspects of human life, including one's place within the family and society at large. In ancient Mediterranean society, one scholar notes, each person possessed a kind of "social card" that determined his place in the world. It told a person who he was, who his relatives were, and how to act and react. In the center of this card was the family, especially the father, then came the village, the town, and so on to the very limits of the created world.[49] The social card

---

[49]Scott, *Hear Then*, 79.

of the prodigal son included his family and his father's home. After he left home, it spread to the limits of the distant country, but he excised the very foundational elements of his identity from his card, especially his connection with his father. And it is not simply that he grew up and began to live independently of his father. No, he actively broke the connection with his father, family, and home, severing himself from the natural context in which he could further develop as a person.

Even in the early Christian era, interpreters gave the parable a universal meaning. Some commentators believed the elder son to be the angels, and the younger son mankind after the fall.[50] Others believed the elder brother represented Israel, and the younger brother represented the Gentiles.[51] Summarizing the various points of view, Theophylact of Bulgaria wrote:

> I am not unaware that some have interpreted the elder son to signify angels, and the younger son, the latter-born nature of men which rebelled against the commandment it was given and went astray. Still others have said that the two sons represent the Israelites and the Gentiles who later believed. But the simple truth is what we have said here, namely, that the person of the elder son should be understood to signify the righteous, and the person of the younger son, to signify sinners who have repented and returned. The entirety of the parable is given for the sake of the Pharisees, to teach them not to be vexed that sinners are received, even if they themselves are righteous.[52]

Interpreting the parable as a symbolic description of what happened to mankind in the person of Adam is typical of both modern and ancient commentators:

---

[50]Ireneaus of Lyons, *Against Heresies* 3.11.8 (PG 7:877; ANF 1:428). Ambrose of Milan equated the younger son with Adam (*Commentary on the Gospel of Luke* 7.234; *Commentary of Saint Ambrose on the Gospel according to Saint Luke*, 265–66; SC 52:96).

[51]Tertullian, *On Modesty* 8–9 (CCSL 2:1294–99; ANF 4:81–84) and Origen, *Homilies on the Gospel of Luke* 38.5 (Origen, *Homilies on Luke, Fragments on Luke*, trans. Joseph T. Lienhard, S.J., FOC 94 [Washington: Catholic University of America Press, 1995], 158; GCS 49:224).

[52]Theophylact, *The Explanation of the Holy Gospel According to Luke* (House Springs, MO: Chrysostom Press, 2007), 204.

Is not the mystery of Adam's short dwelling in Eden hiding behind these words "after the passage of some days"? Having sinned, Adam thereby demanded and achieved separation from God. Having separated from God, he saw his own nakedness, that is, he saw: without God, he is nothing. And God, in his mercy, did not leave him naked, but made clothing for him appropriate to his lessened state; he dressed him and let him go (Gen 3.21). . . . What happened to Adam repeated itself with millions of Adam's sons, who separated from God through sin and with their name walked away into a far country. God forces no one to remain with him, for God created man free, and, being faithful to himself, never desires to transgress human freedom.[53]

The most direct context in which the parable was told was the situation immediately surrounding Christ: on the one hand stood the publicans and sinners who followed him like dogs on a scent, hungry for the word of God, thirsting for healing from their physical and spiritual diseases, and on the other hand stood the Pharisees and scribes who watched this spectacle from the side with doubt and disdain that grew into complaint and anger. Why does he dedicate so much of his attention to the cast-offs of society, while he constantly rebukes and offends the scribes and Pharisees, the bearers of knowledge and piety, the scholars of the law and the Scriptures, the elites of the chosen people, calling them instead hypocrites, children of vipers, and other offensive names? Who was he anyway, to so radically redefine the entire value system that had developed among the Hebrews over the course of centuries?

The Pharisees' complaining and grumbling, their unchanging opposition in both thought and word, constantly followed Jesus. Again and again, he considered it necessary to explain to them that he came "not to call the righteous, but sinners to repentance" (Mt 9.13). Perhaps, desiring to elicit their sympathy, he drew before their mental eyes the picture of a father who equally loves both sons: the righteous elder son who is faithful to his father and never leaves him, who always remains with him (this is how the Pharisees understood their relationship with God) and the younger

---

[53]Nikolai (Velimirovich), *Tvoreniya*, 1:189–90. Translated by DNK.

prodigal son, a sinner who passed through a profound moral fall, but still returned to his father. Jesus hopes that the Pharisees will recognize in these images both themselves and those whom they so despise, and perhaps they will sense that before God all are at fault, and yet God does not love them the less for it.

The parable of the prodigal son begins in the same way as another parable with two sons (Mt 21.28). Yet the situation described in the first verse of the parable is not quite typical for the daily life of Israelites of that time. According to the law of Moses, a rich man's inheritance passes to his son after his death; if he has no son, it passes to his daughter; if he had no children, then it passes to his brothers or other relatives (Num 27.8–11). In a situation when a man had more than one son, the inheritance passed exclusively to the elder son. This was a practical measure intended to preserve large tracts of land undivided for many generations instead of constantly subdividing them into ever-smaller parcels. Furthermore, all real estate found on that land was considered part of the land and therefore part of the inheritance.

There was also another practice in the law. If a man had two sons, then the elder would receive two-thirds of the inheritance, and the younger would receive one-third (Deut 21.17). In any case, being the firstborn meant having significant advantages (see Gen 25.31–34, 27.36–37).

Further, much could also depend on the behavior of the children or the will of the father. As a rule, the children received their inheritance after the father's death, but there were cases when a father could divide his inheritance among his sons during his life. Nevertheless, Jesus ben Sirach criticizes such a practice:

> Hear me, O ye great men of the people, and hearken with your ears, ye rulers of the congregation. Give not thy son and wife, thy brother and friend, power over thee while thou livest, and give not thy goods to another, lest it repent thee, and thou entreat for the same again. As long as thou livest and hast breath in thee, give not thyself over to any. For better it is that thy children should seek to thee, than that thou shouldest stand to their courtesy. In all thy works keep to thyself the preeminence;

The Parable of the Prodigal Son, G. Tucco, 1863

leave not a stain in thine honor. At the time when thou shalt end thy days, and finish thy life, distribute thine inheritance. (Sir 33.18–23)

In the parable, the father ignores the counsel of Sirach and instead grants the son's request to receive his part of the inheritance that he would have received after the father's death. This action on the part of the father transgressed the laws of Israelite society in Jesus' time. By the standards of that time, the father's response was an expression of weakness. Any of Jesus' hearers, especially among the Pharisees, would have expected that the father's response would have been strong resistance to the son's request.[54]

To indicate the inheritance, the parable uses two terms: *ousia* ("property") and *bios* ("life" or "fortune"). The father divides his entire "life" among his two sons, that is, everything that he and his ancestors had gathered.

The expression "he divided unto them his living" should not be understood to mean that the elder brother also received his part of the inheritance. From the parable, it becomes clear that he remained with his father; consequently, he would only receive his portion after the father's death. It is very unlikely that the father simply divided the inheritance in half between his sons; more likely, the younger son received a smaller portion. Moreover, judging by the fact that he managed to waste it all rather quickly, his inheritance was either in money or some other moveable property that he quickly sold off. Even if he did receive some portion of real estate, the expression "gathered all together" can be understood in the sense that he sold everything he received from his father, and only took money with him on his journey.

[54]MacArthur, *A Tale of Two Sons*, 52.

The Prodigal Son,
V. D. Polenov,
1874

In that distant country, he lived beyond his means. The adverb *asōtōs*, which is translated as "riotously" can also be translated as "wastefully." What was this waste exactly? In the end of the parable, we find out that he wasted his fortune on prostitutes.

The distant country to which the younger son journeyed was not simply far away; it was a pagan land. All lands surrounding Israel were pagan lands. Even in Palestine itself, certain regions were thickly settled by pagans, such as the country of the Gadarenes or the Gergesenes on the east shore of the Sea of Galilee. This is why swine were herded there (Mt 8.30; Mk 5.11; Lk 8.32).

While the hero of the tale still had money in his pockets, he wasted it without thinking. When the money ran out, the country was struck by a famine, and he had nothing left to do other than to work in the most despised and underpaid jobs. But even such work did not give him enough money to feed himself. This picture of the younger son's calamitous state is painted in vivid colors: he was hungry, and he did not even have enough money to buy pig feed, even the husks that the pigs ate would not have been enough to satisfy him (some manuscripts have this as "to fill his stomach").[55]

---

[55]The "husks" in question belonged to the bean family, most likely carob, which was widely used as feed for cattle and pigs.

The Prodigal Son,
Pierre Puis de
Chavannes,
19th century

The story takes a sharp turn when the son comes to himself. He suddenly remembers his father's house, and he admits that there even his father's hired servants live better than he, a free man, does in a far country. His motivation seems to be purely pragmatic; he decided to return not because he misses his father, neither for any nostalgia for his fatherland. He remembers his father's house because there he had been fed, dressed, and shod.

He understands that by all the rules of family life, he is worthy of condemnation. And so he prepares a speech for his father in advance, not knowing how his father will react. After all, he had planned never to return. Even now, he does not hope to be restored to the position of sonship; he only wishes for his father to give him bread.

And here something happens that none of the listeners from among the scribes and Pharisees could ever have expected, nor could they be expected to sympathize with it. Instead of punishing the son, condemning him, and at the very least teaching him a harsh lesson, the father runs to him, embraces him and does not even let him finish the speech he prepared: the son's words are interrupted halfway through. The son hears no word of cursing, condemnation, rebuke, or even edification. The father says absolutely nothing to him. He turns to the servants—those whose ranks the son had only recently not even dreamed of joining. And he commands them to return to the unfortunate son all the visible signs of his sonship, including a ring, which was a symbol of power over those same slaves and the property at large. It meant admission back into his family, a return to the father's trust.

It would have been enough to end the parable at this point to once again incite the anger of the Pharisees and scribes. Before, Jesus had offered them the example of publicans and sinful women, but now at the heart of this story, they encounter a person who had wasted his father's inheritance with prostitutes, but they hear not a single word of deserved condemnation from the lips of the Teacher. Yet Jesus did not stop there. He added a final section to the parable, in which the scribes and Pharisees were supposed to recognize themselves.

This is the immediate context of the telling of this parable. It is not difficult to imagine the reaction of the scribes and Pharisees. If the meaning of the parable was limited to this immediate context, however, it would not have touched the hearts of so many people over so many centuries. Jesus' polemic against the scribes and Pharisees is only one of countless examples in human history of ideological opposition between parties of different views, and this particular polemic was limited to a very small nation. But the eternal truths that come to life in that polemic remain real and important for all subsequent generations of people, regardless of their ethnicity. These truths are universal and human in nature.

In the parable, the father symbolizes God, for whom all people are sons and daughters. Every one of his children receives an inheritance—those talents, abilities, and possibilities that a person can realize to their fullest potential while remaining with God and by dedicating all his labors to God. Yet a person can squander that same potential in a place far away from God, using it to acquire earthly or sinful goals. This is the choice that stood before the first people, who could, through obedience to God, flourish in virtue, but instead followed the devil's advice and tasted the forbidden fruit, immediately coming to know their own nakedness. A similar choice stands before each person, and all people, who at some point in their life repeat the mistake of Adam and Eve, falling prey to various forms of temptations inspired by the devil. In this sense, the prodigal son becomes a symbol of every human being who chooses sin.

In the history of the various interpretations of this parable, its original context very quickly took on a secondary role, and in the early Church, commentators examined it through several different prisms: 1) as a universal image of man's fall from God and his subsequent repentance; 2) as an illustration of God's mercy, which knows no bounds; 3) as a short metaphorical description of the entire history of man's salvation by the merciful God through the redemptive suffering of Jesus Christ. Certain details of the parable would necessarily receive slightly different interpretations depending on the point of view of the commentator.

The Prodigal Son,
Dürer, 1496

John Chrysostom examines the parable as it can be applied to those who sinned after baptism. God sometimes allows such people to fall into sin so that they, once they remember him, can come to repentance:

> Therefore, this son bears the image of those who suffer the fall after the Laver [i.e., baptism]. That he represents those who fell after baptism is obvious from the parable. He is called "son"; no one can be called a son without baptism. Furthermore, he inhabited the paternal house, and took his share from all the paternal substance. Before baptism, no one has the right to receive paternal things, nor to obtain an inheritance, so that through all these events he speaks to us about the status of the faithful. He was a brother of the reputable one; he would not have become a brother without spiritual regeneration. Therefore, what does the one say who fell into the worst wickedness? "I will arise and return to my father." His father did not hinder him from departing to the foreign land precisely for this reason: so that he could learn well from the experience how much beneficence he enjoyed while remaining at home.

When he does not convince with his word, God many times per-
mits the experience of things to be the teaching.[56]

According to the commentary of Gregory Palamas (14th century), the
two sons represent two types of people: one person remains in obedience
to God and the Church, faithful in prayer and fulfilling the commands of
God, while the second spends his days in drunkenness and his nights in
unworthy and iniquitous deeds, and hurries to steal money and perform
other evil deeds:

> How did he disperse his wealth? Above all it is our inborn mind that
> is our substance and our wealth. As long as we are faithful to the
> ways of salvation, our mind is at one with itself and with God, the
> first and highest Mind. Whenever we open the door to the passions,
> immediately it is dispersed, wandering continually among fleshly and
> earthly things, all kinds of pleasures and passionate thoughts about
> them. The wealth of mind is prudence, which stays with it, discerning
> between what is better and what is worse, for as long as the mind itself
> stays obedient to the commandments and counsels of the heavenly
> Father. Once the mind rebels, prudence is dispersed in fornication
> and foolishness, shared out between both minds. . . . So the wretched
> man is cut to pieces and tortured by the cares these things bring, and
> cannot even enjoy breathing the air or seeing the sun, the riches we
> all share.[57]

St Philaret of Moscow (19th century) considers the younger son's most
important mistake the fact that he assumed the gift he received from God
was his personal property, which he could waste however he liked:

> Whom does the parable offer as the image of the father? God, with
> reference to mankind. . . . Whom does the parable portray in the per-
> son and actions of the younger son? Mankind the sinner. . . . What
> does the younger son's taking and assuming of his inheritance mean

---

[56]John Chrysostom, *Homilies on Repentance* 1.4.26–27 (PG 49:282–83; FOC 96:11–12).
[57]Gregory Palamas, Homily 3.14–15 (PG 151:40; *Saint Gregory Palamas: The Homilies*, trans.
Christopher Veniamin [Dalton, PA: Mount Thabor Publishing, 2016], 19–20).

The Prodigal Son,
G. I. Semiradsky,
19th century

within the parable? This illustrates the beginning of a sinful state, when a person ceases to look at what he has from the heavenly Father and his providence as a gift of God, instead beginning to look at it as his own personal property. With self-satisfaction, he begins to think, "There are my abilities, my knowledge, my art, my labor, my merits, my dignity, my riches." Naturally, what follows is that he uses these goods given to him only for his own benefit, not for God. . . . What does the separation of the younger son from the father and his house and the journey into a distant country mean? The separation of a sinner from God. . . . What does the hunger in the distant land represent? That in the sinful world the sinful man will find only sensual pleasure for a short time, but soon afterward he will sense a spiritual hunger, because the sinful world offers only perishable, evanescent pleasures, but the soul of man is incorrupt and requires incorruptible food. . . . Who is the inhabitant of that distant country who sent the son out to herd swine? It is the devil.[58]

The sin of the younger son is fornication, and according to Christian teaching, fornication defiles the body of a person, separating him from God. The Apostle Paul includes fornicators in a category of people who

[58]Philaret of Moscow, "Homily for the Sunday of the Prodigal Son and the Commemoration of St Alexis (12 February 1856)," *Pribavleniya k Tvoreniyam sv. Ottsov* [Supplements to the works of the holy fathers] 15 (1856): 23–32. Translated by DNK.

"shall not inherit the kingdom of God" (1 Cor 6.9). The body of a Christian belongs not to himself, but to Christ, and thus fornication is a kind of adultery against Christ:

> Know ye not that your bodies are the members of Christ? Shall I then take the members of Christ, and make them the members of an harlot? God forbid. What? Know ye not that he which is joined to an harlot is one body? For "Two," saith he, "shall be one flesh" (Gen 2.24). But he that is joined unto the Lord is one spirit. Flee fornication. Every sin that a man doeth is outside the body; but he that committeth fornication sinneth against his own body. What? Know ye not that your body is the temple of the Holy Spirit which is in you, which ye have of God, and ye are not your own? For ye are bought with a price: therefore glorify God in your body, and in your spirit, which are God's. (1 Cor 6.15–20)

Fornication is a very serious sin; however, as with other sins, it is capable of being healed with repentance. John Chrysostom calls Christians not to be ashamed of repentance, but of sin:

> Thus, Satan knew that sin has the shame, enough to enable the sinner to rebuff him, and that repentance has the courage, enough to draw to itself the one who repents. He changed the order, giving the shame to repentance and the courage to sin. How does this look? I will tell you. Someone is conquered by a grievous desire for a public prostitute. He follows the prostitute as her prisoner. He goes into the inn. Without being ashamed, without blushing, he entwines himself with the prostitute, he commits the sin. He is not ashamed at all. He does not blush at all. He leaves there after completing the sin, and he is ashamed to repent! You wretched man; when you were entangled with the prostitute you were unashamed, and when you come to repent, then you are ashamed? Tell me, does he feel ashamed? Why was it that when he committed the prostitution he was not ashamed? He commits the act and is unashamed, but in order to say what he did, he blushes? But this is the devil's wickedness: he does not allow the human being to feel

ashamed while publicly committing the sin because he knows that if he were to feel shame, he would avoid the sin.[59]

In the parable, man's falling away from God is described as a process with several stages. First, a person consciously begins to separate his material and spiritual gifts from God, the source of these gifts. He becomes an end unto himself; he wants to use these gifts independently of anyone else. Having received them to use as he wills, he begins to use them to satisfy his own sinful passions. Yet what first seemed so attractive to him soon turns into the exact opposite; what seemed to promise pleasure and satiety in actual fact only leads to spiritual hunger. Man enters into fellowship with demons (in the parable they are symbolized by the swine), and he tries to satisfy himself with the food that they eat, but that food cannot fill him. The lowest pit in the spiritual fall is complete forgetfulness of God, of the father's house, of the possibility of return. The prodigal son did not reach this lowest point. At the second-to-last step of falling away from God, he remembered his father's house, and this begins his long and arduous journey home.

He also accomplishes his return to God in several stages. The first is indicated by the words "when he came to himself." Sin twists a man's personality, as it were replacing it with a false one that effaces his memory of good and the source of good—God himself. The return to God begins with man's remembering his former personality, how he was until the moment he consciously stepped onto the path of sin. In a literal sense, he comes to himself—he returns to his original self, and he again begins to recognize the shade of all former things that used to surround him, that he used to be connected to. He wants to restore the ties that were severed, beginning with his connection to his father. After all, it was the severing of this connection that began his spiritual fall.

The next stage is the willingness to return. It is indicated by the words "I will arise and go." This is not yet action; it is still only intention. Yet God not only accepts actions, he also praises intentions.[60] John Climacus wrote,

---

[59]Chrysostom, *Homilies on Repentance* 8.2.9 (PG 49:339; FOC 96:115–16).

[60]John Chrysostom, *Catechetical Homily* (PG 59:722; *The Paschal Service* [Syosset, NY: Orthodox Church in America, Department of Religious Education, repr. 1986], 45–47).

"Our own strong desire and intention, with God's co-operation, precede every spiritual labor, both visible and mental; for if the first has not paved the way, the second is apt not to follow."[61] On the other hand, the same father also notes, "God is the judge of our intentions; but in his love he does also require us to act as far as we are able."[62] If a good intention does not grow into action, it will not lead a person to the path of repentance:

> As soon as the prodigal son thought of the necessity of turning back, he immediately went in actual fact and approached the father. Thus the parable teaches us that a good intention is only salvific when it is brought into action without deviation and laziness. There are people whose path is sown with good intentions, but these intentions remained unrealized, and that path bent only toward hell.[63]

Finally, the third stage is the passage from thoughts to action. It is indicated by the words "he arose and came." This action becomes the turning point in the fate of the prodigal son. He does not yet know what he can expect upon his return home, but he knows that only the father can save him.

The son is only able to give part of the speech that he had prepared for his father: "Father, I have sinned against heaven, and in thy sight." Here "heaven" is a synonym for the heavenly Father. According to Gregory Palamas,

> We were right when we said at the beginning that this father is God. How could this son who left his father have sinned against heaven unless his father was in heaven? For he says, "I have sinned against heaven," meaning against the saints, the citizens of heaven, "and before thee," who dwellest in heaven with thy saints.[64]

The culmination of the parable comes when the prodigal son and the father meet. This moment is the most unexpected, most vivid, and most

[61]John Climacus, *Ladder* 26.86 (HTM trans., p. 201).
[62]Ibid., 26.164 (p. 213).
[63]Philaret of Moscow, "Homily for the Sunday of the Prodigal Son," 29. Translated by DNK.
[64]Gregory Palamas, *Homily* 3.20 (PG 151:44; *The Homilies*, 21).

touching scene of the entire story. It is at the same time the most shocking moment for the scribes and Pharisees who listened to the parable. The father sees his son from a distance. This means that every day, every passing year, he kept walking out to the threshold of his house to look into the distance and see whether his missing son would return. When he does see him, he breaks all the rules of civility, not thinking at all about his dignity in the eyes of those who surround him. Throwing himself on the neck of his son, hugging and kissing him, he leads him back not as a strict father, but as a loving mother.[65] Instead of deserved punishment, the son receives complete and immediate forgiveness. Instead of condemnation, the father pours his unlimited love over him.

> Therefore, since the prodigal son departed for the foreign land and learned from his own experience how much evil it is for someone to be driven out of his paternal house, he returned, and his father did not remember the wrongs that he had committed against him, but accepted him with open arms. Why? Because he was a father and not a judge. Then, there took place dances, sumptuous feasts, and festivals; and the entire house was beaming with joy and exceeding gladness. What are you saying? These are the rewards of wickedness? Not of wickedness, O man, but of the return. Not of sin, but of repentance. Not of cunningness, but of change toward the better. . . .
>
> No doctor hesitates to administer medicine to one who suffers in order to demand correct and exact vengeance from him for his disorder. Even if it was altogether fitting for the prodigal son to deliver himself up for punishment, he was punished enough by living in the foreign land. At any rate, he was separated from our company for a very long time, and he battled to the finish with famine, dishonor, and the worst evils.[66]

The image of the father who runs to greet his son is proof that repentance is not a one-way street. It is not only a path along which a sinner returns to a God who silently and patiently awaits him at the end of the road. Rather,

[65]Scott, *Hear Then*, 117.
[66]Chrysostom, *Homilies on Repentance* 1.4.28, 30 (PG 49:283; FOC 96:12–13).

repentance is like two-way traffic: God rushing toward man and man moving toward God. According to the words of Philaret of Moscow, a degree of God's prevenient grace is present in a person's repentance:

> The Father greets and gives gifts to the son who returned. This is a bright image of God's wondrous love for the repentant sinner. The father sees the returning, unworthy son from a distance, and walks toward him. God foresees the return of the sinner and helps him with prevenient grace. No sooner does the son restore the necessary obedience to his father in his heart than the father already embraces and kisses him. As soon as the sinner firmly intends in his heart to fulfill the will of God, God already begins to reveal to him his nearness and the signs of his mercy and love. No sooner does the son have time to declare his repentance and self-condemnation—"I have sinned, I am not worthy"—than the father, not allowing him to call himself a hired servant aloud, gives him the bright clothing of sonship, the ring, and shoes for his feet. As soon as the sinner in his humble repentance condemns himself, God mystically in heaven and visibly on earth declares his forgiveness through the servant of the mysteries (i.e., the priest).[67]

The love of God is like the love of a father and mother combined. It does not decrease because the sons act in a way that the parents would not like. Man can deny God, but God will never deny man. The son may forget about the Father, but the Father will never forget the son. The love of the son for the Father can diminish or even disappear, but the love of the heavenly Father for his children never lessens, no matter their evil deeds. Isaac the Syrian (7th century) wrote of this with particular power:

> That God has been eternally the same in all that belongs to him in his nature, that he does not change as a result of what happens within creation—these are points to which I imagine that no one endowed with reason will oppose in his thinking. It is evident to everyone who has rational intelligence that, even if with us (human beings) there exists

---

[67]Philaret of Moscow, "Homily for the Sunday of the Prodigal Son," 29–30. Translated by DNK.

change . . . nevertheless in the mind of the Creator there exists a single, even intention with respect to all rational beings, and there exists with him a single love and compassion which is spread out over all creation, (a love) which is without alteration, timeless and everlasting.

Nor are we able to say that the love of the Creator is . . . less for sinners than for those who are justly named the righteous. This is because (the divine) Nature is not affected by what happens and by opposition, nor does there spring up within it any causal stirring which takes its origin from creation, and which is not to be found with him from eternity; nor does he have a (kind of) love which originates as a result of events which take place in time.

Rather, everyone has a single place in his purpose in the ranking of love, corresponding to the form he beheld in them before he created them. . . . He has a single ranking of complete and impassible love towards everyone, and he has a single caring concern for those who have fallen, just as much as for those who have not fallen.[68]

St Isaac the Syrian,
Fresco, 20th century

The son, even one who is guilty of sin, even one who has betrayed his father, who has wasted his father's inheritance, cannot be lowered to the rank of a hired servant. He always remains a son. This is the mystery of divine love and mercy that the parable reveals.

The return of the prodigal son leads the father to order the fatted calf to be killed. This detail attracted the attention of commentators even in the early Church. Beginning with Irenaeus of Lyons, the image of the fatted calf pointed to the redemptive sacrifice that God the Father brought for the sake of the human race:

[68]Isaac the Syrian, Homily 40.1–3 (CSCO 554:163–64; 'The Second Part', Chapters IV–XLI, 174–75).

For now was made ready the fatted calf, about to be immolated for the finding again of the younger son.[69]

So quickly does he gain forgiveness, that, as he is coming, and is still a great way off, his father meets him, gives him a kiss, which is the sign of sacred peace; orders the robe to be brought forth, which is the marriage garment, which if anyone have not, he is shut out from the marriage feast; places the ring on his hand, which is the pledge of faith and the seal of the Holy Spirit; orders the shoes to be brought out, for he who is about to celebrate the Lord's Passover, about to feast on the Lamb, ought to have his feet protected against all attacks of spiritual wild beasts and the bite of the serpent; bids the calf to be slain, for Christ our Passover has been sacrificed (1 Cor 5.7). For as often as we receive the Blood of the Lord, we proclaim the death of the Lord (1 Cor 11.26). As, then, he was once slain for all, so whenever forgiveness of sins is granted, we receive the sacrament of his Body, that through his Blood there may be remission of sins.[70]

Then he orders the fatted calf to be brought, slain, and offered at table. This calf is the Lord himself who is led out from the hidden place of divinity, from the heavenly Throne set above all things. Having appeared on earth as a man, he is slain like a fatted calf for us sinners, that is, he is offered to us as bread to eat.

God shares his joy and celebration over these events with his saints, making our ways his own, and his extreme love for mankind, and saying, "Come, let us eat and be merry" (Lk 15.23).[71]

The Father accepts him in repentance and does not chide, but displays His divine and paternal compassion by enfolding him in His embrace. He gives him a "garment," Holy Baptism, and as a "seal and token" the grace of the All-Holy Spirit. Furthermore He gives him "footwear" so that his footsteps according to God will no longer be smitten by snakes and scorpions, but rather he will be able to tread on their heads. Then,

[69]Irenaeus, *Against Heresies* 3.11.8 (ANF 1:428).
[70]Ambrose of Milan, *Two Books Concerning Repentance* 2.3.18 (NPNF[2] 10:347).
[71]Gregory Palamas, *Homily* 3.21–22 (PG 151:44; *The Homilies*, 22).

in the height of joy, the Father sacrifices for him the "fatted calf," His only-begotten Son, and He allows him to partake of the "flesh and blood," the Savior's Holy Communion.[72]

For the sake of his lost and found son, the Father killed the fatted calf. For the sake of the lost and found sinner, God gave his own Son as a sacrifice for salvation and as food for life and heavenly joy.[73]

The image of the calf, from the perspective of the Church's commentators, gives the entire parable not only a christological, but also a eucharistic resonance. In the ancient Church, all parables that mention a feast, including the parables of the wedding supper (Mt 22.1–14), those called to the feast (Lk 14.15–24), and the ten virgins (Mt 25.1–13), were understood as images of the Eucharist. The Church included the parable of the prodigal son in this category because the images of the fatted calf and the feast symbolize the redemptive suffering of the Son of God, and the sacrament of the Body and Blood of Christ. In the same way that the story of the son proceeds in stages, so too this symbolism occurs in stages. First comes the confession of sins, then God's forgiveness, and finally Communion, which indicates complete and total reunification with God, a restoration of lost sonship, by which we call God himself our Father.

The parable could easily have ended here, and the story would have been complete. The final section—the elder son's reaction to his own brother's return—is addressed first and foremost to the scribes and Pharisees. In a wider sense, however, it is also directed at everyone who considers himself righteous and yet does not rejoice together with God and the angels at the sinner's repentance.

Several expressive details stress the unfairness of the older son's reaction to his brother's return. The father calls him to the feast, but he does not want to come. The father calls his returned brother "this, thy brother," but he, as though not desiring to acknowledge the relationship, says of him, "this, thy son." The father tells him that the elder is always with him and

[72]Synaxarion for the Sunday of the Prodigal Son: *Synaxarion of the Lenten Triodion and Pentecostarion*, trans. Seraphim Dedes, introd. Roman Braga, ed. David Kidd and Mother Gabriella (Rives Junction, MI: HDM Press, 2005), 19–20.

[73]Philaret of Moscow, "Homily for the Sunday of the Prodigal Son," 30. Translated by DNK.

everything that the father has belongs to him, but the son only notes that the father had not given him enough, in spite of the fact that he remained with him. The elder son "was wise as long as he desired not to leave his father's house, but he did not show himself to be wise when the joy of the father produced sadness in him, when he saw personal offense in the salvation of his lost brother."[74] Yet the father does not condemn even this stubborn and offended son of his. With the same meekness, as though having to justify himself, he patiently explains his actions.

The father has the final word in the parable, expressed in the laconic phrase: "for this thy brother was dead, and is alive again; and was lost, and is found." These words refer to any person who has decided to reject a sinful manner of life, to leave the path of evil and to walk the path of repentance. To such a person God imputes no guilt for his previous way of life, since his transformation and repentance have completely blotted out his previous actions, allowing him to begin again, with a clean slate.

In the final analysis, the parable of the prodigal son speaks eloquently of God's love for man, not because of man's good deeds, but because love is an inalienable quality of God himself. If people often love things that are valuable in and of themselves, then, in the words of the Swedish philosopher A. Nygren, the love of God itself gives value to that which has no value.[75] In the parable, the father's love for both sons is the model of such love; yet the love of God transcends any parental love. Even if one of the sons had decided to kill his father at some point, we can go so far as to imagine that the final words of the father to his own murderer would have been "I love you."[76] The love of the father in the parable is at the same time an image of the love of God the Father and the love of God the Son for mankind—including for those who will soon crucify him.

In the ecclesiastical calendar of the Orthodox Church, the parable of the prodigal son occupies an important place. It is part of the liturgical cycle that prepares the faithful for Great Lent. This cycle begins three weeks before the fast with the Sunday of the Publican and Pharisee, when

[74]Philaret of Moscow, "Homily for the Sunday of the Prodigal Son," 31. Translated by DNK.
[75]Anders Nygren, *Agape and Eros* (Philadelphia: Westminster Press, 1953), 78.
[76]Raymond Angelo Belliotti, *Jesus the Radical: The Parables and Modern Morality* (Lanham, MD: Lexington Books, 2013), 51.

we read about the proud and self-satisfied Pharisee, who is opposed to the repentant tax collector (Lk 18.9–14). The following Sunday is called the Sunday of the Prodigal Son. The hymns for that day interpret the parable of the prodigal son and develop the parable's theological and moral content, using images that call the faithful to repentance:

> Brethren, let us learn the meaning of this mystery. For when the Prodigal Son ran back from sin to his Father's house, his loving Father came out to meet him and kissed him. He restored to the prodigal the tokens of his proper glory, and mystically he made glad on high, sacrificing the fatted calf. Let our lives, then, be worthy of the loving Father who has offered sacrifice, and of the glorious Victim who is the Savior of our souls.[77]

> Foolishly have I run away from thy glory, O Father, wasting in sin the wealth that thou gavest me. Therefore with the words of the prodigal I cry unto thee: I have sinned before thee, compassionate Father. Accept me in repentance and make me as one of thy hired servants.[78]

Identifying ourselves with the prodigal son, we Christians repent for our past life and ask God to open his loving embrace to us as well:

> Make haste to open unto me thy fatherly embrace, for as the prodigal I have wasted my life. In the unfailing wealth of thy mercy, O Savior, reject not my heart in its poverty. For with compunction I cry to thee, O Lord: Father, I have sinned against heaven and before thee.[79]

This same hymn also begins the service of the monastic tonsure. While this hymn is being sung, the future monk, dressed in a long white shirt, crawls from the narthex into the nave of the church, accompanied by older monks who cover him with their own clothes. The procession stops in the middle of the church, where the novice lies face down with his hands extended in the form of the cross. The abbot of the monastery addresses him with the words: "My child, the merciful God, like a father who loves

[77]Second sticheron on "Lord I call" at Vespers of the Sunday of the Prodigal Son.
[78]Kontakion at Matins on the Sunday of the Prodigal Son.
[79]Sessional hymn at Matins on the Sunday of the Prodigal Son.

his child, seeing your humility and true repentance, accepts you like the prodigal son who repented and who prostrated himself before the father with his whole heart."[80]

Thus the monastic tonsure begins with a recapitulation of the scene of the return of the prodigal son. This, however, is not a theatrical staging of the story of the parable. The ecclesiastical life of the Church in no way resembles theater, even if some elements of the services can seem reminiscent of a play. Neither the services nor the sacraments of the Church "reproduce" anything. They actualize the history of the Gospels, helping a person live through it himself, becoming a part of that history in the process. In the services and sacraments of the Church, the events of this history come to life in a person's lived experience, and the parables of Jesus become a guide to real, concrete action. The parable of the prodigal son comes to life in the experience of each person who accepts the monastic tonsure. The Church believes that when a person is tonsured, all his previous sins are forgiven him, and he is able to start life anew.

The same understanding is present at the heart of the sacrament of confession. The Church believes that every person can receive forgiveness of sins through confession, no matter how grave those sins might be. When a person comes to the priest for confession, he should see not the face of a strict judge, but a merciful father. The priest is called not to read a conviction over a sinner for the transgressions he committed, but rather to bear witness that through repentance he is freed from the guilt of his sins.

This same understanding lies at the heart of all pastoral work with the incarcerated. According to civil law, every person must be punished for any crimes he committed. The worse the crime, the more severe the punishment. Repentance does not free a criminal from responsibility before the law, but it is able to reconcile him with God. For this reason, the Church does not deny confession even to those who are awaiting the death penalty. In this way, the Church intercedes before the heavenly Father, asking for a

[80]Cf. *The Great Book of* Needs, trans. St Tikhon's Monastery, vol. 1 (South Canaan, PA: St Tikhon's Seminary Press, 2009), 331.

softening of the conviction that will be read aloud before every person at the final judgment.

The parable of the prodigal son has a universal meaning. Every new generation finds new meaning in it. For example, the state of spiritual hunger described in the parable is well known to many people who live far away from God. In Lermontov's novel *A Hero for Our Time*, we see the description of a character in whose life God plays no part whatsoever. Having wasted his life on his passions and various distractions, he acknowledges that he had not fulfilled his original purpose in life. The night before a duel at which he will kill a former friend, he reminisces over his past life:

> I run through all my past in my memory, and I ask myself unwillingly: why did I live? For what purpose was I born? . . . Truly, that purpose existed, and truly, it was a high calling, because I feel untrammeled power in my soul . . . but I never found that calling. I was distracted by the attractions of empty and ungrateful passions; from their crucible I came out hardened and cold like metal, but I lost forever the ardor of noble striving—that best flower of life. . . . My love brought no one joy, because I never sacrificed anything for those whom I loved. I loved for myself, for my own pleasure: I only satisfied the strange needs of the heart, hungrily inundating those feelings, joys, and pains, and I could never be satisfied. Just so does one suffering from hunger fall asleep in total exhaustion and sees before himself luxurious foods and bubbling wines. He devours these airy gifts of the imagination with ecstasy, and he seems to feel better; but as soon as he wakes up, the dream fades . . . all that remains is redoubled hunger and despair![81]

In this celebrated author's words, we see a vivid description of the spiritual despair and inner emptiness that arise in a person who has wasted on the lure of the passions all the riches and talents given him by God. It is possible that Lermontov, who knew the Bible and Christian literature very well, had the image of the prodigal son in mind when he wrote this passage. In his novel, however, this character does not become a son who

[81]Mikhail Lermontov, *A Hero for Our Time* (St Petersburg, 2008). Translated by DNK.

M. I. Lermontov, dressed in the military attire of the Hussars. F. O. Budkin, 1834

remembers the father, neither does that spiritual transformation take place that is only possible after repentance.

In Russia in the nineteenth century, when Lermontov wrote his novel, the Church's teaching about repentance was universally known. The intelligentsia, however, who for the most part had fallen away from the Church, lived another life, filled with interests that were different from the community of the faithful. The intelligentsia itself became the prodigal son who wasted the father's inheritance, falling ever deeper into the abyss of godlessness. The Church, in the person of its best representatives such as Philaret of Moscow, continued to call all people, including the intelligentsia, to the path of repentance.

In the teachings and parables of Jesus Christ, we will not find a clearly articulated doctrine of repentance. Jesus preferred to reveal the mystery of repentance not through concrete rules, but through various metaphors, each of which illustrated some aspect of his teaching. For example, the parable of the workers in the vineyard (Mt 20.1–16) emphasizes that it is never too late to enter the path of service to God. In the parable of the two sons (Mt 21.28–32), he shows that even those who refuse to follow God can later change their mind and follow the path of repentance. The parable of the barren fig tree (Lk 13.6–9) demonstrates that even if a person did not take advantage of the chances God gave him, while he yet lives, he still has an opportunity to change his way of life to bring forth fruits of repentance.

All these parables, together with the story of the prodigal son, can be called parables of hope. The term "hope" (*elpis* in Greek) is not found in the Gospels, nor in Jesus' direct words or stories. Yet it plays an important role in the theology of the early Church, especially in the work of the Apostle Paul, who said that "we are saved by hope" (Rom 8.24). He calls the Christians of Rome to be comforted by hope (Rom 12.12), addressing them with words of blessing: "Now the God of hope fill you with all joy and peace in believing, that ye may abound in hope, through the power of the Holy Spirit" (Rom 15.13). Paul includes hope, together with faith and love, in his list of cardinal virtues (1 Cor 13.13) that constitute the essence of Christian faith.

Christianity reveals itself as a religion of hope through the examples of people who encountered Jesus and received the forgiveness of their sins: the sinful woman (Lk 7.36–50), the woman caught in the act of adultery (Jn 8.3–11), the publican (Lk 19.1–9), the thief on the cross (Lk 23.43), and others. In parallel with these real people depicted in the Gospels, the reader also meets a series of characters in parables who encounter God in the same way that

Christ Enthroned, Icon by St Andrei Rublev, 1410

these real people do. Among these characters there are both positive and negative figures; in many situations, however, just as in real life, these characters have good and bad qualities intertwined within them. Neither of the two sons of this parable can be called a completely positive character.

The only completely positive character in the parable is the father. He loves both sons, regardless of their merits or their failings. He loves them with that absolute and unconditional love that only God is capable of extending to his sons and daughters.

9. The Unjust Steward

The last in the fourfold series of parables that we have been examining in the Gospel of Luke is the parable of the unjust steward. It is separated from the parable of the prodigal son by a single phrase: "And he said also unto his disciples" (Lk 16.1). This remark could indicate a change of context, such as we see in the series of parables in the Gospel of Matthew, where the first four parables are told to the people (Mt 13.3–35), while the next three are told to the disciples (Mt 13.36, 44–52). In that case, however, the change of intended audience accompanied a change of place (the first four were told outside, the last three inside a house). In this case, no external change is evident in context.

Moreover, after the parable and its attendant interpretation these words follow: "And the Pharisees also, who were covetous, heard all these things and they derided him" (Lk 16.14). This phrase makes it clear that Jesus told the parable of the unjust steward to the disciples, but the conversation took place within hearing of the Pharisees. Suggestions that the parable was initially told to the large crowd and only later given the form of an address to the disciples alone by the evangelist,[82] or that it was addressed to the opponents of Jesus,[83] have no basis in the text of the Gospel.

Commentators often anazlye this parable in isolation from the parable of the prodigal son. Such commentators pay great attention to the unusual nature of the story and the many possible interpretations of its content, in the process ignoring any possible connection between it and the preceding parable. But such a connection definitely exists. In both parables, the lesser is guilty before the greater, having squandered his property. The fate of the lesser is entirely based on the decision of the greater. The greater shows unexpected condescension to the guilty party. Also, both parables speak of broken trust. According to one scholar, the themes that began in the parable of the prodigal son are further developed in the parable of the unjust steward. These themes include God, sin, mercy, and salvation, and a definite lack of integrity in financial matters.[84] Another scholar argues that the parable of the unjust steward can be considered almost as a continuation of the parable of the prodigal son.[85]

The parable should be analyzed together with the internal commentary provided by Jesus himself:

> There was a certain rich man, which had a steward, and the same was accused unto him that he had wasted his goods. And he called him, and said unto him, "How is it that I hear this of thee? Give an account

---

[82]Jeremias, *Parables*, 47–48.

[83]Dodd, *Parables*, 18; A. T. Cadoux, *The Parables of Jesus: Their Art and Use* (London: Clarke, 1930), 135–37.

[84]Bailey, *Jesus through Middle Eastern Eyes*, 332.

[85]Manson, *The Sayings*, 291.

The Unjust Steward, Jan Leychen, 1791–1826

of thy stewardship; for thou mayest be no longer steward." Then the steward said within himself, "What shall I do? For my lord taketh away from me the stewardship. I cannot dig; to beg I am ashamed. I am resolved what to do, that, when I am put out of the stewardship, they may receive me into their houses." So he called every one of his lord's debtors unto him, and said unto the first, "How much owest thou unto my lord?" And he said, "An hundred measures of oil." And he said unto him, "Take thy bill, and sit down quickly, and write fifty." Then said he to another, "And how much owest thou?" And he said, "An hundred measures of wheat." And he said unto him, "Take thy bill, and write fourscore." And the lord commended the unjust steward, because he had done wisely: for the children of this world are in their generation wiser than the children of light.

And I say unto you, make to yourselves friends of the mammon of unrighteousness, that, when ye fail, they may receive you into everlasting habitations. He that is faithful in that which is least is faithful also in much; and he that is unjust in the least is unjust also in much. If therefore ye have not been faithful in the unrighteous mammon, who will commit to your trust the true riches? And if ye have not been faithful in that which is another man's, who shall give you that which is your own? No servant can serve two masters: for either he will hate the one, and love the other; or else he will hold to the one, and despise the other. Ye cannot serve God and mammon. (Lk 16.1–13)

The text of the parable itself ends with the phrase "he had done wisely." After it follows Jesus' own commentary, in which the theme of riches plays a prominent role. Three times in the Greek text of the Gospel of Luke the word "mammon" is used, which is a direct transliteration of an Aramaic term.[86] But in contrast with its use in the Sermon on the Mount, where the word appears in a teaching on riches, here Jesus uses it in a more complex commentary, in which the theme of riches, though prominent, is not the most important.

What is the main point of the parable, then? Why is a man who acts dishonestly and dishonorably presented as a positive example? And why does the word "mammon," which in Jesus' teaching has such a negative meaning, suddenly appear to have positive connotations?

To answer this question, we must first of all pay attention to the external structure of the parable. Unlike many other parables, in which the characters are described conditionally, partially, with only a few key characteristics, in this case the main character is much more fleshed out. This seemingly excessive detail could make the reader incorrectly assume that the Storyteller wanted to give this story more authenticity. In point of fact, we believe that the detailed characterization of the unjust steward is instead meant to stress the almost fairytale quality of this story. The situation described in the story is wittingly unrealistic. We believe this was the Author's initial intention. By doing this, it is as though he wanted to tell his listeners: you need to learn to act in a way that nearly no one does in real life. The heart of the metaphor, then, is not the principle of similitude, but rather, the principle of opposition, which is emphasized by the epilogue of the parable. The expression "in their generation" indicates the categorical and qualitative difference between the image and the reality it is supposed to make clear. This fact alone makes it clear that the image of the unjust steward should not be interpreted literally.

[86]We have already spoken of this term in Alfeyev, *Jesus Christ: His Life and Teaching*, 2:315–19.

The master of the parable is very rich. This is shown by the amounts owed to him by various parties. The text of the Gospel uses the term *batos* (Hebrew *bat*) to indicate a measure of oil, and the term *koros* (Hebrew *kor*) to indicate a measure of wheat.[87] One hundred measures (*batoi*) of oil is about 900 to 1000 gallons, that is, around 3500 liters. One hundred measures of wheat (*koroi*) is also a massive amount.[88] Such huge debts have a symbolic meaning in the parable, similar to the ten thousand talents in the parable of the two debtors (Mt 18.24). This simply underlines the fact that here any reduction of such a debt would be a significant boon to the debtor.

The Worship of Mammon, Evelyn de Morgan, 1909

The steward in this parable is not a slave, but a freeman who works for wages. His welfare depends entirely on whether or not his master is pleased with his work. His master receives word that the steward has been squandering his property: we do not know whether this information is fair or whether the steward was slandered (the verb *dieblēthē* is the passive form of the verb *diaballō*, which means "to slander," this is where we get the word "devil"). Whatever the case may be, as a result of this report the master fires his steward, while simultaneously demanding that he present a report of his stewardship. The steward is left with no time or space to find a way out of his dilemma.

Nevertheless, he acts quickly and ingeniously. Knowing that he has no chance of presenting his case before his master, he decides to secure possible future employment through the debtors of his former master. The dialogue that he has with himself is similar to such interior dialogues in other parables of Luke's Gospel (Lk 12.17–19, 45; 15.17–19; 18.4–5; 20.13). In this dialogue, he admits to himself that he is incapable of hard physical labor, and he is ashamed to become a beggar. Therefore he decides on cunning: he goes to the various debtors of his former master, as if on behalf

---

[87]Josephus uses the same measures in his *Antiquities of the Jews* 8.2.9; *Works of Josephus*, 215.

[88]Cf. Fitzmeyer, *Luke*, 1100–1101; and Hultgren, *Parables*, 150–51.

of his master (they still think he is employed as a steward) and offers all of
them to write off part of their debt: to some he offers a fifty percent reduction, to some twenty. He returns the original receipts to the debtors and
asks them to provide him with new receipts containing the new amounts.
With each of these debtors, he works without witnesses. Considering the
urgency of his errand, this entire project must have been performed very
quickly. We do not know how many debtors he managed to go to: the parable only mentions two to provide examples.

Commentators interpret the actions of this steward in different ways.
Most consider them unjust and fraudulent, while others consider them
just and fair. A third group consider that Jesus speaks with a measure of
irony.[89] As a rule, these differences are determined from the point of view
that the commentator takes. The large number of different opinions indicates that this is a particularly difficult parable to interpret.

To make this task easier, some suggest that by reducing the debt from
one hundred measures to eighty or fifty, the steward was simply taking out
his lawful commission from the transaction, which in one case would be
twenty-five percent, and in the other, one hundred percent.[90] Yet such an
interpretation contradicts the meaning of the questions that the steward
asks of his master's debtors, i.e., "How much do *you* owe my master?"
These questions reveal that the cunning steward was showing generosity
not at the expense of his own funds, but rather his master's. The receipts
that the debtors were supposed to destroy, now replaced with new ones,
contain only the sum owed by each to the master; nothing is said about
any commission to be paid to the steward.

Against all rational expectations, the master not only does not condemn his steward for his fraudulent behavior, but praises him for acting
intelligently (the adverb *phronimōs* can be translated as either "intelligently" or "cunningly"). Here the parable, as often happens, exceeds the
bounds of historical realism. The master acts in a way that no actual master

---

[89]Dennis J. Ireland, *Stewardship and the Kingdom of God: An Historical, Exegetical, and
Contextual Study of the Parable of the Unjust Steward in Luke 16:1–13* (Leiden: E. J. Brill, 1992),
73–82.
    [90]Fitzmeyer, *Luke*, 1101.

would ever act. The word *kyrios*, which is used to describe the master, also underlines that in this parable he symbolizes God.

In the parable and in its interpretations, the word *adikia* ("untruth," "dishonesty," "unfaithfulness") is constantly used, as well as the adjective derived from it, *adikos*. The antonym of the word is not *dikaios* ("righteous") as might be expected, but *pistos* ("faithful"). Thus, the literal translation of the expression *oikonomos tēs adikias* is "untruthful" or "unfaithful steward."

The key to understanding the meaning of the parable is the following phrase: "Make to yourselves friends of the mammon of unrighteousness." The mammon of unrighteousness here indicates material success—what Jesus considered to be almost an insuperable obstacle for entering the kingdom of heaven. We have already mentioned the words Jesus spoke to the disciples after his conversation with the rich young ruler: "It is easier for a camel to go through the eye of a needle, than for a rich man to enter the kingdom of God" (Mt 19.24). It may seem that these words negate any possibility for rich people to receive heavenly rewards. Yet this parable adds a bit of nuance to an otherwise one-sided argument. Material goods may help someone acquire the friends who will help him secure a place in the eternal mansions.

Thanks to the mention of these mansions, it is possible to see a thematic connection between this parable and the one that follows—the parable of the rich man and Lazarus (Lk 16.19–31). In that parable, we will see a rich man who is condemned not so much for his riches as for failing to help the poor man Lazarus during his life. In the end, the poor man finds himself in the bosom of Abraham—those same eternal mansions—while the rich man finds himself suffering in hell. If the rich man from the parable had shared at least a small percentage of his "mammon of unrighteousness" with Lazarus, it is possible that Lazarus might have become a friend who would have interceded before God for the rich man's sake after death.

As we see from its general context in a series of parables in the Gospel of Luke, the main idea of the parable of the unjust steward is that material wealth does not belong to man; it is the property of God and is only given to man for temporary stewardship. This is forgotten by those who are like the rich fool we discussed above, who say to themselves, "Soul, thou hast much goods laid up for many years; take thine ease, eat, drink, and be merry" (Lk 12.19). Considering themselves to be the rightful owners of their own riches, such people forget that sooner or later they will lose all of it, and at that moment, they will need friends who will welcome them into the eternal mansions. He can only find such friends by giving alms. To share his wealth, to share his money with those who have less and who are in need—this means to live not only for oneself, but to be "rich toward God" (Lk 12.21).

In his commentary on this parable, Cyril of Alexandria stresses that it shows a path to salvation for all rich people:

> For as long as a man lives in wealth and pleasure, he is careless about piety to God. For wealth renders men contemptuous, and sows in the minds of those that possess it the seeds of all voluptuousness. Is there then no way of salvation for the rich, and no means of making them partakers of the hope of the saints? Have they fallen completely from God's grace? Is hell and the fire necessarily prepared for them, such as is the fitting lot of the devil and his angels? Not so: for lo! the Savior has shown them a means of salvation in the present parable. They have been entrusted with worldly wealth by the merciful permission of Almighty God: according nevertheless to his intention they have been appointed stewards for the poor. But they discharge not their stewardship rightly, in that they scatter, so to speak, what has been given them of the Lord; for they waste it solely on their pleasures, and purchase temporal honors. . . . What therefore would Christ have them to do? It is, that while they are yet in this world, if they are unwilling to divide all their wealth among the poor, that at least they should gain friends by a part of it; and numerous witnesses to their charitableness, even those who have received well at their hands: that when their earthly wealth fails them, they may gain a place in their tabernacles. For it is impossible for love of the poor ever to remain unrewarded. Whether therefore a man give away all his wealth, or but a part, he will certainly benefit his soul.[91]

[91]Cyril of Alexandria, *Commentary upon the Gospel of St. Luke*, trans. R. Payne Smith (Oxford: Oxford University Press, 1859), 508–509.

It seems to us that this is the interpretation that best expresses the content of the parable. It also helps us understand these words of Jesus: "If therefore ye have not been faithful in the unrighteous mammon, who will commit to your trust the true riches? And if ye have not been faithful in that which is another man's who shall give you that which is your own?" (Lk 16.11–12). The meaning of these words is the following: if a person on earth has found a way to correctly use that which he received from God, then he will be found worthy of eternal riches. All earthly good things should be acknowledged as belonging to another, even if by earthly standards a person is their rightful owner. First, this is because all such things belong not to him, but to God, but second, because sooner or later he will lose them all.

Another interpretation is offered by a seventh-century writer, Anastasius of Sinai:

The Lord did not say these things giving permission nor giving orders for you to accumulate money from injustice and to give alms out of it; but aware that the whole world is involved in injustice and that almost all the wealth of those who are rich and in positions of government comes from injustice—usury, confiscations, enforced gifts, robberies. That is why he gave utterance to such a saying, so that one might choose the lesser evil by comparison. It is a beautiful act and pleasing to God that one should give alms from one's just and sinless labors and pains. . . . However if it appears that a certain wealth has come to us through some injustice, it is better that what has been accumulated from evil sources be distributed for good purposes, and not that what has come from evil sources should go once more into evil practices, and luxury, and fornication, and drunkenness, and profligacy, and houses with golden ceilings and silken hangings, and all the other deceit of life.[92]

The words "He that is faithful in that which is least is faithful also in much, and he that is unjust in the least is unjust also in much" mean the

---

[92]Anastasios of Sinai, *Questions and Answers*, trans. Joseph A. Munitiz (Turnhout: Brepols Publishers, 2011), 201.

St Anastasius in
the Monastery,
Rembrandt, 1631

same thing: a person who has managed to properly dispose of lesser things, that is, his earthly wealth, will receive heavenly wealth. These words remind us that in another parable the master tells each of his two slaves who properly disposed of their talents: "Well done, thou good and faithful servant: thou hast been faithful over a few things, I will make thee ruler over many things: enter thou into the joy of thy Lord" (Mt 25.21).

In the context of what we have said here, the phrase that Jesus earlier used in the Sermon on the Mount (that a man cannot serve two masters) gathers additional subtext. Mammon exists not so that a person will serve it as though it were his master, but so that a person may dispose of it as the steward disposed of his master's property. Man can create nothing out of nothing. Even if he acquired something by his own labors, this was thanks to the fact that God gave him those abilities, opportunities, and beneficial circumstances. And God expects that man will return at least part of those riches to him through almsgiving.

God calls man to be just as generous to his neighbors as he reveals himself to be toward man. This generosity can refer not only to material wealth: a person is called to share his intellectual, emotional, and spiritual gifts with others. By acting thus, he also models the wise steward who disposed of his master's income in the most beneficial way for himself.

Julian the Apostate used the parable of the unjust steward to accuse Christians of dishonesty.[93] One of the measures that Julian adopted against Christians was denying them admission to pagan places of learning. As Gregory the Theologian recounts, he said that learning and culture, as well as worship of the gods, belonged exclusively to the pagans, while the lot of the Christians was ignorance and crudeness, because there is nothing in Christian wisdom outside of "I believe."[94] In answering this critique of the apostate emperor, Gregory the Theologian used the image of the Egyptian treasures that the Israelites took with them into the desert (Ex 3.21–22). These

St Gregory the Theologian,
Fresco, 14th century

riches are symbolic of pagan learning, which the new Israel (Christians) should not abandon in the hands of the "Egyptians" (the pagans). Christians should instead use them, assimilate them, make them their own, while of course rejecting the worship of idols. As he makes this argument, Gregory references the parable of the unjust steward:

> Borrow from the Egyptians vessels of gold and silver [Ex 11.2]; with these take your journey; supply yourself for the road with the goods of strangers, or rather with your own. . . . What then? Do you come out for nothing and without wages? But why will you leave to the Egyptians

[93]Bailey, *Jesus through Middle Eastern Eyes,* 333.

[94]Gregory the Theologian, *Homily* 4.102 (SC 309:250; see *Julian the Emperor, Containing Gregory Nazianzen's Two Invectives and Libanius' Monody with Julian's Extant Theosophical Works,* trans. C. W. King [London: George Bell and Sons, 1888], 68).

and to the powers of your adversaries that which they have gained by wickedness, and will spend with yet greater wickedness? It does not belong to them: they have ravished it, and have sacrilegiously taken it as plunder from him who says, "The silver is mine and the gold is mine" [Hag 2.8], and I give it to whom I will. Yesterday it was theirs, for it was permitted to be so; today the Master takes it and gives it to you [Mt 20.14], that you may make a good and saving use of it. Let us make to ourselves friends of the Mammon of unrighteousness [Lk 16.9], that when we fail, they may receive us in the time of judgment.[95]

Here the image from the parable is used more broadly—as an indication that man can use any wealth at all to acquire "heavenly riches" (Mt 6:20). In this case, Gregory speaks of intellectual riches. They too, like material riches, are not the property of the person who happens to have them. They are borrowed for a time either from God or from other people thanks to God's good will, and such people are called to dispose of their goods for the benefit of their neighbors.

Other than the thought that man is not the master, but the steward of riches entrusted him by God, the parable contains an indication that all of life is merely a short period of time given to man so that he may prepare to meet the Lord at the final judgment. Like the steward who received notice from his master, every person stands before the real fact of his own mortality, a death that can occur at any moment and after which the judgment will inexorably follow. He should maximize the profits, so to speak, out of the time allotted to him, following the example of the cunning steward. In the space of a few hours, he acquired friends for himself after he shared the wealth of his master with them. In the same way, every person is called to acquire friends with whom he will be able to share his fate in eternity.

In Jesus' parables, people are often depicted as connected to one another based on mutual responsibilities. The fate of one person depends on his relationship with other people and how they, in their turn, relate to him when he finds himself in a crisis. The good Samaritan showed himself to be a true neighbor to the man who was attacked by robbers. We can

---

[95]Gregory the Theologian, *Oration* 45.20 (NPNF[2] 7:430).

safely assume that at the final judgment, the unfortunate man will appear as a witness for the Samaritan's defense. The rich man, however, was not a neighbor to Lazarus, and so that poor man cannot lessen the rich man's sufferings.

Jesus challenges the "sons of light," that is, his disciples, to take the example of the "sons of this generation," but not in the sense of cunning and unrighteousness. There is a degree of humor in Jesus' telling of this story: the swindler, after all, ensures his future prosperity using the precise methods that got him fired in the first place:[96] he was accused of improperly disposing of his master's wealth, and it was exactly through doing that that he now finds new friends. But in fact this character, whose actions have a grotesque element to them, is a symbol of a different kind of action. He symbolizes those who strive to attain to the eternal mansions. A disciple of Jesus is called to care for his own future in heaven, just as the unjust steward took pains to ensure his future on earth.

The verb "to squander" (or "scatter," *diaskorpizō*), used in the parable, reminds us of another phrase of Jesus: "He that is not with me is against me, and he that gathereth not with me scattereth abroad [*skorpizei*]" (Mt 12.30). What seems wasteful in earthly terms becomes acquisition in terms of the kingdom of heaven. The opposite is also true: the person who enriches himself only on earth becomes a pauper at the moment of his death and passes into eternity with nothing. At the final judgment, he will have nothing to justify himself, and no beneficiaries (who have become benefactors) to await him in the eternal mansions.

[96]Tannehill, *Luke*, 247.

10. The Rich Man and Lazarus

Jesus' warning that one cannot serve both God and mammon becomes the connective tissue between the parable of the unjust steward and the parable of the rich man and Lazarus. As we remember, the parable of the unjust steward led the Pharisees to laugh at Jesus (Lk 16.14). Jesus did not immediately respond to that laughter. At first, he rebuked the Pharisees for their superficial righteousness, and then he speaks of the importance of the Mosaic law, as well as the inadmissibility of divorce (Lk 16.15–18), and he briefly repeats what he had already said in the Sermon on the Mount (Mt 5.18, 32) and at other times (Mt 11.12–13, 19.19; Mk 10.11–12). Only after this does he return to the theme of greed and tells his most important parable dedicated to this theme:

> There was a certain rich man, which was clothed in purple and fine linen, and fared sumptuously every day. And there was a certain beggar named Lazarus, which was laid at his gate, full of sores, and desiring to be fed with the crumbs which fell from the rich man's table; moreover the dogs came and licked his sores. And it came to pass, that the beggar died, and was carried by the angels into Abraham's bosom. The rich man also died, and was buried; and in hell he lift up his eyes, being in torments, and seeth Abraham afar off, and Lazarus in his bosom. And he cried and said, "Father Abraham, have mercy on me, and send Lazarus, that he may dip the tip of his finger in water, and cool my tongue; for I am tormented in this flame." But Abraham said, "Son, remember that thou in thy lifetime receivedst thy good things, and likewise Lazarus evil things, but now he is comforted, and thou art tormented. And beside all this, between us and you there is a great gulf fixed, so that they which would pass from hence to you cannot, neither can they pass to us, that would come from thence." Then he said, "I pray thee therefore, father, that thou wouldest send him to my father's house, for I have five brethren, that he may testify unto them, lest they also come into this

*The Parable of
the Rich Man
and Lazarus,*
Codex Aureus
Epternacensis,
1035–44

place of torment." Abraham saith unto him, "They have Moses and the prophets; let them hear them." And he said, "Nay, father Abraham, but if one went unto them from the dead, they will repent." And he said unto him, "If they hear not Moses and the prophets, neither will they be persuaded, though one rose from the dead." (Lk 16.19–31)

The parable begins in the same way as the previous one: at the heart of this story is a rich man. Unlike some other rich men in parables, however, this rich man does not symbolize God. Abraham appears in God's name, and his words symbolize the voice of God to the rich man. This same voice is also addressed to his brothers who are still alive, but through the medium of the Holy Scriptures (Moses and the prophets).

Jesus knowingly uses names and images that are familiar to the primary audience of this parable: the avaricious Pharisees. They proudly said concerning themselves: "We have Abraham to our father," (Mt 3.9) "We are Abraham's seed" (Jn 8.33), "We are Moses' disciples" (Jn 9.28). While rebuking his opponents, Jesus frequently referred to these two Old Testament righteous men, who had an absolute and indisputable authority for the scribes and Pharisees. Yet in his parables, as a rule, he quotes neither of them. This parable is an exception.

Another unique feature of this parable is that one of the characters has a proper name. Usually, the characters in parables remain without proper names: a man, a certain man, a rich man, a master, a steward, a slave, a younger brother, an elder brother, the workers in a vineyard, some virgins, workers, a sower. In this case, the poor man has a name, while the rich man remains without a name. This emphasizes the contrast between these two characters and between their fate after death: it is unlikely that many people knew the poor man's name during his life, while the name of the rich man was universally acknowledged. In eternity, however, the opposite is true.[97]

Some commentators, beginning with Origen,[98] wondered if there may be a connection between the Lazarus of the parable and the Lazarus that Jesus (in the Gospel of John) raised from the dead (Jn 11.1–44, 12.1). Modern scholars offer various opinions on the subject, generally falling into four groups:

1) The name "Lazarus" was added to the Gospel according to Luke at an early stage under the influence of the account of Lazarus' resurrection in Gospel of John;

2) The account of Lazarus' resurrection in the Gospel of John is a theological fantasy based on the final section of the parable of the rich man and Lazarus;

---

[97]We will mention here the most ancient extant manuscript of the Gospel according to Luke (P75), where the rich man has a name, Nevis, while in the Coptic version, his name is Nineves.
[98]Cf. Origen, *Fragments on John* 77 (GCS 10:543–44).

The Rich Man
and Lazarus,
F. A. Bronnikov,
1886

3) The final section of the parable, especially the words about the resurrection of the dead, were added to the original Lucan text under
the influence of the account of Lazarus' resurrection;

4) There is no connection between the two Lazaruses other than the
coincidence of name.

We hold to the fourth point of view; any of the other three requires too
many guesses and extrapolations to prove.

As in other parables, the images of the rich man and Lazarus are
described with some vivid details. The former wears clothing from very
expensive materials—the silks (or fine linens) and purples are referred to
in the Old Testament (Prov 31.22). This clothing symbolizes kingly status
(Gen 41.42; 1 Macc 8.14). Linen was also used as part of the decoration of
the tabernacle and the sewing of priestly garments (Ex 26.1, 28.39). In this
case, linen and purple are synonymous with the most expensive material
that money can buy. This reference, together with the detail that the rich
man feasted every day, are elements that underline the rich man's luxuri-
ous life. The contrast between the rich man and Lazarus is stark: the latter
lay "full of sores" on the ground (*heilkōmenos*, covered with sores), and the
dogs licked his wounds.

The lives of the rich and poor often represent two realities that do not
intersect in any way: each lives in his own world. In this case, however, the
poor man was lying at the gates of the rich man. This means that the rich
man could see him whenever he walked in or out of his home. The poor

An image of Jesus Christ
painted on linen

man, naturally, would never have been allowed to
approach the table of the rich man. Even the crumbs
that fall off the rich man's table were nothing more
than figments of the poor man's imagination.[99]

From the beginning, the parable points to the
invisible mutual connection between the rich man
and Lazarus. The rich man did not feel it at all; for
Lazarus, it was expressed solely in the fact of his
lying at the gates of the rich man. The connection
between their fates becomes clear only after death,
when the rich man sees Lazarus in Abraham's
bosom and recognizes him.

Nothing is said about the poor man's burial after death; all that is mentioned is that he is carried to the bosom of Abraham by the angels. In
contrast, the rich man's funeral is mentioned, but nothing is said about
the presence of angels in his fate after death. The turning point in the fates
of both is their death.

The first act of the story ends with the funeral of the rich man. We can
only guess that it was a grand and opulent event.

The second act begins in hell, where the rich man and Lazarus have
switched roles. Now Lazarus rests in the bosom of Abraham. This expression, absent in earlier Jewish sources, indicates a place where, according
to Jewish belief, the righteous found repose after death. There are hints
of this belief in the Biblical expression "gathered to his people" (Gen 25.8,
17; 35.29; 49.33; Num 27.13; Deut 32.50) and "shall sleep with his fathers"
(1 Kings 1.21, 2.10, 11.21). The Hebrews saw their fate after death only in
terms of the general context of the fate of their nation. Being members of
the chosen nation on earth, they wanted that connection to continue after
death. The assumption was that Israel, as God's chosen nation, would be
preserved in a life after death, where they would be separated from the
Gentiles in the same way that they were on earth.

---

[99]In many ancient manuscripts the word "crumbs" is not present. The text thus reads "desiring to be fed with what fell from the rich man's table."

The Parable of the Rich Man and Lazarus, Gustave Doré, 1891.

Jesus' teaching about life after death subverts the expectations that the bosom of Abraham would be a place set aside for the sons of Israel. To the indignation of the Pharisees, Jesus said that "Many shall come from the east and west, and shall sit down with Abraham, and Isaac, and Jacob, in the kingdom of heaven. But the children of the kingdom shall be cast out into outer darkness; there shall be weeping and gnashing of teeth" (Mt 8.11–12). Sometimes this warning was addressed directly to the audience: "There shall be weeping and gnashing of teeth, when ye shall see Abraham, and Isaac, and Jacob, and all the prophets, in the kingdom of God, and you yourselves thrust out. And they shall come from the east, and from the west, and from the north, and from the south, and shall sit down in the kingdom of God" (Lk 13.28–29). The criterion that separates the sheep from the goats at the dread judgment was not belonging to the chosen nation of Israel, but virtuous deeds (Mt 25.31–46).

The Bosom of Abraham,
Icon, 1830.

The word *kolpoi*, translated as "bosom," is a plural form of the noun *kolpos*, which means "breast." This same noun is used to indicate a mother's breast (or womb) in Greek. The use of this term in the given context, together with the idea that the righteous will "recline" together with Abraham in the kingdom of heaven, corresponds to the pose most often assumed by an intimate friend of the host at dinner, where people did not sit, but reclined. This same term (in the singular) appears in the account of how the favorite disciple of Jesus reclined on his breast at the Last Supper (Jn 13.23).

In the parable, the obscure poor man ends up in the closest intimacy with Abraham himself, the father of the Jewish nation. Together with Abraham, he is reclining at a feast, much as the rich man used to recline at feasts every day while he was still alive. But the rich man finds himself in flames and torment. Just as the poor man used to fantasize about the crumbs falling off the rich man's table, now the rich man begs Abraham to send the poor man to him, to lessen his sufferings. But Abraham announces an inexorable verdict: the rich man had already received all good things during life; he has nothing more to hope for. And he adds words about the unbridgeable abyss between those who are in hell and those in bosom of Abraham.

This abyss opens up at the feet of a person even during his life. The radiance and splendor of a rich life dim the spiritual eyes of a person, obscuring the reality awaiting him after death. It seems to him that his house is built on a firm foundation, that his gates are shut fast, and he can calmly enjoy his life. Only death opens his eyes to the true nature of things. It turns out that his house was built not even on sand. It stood at the edge of an abyss, into which it falls with all it contains.

When Abraham answers the rich man, he uses a gentle word, *teknon* ("child"). By this, he seems to acknowledge that the rich man belongs to his people. In the words of Abraham we can hear compassion and regret; he patiently explains the reasons why the rich man ended up in hell. But he has no power to change the situation: the abyss between hell and the kingdom of heaven was not made by him.

The third act of the story also takes place in the world after death, but it refers to earthly life. Now the conversation no longer concerns the rich man or Lazarus, but the brothers of the rich man, who are still alive and do not suspect that the same fate awaits them as their brother. The followers of the historical-critical school of criticism consider this section of the parable to be a later addition to an original authentic text.[100] Yet their opponents make the case that the hypothesis of the two stages of development of this parable is dubious:

> It is perhaps doubtful whether any two-stage development of the parable should be posited. . . . The theme of "too late" winds through all the portions of the passage, weaving it into a tightly knit unity. The rich man pays attention to Lazarus too late, he sees the unbridgeable chasm too late, he worries about his brothers too late, and he heeds the Law and the prophets too late.[101]

Jesus constantly mentions the "law and prophets." This phrase refers to the Hebrew Scriptures. He dedicates an entire section of the Sermon on the Mount to the theme of the law and the prophets. Jesus triumphantly announced the enduring worth of the Law of Moses at the beginning of the sermon, immediately after the Beatitudes (Mt 5.17–19). After this, however, he criticizes the righteousness of the scribes and Pharisees (Mt 5.20), then he gives his own personal interpretation of some aspects of the Old Testament law (Mt 5.21–47). The Sermon on the Mount includes also a section about almsgiving, which is connected with the theme of heavenly rewards (Mt 6.1–4).

When speaking of the law and the prophets, Jesus reminds us of the many Old Testament admonitions to give alms and care for the poor. Here are merely two of them:

---

[100]Rudolf Bultmann, *History of the Synoptic Tradition,* trans. John Marsh (Oxford: Basil Blackwell, 1963), 196–97; John Dominic Crossan, *In Parables: The Challenge of the Historical Jesus* (Sonoma, CA: Polebridge Press, 1992), 66–67; Scott, *Hear Then,* 142–46.

[101]Blomberg, *Interpreting the Parables,* 257.

If there be among you a poor man of one of thy brethren within any of thy gates in thy land which the Lord thy God giveth thee, thou shalt not harden thine heart, nor shut thine hand from thy poor brother. But thou shalt open thine hand wide unto him, and shalt surely lend him sufficient for his need, in that which he wanteth. Beware that there be not a thought in thy wicked heart, saying, "The seventh year, the year of release, is at hand," and thine eye be evil against thy poor brother, and thou givest him nought, and he cry unto the Lord against thee, and it be sin unto thee. Thou shalt surely give him, and thine heart shall not be grieved when thou givest unto him, because that for this thing the Lord thy God shall bless thee in all thy works, and in all that thou puttest thine hand unto. For the poor shall never cease out of the land. Therefore I command thee, saying, "Thou shalt open thine hand wide unto thy brother, to thy poor, and to thy needy, in thy land." (Deut 15.7–11)

Is it not to deal thy bread to the hungry, and that thou bring the poor that are cast out to thy house? When thou seest the naked, that thou cover him, and that thou hide not thyself from thine own flesh? (Is 58.7)

It is the absence of these virtues, not wealth itself, that becomes the reason for the rich man's condemnation to eternal torments. This is the conclusion that emerges from the context of the parable itself, as well as Jesus' teaching in general. Jesus was very critical of wealth, but as we see in the parable of the unjust steward, he also challenged his listeners to find friends "among unrighteous mammon," so that those who had been helped with alms might then welcome their benefactors into the eternal mansions. Let us not forget that Abraham himself "was very rich in cattle, in silver, and in gold" (Gen 13.2). This wealth, however, not only did not prevent him from entering the kingdom of heaven, or even from standing at the head of the community of the saved, to become a kind of host of the wedding feast in heaven.

N. T. Wright notes that the parable of the rich man and Lazarus is one of many parables where Jesus speaks about repentance. Some aspects of the parable are similar to the parable of the prodigal son. Abraham, who welcomes the poor man into his bosom, reminds the reader of the father who embraces and kisses his son. The five brothers who remain on earth remind one of the elder brother. A resurrection, of sorts, occurs, but they do not see it. It is difficult to disagree with these points. Yet Wright's insistence that the parables do not at all speak about life after death and the final fate of mankind is dubious.[102]

The Bosom of Abraham,
Icon, 19th century

A significant portion of the parable is dedicated to life after death: the second and third acts of the story occur entirely in the world after death. Thus the parable is a call to repentance that must be expressed in specific ways. This challenge is directed at both the rich and the poor, at the disciples of Jesus and his opponents. Yet this teaching about repentance is only fully revealed in light of the reality of life after death, which the parable depicts very vividly and visually.

In the finale of the story, he who will soon rise from the dead makes an appearance. The words that conclude the parable: "neither will they be persuaded, though one rose from the dead," refer to Jesus himself. Once again, as with several other parables, we see Jesus at the epicenter of events. He does not watch people passively from the sidelines; he intervenes in the fate of men, by his death and resurrection he vividly witnesses to the same truths he expressed in his parables about eternal life, for which earthly life must become a training ground.

The parable of the rich man and Lazarus has a long history of commentary among the Fathers of the Church. The most detailed such commentary is a series of seven homilies "On Lazarus," given by John Chrysostom in Antioch in AD 387. The large size of this collection of homilies and the many different themes they touch upon do not allow us to summarize their content completely, or even superficially. We will only point out several important moments that can help us understand how the parable of the

---

[102]Wright, *Jesus and the Victory of God*, 255.

rich man and Lazarus was understood three and a half centuries after it was told.

The most important sin of the rich man, according to Chrysostom, is cruelty and inhumanity:

> He himself has demonstrated that not only did he neglect that man by the gate but he did not give alms to anyone else either. For if he did not give alms to this man who was continually prostrate at his gate, lying before his eyes, whom he had to see every day once or twice or many times as he went in and out, for the man was not lying in the street nor in a hidden or narrow place, but where the rich man whenever he made his entrance or exit was forced unwillingly to see him, if (I say) he did not give alms to this man, who lay in such grievous suffering, and lived in such destitution, or rather for his whole life was troubled by chronic illness of the most serious kind, whom of those he encountered would he ever have been moved to pity? If we suppose that he passed the man by on the first day, he would probably have felt some pity on the second day; if he overlooked him even on that day, he surely ought to have been moved on the third or the fourth or the day after that, even if he were more cruel than the wild beasts. But he felt no such emotion, but became harder-hearted and more reckless even than that unjust judge who knew neither fear of God nor shame before men.[103]

Another sin of the rich man, according to Chrysostom, was that he feasted every day without fear. He was bound by his drunkenness and gluttony as though they were chains, making his soul dead even in life. The vanity of his earthly values and interests become fully obvious when he dies:

> Do not simply pass over that phrase "he was buried," beloved: by it you should understand that the silver-inlaid tables, couches, rugs, tapestries, all other kinds of furnishings, sweet oils, perfumes, large quantities of undiluted wine, great varieties of food, rich dishes, cooks,

---

[103]John Chrysostom, *Homily 1 on the Rich Man and Lazarus*; John Chrysostom, *On Wealth and Poverty*, trans. Catharine P. Roth, PPS 9 (Yonkers, NY: St Vladimir's Seminary Press, 2020), 22–23.

flatterers, body-guards, household servants, and all the rest of his ostentation have been quenched and withered up. Now everything is ashes, all is dust and ashes, dirges and mourning, as no one is able to help any more, nor to bring back the soul that has departed. Then the power of gold is tested, and of all superfluous wealth. From such a crowd of attendants he was led away naked and alone, since he could not take anything with him out of such abundance; but he was led away without any companion or guide. None of those who had attended him, none of those who had assisted him was able to save him from the punishment and retribution; but removed from all those followers, he was taken away alone to endure the unbearable retribution. Truly, "All flesh is as the grass, and all the glory of mankind is as the flower of grass. The grass has withered, and its flower has faded; but the word of the Lord remains forever." Death came and quenched all those luxuries; it took him like a captive and led him, hanging his head low, groaning with shame, unable to speak, trembling, afraid, as if he had enjoyed all that luxury in a dream. Finally the rich man became a suppliant to the poor man and begged from the table of this man who earlier had gone hungry and been exposed to the mouths of dogs. The situation was reversed, and everyone learned who was really the rich man and who was really the poor man, and that Lazarus was the most affluent of all but the other was the poorest of all.[104]

Chrysostom points out that some people are punished for their sins on earth, while others suffer nothing on earth, but receive their full recompense in the other life, and some are punished in both places. Temporal punishments free a person from eternal ones. This is shown by Lazarus' example: if he had done anything evil in this life, the guilt of it was washed away completely in this life and he passed into the next life pure.[105]

The parable of the rich man and Lazarus contains an important moral lesson that has universal value:

---

[104]John Chrysostom, *Homily 2 on the Rich Man and Lazarus* (PPS 9:44–45).
[105]Ibid. (PPS 9:62).

He lies at your entrance, the pearl in the mud, and do you not see him? The physician is at your gate, and do you not accept the treatment? The pilot is in the harbor, and do you endure shipwreck? Do you feed parasites, and do you not feed the poor? This happened in the past, and it happens even now. This is why this story is written, so that those who come later may learn from the events and may not suffer the same disaster as this man did. The poor man lay at the gate, you see: poor outwardly, but rich inwardly. . . . Let the poor hear and not be suffocated by discouragement. Let the rich hear and change from their wickedness. This is why the two images are set before us, the images of wealth and poverty, of cruelty and endurance, of patience and greed, so that when you see a poor man injured and despised, you may not consider him unfortunate; and when you see a rich man adorning himself, you may not consider him fortunate. Run back to the parable. If the shipwreck of thoughts confuses you, rush to the harbor, take comfort from the explanation, think how Lazarus was despised, think how the rich man prospered and enjoyed luxury, and do not let any of the things that happen in life confuse you.[106]

Chrysostom compares earthly life with a play and life after death with what happens after the play ends. Death reveals the true face of every human being.

Both men departed to that place where everything is true. The stage sets were removed and the masks were taken off. In a theater of this world one becomes a philosopher, though he is not a philosopher. Another becomes a king, though he is not a king, but has the appearance of a king for the story. Another becomes a physician without knowing how to handle even a piece of wood, but wearing the garments of a physician. Another becomes a slave, though he is free; another a teacher, though he does not even know his letters. But when evening overtakes them, and the play is ended, and everyone goes out, the masks are cast aside. He who is king inside the theater is found to be a coppersmith outside. The masks are removed, the deceit departs, the truth

[106]John Chrysostom, *Homily 6 on the Rich Man and Lazarus* (PPS 9:99).

The Rich Man
and Lazarus,
Jacobo Bassano,
1550

is revealed. He who is a free man inside the theater is found to be a slave outside. . . . So it is also in life and its end. The present world is a theater, the conditions of men are roles: wealth and poverty, ruler and ruled, and so forth. When this day is cast aside . . . when each person is judged with his works—not each person with his wealth, not each person with his office, not each person with his authority, not each person with his power, but each person with his works, whether he is a ruler or a king, a woman or a man . . . then the truly rich and the truly poor are revealed.[107]

In this commentary, earthly life is a kind of virtual reality in which every person is assigned a specific role to play, and every person wears his own mask.

This image can also be extended to the situation in which the Son of God found himself when he became man. He found himself in the company of the Pharisees and scribes, a world where everyone's roles were strictly assigned, where everyone had his own mask: a mask of prayer to assume when you stop at street corners (Mt 6.5), a sad mask to assume during fasting periods (Mt 6.16). They liked to broaden the hem of their garments, they loved to feast and to be greeted in public and to be called *Teacher! Teacher!* (Mt 23.5–7). In this community of hypocrites, he appeared— without a mask or a role—as an uncompromising radical, ready to stand for the truth even at the cost of his own life.

[107]Ibid. (PPS 9:102).

Poor Lazarus, Paolo Pagani,
18th century

His preaching tore the masks off those who had become accustomed to hiding their true faces; it revealed their inner content, bringing out their spiritual and moral emptiness. Every parable was another strike against Pharisaic pietism, which he denounced sharply and mercilessly. "Ye are they which justify yourselves before men; but God knoweth your hearts: for that which is highly esteemed among men is abomination in the sight of God" (Lk 16.15). This is what he said to the Pharisees, and they did not know how to answer him.

In the Pharisaic theater of the absurd, Jesus was a foreign body, like a person who comes out on the stage, stops the show, and begins to call everyone in the theater to repentance. The audience was divided in two by this preaching: some responded with sympathy, but others were only filled with sadness and irritation, because the play had stopped while they were invested in the familiar script. As for the group of actors themselves, so to speak, with one voice they attacked the one who destroyed all the rules of the genre, deciding to take away the actors' livelihood (after all, they were being paid to inhabit those roles that they played on stage) and to pull off their masks.

They had forgotten that for each of them, the play was bound to end, and from the virtual reality of earthly life, they would have to pass into a different reality, one where the point of view is inverted, where the rich man becomes a pauper, while the poor man reclines in the bosom of Abraham. Jesus constantly reminded them of this reality through his parables.

11. The Unprofitable Servant

Continuing his account of Jesus' final journey to Jerusalem, the evangelist Luke records how the disciples turned to him with a request: "Increase our faith." Jesus' answer is given by the other two synoptic evangelists in different contexts: "If ye had faith as a grain of mustard seed, ye might say unto this sycamine tree, 'Be thou plucked up by the root, and be thou planted in the sea,' and it should obey you" (Lk 17.5–6). In Matthew and Mark's accounts, Jesus speaks not of a tree, but of a mountain: "If ye have faith as a grain of mustard seed, ye shall say unto this mountain, 'Remove hence to yonder place,' and it shall remove; and nothing shall be impossible unto you" (Mt 17.20) In Mark's account, these words form part of the episode of the withering fig tree. In Matthew, they are a part of Jesus' dialogue with the disciples after he cast the demon out of a possessed boy; then Jesus repeats them in Matthew's account of the withering of the fig tree as well.

Thus, according to the synoptic Gospels, Jesus spoke the same hyperbolic aphorism in three different places, thereby illustrating an idea that forms the basis of much of his preaching: faith is capable of performing miracles. This image firmly lodged itself in the imagination of early Christians. We find hints of it in the Apostle Paul's words: "Though I have . . . all knowledge, and though I have all faith, so that I could remove mountains, and have not charity, I am nothing" (1 Cor 13.2).

In the Gospel according to Luke, what immediately follows this aphorism on faith is a short teaching that at first glance seems to have little to do with faith:

> But which of you, having a servant plowing or feeding cattle, will say unto him by and by, when he is come from the field, "Go and sit down to meat," and will not rather say unto him, "Make ready wherewith I may sup, and gird thyself, and serve me, till I have eaten and drunken, and afterward thou shalt eat and drink"? Doth he thank that servant

*Jesus Christ
Sends the
Apostles to
Preach*, Fresco,
12th century

because he did the things that were commanded him? I trow not. So
likewise ye, when ye shall have done all those things which are commanded you, say, "We are unprofitable servants: we have done that
which was our duty to do." (Lk 17.7–10)

This short teaching lacks several characteristic elements of the parable
genre. It does not begin with the usual introduction, such as "There was a
certain rich man," (Lk 16.1) or "A certain man had two sons" (Mt 21.28), or
"Behold, a sower went forth to sow" (Mt 13.3). It does not contain questions like "Unto what is the kingdom of God like? And whereunto shall
I resemble it?" (Lk 13.18) or declarative statements that the kingdom of
heaven is like some particular image or example (Mt 13.24, 31, 33, 44, 45,
47). There is no plot, there are no characters; there is only a situation taken
from daily life. If we use Origen's classification,[108] this is not a parable, but
a simile.

Nevertheless, many scholars include this in their list of parables because
it uses a comparison in figurative language. The question "who among
you," as we have seen above, begins two other parables: the parable of

---

[108]Origen, *Commentary on the Gospel of Matthew* 10.4 (SC 162:152–54; ANF 9:415–416).

the tower builder (Lk 14.28) and the lost sheep (Mt 12.11; Lk 15.4). It also begins certain other teachings that do not have the parable form (Mt 6.27; Lk 12.24; Jn 8.7, 46).

Some scholars believe that the teaching was addressed to the Pharisees[109] or the people,[110] although in the text of the Gospel of Luke, it follows a question asked by the disciples. It is possible that, as often happened, a conversation between the disciples and Jesus took place in the presence of many other people, and having answered the question, Jesus could then have turned to the crowd. As far as we can tell, not one of the disciples belonged to a social class that could afford to have a slave work the fields. But among Jesus' listeners at large, there probably were many people who had at least one servant.[111]

The scene Jesus describes is typical of the society in which he lived and preached. As we have said before, in this age slavery had reached its widest spread in the Roman empire. Not a single teaching of Jesus contests the institution of slavery, just as he never contested other aspects of the social-political structures of that empire. As a reformer of human souls, Jesus was not in the business of reforming social institutions, neither did he offer recommendations about societal reorganization.

When speaking with the Jews, Jesus said, "Verily, verily, I say unto you, whosoever committeth sin is the servant of sin. And the servant abideth not in the house for ever, but the Son abideth forever. If the Son therefore shall make you free, ye shall be free indeed" (Jn 8.34–36). Thus Jesus introduces a teaching that views slavery as spiritual bondage to sin and freedom as liberation from sin. The Apostle Paul develops this in greater detail:

Know ye not, that to whom ye yield yourselves servants to obey, his servants ye are to whom ye obey: whether of sin unto death, or of obedience unto righteousness? But God be thanked, that ye were the servants of sin, but ye have obeyed from the heart that form of doctrine

[109]Jeremias, *Parables*, 193.

[110]P. A. Minear, "A Note on Luke 17:7–10," *Journal of Biblical Literature* 93 (1974): 82–87, at 84.

[111]Kenneth E. Bailey, *Through Peasant Eyes: More Lucan Parables, Their Culture and Style* (Grand Rapids, MI: William B. Eerdmans Publishing Company, 1980), 114–15.

Christ and the Pharisees, K. V. Lebedev, 19th century

which was delivered you. Being then made free from sin, ye became the servants of righteousness. (Rom 6.16–18)

Paul believed that freedom is better than slavery, but higher than all he placed freedom in Christ: "Art thou called being a servant? Care not for it, but if thou mayest be made free, use it rather. For he that is called in the Lord, being a servant, is the Lord's freeman; likewise also he that is called, being free, is Christ's servant" (1 Cor 7.21–22). As he told slaves to be submissive to their masters (Eph 6.5–7), Paul stressed that in the Church there is neither slave, nor freeman, but all are "one in Christ Jesus" (Gal 3.28). Most of his Epistle to Philemon is dedicated to the fate of Onesimus, who, judging by the letter, was Philemon's slave and had become "useless" to him (evidently, he ran away), but he became useful to Paul in his bondage. Together with the letter, Paul returned the slave to his master, but he asked that he "receive him forever, not now as a servant, but above a servant, a brother beloved" (Philem 1.15–16).

In the fourth century, when John Chrysostom pondered the existence of slavery, he insisted that it was not instituted by God: "When God formed man, he did not make him a slave, but free. He made Adam and Eve, and both were free." As for the question of how slavery started, he said,

> The race of men drifted off course, passed beyond the proper limits of desire, and were carried away with licentiousness.[112]

Slavery came about as a result of sin and iniquity. And true slavery is slavery to sin, just as the only true freedom is freedom from sin:

> What is a slave? It is a mere name. How many masters lie drunken on their beds, while slaves stand by sober? Whom shall I call a slave? The one who is sober, or the one who is drunk? The one who is the slave of a man, or the one who is the captive of passion? The former has his slavery on the outside; the latter wears his captivity on the inside.[113]

The parable of the unprofitable servant could be interpreted as an allegory of slavery itself. At first glance, it seems to justify the slave's hard labor: the one who worked all day in the fields or herding cattle must serve his master before he himself can sit down to eat; moreover, he is not due even normal human gratitude. Judging by the fact that the same slave must both herd cattle and serve his master at table, his master is not a rich landowner, since he only has one slave in his service.

In our opinion, however, this story should indeed be considered a parable, because it uses one example from daily life to illustrate a completely different idea. The theme of this parable is not slavery at all, nor is it agricultural labor, nor is it serving at table, nor is it gratitude. The most important theme is man's relationship to God. The image of the slave who serves his master at table is only necessary because it demonstrates that man cannot take credit for fulfilling God's commands.

Judging by the description, this slave is useful to his master because he fulfills various functions. At the same time, having done everything that is required of them, the disciples must still acknowledge themselves to be "unprofitable servants." This is the meaning of the term *achreioi*, translated as "unprofitable" (or sometimes as "worthless"). The overall logic of the

---

[112]John Chrysostom, *Homily 6 on the Rich Man and Lazarus* (PPS 9:104–105).
[113]Ibid. (PPS 9:107).

parable is thus strengthened by the principle of comparison *a fortiori*: the slave does not expect gratitude, even if he is useful, and so we not only should not take any credit or expect any gratitude, but we should also acknowledge ourselves to be worthless and useless.

By asking the question, "Who among you," Jesus forces the listener to imagine himself in the place of the master. By the end of the story, however, the focal point shifts to the slave, with whom the listener must identify. This switch of focus occurs thanks to the verbal formula "so likewise ye," which helps lead the listeners to the point of the parable.

This teaching is dedicated to a quality that Jesus speaks of constantly: humility. The theme is present in the Sermon on the Mount, when Jesus speaks of the blessedness of those who are poor in spirit (Mt 5.3), putting humility in the first place among the other virtues. Jesus said of himself: "Learn of me, for I am meek and lowly in heart" (Mt 11.29). He also constantly speaks of his complete obedience to the Father (Jn 6.38).

The image of the slave was applied to Jesus at the earliest stages of the Church's existence. According to St Paul, he "made himself of no reputation, and took upon him the form of a servant, and was made in the likeness of men, and being found in fashion as a man, he humbled himself, and became obedient unto death, even the death of the cross" (Phil 2.7–8). These words inspired a series of commentaries among the early Church Fathers, in which the service of the Son of God is compared to a slave's service.[114]

The parable teaches that all people are slaves before God. Any difference in social status refers only to human interactions, not one's relationship to God, before whom all are equal. The phrase "servant of God" became part of the language of the Church at a very early stage and is preserved to this day. To a modern ear it may sound degrading, but its original meaning was quite the opposite—it underlined those qualities that a slave must have: humility, obedience, and faithfulness.

The slave is a symbol of those qualities. Slave labor, in this parable, symbolizes the fulfillment of God's commandments, for which a person should not expect thanks. Considering that this teaching follows immediately after the apostles' request to increase their faith, we can also interpret this

[114]G. W. H. Lampe, *A Patristic Greek Lexicon* (Oxford: Clarendon, 1961), 385.

parable as a lesson about faith: if you are humble and do not take credit for anything you do, this will help increase your faith.

The teaching about the unprofitable servant can be read as a prelude to the parable of the publican and the Pharisee, because the Pharisee takes credit for all his virtues (Lk 18.11–12). It is also an introduction to the difficult parable of the workers in the vineyard, where every worker receives a reward not according to his labor, but according to God's mercy alone (Mt 20.1–16). We will now analyze these two parables.

12. The Publican and the Pharisee

In the liturgical calendar of the Orthodox Church, the Sunday of the Publican and Pharisee precedes the Sunday of the Prodigal Son. In the Gospel of Luke, however, the parable of the publican and the Pharisee follows it, divided by two chapters of text. There is a certain logic to putting these two parables together. Both are built on the principle of opposing two functionally similar images. On the one hand, the Pharisee and the elder brother personify Pharisaic piety, on the other hand, the publican and the younger son symbolize repentance. It is no coincidence that the Church, when it was still working out the details of the liturgical calendar, saw the similarity between the two parables and placed them in the same part of the liturgical year—the preparatory period to Great Lent. In the Gospel of Luke, they are even placed in a single chronological interval: Jesus' final journey to Jerusalem.

Three events precede the telling of the parable: the healing of the ten lepers (Lk 17.11–19), the teaching on the second coming (Lk 17.20–37), and the parable of the persistent widow (Lk 18.1–8). According to the Gospel of Luke, the parable of the publican and the Pharisee is the last in a series of parables that Jesus told on the way to Jerusalem. It is the only parable in which a Pharisee[115] plays a significant role:

[115]Concerning Pharisees, see, in particular, Hilarion Alfeyev, *Jesus Christ: His Life and Teaching*, 1:468–69.

And he spake this parable unto certain which trusted in themselves that they were righteous, and despised others: "Two men went up into the temple to pray: the one a Pharisee, and the other a publican. The Pharisee stood and prayed thus with himself, 'God, I thank thee, that I am not as other men are, extortioners, unjust, adulterers, or even as this publican. I fast twice in the week; I give tithes of all that I possess.' And the publican, standing afar off, would not lift up so much as his eyes unto heaven, but smote upon his breast, saying, 'God be merciful to me a sinner.' I tell you, this man went down to his house justified rather than the other: for everyone that exalteth himself shall be abased; and he that humbleth himself shall be exalted." (Lk 18.9–14)

The primary audience of this parable are the Pharisees. It is they who considered themselves righteous and took credit for their virtues. The Pharisees loved to pray, but they did it ostentatiously, for which Jesus harshly criticized them in the Sermon on the Mount. In that same sermon, he counseled his disciples on the proper way to pray—not publicly, but secretly, and not like the pagans in wordiness (Mt 6.5–8). The parable of the publican and the Pharisee is an illustration of these words.

The action of the story occurs in the temple of Jerusalem, the only place that could be described by the term *to hieron* (literally "the holy place"). The restored temple that was in large part rebuilt by Herod the Great was an impressive architectural complex that included both interior and exterior elements. From the southern side, one entered the temple through a double door, beyond which stood the Court of the Gentiles, the only place admissible to pagans. Beyond this outdoor square was a covered courtyard called the Court of the Women. All Jews could enter here, including women, but no pagans were allowed. Only ritually purified men could enter the Court of Israel; only priests could enter into the Court of the Priests; and only the high priest could enter the holy of holies inside the sanctuary, and that only once a year. The Pharisees, then, prayed in the Court of Israel, as close as possible to the sacrificial altar.[116]

[116]"Temple" entry, subsection "1.3 The Temple of Herod," in Joel B. Green, I. Howard Marshall and Scot McKnight, eds, *Dictionary of Jesus and the Gospels: A Compendium of Contemporary Biblical Scholarship*, 2nd ed. (Downers Grove, IL: InterVarsity Press, 2013).

We do not know where the publican prayed—it is possible he entered into the Court of Israel. He stood far away from the Pharisee, but close enough for the Pharisee to notice him.

Vivid details stress the contrast between the two characters of the parable. The Pharisee stood close to the altar, the publican far away from it. The Pharisee evidently prayed with his eyes lifted up, as was customary; the publican did not dare lift his eyes to heaven. The Pharisee stood straight and did not move (suggested by the adverb *statheis*, "having stood up," that is, standing unmoving). The publican prayed and struck himself on the chest. The prayer of the Pharisee was rational; the prayer of the publican was emotional. The Pharisee's prayer was long, listing his virtues, but not repeating himself. The publican repeated the same short prayer over and over again. The Pharisee prayed quietly (*pros heauton*, literally "to himself"); the publican prayed aloud (*legōn*, "speaking"). The Pharisee could watch the publican, see his movements, and probably hear his voice; the publican did not watch the Pharisee and probably did not even notice him. The Pharisee was focused on himself; the publican was focused on God.

Pointing out the universal Jewish custom of praying aloud, one scholar insists that the Pharisee followed the custom, and the expression *pros heauton* should be understood as "with himself." By praying aloud, the Pharisee was advertising his virtues, turning his prayers into an instructive lesson for everyone else.[117] Such a reading is certainly possible, though it does not come directly from the context of the parable.

We will note that the expression *ho pharisaios statheis pros heauton tauta prosēycheto* does allow for at least three different translations, depending on what *pros heauton* modifies—what preceded it or what follows it, and, furthermore, the expression *pros heauton* can be understood in different ways:

1) "having stood, he prayed to himself, saying"
2) "having stood by himself, he prayed, saying"
3) "having stood, he prayed concerning himself, saying"[118]

---

[117]Bailey, *Jesus through Middle Eastern Eyes*, 347.
[118]Hultgren, *Parables*, 122.

The Publican and the Pharisee, Tucco, 1886, 1894

In the eyes of the Pharisee, the publican represented a category of people who deserved total contempt. Publicans collected taxes for the Roman authorities: this alone made them hateful in the eyes of faithful Jews. For the Pharisee, the publican was synonymous with "sinner." We note that the expression "publicans and sinners" (Mt 9.10; Mk 2.15; Lk 15.1), which appears in the Gospels, is not a phrase invented by the evangelists. They took it from the vocabulary of the scribes and Pharisees (Mt 9.11; Mk 2.16; Lk 5.30). This was a widely used phrase, similar to other semantic pairs that Jesus used, such as "publicans and harlots" (Mt 21.31–32), "Gentile and publican" (Mt 18.17). The publicans, harlots, and Gentiles were roughly all on the same level for a right-believing Jew, that is, the lowest possible level of the social ladder.

John Chrysostom expresses the way Pharisees related to publicans in the following words:

Tell me, who is worse than the publican? He is a dealer in the misfortunes of others. He is a participant in unnatural toils. Although the publican does not experience labor, he participates in the profit; consequently, his sin is the worst. For the publican is none other than a plain extortioner, sin incarnate, and the epitome of all greediness. What is worse than a publican who sits by the roadside and gathers the fruits of someone else's labor, and when it is the season for toil does not care at all, and when the profit is from things he did not toil to obtain, takes his share?[119]

The prayer of the Pharisee corresponds to the form of other prayers typical of the Jewish tradition (scholars note the presence of similar prayers in Talmudic literature).[120] It began with thanksgiving to God, as is appropriate for the prayer of a righteous man. Yet this gratitude in the

[119]Chrysostom, *Homilies on Repentance* 2.5.26 (PG 49:290; FOC 96:25–26).
[120]Jeremias, *Parables*, 142; Manson, *The Sayings*, 311.

first phrase of the prayer is immediately connected to his condemnation of other people: the Pharisee sees nothing positive in them, they are "thieves, offenders, adulterers." As an example of the sort of people the Pharisee distances himself from, he offers the publican who caught his eye, standing afar off. He knows nothing about that man other than that he is a publican; consequently, he is deserving of contempt, just like all the other categories of people he already mentioned.

Then the Pharisee lists his own merits, among which he includes fasting twice a week (which means total abstinence from food from sunrise to sunset, presumably on Mondays and Thursdays).[121] Then he takes credit for strictly following the law concerning tithing, which is listed in the book of Deuteronomy in the following terms:

> Thou shalt truly tithe all the increase of thy seed, that the field bringeth forth year by year. And thou shalt eat before the Lord thy God, in the place which he shall choose to place his name there, the tithe of thy corn, of thy wine, and of thine oil, and the firstlings of thy herds and of thy flocks, that thou mayest learn to fear the Lord thy God always. (Deut 14.22–23)

It is possible that the Pharisee puts special emphasis on "all that I possess"; in other words, he gives a tithe not only of the things that the law requires, but even including things the law makes no mention of.

In the parable, the Pharisee is first of all a symbol of pride. The Apostle Paul, who himself was a Pharisee before his conversion, described Pharisaic pride in one of his letters: "If any other man thinketh that he hath whereof he might trust in the flesh, I more: circumcised the eighth day, of the stock of Israel, of the tribe of Benjamin, an Hebrew of the Hebrews as touching the law, a Pharisee; concerning zeal, persecuting the church; touching the righteousness which is the law, blameless" (Phil 3.4–6).

The Pharisee of the parable is similar to Paul's description. Following all the dictates of the law, and even more than the law, leading an ascetic life (fasting twice a week is not part of the law), the Pharisee was sure of

---

[121]*Didache* 8.1.

The Publican and the Pharisee, Gustave Doré, 1865

his own blamelessness, which so clearly separated him from all the others. John Chrysostom wrote:

> Scripture says that the Pharisee and the publican went up into the temple to pray, and the Pharisee began to enumerate his virtues. He said, "I am not sinful like the whole world, nor like this publican."
>
> O you miserable and wretched soul, you condemned the entire world! Why did you also afflict your neighbor? The world was insufficient for you. Surely you do not mean to say that you condemned even the publican? In this manner, you slandered everyone and did not grieve for a single human being. "I am not like the rest of the world, nor

like this publican. I fast twice a week. I give a tithe of all my possessions to the poor." He made false pretensions. You wretched man, so be it, you condemned the whole world.[122]

The publican, on the contrary, is a symbol of humility. He personifies that inner disposition that Isaiah expresses in these words: "The heaven is my throne, and the earth is my footstool: where is the house that ye build unto me? And where is the place of my rest? . . . But to this man will I look, even to him that is poor and of a contrite spirit, and trembleth at my word" (Is 66.1–2). Those who heard the parable could have easily recognized Isaiah's description in the image of the publican. He is one of those who are poor in spirit, whose blessedness Jesus speaks of in the Sermon on the Mount (Mt 5.3). Once again we will quote Chrysostom:

> Therefore, how did the publican answer? As he heard these things, he did not say, "Who are you to tell me such things? From what source did you learn of my life? You did not keep company with me. You did not live with me. We did not spend time together. Why are you so haughty? Who witnesses your beneficence? Why do you praise yourself? Why do you indulge yourself?" The publican said nothing like this. However, bowing, he worshipped and said, "God have mercy upon me a sinner."
>
> By being humble, the publican became righteous. The Pharisee descended from the temple utterly deprived of righteousness; and the publican came down having acquired righteousness. Words prevailed over deeds. For the Pharisee totally ruined the righteousness of his deeds, and the publican acquired righteousness with the word of humility.[123]

We should note that Chrysostom somewhat ignores the effect produced by both men's prayers. According to the Gospel, each of the two went home after visiting the temple, but one of them was "justified rather than the other." Nothing is said about one being condemned, the other justified; all we hear about is various stages of justification. It is possible

---

[122]Chrystosom, *Homilies on Repentance* 2.4 (PG 49:289; FOC 96:24).

[123]Chrysostom, *Homilies on Repentance* 2.4.24–25 (PG 49:290; FOC 96:25).

that the less harsh formulation of the parable is intended to underline that God accepts all prayer, though the prayer of the humble is more pleasing to him.

The prayer of the publican—"God, be merciful to me, a sinner!"—became one of the favorite prayers of the early Church. It became a common practice for both monks and laypeople, along with other short prayers, including the Jesus Prayer, which started to be widely practiced in the fifth century. The Jesus Prayer—"Lord, Jesus Christ, Son of God, have mercy on me, the sinner"—has obvious similarities with the prayer of the publican and likely used that prayer as a model.

We should also note than in contrast to the Pharisee, the publican says nothing of himself in the prayer, other than that he is a sinner (*hamartolos*). Calling himself by that name, the publican confesses his sinfulness, not considering it necessary to list out all his sins as the Pharisee listed his virtues. A confession of one's own sinfulness is the all-encompassing sense that justified the publican in the eyes of God.

The parable ends with a short aphorism: "for every one that exalteth himself shall be abased; and he that humbleth himself shall be exalted." In the Gospel of Luke, Jesus speaks the same words at a meal in the house of one of the leaders of the Pharisees, when Jesus noticed that those called to the meal chose the best places at table (Lk 14.7–11). In the Gospel according to Matthew, these same words occur in Jesus' teaching addressed to the people and to his disciples (Mt 23.12). One of the most important themes of this teaching is his accusation of the hypocrisy and sanctimoniousness of the scribes and Pharisees. Thus, this phrase appears in three separate events in the two Gospels of Matthew and Luke, which suggests it is one of the most characteristic expressions of Jesus, summarizing the essence of his teaching.

The main idea of the parable can be summarized in several simple phrases:

1) God looks not at the merits of a human being, but at his heart;

2) A sacrifice to God is a contrite spirit; God will not despise a heart that is contrite and humble (see Ps 50.19);

3) Every person is sinful in the eyes of God; confessing one's own sinfulness with repentance justifies a man more before God than the works of the law (Rom 3.28);

4) A person cannot take credit for any virtues, no matter how worthy they may be in and of themselves;

5) Man's salvation does not depend on the sum of his merits, but on the mercy of God.

This last theme links the parable of the publican and the Pharisee in Luke and the parable of the workers in the vineyard in Matthew.

13. The Laborers in the Vineyard

In the Gospel according to Matthew, this parable is preceded by an episode in which Peter asks Jesus, "Behold, we have forsaken all, and followed thee; what shall we have therefore?" Jesus answered that the twelve apostles, "in the regeneration . . . [ye] shall sit upon twelve thrones, judging the twelve tribes of Israel." He adds that anyone who forsakes anything for his sake "shall receive an hundredfold, and shall inherit everlasting life" (Mt 19.27–30). In the Gospel of Luke, this takes place soon after the parable of the publican and the Pharisee (Lk 18.28–30). In Matthew, Luke, and Mark (Mk 10.28–30), this dialogue occurs before Jesus' entry into Jerusalem.

In Matthew and Mark's versions, the episode ends with the following words: "But many that are first shall be last; and the last shall be first" (Mt 19.30; Mk 10.31). These words in Matthew connect Jesus' answer to Peter's question with the parable of the workers in the vineyard. The connection is further underlined by the usage of the conjunction "for" (*gar*), and also by the repetition of a similar phrase at the end of the parable:

For the kingdom of heaven is like unto a man that is a householder, which went out early in the morning to hire laborers into his vine-

*The Parable of
the Workers in
the Vineyard,*
Patrick de Wet,
mid-17th century

yard. And when he had agreed with the laborers for a penny a day, he sent them into his vineyard. And he went out about the third hour, and saw others standing idle in the marketplace, and said unto them, "Go ye also into the vineyard, and whatsoever is right I will give you." And they went their way. Again he went out about the sixth and ninth hour, and did likewise. And about the eleventh hour he went out, and found others standing idle, and saith unto them, "Why stand ye here all the day idle?" They say unto him, "Because no man hath hired us." He saith unto them, "Go ye also into the vineyard, and whatsoever is right, that shall ye receive." So when even was come, the lord of the vineyard saith unto his steward, "Call the laborers, and give them their hire, beginning from the last unto the first." And when they came that were hired about the eleventh hour, they received every man a penny. But when the first came, they supposed that they should have received more; and they likewise received every man a penny. And when they had received it, they murmured against the goodman of the house, saying, "These last have wrought but one hour, and thou hast made them equal unto us, which have borne the burden and heat of the day." But he answered one of them, and said, "Friend, I do thee no wrong. Didst not thou agree with me for a penny? Take what thine is, and go thy way. I will give unto this last, even as unto thee. Is it not lawful for me to do what I will with mine own? Is thine eye evil, because I am good?" So the last shall be first, and the first last: for many be called, but few chosen. (Mt 20.1–16)

In the most authoritative manuscripts, the phrase about many being called and few chosen is missing.[124] It is believed to have been taken from another parable—those called to the bridal feast, where it provides the moral lesson at the end of the parable (Mt 22.14).[125] In this parable, the summary phrase is "the last shall be first, and the first last," which forms a thematic arc with the analogous phrase that occurs directly before the parable. These words are also found in two other synoptic Gospels (Mk 10.31; Lk 13.30).

The main character of the parable in the original Greek text is called a "master of the house." The term *oikodespotēs* indicates a man who owns a piece of land with a vineyard on it. Winemaking was one of the most important parts of agriculture, since wine (which was, as a rule, not heavily alcoholic and was diluted with water before consumption) was the main drink given at table. To take care of a vineyard and collect grapes, day laborers were generally hired. A denarius—a Roman silver coin—was the usual wage for a full day (sunrise to sunset) of working in the vineyard.

The parable draws a picture that fully reflects a real-life situation typical of Palestine at that time. The general level of unemployment was high, and many people who wanted to earn a denarius would stand outside in central places hoping to get hired (a picture that is familiar in many places in our time as well, including in the Middle East). On the other hand, many farmers who did not have enough hired help had to constantly go to market throughout the day in search of more workers. The need for such day laborers grew especially high during the autumn period of harvest.[126]

The first time the master of the vineyard goes looking for workers is early in the morning, that is, around six o'clock in the morning by our

---

[124]See *Novum Testamentum graece*, 28th rev. ed.

[125]Nevertheless, even in the fourth century, the phrase's appearance in this parable was considered canonical. Cf. John Chrysostom, *Homilies on the Gospel of Matthew* 64.3 (PG 58:612; NPNF¹ 10:393–94).

[126]Craig S. Keener, *The Gospel of Matthew: A Socio-Rhetorical Commentary* (Grand Rapids, MI: William B. Eerdmans Publishing Company, 1999), 481–82.

reckoning. Then he comes out four more times, at nine, noon, three in the afternoon, and five in the afternoon. Scholars have tried to find many different natural explanations for the master's behavior. For example, they point out that the work had a deadline, because the harvest needed to be finished by the rainy season,[127] or they argue that the master's subsequent trips were intended to find cheaper labor.[128] But the end of the parable clearly contradicts such a reading.

The actions of the master of the vineyard cannot be explained by historical realism, and that is one of the most important thematic elements of the parable. If hiring workers at nine in the morning or even near midday can be explained by a great need for additional labor, his subsequent choice to continue hiring people even at the eleventh hour does not follow any norms of common sense or economic expedience. By the time he is speaking to the final group of hired workers, the listener is very much aware that this is not a typical master of a vineyard, but a person whose actions are motivated by non-financial considerations.

The parable mentions only that the first group of workers is hired for a specific amount of money. All the other groups are promised that they will receive "whatsoever is right." They could easily have assumed it would have been less than a denarius. The exchange with the workers who had stood all day without working almost seems to be a charitable act, since hiring them could hardly have any practical use. Evidently, the master simply felt sorry for them. He promises them nothing, only saying, "Go ye also into the vineyard." (The words present in the KJV about receiving "whatsoever is right" are absent in most ancient manuscripts;[129] they are believed to have been added later to provide an analogy to what the master said when he hired the workers of the third hour.)

As in other parables, the most important event occurs at the climax. The master calls his steward and commands him to pay all the workers, starting with those called last. To their surprise, they, who only worked an hour, receive a full day's wage. But so do all the others, including those

---

[127]Jeremias, *Parables*, 136.
[128]Herzog, *Parables*, 85–86.
[129]See *Novum Testamentum graece*, 28th rev. ed.

The Parable of the Workers in the Vineyard, Rembrandt, 1637

who had spent the entire day enduring the hardship of outdoor work in a hot climate. Their surprise is transformed to anger, because they cannot understand why they did not receive more than the rest.

The workers' reaction is totally realistic; it is the behavior of the master that goes beyond all realism. Not only does he pay everyone the same wage, but he also justifies himself before those who rebuke him in his unfairness. His explanation is directed to one of the workers, probably the one who complained the loudest. The master addresses him with the word *hetairos*, which is a gentle word in Greek that can be translated either as "friend" or "fellow traveler" or even "beloved."

The primary meaning of the parable is that God does not act toward us as we act toward each other. The laws of fair recompense for labor do not apply to God. The way God establishes his own relationship with humankind does not fit within the bounds of human logic. Market considerations may be possible in human society, but they are impossible in the relationship of God and humanity. You cannot make a deal with God, and his reward is never proportionate to your efforts.

Jesus tells his parables and sermons in a context of constant and ever-increasing antagonism between him and the Pharisees. They could easily have recognized themselves in the image of the workers who had labored

The Savior of Svenigorod,
St Andrei Rublev, 1410s

from early morning. And they sincerely did not understand why Jesus preferred publicans and harlots—who came to Jesus without any merits and still immediately received his blessing—to them, in spite of the fact that they labored day and night to acquire righteousness and goodwill in the eyes of God. Simon the Pharisee's response to Jesus' interaction with the sinful woman who had anointed his feet with precious myrrh reminds us of the complaining workers in the parable, while Jesus' words to the Pharisees, which seem to justify his actions, are similar even in tone to the words of the master of the vineyard (Lk 7.37–47).

The image of the master of the vineyard makes it obvious that this parable was told to the Pharisees. The image of the vineyard symbolizes the chosen nation in the Old Testament (Is 5.1–7; Jer 12.10). Jesus plays upon the same symbolic resonance in the parable of the wicked tenants (Mt 21.33–46; Mk 12.1–12; Lk 20.9–19). In the parable of the laborers in the vineyard, the same symbolism acts as a reminder that the parable is told directly to the Pharisees. In the general context of the history of Israel, it can also indicate that this people, having been called to faith in the one true God from the beginning, will receive its reward if it preserves this faith; but those who were called much later will receive no less a reward in the kingdom of heaven (this is the most important point of the parable). This is how Cyril of Alexandria reads it. He considered that those who were called from the first to the ninth hour symbolize various eras of ancient Israel, while those who came at the eleventh house are those called by Christ himself to salvation.[130]

Another widely held interpretation is that the times of calling symbolize those who come to faith at different ages of life. John Chrysostom writes:

---

[130]Cyril of Alexandria, *Fragments* 226 (TU 61:229–30).

Wherefore then was this parable thus composed? What is its object to effect? To render more earnest them that are converted and become better men in extreme old age, and not to allow them to suppose they have a less portion. . . . But wherefore can it have been that he did not hire all at once? As far as concerned him, he did hire all; but if all did not hearken at once, the difference was made by the disposition of them that were called. For this cause, some are called early in the morning, some at the third hour, some at the sixth, some at the ninth, some at the eleventh, when they would obey. . . . From everything then it is manifest to us, that the parable is spoken with reference to them who from earliest youth, and those who in old age and more tardily, lay hold on virtue; to the former, that they may not be proud, neither reproach those called at the eleventh hour; to the latter, that they may learn that it is possible even in a short time to recover all. For since he had been speaking about earnestness, and the casting away of riches, and contempt of all one's possessions, but this needed much vigor of mind and youthful ardor; in order to kindle in them a fire of love, and to give vigor to their will, he shows that it is possible even for men coming later to receive the hire of the whole day.[131]

The catechetical sermon that is read in all Orthodox churches on Pascha night is also attributed to St John Chrysostom. It is woven together with allusions to various Gospel parables, and the majority of these allusions refer to the parable of the workers in the vineyard:

If any man be devout and love God, let him enjoy this fair and radiant triumphal feast. If any man be a wise servant, let him rejoicing enter into the joy of his Lord. If any have labored long in fasting, let him now receive his recompense. If any have wrought from the first hour, let him today receive his just reward. If any have come at the third hour, let him with thankfulness keep the feast. If any have arrived at the sixth hour, let him have no misgivings; because he shall in nowise be deprived thereof. If any have delayed until the ninth hour, let him draw near,

[131]John Chrysostom, *Homilies on the Gospel of Matthew* 64.3–4 (NPNF[1] 10:394–95).

fearing nothing. If any have tarried even until the eleventh hour, let him, also, be not alarmed at his tardiness; for the Lord, who is jealous of his honor, will accept the last even as the first; he gives rest unto him who comes at the eleventh hour, even as unto him who has wrought from the first hour. And he shows mercy upon the last, and cares for the first; and to the one he gives, and upon the other he bestows gifts. And he both accepts the deeds, and welcomes the intention, and honors the acts and praises the offering. Wherefore, enter you all into the joy of your Lord; and receive your reward, both the first, and likewise the second. You rich and poor together, hold high festival. You sober and you heedless, honor the day. Rejoice today, both you who have fasted and you who have disregarded the fast.[132]

Thus, even minimal efforts, or even a good intention, are put on an equal footing with prolonged labors. The Paschal triumph in this text is painted as a participation in a feast of faith, which God prepared for all mankind. All, no matter whether they fasted before Pascha or not, are called to this feast. "The table is full-laden; feast ye all sumptuously. The calf is fatted; let no one go hungry away. Enjoy ye all the feast of faith: Receive ye all the riches of loving-kindness. Let no one bewail his poverty, for the universal kingdom has been revealed. Let no one weep for his iniquities, for pardon has shone forth from the grave."[133]

The celebration of Pascha on earth becomes a foreshadowing of the universal kingdom—the same kingdom of heaven that Jesus preached in his parables. In this kingdom, the laws of earthly fairness do not apply. Only a single law applies—the law of divine love. By his love, God embraces all people that come to him. God loves every person regardless of his spiritual state or whether or not he managed to accomplish much good during his life.

Maximus the Confessor poses the following question in *Questions and Doubts*: "What is the parable, in the Gospel, of the hired workers in the vineyard and what is the seeming inequality?" He answers this question

The Resurrection of Christ, Icon, 15th century

by applying the parable to different amounts of time spent by different persons in monastic life:

> Often, there is someone who has had seventy years in the monastic life and another who has had a single day. But since the aim of the profession is that having pulled away from the passionate attachment and attitude toward material things one may transfer one's entire soul to God, and the one who had seventy years died without having striven completely for such detachment, whereas the other, who had one day, because he drew away all his passionate thought (*dianoia*) from material things and placed it completely in the bosom of God, died perfected (*eteleiōthē*). And so, in the disbursal [that occurs] during the judgment, one of them receives the wage worthily as he has completed the aim

of the profession, while the other receives according to grace, and only because he endured the toil of *askesis*.[134]

Yet the equal pay that the workers received does not mean that everyone will be equal in the kingdom of heaven. Jesus constantly reminded his readers that there will be many mansions in the kingdom (Jn 14.2), that there are greater and lesser in the kingdom (Mt 11.11). The eastern Church Fathers taught that those who enter the kingdom of heaven will find themselves in different degrees of nearness to God, depending on each person's ability to contain the light of the divinity. But these different stages do not constitute a hierarchal inequality between the saved; for each, his personal degree of communion with God will be the greatest possible:

> The Saviour calls the *many mansions* of his Father's house the noetic levels of those who dwell in that land, that is, the distinctions of the gifts and the spiritual degrees which they noetically take delight in, as well as the diversity of the ranks of the gifts. But by this he did not mean that each person [yonder] will be confined in his existence by a separate spatial dwelling and by the manifest distinguishing mark of the diverse placement of each man's abode. Rather, it resembles how each one of us derives a unique benefit from this visible sun through a single enjoyment of it common to all, each according to the clarity of his eyesight and the ability of his pupils to contain the sun's constant effusion of light. . . . For, in the same manner, those who at the appointed time will be deemed worthy of that realm will dwell in one abode which will not be divided into a multitude of separate parts. . . .
>
> He whose measure is less will not see the great measure of his neighbour's rank, lest [he should think that] this arises from the multitude of his neighbour's gifts and the fewness of his own, and this very thing should become for him a cause of sadness and mental anguish. Far be it that one should suppose such a thing to occur in that realm of

---

[134]Maximus the Confessor, *Questions and Doubts* 127 (CCSG 10:93–94; *St. Maximus the Confessor's Questions and Doubts*, trans. Despina D. Prassas [DeKalb, IL: Northern Illinois University Press, 2010], 109–10).

delights! Each man inwardly takes delight in the gift and the lofty rank whereof he has been deemed worthy.[135]

Such an interpretation shows that in the kingdom of heaven, all earthly assumptions of God as a righteous judge who gives to each according to his deeds or sins, will be transcended. Moreover, all feelings that darken interpersonal relationships will also disappear, among them envy, which is so vividly expressed in this parable. In the parable of the prodigal son, the elder son plays the same role as the workers who toiled from early morning, since he cannot understand the actions of a father who forgives his younger son and who arranges a feast for him. And just as in this parable of the laborers in the vineyard, the master explains his behavior to those who complain to him, so also the father justifies his actions before his elder son as expressing goodness and mercy (Lk 15.25–32).

From one parable to the next, from one sermon to another, Jesus continues the theme of God's unutterable love for mankind. It is a love that does not fit into human categories or assumptions about justice, rewards, and retribution. One modern commentator sees in this parable "a striking picture of the divine generosity which gives without regard to the measures of strict justice."[136] Thirteen centuries before him, another commentator wrote that God's dealings with people cannot possibly be expressed in the terminology of fairness, justice, or retribution. This understanding, according to Isaac the Syrian, is completely rejected by the parables of the workers in the vineyard and the prodigal son, but even more so by the redemptive sacrifice of Jesus Christ himself. Instead of repaying people for their sins, he died for them on the cross.[137]

The contrast between divine and human logic is underlined by the words with which the master of the house concludes his conversation with the complaining workers: "Is thine eye evil [*ponēros*], because I am good [*agathos*]?" Here there is a strong contrast drawn between evil—whose source and primary expression is the evil one, the devil—and good, whose

---

[135]Isaac the Syrian, Homily 6 (HTM trans., 172–73).
[136]Dodd, *Parables*, 94–95.
[137]Isaac the Syrian, Homily 51 (*The Ascetical Homilies*, 387).

source is God himself. Man, as in many other parables, finds himself at the division between the two extremes. Jesus invites his listeners to think about the goodness of God, and being inspired by such thoughts, to emulate God in his mercy and love. He also insistently warns his listeners against every manifestation of human envy, whose source is the devil.

It is also necessary to note that immediately after this parable, Matthew recounts one of Jesus' prophecies of his death and resurrection (Mt 20.17–19), followed by the account of the mother of the sons of Zebedee asking him, on behalf of her sons, to seat them at his right and left hand in the kingdom. When the rest of the disciples heard this, they "were moved with indignation against the two brethren." But Jesus spoke to them all and said, "Ye know that the princes of the Gentiles exercise dominion over them, and they that are great exercise authority upon them. But it shall not be so among you: but whosoever will be great among you, let him be your minister, and whosoever will be chief among you, let him be your servant" (Mt 20.26–27).

The similarity between this episode and the parable of the laborers in the vineyard is quite obvious. Both describe human envy. In the first case, the workers complained to the master because of his generosity, and in the second, the disciples grew angry at the brothers for their brazenness. In both places, Jesus speaks of those who are first: in the first case, those who are first will be last, and in the second, those who are first will become the slaves of all. We see how the parable's teaching almost immediately extended to a real-world example involving the disciples of Jesus himself.

This lesson that they learned concluded with these words: "the Son of Man came not to be ministered unto, but to minister, and to give his life a ransom for many" (Mt 20.28). These words forge a thematic connection between four different accounts that follow each other: the dialogue with Peter, the parable of the laborers in the vineyard, the prophecy of Jesus' impending death, and the account of the wife of Zebedee interceding for her sons (Mt 19.27–20.28). In the first case, Jesus promises his disciples that the Son of Man will sit on the throne of his glory, and they will sit on the thrones of the twelve tribes of Israel; in the last, two brothers seek to secure the best seats in this council of twelve. But Jesus' answer concerns the cup from which he will soon drink, and the baptism that he is about to be baptized with. Evidently, Jesus and his disciples are speaking different languages: they are still thinking of primacy, glory, and honor. He sees before him the cup of suffering and his impending death "as a ransom for many."

The parable of the workers in the vineyard puts in very sharp relief the question of what is necessary for salvation: one's own works or God's mercy? Christian theology, beginning with the times of the apostles, always sought to strike a balance between these two extremes. The Apostle Paul insisted that "man is not justified by the works of the law, but

The Harlot from Jericho and the Two Spies, Tucco, 1902

by the faith of Jesus Christ, even we have believed in Jesus Christ, that we might be justified by the faith of Christ, and not by the works of the law: for by the works of the law shall no flesh be justified" (Gal 2.16). The Apostle James, in contrast, stresses that faith cannot save a person unless it is accompanied by works:

> What doth it profit, my brethren, though a man say he hath faith, and have not works? Can faith save him? If a brother or sister be naked, and destitute of daily food, and one of you say unto them, "Depart in peace, be ye warmed and filled," notwithstanding ye give them not those things which are needful to the body; what doth it profit? Even so faith, if it hath not works, is dead, being alone. Thou believest that there is one God; thou doest well: the devils also believe, and tremble. But wilt thou know, O vain man, that faith without works is dead? Was not Abraham our father justified by works, when he had offered Isaac his son upon the altar? Seest thou how faith wrought with his works, and by works was faith made perfect? And the Scripture was fulfilled which saith, "Abraham believed God, and it was imputed unto him for righteousness," and he was called the friend of God. Ye see then how that by works a man is justified, and not by faith only. Likewise also was not Rahab the harlot justified by works, when she had received the

Joshua has Mercy on the Harlot Rahab, Gustave Doré, 1902

messengers, and had sent them out another way? For as the body without the spirit is dead, so faith without works is dead also. (Jas 2.14–17, 19–26)

In apostolic times, the argument primarily concerned salvation through faith in Jesus Christ and the fulfillment of the works of the law, that is, the requirements of the law of Moses, which continued to hold significance for members of some communities, while losing all relevance for others. It was for this reason that Paul accused Peter and other disciples of hypocrisy and of walking "not uprightly according to the truth of Gospel" when they first ate together with the Gentiles, but later in the presence of the Jewish members of the community they "withdrew and separated [themselves]" (Gal 2.11–15). Paul's famous assertion that man is justified by faith in Jesus Christ, not by blindly following Old Testament customs and rules, came out of this specific context.

Many centuries later, in the polemic between Catholics and Protestants, this issue broadened considerably. It no longer concerned the relationship between faith in Jesus Christ and the fulfillment of the dictates of the Old Testament law, but instead, it became an argument about the relationship, in general, between human righteousness and the redemptive sacrifice of Jesus. In the broadest terms, one can summarize the arguments in the following way.

In the Middle Ages, the Catholic Church developed a doctrine concerning the need for a certain number of good deeds that each person must perform for salvation to be possible. These works were credited as "merits" to each human being. This teaching about the need for merits to attain salvation was often expressed in a formal, even juridical, manner. For example, the saints were thought to have surpassed their "quota" of good deeds, and so they could share their merits with others who did not have so many. The combined store of the merits of all the saints, including the most holy Virgin, comprised a kind of treasury of merit (*thesaurus meritorum*), and the pope alone could distribute merits from this treasury to whomever he wished. Whoever did not have enough personal merits could use the treasure house of merits to "pay off his debt" before God's justice. This became the reason for the practice of the sale of indulgences.

Protestantism, in the person of Martin Luther and other reformers, offered a counter-proposal to this deviation from the original Christian teaching. They suggested that no personal merits of any human being could possibly intercede before the justice of God, since both justification and redemp-

Martin Luther, Lucas Cranach the elder, 1526

tion were accomplished once and for all by Jesus Christ. As proof of this position, the Lutherans quoted the Apostle Paul's words concerning salvation through faith in Jesus, not because of some collection of good deeds. Finally, the juridical nature of Catholic doctrine concerning salvation led the Protestants to formulate a teaching that completely diminished the role of one's personal efforts in acquiring salvation.

Orthodox tradition, as expressed by the Fathers of the Eastern Church, is and always has been far from both of these extremes. It has always underlined that without faith in Jesus Christ and without the Church, salvation is impossible. At the same time, each individual person's participation in his own salvation cannot simply be reduced to passive assimilation of the fruits of the redemptive sacrifice of Jesus Christ. People are fellow-laborers of God (1 Cor 3.9), and this common work (*synergeia*; "synergy" or "cooperation") between God and man is necessary for anyone to approach God and become worthy of the kingdom of heaven.

It may seem that the parable of the workers in the vineyard also diminishes the importance, significance, and duration of personal efforts toward salvation, putting an accent on God's good will, mercy, and his readiness to reward each person equally, with no reference to how much that person worked. Such a literal reading of the parable, however, can easily lead one to a mistaken interpretation of the reason why this parable was told in the first place.

Doubtless, God, who is bound by no obligation before mankind, can reward each person not according to his merits or even according to justice, but according to his own mercy and love alone. At the same time, the workers in the parable are in no way presented as passive recipients of God's gifts. They all work: some work more, some less. They are all fellow laborers in God's vineyard. Each of them, having worked, receives a reward for that work, but not for idleness and sloth. In the parable of the talents, which we will examine soon, those who put their money to work are rewarded, while the one who buried his talent in the earth is condemned (Mt 25.14–30). This means that God expects every human being to struggle actively for virtue. If that were not so, Jesus would not have said to his disciples, "Let your light so shine before men, that they may see your good works, and glorify your Father which is in heaven" (Mt 5.16).

At the same time, a person must not simply trust in his own strength, talents, good deeds, or merits. When people accomplish what God commanded, they must humbly say, "We are unprofitable servants: we have done that which was our duty to do" (Lk 17.10). No amount of good works or merits can by themselves, because of some kind of legal necessity, accomplish man's redemption, justification, or salvation. Only God can pass judgment on each person's fate in eternity, his place in the Father's mansions in the kingdom of heaven. God is absolutely unconstrained in this decision; this is the main idea of the parable of the laborers in the vineyard.

Chapter 5

PARABLES TOLD IN JERUSALEM

I n this chapter, we will examine the parables that Jesus told in Jerusalem in the final days of his earthly life. There are six such parables in the Gospel according to Matthew, and they can be divided into two groups of three. The first group includes the parables of the two sons, the wicked tenants, and the wedding feast (Mt 21.28–22.14). The second group includes the parables of the wise servant, the ten virgins, and the talents (Mt 24.45–25.30). In the Gospel of Mark, only one parable comes from his time in Jerusalem: the expectation of the return of the master (Mk 13.32–37). In Luke's account, Jesus tells no parables in Jerusalem.

Of the six parables in Matthew, one (the wise servant) we already examined together with its telling in the Gospel of Luke. Thus, we have five parables left to examine in the Gospel of Matthew, and one in the Gospel of Mark.

1. The Two Sons

The first group of three parables is often examined as a single composition in the critical literature.[1] This compositional unity is, as a rule, ascribed to the editing hand of Matthew.[2] According to some scholars, he

---

[1]Wesley G. Olmstead, *Matthew's Trilogy of Parables: The Nation, the Nations and the Reader in Matthew 21:28–22:14* (Cambridge: Cambridge University Press, 2003), 22–46.

[2]S. van Tilborg, *The Jewish Leaders in Matthew* (Leiden: Brill, 1972), 49.

systematically used the triadic structure when organizing his text to help his readers better assimilate the information.[3]

As in other, similar cases, such scholarly assertions are largely speculative, as though intentionally ignoring the possibility that Jesus himself could have told the parables in the order in which they appear in the Gospel. Indeed, there is no good reason to ignore such a possibility. The fact that Jesus frequently told several parables in a row is further confirmed by multiple examples of this pattern in the Gospels. The most obvious of these is the sermon on the boat, which in Matthew's account includes four parables, after which Jesus told another three parables in a house where the disciples were present (Mt 13). There are no good reasons to believe that Matthew, or the other disciples, failed to accurately reproduce not only individual portions of Jesus' direct speech, but entire thematic blocks as well, in which the connection between the individual parts of the text are formed not by the editor's pen, but by the personal will of Jesus, who structured his teachings in a specific and intentional manner.

All three parables form part of a larger sermon given in the temple of Jerusalem. He delivered this sermon in the final days of his earthly life, and it has a single theme: the relationship of the chosen Israelite nation to God, his commands, and to the Son of God whom he sent. This teaching cannot be examined outside the context of Jesus' polemic with the spiritual elite of Israel, to whom this sermon is primarily addressed. Each of the three parables adds its own element to the polemic.

The teaching follows after Jesus' triumphant entry into Jerusalem (Mt 21.1–11), the casting out of the merchants from the temple (Mt 21.12–17), and the cursing of the fig tree (Mt 21.18–22). The question by the chief priests and elders leads to this sermon: "By what authority do you do these things?" As Jesus often did, he answered their question with a question: "The baptism of John, whence was it? From heaven, or of men?" (Mt 21.25). When the chief priests and elders refuse to answer, Jesus, in turn, refuses to answer the question they asked about his authority.

---

[3]W. D. Davies and Dale C. Allison, *A Critical and Exegetical Commentary on the Gospel according to Saint Matthew*, vol. 1 (London: T & T Clarke, 1988), 70.

Continuing to speak, Jesus then tells the first of three parables. He offers an interpretation in a subsequent exchange with the chief priests and elders:

> But what think ye? A certain man had two sons; and he came to the first, and said, "Son, go work today in my vineyard." He answered and said, "I will not," but afterward he repented, and went. And he came to the second, and said likewise. And he answered and said, "I go, sir," and went not. Which of the two did the will of his father? They say unto him, "The first." Jesus saith unto them, "Verily I say unto you, that the publicans and the harlots go into the kingdom of God before you. For John came unto you in the way of righteousness, and ye believed him not, but the publicans and the harlots believed him; and ye, when ye had seen it, repented not afterward, that ye might believe him." (Mt 21.28–32)

As in the parable of the laborers, the setting is a vineyard; this means that once again Jesus is speaking of the fate of Israel. Since this parable includes an interpretation, the meaning behind the contrast between the two brothers is easy to understand. It illustrates the difference between the chief priests and elders with whom Jesus is speaking, on the one hand, and the publicans and harlots on the other. The first son (not necessarily the elder) symbolizes the latter; the second son symbolizes the former.

The image of John the Baptist connects the dialogue that precedes the parable with the parable itself. As we see in the end of the parable, however, in both cases, he plays a secondary role. The reaction of the chief priests and elders to John's preaching is only important insofar as it precedes a similar reaction to Jesus' own preaching. John called his listeners to repentance; sinners answered the call, while those who considered themselves already righteous did not. In the same way, those who respond to Jesus' preaching are not at all those who seem to be righteous on the surface while "within [they] are full of hypocrisy and iniquity" (Mt 23.28).

The word "later" (*hysteron*) used at the beginning of the parable, and then again in its interpretations, indicates a certain transformation in the

St John the Baptist,
Icon, 14th century

consciousness of one of the two main characters. The first son initially refused, then later, having repented (*metamelētheis*, literally, "having changed his mind"),[4] went to work. The second, on the contrary, first agreed, but then later did not go. When John the Baptist came, the elders and chief priests did not believe him, while the publicans and harlots did. The first division of the faithful and the unfaithful was, however, not final: the first still had the opportunity to believe "later," when they saw that the sinners had also believed. But this did not occur; they availed themselves neither of the first, nor of the second opportunity.

In the Gospel according to Luke, Jesus says the following: "Among those that are born of women there is not a greater prophet than John the Baptist, but he that is least in the kingdom of God is greater than he" (Lk 7.28). These words do appear in Matthew's account (11.11), but only in Luke are they accompanied by a further clarification, which is similar to the parable of the two sons: "And all the people that heard him, and the publicans, justified God, being baptized with the baptism of John. But the Pharisees and lawyers rejected the counsel of God against themselves, being not baptized of him" (Lk 7.29–30). In both cases, Jesus speaks of God's will, which the spiritual leaders of Israel rejected, because they had not believed in what John the Baptist preached.

John's preaching was a call to repentance. In the Greek, the understanding of repentance (*metanoia*) and remorse (*metameleia*) both have the prefix "meta-," which points to transformation, change. To repent means to change your mind, your manner of thinking, to transform your life. This prefix divides a person's life into two stages: before and after. The word "later" has the same purpose in the parable. It is a turning point between what preceded God's call and what followed it.

[4]Matthew is the only evangelist who uses this participle, which comes from the word *metamelomai* (to repent). The second time he used it with reference to Judas (Mt 27.3). Cf. Guy D. Nave, *The Role and Function of Repentance in Luke-Acts* (Leiden: Brill, 2002), 135.

John's preaching was only a prelude to the preaching and ministry of Jesus. It was through Jesus that the nation of Israel heard the divine call that each person must individually respond to. As with John the Baptist's preaching, however, those who responded to Jesus' call were not those who seemed to be righteous in their own eyes or in the eyes of those who surrounded them.

St John the Baptist,
Icon, 15th century

The expression "the way of righteousness" deserves special attention. In the Greek text of the Gospel according to Matthew, the term *dikaiosynē*, which corresponds to the Hebrew *tsedaqa*, occurs seven times. The English translation is "righteousness." We first encounter this term in Jesus' answer to John the Baptist's words when he tried to stop Jesus from approaching baptism: "Suffer it to be so now: for thus it becometh us to fulfill all righteousness" (Mt 3.15). The term appears in the Sermon on the Mount five times, including twice in the Beatitudes: "Blessed are they which do hunger and thirst after righteousness: for they shall be filled. . . . Blessed are they which are persecuted for righteousness' sake: for theirs is the kingdom of heaven" (Mt 5.6, 10). Later, Jesus says, "Except your righteousness shall exceed the righteousness of the scribes and Pharisees, ye shall in no case enter into the kingdom of heaven" (Mt 5.20). In the next chapter, he says, "But seek ye first the kingdom of God, and his righteousness; and all these things shall be added unto you" (Mt 6.33). Finally, the last time we find this term in Matthew is in the parable we are now discussing.

Thus, outside the Sermon on the Mount, the term occurs only twice in Matthew, and both times it occurs together with a mention of John the Baptist. Is this a coincidence or a pattern? In our opinion, there is such a consistent pattern in Matthew, even if it was not intentional. In the first of these two cases, Jesus speaks to John about the need to fulfill all righteousness, meaning the mission laid upon him and John by God the Father. In the latter case, John is said to have traveled the way of righteousness. Thus, a clear connection is made between God's plan and its accomplishment in action, between the call to undertake the mission and the mission's accomplishment. Righteousness describes the way that John the Baptist lived and the way in which every disciple of Jesus is called to walk. He must hunger and thirst after that righteousness, and not be afraid to suffer for its sake.

Thrice in the Sermon on the Mount the term "righteousness" accompanies the expression "kingdom of heaven," which Jesus and John both used in their preaching. This also seems to be no coincidence. The way of righteousness is a path that leads to the kingdom of heaven. Yet Jesus stresses that what he speaks of is not superficial righteousness; the righteousness he requires is radically different from the righteousness of the scribes and Pharisees. It is completely other than the sort of righteousness that consists in fulfilling a certain number of external moral rules. It is the righteousness of God, and man must be ready, if required, to lay down his life for its sake, as the Son of God himself did.

The righteousness that Jesus preaches assumes a complete conformity between one's inner and outer realities, between words and deeds. The second son, who personified the chief priests and Pharisees, responded to God's call only with words, but did not fulfill that call in action. The first son, on the contrary, fulfilled the will of the father and went to work in the vineyard. The accent is placed on action, on practice, not only on faith.[5] This is the difference between the parable of the two sons and the parable of the laborers in the vineyard. In the latter, Jesus places the emphasis not so much on active work as on the saving grace of God that rewards man, as it seems, without any direct reference to the degree of his righteousness or the amount of his efforts.

Commentators have often seen an opposition between Gentiles and Jews in this parable. John Chrysostom, for example, believed that in this parable, "these two children declare what came to pass with respect to both the Gentiles and the Jews. For the former not having undertaken to obey, neither having become hearers of the law, showed forth their obedience in their works; and the latter having said, 'All that the Lord shall speak, we will do, and will hearken' (Ex 19.8) in their works were disobedient. And for this reason, let me add, that they might not think the law would benefit

[5]Olmstead, *Matthew's Trilogy*, 103.

them, he shows that this self-same thing condemns them, as Paul also says, 'Not the hearers of the law are just before God, but the doers of the law shall be justified' (Rom 2.13)."[6]

John the Baptist,
Icon, 14th century

Such a reading is completely valid, if only because Jesus frequently offered the Gentiles as models of emulation for the Jews. In this case, however, Jesus offers not Gentiles, but publicans and harlots, which are two types of people that the Jews despised the most: the publicans because they worked for the invaders and collected taxes for them, and the harlots because they led a publicly sinful life.

When speaking of the fact that the publicans and harlots would enter the kingdom of heaven before the chief priests and Pharisees, Jesus did not mean *all* publicans and harlots. As he later clarifies, he only spoke of those who answered the call of John the Baptist's preaching and who repented and changed their way of life. It is repentance that erases one's previous way of life and blots out one's past guilt before God.

This understanding formed the basis of the Christian teaching on repentance as the expression of a person's free will, born of his desire to change his way of life completely. If a person offers sincere repentance, his sins are forgiven, no matter their severity or quantity. At any moment, if he wants, a person can begin a new life. It is never too late to come to work in the Lord's vineyard, even if someone has come to God at the twilight of his earthly days, like the workers hired at the eleventh hour (Mt 20.6–9), or even if such a person has spent his entire life in sin up to that moment, like the sinful woman who anointed the feet of Jesus (Lk 7.37–47) and the repentant good thief (Lk 23.40–43).

The expression "publicans and harlots," moreover, is a kind of generalization: it should not be understood to be limited only to members of those groups. Publicans and harlots are only examples of those kinds of men and women who lived in sin, but then embraced repentance.

[6]John Chrysostom, *Homilies on the Gospel of Matthew* 67.2 (NPNF[1] 10:411).

The chief priests and Pharisees were extremely offended to hear Jesus offer them the moral examples of publicans and harlots. But this was Jesus' teaching, which he persistently and consistently developed from one parable to another. Even considering all the many interpretations that are possible, each new parable in which Jesus' opponents heard a harsh rejection of their assumptions about righteousness made them increasingly intransigent in their opposition to him. The parable of the wicked tenants, which follows the parable of the two sons, completely fits the logical sequence of the growing conflict between Jesus and the Jewish leaders, which was to lead to an imminent and violent end.

2. The Wicked Tenants

Of the three parables in the first trilogy, the second parable depicts the Jews' opposition to Jesus and his mission in the starkest terms. In his own interpretation of the parable, Jesus openly says that the kingdom of heaven will be taken away from the people who reject the Son of God:

> There was a certain householder, which planted a vineyard, and hedged it round about, and digged a winepress in it, and built a tower, and let it out to husbandmen, and went into a far country. And when the time of the fruit drew near, he sent his servants to the husbandmen, that they might receive the fruits of it. And the husbandmen took his servants, and beat one, and killed another, and stoned another. Again, he sent other servants more than the first, and they did unto them likewise. But last of all he sent unto them his son, saying, "They will reverence my son." But when the husbandmen saw the son, they said among themselves, "This is the heir: come, let us kill him, and let us seize on his inheritance." And they caught him, and cast him out of the vineyard, and slew him. When the lord therefore of the vineyard cometh, what will he do unto those husbandmen? They say unto him, "He will miserably destroy those wicked men, and will let out his vineyard unto other husbandmen,

which shall render him the fruits in their seasons." Jesus saith unto them, "Did ye never read in the scriptures, 'The stone which the builders rejected, the same is become the head of the corner: this is the Lord's doing, and it is marvelous in our eyes'? Therefore say I unto you, the kingdom of God shall be taken from you, and given to a nation bringing forth the fruits thereof. And whosoever shall fall on this stone shall be broken; but on whomsoever it shall fall, it will grind him to powder." And when the chief priests and Pharisees had heard his parables, they perceived that he spake of them. But when they sought to lay hands on him, they feared the multitude, because they took him for a prophet. (Mt 21.33–46)

The Parable of the Wicked Tenants, Sir John Everett Millais, engraving, 1864

In the Gospels of Mark and Luke, this parable is slightly different (Mk 12.1–12; Lk 20.9–19). In Matthew's version, the master of the vineyard at first sends not many slaves to the husbandmen, but a single servant: the workers beat him and send him away with nothing. Then, he sends them another one, whom they also beat and insult. According to Mark, the third was killed, and "many others: beating some, and killing some" (Mk 12.5). According to Luke, the third slave was wounded and cast out. Then, the master sends his own beloved son. They seize him, take him out of the vineyard, and kill him (Luke's version agrees with Matthew's; in Mark's version, they first kill him, then cast his body out of the vineyard). Again, in Luke's version, Jesus does not wait for the answer to the question of what the master will do, but himself offers the answer: "He shall come and destroy these husbandmen, and shall give the vineyard to others." Jesus' listeners respond, "God forbid" (Lk 20.16). Then Jesus speaks of the stone that the builders rejected, and in Mark and Luke's account, this concludes the telling. His words about the kingdom being taken away from the Jews to be given to another nation are absent in Mark and Luke. But both of these evangelists agree with Matthew in that the listeners recognized themselves in the characters of the parable.

Matthew's version, in this case, is the fullest both in the telling of the parable and in its interpretation. It is in this version that we see the source of the teaching that modern liberal critics call replacement theology (or supersessionism), meaning that the Church, as it were, replaced or superseded the nation of Israel. But the Apostle Paul offered a different contrast: the Israel of God (Gal 6.16) as opposed to the Israel of the flesh (1 Cor 10.18), that is, the nation of Israel. This concept appears in the works of the patristic tradition, including works written as polemics specifically against Jews. Modern western theology—both Protestant and post-Vatican II Catholic—has seen in this "replacement theology" signs of antisemitism, and has consequently rejected it completely.[7] From the point of view of the Orthodox Church, however, the teaching of the New Israel has no antisemitic subtext, just as one cannot call the writings of the fathers who engaged in polemics with Judaism antisemitic.

The understanding of the Church as the New Israel constitutes an integral part of church tradition and comes from Jesus himself in this parable, but only if you do not consider these words—"the kingdom of God shall be taken from you, and given to a nation bringing forth the fruits thereof"—as an editorial addition. Attempts to do exactly this continued throughout the twentieth century. Summarizing these attempts, one modern scholar notes that it is nearly impossible to reject the argument that this verse and those that follow are secondary commentaries. He claims that Matthew's usual description of the kingdom as the community of all the chosen in the kingdom of the Father is inappropriate here. In fact, this scholar goes so far as to suggest that the editorial addition actually breaks the logical sequence of Jesus' preaching.[8] Other scholars also believe that this verse does not fit with Matthew's usual tone, which was generally quite pro-Jewish.[9]

---

[7]Walter Kasper has said that it is impossible to say that the New Covenant replaced Israel. One can only say that the New Covenant is a *fulfillment* of the Old Covenant. Cf. Walter Cardinal Kasper, "Foreword," *Christ Jesus and the Jewish People Today: New Explorations of Theological Interrelationships*, ed. Philip A. Cunningham, Joseph Sievers, Mary Boys, and Hans Hermann Hendrix (Grand Rapids, MI: William B. Eerdmans Publishing Company, 2011), x–xviii, at xiv.

[8]Albright and Mann, *Matthew*, 265.

[9]Craig A. Evans, *Matthew* (Cambridge: Cambridge University Press, 2012), 375.

Nevertheless, we believe the opposite is true. This verse in no way contradicts either the teaching of Jesus or the position Matthew adopts in the rest of his Gospel (if indeed we can accept that his point of view would in any way differ from the teaching of Jesus in the first place). This verse, even if it is not present in Mark and Luke, is in fact a summary exposition of the meaning of the entire parable, and provides a key to understanding not only the parable, but many other New Testament texts that concern the consequences of the chosen people's rejection of Jesus and his mission. We will try to substantiate this claim by closely examining the parable.

God and His Vineyard

According to many scholars, the parable of the wicked tenants is "one of the most significant, most discussed, and most complicated of all the parables."[10] This is the only parable in which the main character is a father with a single son; in two other parables that concern parents and children (Mt 21.28–32; Lk 11.15–32), the father has two sons.[11] This fact alone gives the parable a personal and autobiographical element.[12]

The plot once again unfolds in a vineyard; as we mentioned before, this underlines that it speaks of the chosen nation of Israel. This context would have been obvious also to the listeners who, according to all three synoptic evangelists, understood that Jesus was speaking about them. We have already mentioned several texts that compare the nation of Israel to a vineyard. The most important of these occurs in the Book of Isaiah, and we offer the complete text here:

> Now will I sing to my well-beloved a song of my beloved touching his vineyard. My well-beloved hath a vineyard in a very fruitful hill, and he fenced it, and gathered out the stones thereof, and planted it with the choicest vine, and built a tower in the midst of it, and also made a winepress therein; and he looked that it should bring forth grapes, and

[10]Snodgrass, *Stories with Intent*, 276.

[11]A. Puig i Tàrrech, "The Parable of the Tenants in the Vineyard," *Biblische Notizen* 158 (2013): 85–112, at 86–87.

[12]A. Puig i Tàrrech, "Metaphors, First Context and Jesus Tradition," *Biblische Notizen* 159 (2013): 73–120, at 91.

Christ before Caiaphas, Matthias Stom, 1630s

it brought forth wild grapes. And now, O inhabitants of Jerusalem, and men of Judah, judge, I pray you, betwixt me and my vineyard. What could have been done more to my vineyard, that I have not done in it? Wherefore, when I looked that it should bring forth grapes, brought it forth wild grapes? And now go to, I will tell you what I will do to my vineyard: I will take away the hedge thereof, and it shall be eaten up, and break down the wall thereof, and it shall be trodden down, and I will lay it waste; it shall not be pruned, nor digged; but there shall come up briers and thorns; I will also command the clouds that they rain no rain upon it. For the vineyard of the Lord of hosts is the house of Israel, and the men of Judah his pleasant plant. And he looked for judgment, but behold oppression, for righteousness, but behold a cry. (Is 5.1–7)

The chief priests and elders to whom Jesus told the parable could not fail to remember this text when he began his telling. The textual similarity is especially evident if we compare the words of the prophet with the text of the version of this parable in Matthew and Mark. In both places, the master planted the vineyard, surrounded it with a fence, dug a winepress, and put a tower within it. From that point, the plots diverge. In Isaiah's prophecy, the vineyard never produces grapes, and God leaves it desolate. In the parable, the husbandmen cruelly misuse the servants of the master, and the master condemns them to a horrible death, and the vineyard he gives to other husbandmen. In the end, both accounts come to a resounding ending: both the prophecy and the parable speak of punishment that awaits the chosen nation for its lack of faith and its disobedience before God.

If we are to interpret the parable literally, the plot does not directly reflect analogous real-life situations. Joachim Jeremias offers two possible literal interpretations:

1) The husbandmen rose up against the master because he was a foreigner and left to his own country;

2) Having seen the son, they decided that the master had died, and if they kill the only heir, then they could become owners of the land.[13]

These two scenarios contradict one another. In the first case, the scenario assumes a post-war situation, while the second can only be true in times of peace. Moroever, neither Roman nor Jewish law would ever legitimize the husbandmen's claim to the land based on their having killed the heir.[14] Other scholars offer the suggestion that the master of the vineyard, being a Jew, could easily have gone to a place not far from his home, such as Galilee or Jerusalem.[15]

Neither of these two interpretations in any way helps us understand the meaning of the parable, because its entire plot is a single extended metaphor related to Jesus' imminent death.

In the parable of the wicked tenants, we see the entire history of the relationship between God and his chosen nation. This history, which is described in detail in the Old Testament, was filled with examples of God's beneficence to the people at large and to individuals. God separated the people of Israel in a special way from other nations, gave them knowledge

---

[13]Jeremias, *Parables,* 74–76. The second possibility is also developed by Klyne Snodgrass, *The Parable of the Wicked Tenants* (Tübingen: Mohr Siebeck, 1983), 31–40.

[14]Joel Marcus, *Mark 1–16, A New Translation with Introduction and Commentary* (New Haven and London: Yale University Press, 2000), 804.

[15]Herzog, *Parables,* 104.

*The Parable
of the Wicked
Tenants,*
Miniature,
11th century

concerning himself, gave them commandments that they were called to
fulfill. At the same time, the Bible is filled with stories of how the people
turned aside from the true faith and how the Lord poured out his wrath
on them for it. There are also many prophecies of future calamities that
the Lord would pour out on his people if they continued to be stubborn
in their unfaithfulness.

In the Old Testament, the relationship between God and his people is
likened to the relationship between a man and his wife. The God of Israel
is a jealous God (Ex 34.14, 20.5) in the sense that he is jealous of his people
in relation to other gods.[16] He takes the people of Israel as his bride (Jer
2.2), and calls himself her husband (Is 54.5). Any turning aside to idolatry
he considers tantamount to adultery and fornication (Ex 34.15–17). The
Prophet Jeremiah compares the daughter of Israel to a harlot who "has
gone up upon every high mountain and under every green tree, and there
hath played the harlot," while Judea he calls her sister, who "defiled the land,
and committed adultery with stones and with stocks"[17] (Jer 3.6–9). Ezekiel
develops these images further, describing various kinds of fornication that
the daughter of Israel has fallen into, in spite of all the mercy poured out
on her by God (Ezek 16.1–43).

Over the course of centuries, God sent to the nation of Israel various
prophets, leaders, and teachers, through whom he informed them of his
will. But the fate of these prophets was often tragic: they were disregarded,
they were "stoned, they were sawn asunder, were tempted, were slain with
sword; they wandered about in sheepskins and goatskins, being destitute,

[16]The Old Testament term *qanna* literally means "jealous one."

[17]This references the idols that were made from wood or stone worshipped by the Jews who
turned away from God.

afflicted, tormented" (Heb 11.37). Here the text refers in part to the fate of Isaiah, who, according to tradition was sawn in half with a wooden saw,[18] and to Jeremiah, who, according to some sources, was stoned.[19] Blessed Jerome wrote,

> He had given the Law to them and had commanded them to labor in this vineyard that they might exhibit the fruit of the Law by their works. Later he sent servants to them, whom they seized and beat, such as Jeremiah, or killed such as Isaiah, or stoned, such as Naboth and Zechariah, whom they killed between the sanctuary and the altar. Let us read Paul's letter to the Hebrews and out of it learn in great detail which of the Lord's servant have endured what sorts of things.[20]

The Old Testament also speaks about the death of the prophets. The prophet Elijah complained, "I have been very jealous for the Lord God of hosts, for the children of Israel have forsaken their covenant, thrown down thine altars, and slain thy prophets with the sword; and I, even I only, am left; and they seek my life, to take it away" (1 Kgs 19.10). We find similar complaints against the sons of Israel in a prayer to God spoken by the Levites in the presence of Ezra and Nehemiah:

> They did eat, and were filled, and became fat, and delighted themselves in thy great goodness. Nevertheless they were disobedient, and rebelled against thee, and cast thy law behind their backs, and slew thy prophets which testified against them to turn them to thee, and they wrought great provocations. . . . They dealt proudly, and hearkened not unto thy commandments, but sinned against thy judgments (which if a man do, he shall live in them), and withdrew the shoulder, and hardened their neck, and would not hear. Yet many years didst thou forbear them, and testifiedst against them by thy Spirit in thy prophets,

---

[18]Justin Martyr, *Dialogue of Justin, Philosopher and Martyr, with Trypho. a Jew* 120 (ANF 1:259); Tertullian, *Against the Gnostics* 8.3 (CCSL 2:1083); Origen, *Commentary on Isaiah* 1.5 (GCS 33:247).

[19]Epiphanius the Latin, *Commentary on the Gospels* 31 (PLS 3:876–77).

[20]Jerome, *Commentary on Matthew* 3.21.34–35 (CCSL 77:195; St Jerome, *Commentary on Matthew*, trans. Thomas P. Scheck, FOC 117 [Washington: The Catholic University of America Press, 2008], 245).

Prophet Elijah,
Icon 13th–14th
century

yet would they not give ear; therefore gavest thou them into the hand of the people of the lands. Nevertheless for thy great mercies' sake thou didst not utterly consume them, nor forsake them; for thou art a gracious and merciful God. (Neh 9.25–26, 29–31)

John the Baptist became the last in this chain of prophet-martyrs, beheaded by the tetrarch Herod Antipas (Mt 14.1–12; Mk 6.16–29; Lk 9.7–9).

Jesus makes a direct genealogical connection between those who killed the prophets in the Old Testament and the scribes and Pharisees of his own time. After the three parables we have already examined, Jesus turned to them with these frightening words:

Woe unto you, scribes and Pharisees, hypocrites! Because ye build the tombs of the prophets, and garnish the sepulchers of the righteous, and say, "If we had been in the days of our fathers, we would not have been partakers with them in the blood of the prophets." Wherefore ye be witnesses unto yourselves, that ye are the children of them which killed the prophets. Fill ye up then the measure of your fathers. Ye serpents, ye generation of vipers, how can ye escape the damnation of hell? Wherefore, behold, I send unto you prophets, and wise men, and scribes, and some of them ye shall kill and crucify, and some of them shall ye scourge in your synagogues, and persecute them from city to city. (Mt 23.29–34)

The parable of the wicked tenants is the prelude to these words, and thus they are the direct continuation of the parable. As he neared the end, Jesus speaks to his opponents more openly. In Matthew, Jesus continues with prophecies concerning the fall of Jerusalem and the destruction of the temple immediately after these denunciations (Mt 24.2). These rebukes and prophecies are completely consonant with everything that Jesus told the Jews more than once during his public ministry. Let us remember the words he spoke soon after the healing of the centurion's servant: "Many shall come from the east and west, and shall sit down with Abraham, and Isaac, and Jacob, in the kingdom of heaven. But the children of the kingdom shall be cast out into outer darkness: there shall be weeping and gnashing of teeth" (Mt 8.11–12). In these words, we can see the so-called replacement or supersessionist theology in stark terms: the place that used to be set aside for one group will be taken by another. The same thought will be repeated in the parable of those called to the wedding feast, which is the third in the first trilogy we are now discussing (Mt 22.1–14).

Ancient commentators saw a collection of themes in this parable, all of which refer to the fate of the people of Israel. John Chrysostom finds eight such themes:

Many things does he intimate by this parable: God's providence, which had been exercised towards them from the first; their murderous disposition from the beginning; that nothing had been omitted of whatever pertained to a heedful care of them; that even when prophets had been slain, he had not turned away from them, but had sent his very Son; that the God both of the New and of the Old Testament was one and the same; that his death should effect great blessings; that they were to endure extreme punishment for the crucifixion, and their crime; the calling of the Gentiles, the casting out of the Jews.[21]

Modern scholars usually find only two or three main ideas in the parable. Blomberg, for example, sees three main themes in the parable:

1) God is greatly merciful and patiently waits for his people to bring forth fruits, even when people constantly rise against him;

2) A day will come when the patience of God will run out and all who reject him will be destroyed;

3) God's original plan was not frustrated, because he will put new leaders in place, and these will cultivate the fruits that the first husbandmen were not able to produce.[22]

Naturally, all of these themes are present in the parable. And still, if we try to listen to the parable with the ears of those who heard it from the mouth of Jesus, then it seems to us that the most sensitive topic that he touched upon was the theme of the land: his listeners could not have failed to hear his prophecy that the Jews would lose the promised land that was so precious to them. This was what resonated in their hearts the most. They probably were not all that worried that some hypothetical kingdom of God, which Jesus spoke of so often, would be taken from them. But that they would lose their vineyard—the one that God himself put in their hands—that they would lose the land that they had lost already so many times, which they continued to return to stubbornly—this was a thought that could not fail to grab them.

Let us not forget that the land was currently occupied, and the threat of expulsion constantly hung over them. This threat was realized in the days of the Jewish wars in the years 66–73, during which Jerusalem was

---

[21]John Chrysostom, *Homilies on the Gospel of Matthew* 68.1 (NPNF[1] 10:414–15).
[22]Blomberg, *Interpreting the Parables*, 267.

The captive Jews
on the interior
wall of the arch
of Titus, 1st
century AD

seized by Roman forces, and all its inhabitants were either slaughtered or deported and sold into slavery. This occurred about forty years after Jesus told his last parable. The general situation of Roman dominion and a general sense of political instability gave these parables a strong sense that is not always obvious to those who read them two thousand years later.

Whom do the evil husbandmen in the parable symbolize? Often, the answer offered is the chief priests and elders, the spiritual elite of Israel, against whom the parable is directed. The general context of the Gospel story, however, as well as the image of the vineyard as a symbol of the entire nation (not just a specific subset of it), forces us to see the wicked tenants as a symbol of all the Jews who rejected Jesus. Such a reading is confirmed, first of all, by the evangelists' testimony regarding the Jews' collective responsibility for Jesus' death, and the consequences of that guilt on future generations. After all, the people took responsibility on themselves when they said, "His blood be on us, and on our children" (Mt 27.25). Second, this is exactly how ancient commentators understood the parable.[23] Third, even some modern scholars, contrary to mainstream opinion, also hold an analogous point of view. One of them, a Jewish rabbi, wrote:

> The leaders alone were not responsible for the son's death—any more than they were responsible for John's death or the death of the prophets. The people had strayed and become as rebellious and destructive as wild grapes. . . . Therefore, the entire vineyard needed to be destroyed—Jerusalem, the Temple, its priests, the elders of the city, the merchants, bakers, cheese makers, potters, builders, and masons. In short, Jesus condemned everyone who disobeyed God and refused to repent.[24]

[23]John Chrysostom, *Homilies on the Gospel of Matthew* 68.1–2 (NPNF[1] 10:414–15).
[24]Frank Stern, *A Rabbi Looks at Jesus' Parables* (Oxford: Rowman & Littlefield Publishers, Inc., 2006), 118.

The theme of the collective responsibility of Israel for Jesus' death is one of the most hotly-contested and painful subjects in the history of the interpretation of the Gospels. This responsibility is completely rejected by the vast majority of modern scholars in the West, because they believe that such an interpretation has led to persecution against the Jews in different places over the centuries. The very idea of collective responsibility is subject to debate, since every person can answer only for his own actions. Nevertheless, this theme does exist in the Gospel account of Christ's passion; it is implicit in this parable as well. It is no coincidence that Jesus ends the parable (in Matthew's account) by saying that the vineyard will be given to a different people (*ethnei*). If the responsibility for what happened in the vineyard was not shared by the entire nation, then some other image or word would have been used, not "people."

At the same time, every nation has its leaders, its political, spiritual, and intellectual elite. Very often, the elite is responsible for fateful decisions that the entire nation has to pay for later on. Matthew underlined this by adding his own commentary to Jesus' words that the kingdom of heaven would be given to a people who bring forth the fruits thereof. He stresses that Jesus spoke of the chief priests and Pharisees, and that they understood this perfectly well. Consequently, most of the responsibility for the death of the Son of God is laid at their feet.

The story of the parable leads to a climactic moment, when the master of the vineyard sends his own son to the tenants. In Luke, he is the "beloved *(agapētos)* son," which cannot fail to remind us of two events, described in the Synoptic Gospels, when the voice of the Father was heard from heaven: at Jesus' baptism and his transfiguration.[25] In both cases, the phrase "beloved Son" is prominent (Mt 3.17; Mk 1.11; Lk 3.22; Mt 17.5; Mk 9.7; Lk 9.35).

In the parable, Jesus speaks of himself and predicts his own death at the hands of those to whom he told the parable. As their reaction shows (they tried to seize him, but were afraid of the crowd), they also saw the parable as a direct provocation. The main message of the parable in some ways reminds us of the words that Jesus spoke to Judas at the Last Supper:

[25]Puig i Tàrrech, "Metaphors," 108–109.

"What thou doest, do quickly" (Jn 13.27). These words were not a call to action, just as the parable was not a call to the elders to bring about what Jesus predicted. Judas could have set aside his intention to betray Jesus, and the chief priests and elders could have abandoned their intention to seize and kill him. Nevertheless, they acted exactly as Jesus predicted. His prophecy thus constitutes an inevitable and irreversible fact.

God's Apparent Powerlessness and the Cornerstone

What we see here is something that can be described as God's "powerlessness" before human freedom. This is not a forced powerlessness, but a willing one. God knows in advance what evil people will do, but this knowledge does not mean that those people are predestined to commit such actions. God can intervene in a situation and prevent evil, and in some cases he does so. At other times, however, he sends such people signs, hoping they will react to them and consciously reject their evil intentions. This rejection completely and totally depends on their free will. God does not force them to reject their intentions; he merely indicates that he is aware of them, and perhaps this will shame them and lead them to repentance. The Jews' reaction to the parable of the wicked tenants could have been repentance. This is not what happened, however, and Jesus knew that it would not happen.

The wicked tenants take what seems to them the easiest decision before them: "This is the heir: come, let us kill him, and let us seize on his inheritance." Similar decisions were made by many people who killed their fellow men from a desire to take their property or because of envy, jealousy, or hatred, or any number of other reasons. Many philosophical works have been written on the theme of murder, as well as many literary works.

In Fyodor Dostoyevsky's novel *Crime and Punishment*, the question is raised: is it allowable for a man to step over the corpse of another person to attain his own goals, whether they are noble and exalted, or merely materialistic and mercenary. The student Raskolnikov asks himself such questions as he contemplates killing the old woman pawnbroker. "I wanted to find out something else . . . Whether I can step over barriers or not,

Pietà,
Michealangelo,
c. 1498

whether I dare stoop to pick up or not, whether I am a trembling creature or whether I have the *right . . ."*[26]

In the parable, the wicked tenants were able to step over barriers, because they believed that they "had the right." Many philosophical and political theories justify murder if it is motivated by a particular goal, for example, class warfare or just war against a tyrant. In the Christian tradition, however, God's sixth commandment always remains: "Thou shalt not murder" (Ex 20.13; Deut 5.17). All human life has value, and any death, especially a violent one, is a wound for all mankind. This is what the seventeenth-century English poet and clergyman John Donne believed:

> No man is an Island, entire of itself, every man is a piece of the Continent, a part of the main; if a clod be washed away by the sea, Europe is the less, as well as if a Promontory were, as well as if a Manor of thy friends, or of thine own were; Any Mans death diminishes me, because I am involved in Mankind; And therefore never send to know for whom the bell tolls; It tolls for thee.[27]

[26]Fyodor Dostoevsky, *Crime and Punishment*, Part 5, chapter 4; Fyodor Dostoevsky, *Crime and Punishment*, trans. Constance Garnett (London: Heinemann, 1914), 369.

[27]John Donne, *Selections from Divine Poems, Sermons, Devotions, and Prayers* (Mahwah, NJ: Paulist Press, 1990), 58.

The traditional Christian understanding, expressed so poignantly in these words, that mankind is a single large family, was foreign to the Hebrew nation of Jesus' time. Neither is it familiar to many modern ethnic or social groups, who are ready, for the sake of their group's agenda, to walk over the corpses of other people that belong to groups of "others."

The Son of the Master of the Vineyard, Tucco, 1886–94

Any violent death encroaches upon God's plan, according to which every person has his own date of birth and death, determined by God himself. Jesus' parables, like his other sermons, were like a bell that tolled certain simple, eternal truths, which mankind, in spite of the constantly resounding voice of God, violates again and again. One of these eternal truths is the commandment not to murder, a commandment that was broken in the first generation after Adam. The inevitable continuation of murders, beginning with Cain's murder of Abel, and continuing through the murder of John the Baptist, culminates with the murder of the Son of God, who was sent into the world by the Father to save mankind.

The figure of the beloved son is the central image of the parable. It seems to move the figure of the master to the side, and he does remain off camera for the entirety of the parable. He makes all the decisions, he sends one servant after another, but he never appears on the scene. Instead of coming himself, he sends his son, and in this it is impossible to miss the direct reflection of what Jesus said to the Jews many times about his own Father. The relationship between the Father and the Son, as expressed in Jesus' sermons in the Gospel of John, can be summarized in several frequently-repeated phrases: The Father sent the Son into the world (Jn 5.36–37), the Son acts in the name of the Father (Jn 5.17–19), the Son does not do his own will, but the will of the Father (Jn 6.38).

The central importance of the son in the parable is underlined by the use of the image of the stone that the builders rejected, which became the head of the corner. This image, taken from the Psalms (Ps 117.22), indicates

The Parable
of the Wicked
Tenants,
Jan Leychen,
1791–1826

a stone that is placed in the foundation of a house. Even in the Old Testament, the image of the cornerstone had a religious connotation: "Behold, I lay in Zion for a foundation a stone, a tried stone, a precious corner stone, a sure foundation: he that believeth shall not make haste" (Is 28.16). The Apostle Peter spoke of Jesus Christ as the cornerstone of faith, citing both of these Old Testament sources (1 Pet 2.6–8).

Earlier, in Caesarea Philippi, Jesus used the image of the stone to refer to Peter (Mt 16.18). In the parable of the wicked tenants, he applies the image to himself, indicating the central importance of his own coming into the world, not for the history of Israel, but for the history of that nation that would bring forth fruits—that is, saved mankind that is gathered into the Church as the New Israel. Therefore, the parable gradually leads the listeners far away from the theme of the relationship of God and a specific nation, taking on a universal character.

As with many of Jesus' other teachings and parables, this parable finishes with the listeners divided into two groups: those who believe and those who do not, those who repent and those who do not, the sheep and the goats, the saved and those who rejected salvaion. The final division will occur at the dread judgment, but it began on earth, where some responded to Jesus' preaching and his miracles, while others were only increasingly irritated by his words and actions. This mixed reaction is evident both in the examination of Jesus' miracles and in the analysis of his parables. This is what Jesus himself pointed to when he said, "Suppose ye that I am come to give peace on earth? I tell you, nay, but rather division" (Lk 12.51). In this case, the judgment of those who do not believe is expressed in the fact that they will lose the vineyard, while the blessing upon those who believe is expressed in the fact that they become the new tenants of the vineyard.

The Savior not Made with Hands, Icon of the Novgorod school, 12th century

If the vineyard symbolizes the nation of Israel, then the image of the stone refers to the temple in Jerusalem. Not long before telling this parable, Jesus entered into the temple, cast out the buyers and sellers, and turned over the tables of the money-changers (Mt 21.12; Mk 11.14; Lk 19.45). Soon after he told the parable, he would point to the walls of the temple and say that not one stone would remain upon another (Mt 24.2). If his actions in the temple can be seen as symbolizing the coming destruction of the temple, then his words were a direct prophecy of this event.

Together with some other scholars, we must also note that in Hebrew the word "son" (*ben*) and "stone" (*eben*) sound similar.[28] It is possible that this resonance led to these two images being used in the same teaching. The stone, in this context, can be interpreted as an image with several meanings. On the one hand, it points to Jesus as the cornerstone that the builders rejected. On the other hand, it is connected to the idea of the new, eschatological temple, the new community of the nation of the Lord. The Son is thus a messianic stone that is cast aside by the builders, but ends up taking the most important place. His opponents will see that their regime and their temple will be destroyed, while his kingdom will be established.[29]

[28]Matthew Black, "The Theological Appropriation of the Old Testament by the New Testament," *Scottish Journal of Theology* 39 (1986): 1–17, at 12; Snodgrass, *Wicked Tenants*, 113–18; Seyoon Kim, "Jesus—the Son of God, the Stone, the Son of Man and the Servant: The Role of Zechariah in the Self-Identification of Jesus," *Tradition and Interpretation in the New Testament: Essays in Honor of E. Earle Ellis*, ed. Gerald F. Hawthorne and Otto Betz (Grand Rapids, MI: William B. Eerdmans Publishing Company, 1987), 134–48, at 135; Robert D. Rowe, *God's Kingdom and God's Son: The Background to Mark's Christology from Concepts of Kingship to the Psalms* (Leiden: Brill, 2002), 265–70.

[29]Wright, *Jesus and the Victory of God*, 452–53, 455.

3. The Wedding Feast

The parable of the wedding feast in the Gospel of Matthew follows immediately after the parable of the wicked tenants in the vineyard. The Gospel
of Luke has a similar parable. Comparing the texts of both parables and
the circumstances of their telling allows us to conclude that Jesus told
the same parable twice. Moreover, when Jesus told it the second time, he
added to it significantly, and ended up changing its meaning, as well as its
general tone and character. We believe it is useful to look at both versions
of the parable, beginning with Luke's, since it belongs to an earlier period
in Jesus' ministry.

Two versions of the parable

Luke tells us that Jesus, on the way from Galilee to Jerusalem, came to
the home of one of the leaders of the Pharisees on a Sabbath to eat bread.
There he first healed a man sick with dropsy (Lk 14.1–6). Then, seeing how
those who were called to the feast were choosing the best places at table,
he tells them a "parable":

> When thou art bidden of any man to a wedding, sit not down in the
> highest room, lest a more honorable man than thou be bidden of him,
> and he that bade thee and him come and say to thee, "Give this man
> place," and thou begin with shame to take the lowest room. But when
> thou art bidden, go and sit down in the lowest room, that when he
> that bade thee cometh, he may say unto thee, "Friend, go up higher."
> Then shalt thou have worship in the presence of them that sit at meat
> with thee. For whosoever exalteth himself shall be abased, and he that
> humbleth himself shall be exalted. (Lk 14.8–11)

This account does not have the character of a parable, even though
Luke names it as such. The teaching that follows, directed to the master of
the house, is also not a parable:

The Parable of the Wedding Feast, Fresco, 14th century

When thou makest a dinner or a supper, call not thy friends, nor thy brethren, neither thy kinsmen, nor thy rich neighbors, lest they also bid thee again, and a recompense be made thee. But when thou makest a feast, call the poor, the maimed, the lame, the blind, and thou shalt be blessed; for they cannot recompense thee, for thou shalt be recompensed at the resurrection of the just. (Lk 14.12–14)

When he heard these words, one of those who reclined at table with Jesus said, "Blessed is he that shall eat bread in the kingdom of God!" (Lk 14.15) Here we see a typical Lukan stylistic flourish: he focuses on a "voice from the crowd," which expresses a spontaneous emotional reaction to Jesus' words (in many translations, this emotional character is expressed with an exclamation point). Thus, for example, only Luke mentions that in answer to Jesus' teaching about the unclean spirit that takes with him seven other spirits, more evil than he, and returns to his former house (Mt 12.43–45; Lk 11.24–26), "a certain woman of the company lifted up her voice, and said unto him, 'Blessed is the womb that bare thee, and the breasts which thou has sucked!'" (Lk 11.27) Luke is also the only evangelist who notes that the listeners exclaimed "God forbid!" after Jesus told them the parable of the evil husbandmen.

As a rule, Jesus does not leave these voices from the crowd without an answer. His response to the exclamation "God forbid!" is the teaching about the stone that the builders rejected (Lk 20.17–18). Jesus responds to the exclamation of the person sitting at table with him in the home of the Pharisee by telling the parable of the wedding feast:

> Then said he unto him, "A certain man made a great supper, and bade many, and sent his servant at supper time to say to them that were bidden, 'Come, for all things are now ready.' And they all with one consent began to make excuse. The first said unto him, 'I have bought a piece of ground, and I must needs go and see it. I pray thee have me excused.' And another said, 'I have bought five yoke of oxen, and I go to prove them. I pray thee have me excused.' And another said, 'I have married a wife, and therefore I cannot come.' So that servant came, and showed his lord these things. Then the master of the house being angry said to his servant, 'Go out quickly into the streets and lanes of the city, and bring in hither the poor, and the maimed, and the halt, and the blind.' And the servant said, 'Lord, it is done as thou hast commanded, and yet there is room.' And the lord said unto the servant, 'Go out into the highways and hedges, and compel them to come in, that my house may be filled.' For I say unto you, that none of those men which were bidden shall taste of my supper." (Lk 14.16–24)

Thus the parable of those called to the feast in the Gospel of Luke finishes a series of events, all of which are thematically connected to this parable.[30] The general context is the feast in the home of a Pharisee. Within that context, the telling of the parable intertwines with Jesus' broader teaching, which consists of variations on the theme of feasting or of bread. Another element that ties together the entire episode is the repetition of the words "the poor, the maimed, the halt, and the blind" in the teaching that he addresses the master of the feast and that he includes in the parable of those called to the wedding feast.[31]

---

[30]Willi Braun, *Feasting and Social Rhetoric in Luke 14* (Cambridge: Cambridge University Press, 1995), 15.
   [31]Ibid., 18.

The Parable of the Wedding Feast, Johann Georg Platzer, 1737

In the Gospel according to Matthew, Jesus tell an analogous parable in the temple in Jerusalem, and the listeners are those same chief priests and elders who were the primary audience of the parable of the wicked tenants:

> The kingdom of heaven is like unto a certain king, which made a marriage for his son, and sent forth his servants to call them that were bidden to the wedding: and they would not come. Again, he sent forth other servants, saying, "Tell them which are bidden, 'Behold, I have prepared my dinner: my oxen and my fatlings are killed, and all things are ready; come unto the marriage.'" But they made light of it, and went their ways, one to his farm, another to his merchandise. And the remnant took his servants, and entreated them spitefully, and slew them. But when the king heard thereof, he was wroth, and he sent forth his armies, and destroyed those murderers, and burned up their city. Then saith he to his servants, "The wedding is ready, but they which were bidden were not worthy. Go ye therefore into the highways, and as many as ye shall find, bid to the marriage." So those servants went out into the highways, and gathered together all as many as they found, both bad and good: and the wedding was furnished with guests. And when the king came in to see the guests, he saw there a man which had not on a wedding garment, and he saith unto him, "Friend, how camest thou in hither not having a wedding garment?" And he was

speechless. Then said the king to the servants, "Bind him hand and foot, and take him away, and cast him into outer darkness, there shall be weeping and gnashing of teeth." For many are called, but few are chosen." (Mt 22.2–14)

Before us we see a good example of how similar plots can serve different functions, depending on the context of the parable's telling. In the first case, the parable was told in the peaceful and genial context of a friendly meal. This fact is underlined by the conspicuous lack of any mention of the Pharisees' unhappiness with Jesus' words and actions, in spite of the fact that he healed someone on the Sabbath. In answer to his question—is it permissible to heal on the Sabbath?—they remain silent. Neither does his teaching about how to properly choose a place at table, or whom to invite to that table, inspire any negative reaction. In this situation, then, the parable, though it does not have a conciliatory message at all, is still spoken in a calm, irenic tone. When asked to come to the feast, those who were invited ask to be excused and provide justification for their not being able to come. Even though the master does get angry at them, he does not punish them in any way, which merely means they will not eat at his table, as is quite obvious from the context of the story.

Yet when Jesus tells a similar parable in the temple of Jerusalem, the picture he draws is completely different. First of all, the master of the feast is not just anyone, but a king, which gives the entire story more significance, because kings in Jesus' parables always symbolize God. Second, other than the king, Jesus adds further detail: the king is not simply preparing a feast, but a wedding feast for his son. So, from the first words of the parable, we recognize a christological aspect to the story. Third, the king calls those whom he invited not once, but twice, yet they refuse both times. Fourth, they refuse in a very rude way: their actions in response to the repeated invitation remind the audience of the actions of the wicked tenants. Fifth, the reaction of the king is not limited to announcing that those who were called will not take part in the dinner; the king acts decisively and harshly, destroying "those murderers" and burning down their city.

Finally, in this version told in the temple of Jerusalem, Jesus adds an entire episode that is absent in Luke's version: the man who comes to the feast without a wedding garment. This has its own unique meaning.

Both parables share the same replacement theology that is so disdained by modern Western scholars,[32] but which permeates the entire story of the Gospels. The place of those who refused to come to the feast will be taken by others, just as the master of the vineyard replaces the wicked tenants with others: a nation that is capable of bringing forth the fruits of the vineyard.

Similar, but not identical, is the motivation of those who refuse the call to attend the wedding feast. In Luke, one of the invited guests refuses because he has purchased land, another because he has bought oxen, and a third cites his own recent marriage. In Matthew, some of those who refused the call of the king, went "their ways, one to his farm, another to his merchandise, and the remnant took his servants, and entreated them spitefully, and slew them." In Luke's version, it seems that financial concerns take the forefront: it does not look like the guests have any evil intentions. They simply prefer to serve mammon rather than God. In Matthew's version, however, things are somewhat different: those who are called refuse to come because of an intentional and blatant disregard of the king's will. This disregard extends to the shameful treatment and even murder of the king's servants.

This last detail takes the parable out of the realm of the realistic and historical: one could only realistically expect such a reaction if the king were inviting his sworn enemies, which is difficult to imagine. Neither can one agree with scholars who think that the king invited people from the street merely to save face and preserve his reputation.[33] Any attempt to explain the parable in historical terms cannot fail to founder in the face of an entire series of details that make it clear that the story is entirely ahistorical.

[32]Cf. Mary C. Boys, "Beyond 'Removing' Anti-Judaism: The Theological and Educational Task of Reframing Christian Identity," *Removing the Anti-Judaism from the New Testament*, ed. Howard Clark Kee and Irvin J. Borovsky (Philadelphia: American Interfaith Institute, 1998), 88–102, at 94–95. (The author laments that in spite of a total redaction of theological texts in both the Protestant and Catholic traditions, replacement theology persists in certain liturgical hymns.)

[33]Wright, *Jesus the Storyteller*, 163.

The Wedding of the King's Son, Miniature, 13th century

Nevertheless, only the plot of the parable is invented. The reality that the parable reflects is in no way imaginary. As with the parable of the wicked tenants, Jesus once again speaks of himself and his mission. In the parable of the wicked tenants, the figure of the son is central; in this parable, however, the son is only mentioned as the one for whom the king prepared a wedding feast. If in the former parable the father remains in the shadows, here, the son does. Moreover, in both parables, the conflict develops between one person (either the master or the king) and a group of people (the tenants or those invited to the feast). The entire story hinges on this main conflict.

The essentially different roles that the son plays in the two parables forces commentators to examine the role of the servants differently in each parable. In the parable of the wicked tenants, the master first sends three groups of servants, and only later his son. In the second parable, the son is mentioned first, but then no longer takes part in the story; moreover, the first group of servants are simply ignored, the second are variously mistreated, even killed. This may show that the first group symbolizes the Old Testament prophets, and the second group represents Christian preachers, the disciples of Jesus, to whom he frequently prophesied future sufferings and martyrdom. This is how many ancient commentators understood the parable, both in the East and the West.

Gregory the Great sees the wedding feast prepared by the king for his son as an allegory of the birth of the Son of God from the Virgin. Having come from the womb of the Virgin, as from a bridal chamber, the Bridegroom is to be united with his bride, the Church. God the Father sent his servants to invite his friends to the feast: "He sent once, and he sent again, because first he made the prophets, and later the apostles, preachers of the Lord's incarnation. He sent his servants twice with the invitation, because he said through the prophets that his only Son's incarnation would come about, and he proclaimed through the apostles that he had."[34] Symeon the New Theologian wrote, "Who, then, were those who had been sent? The prophets, he says. Who were those who had been called? The children of the Jews, for they were those who then and from the beginning had been called, and they did not want to listen to them. . . . Whom does he call servants here? His apostles."[35]

Anti-Judaic Context

John Chrysostom sees in the parable of the wedding feast a direct continuation of the parable of the wicked tenants. In his opinion, the events described in the parable of the wedding feast refer to the first generation of Christians. Moreover, both parables are directed against the Jews, and the climax of both parables is the destruction of Jerusalem in AD 70, accompanied by the exile of the Jews from the promised land:

> Since they were not willing to come, yea and also slew those that came unto them, he burns up their cities, and sent his armies and slew them. And these things he says, declaring beforehand the things that took place under Vespasian and Titus, and that they provoked the father also, by not believing in him; it is the father at any rate who was avenging. And for this reason let me add, not straightway after Christ was

[34]Gregory the Great, *Forty Gospel Homilies*, 38.3 (PL 76:1283; Gregory the Great, *Forty Gospel Homilies*, trans. Dom David Hurst, Cistercian Studies Series 123 [Kalamazoo, MI: Cistercian Publications, 1990], 341).

[35]St Symeon the New Theologian, *First Ethical Discourse* 11 (Symeon the New Theologian, *On the Mystical Life: The Ethical Discourses, vol. 1: The Church and the Last Things*, trans. Alexander Golitzin, PPS 14 [Crestwood, NY: Saint Vladimir Seminary Press, 1995], 60–61).

slain did the capture take place, but after forty years, that he might
show his long suffering, when they had slain Stephen, when they had
put James to death, when they had spitefully entreated the apostles. Do
you see the truth of the event, and its quickness? For while John was
yet living, and many other of them that were with Christ, these things
came to pass, and they that had heard these words were witnesses of
the events. See then care utterable. He had planted a vineyard; he had
done all things, and finished; when his servants had been put to death,
he sent other servants; when those had been slain, he sent the son; and
when he was put to death, he bids them to the marriage. They would
not come. After this he sends other servants, and they slew these also.
Then upon this he slays them, as being incurably diseased.[36]

In spite of the fact that in modern scholarship it is common to dismiss
such attacks on the Jews as evidence of antisemitism that has ostensibly
infected the Fathers of the Church, this same interpretation of the parable
of the wedding feast—that it refers to the Old Testament prophets and
the first generation of Christian preachers—is also found in some modern
scholarship.[37] St Nikolai Velimirovich, a renowned Serbian theologian of
the twentieth century, wrote the following:

As is usually the case in the parables of Christ, this spans the entire
history of mankind from beginning to end. . . . The Kingdom of Heaven
cannot be expressed in words—it can only be likened to something
that exists in this life. Among other things, it can be likened to a wedding feast. A wedding is a joyful event for people, and the Kingdom
of Heaven is joy itself. . . . Christ's coming into the world is the most
joyful event for mankind as a whole and for each soul individually, like
the coming of the betrothed to his bride. Of all the nations on earth,
the Jewish people should have greeted the coming of the Bridegroom
Christ most joyfully, for this people had been the most prepared by
God to meet him. This nation was faced with the task of being the

[36]John Chrysostom, *Homilies on the Gospel of Matthew* 69.1 (NPNF[1] 10:422).
[37]Cf. Douglas R. A. Hare, *The Theme of Jewish Persecution of Christians in the Gospel According to St Matthew* (Cambridge: Cambridge University Press, 1967), 121.

first to go out to meet Christ, be the first to recognize and accept him, and then to proclaim joy
and salvation to all peoples and tribes on earth. . . .
But this people did not know him, did not recognize him, despised and rejected him. . . . But
they neglected this: some went to their field, and
some to their trade; the rest, seizing his servants,
insulted and killed them. . . . Hearing this, the king
was angry and, sending his troops, destroyed these
murderers and burned their city. This king is God;
his anger finally exhausts his patience and mercy
gives place to justice; the troops are Roman troops;
the murderers are Jews, and their city is Jerusalem.

St Nikolai (Velimirovich)

God's longsuffering is immeasurable. God did not want to punish the
Jews immediately after the murder of our Lord Jesus Christ, but waited
another forty years. . . . *Then saith he to his servants, "The wedding is
ready, but they which were bidden were not worthy. Go ye therefore
into the highways, and as many as ye shall find, bid to the marriage."*
. . . The "highways" means the pagan world, where the ways of good
and evil, rapids and cliffs, stony and thorny places, where the seed of
God was exposed to all kinds of dangers, crossed and intertwined. God
looked at this vast and manifold world with the same paternal concern
with which he looked at Israel, and provided for it—only in a different way. . . . And those servants, going out onto the roads, gathered
everyone they could find, both evil and good; and the wedding feast
was filled with guests. This is the Church of God on earth. This is a
new union of God with people in the name of his Son, our Lord Jesus
Christ. . . . This is a new people chosen by God, a New Israel, a new
tribe of righteous Abraham. Old Israel changed and lost its elect role
in the history of mankind, and God created a new channel of human
salvation, a New Israel.[38]

---

[38]Nikolai Velirimovich, *Tvoreniya*, 2:215–23.

We must stress that there is nothing antisemitic in the traditional interpretation of the parable of those called to the wedding feast, just as we cannot call Jesus' denunciation of the Jews in the Gospels antisemitic, either.[39]
Yet an anti-Judaic subtext is evident in this parable.

In modern scholarly literature, antisemitism and anti-Judaism are often
conflated.[40] Scholars who do this insist that antisemitism and anti-Judaism
are expressions of the same hatred for Jews and Judaism.[41] In reality, they
truly are different phenomena, and each needs its own proper treatment.[42]
Antisemitism as hatred for the Jews as an ethnic group (or for the larger
group of Semitic peoples) should be justly rejected (in many countries
its extreme manifestations are criminally prosecuted). But the polemic
against Judaism as a religious tradition is a major theme of most of the
books of the New Testament, permeating early Christian theology, and it
is even reflected in liturgical texts. To simply erase it from Christian history would mean to remove an important element of Christian identity.
In exactly the same way, the polemic against Christianity constitutes an
important part of Judaism's religious tradition.

Modern Christian-Jewish dialogue has called for the removal of a
centuries-brewing tension between the two religious traditions to help
them coexist peacefully in the future. But this cannot be done by radically

[39]G. Baum, *The Jews and the Gospel: A Re-Examination of the New Testament* (Westminster,
MD: The Newman Press, 1961), 45. (The author underlines that one cannot confuse "prophetic
wrath" with anti-Semitic feelings.)

[40]Cf. Irvin J. Borovsky, "Introduction," in *Removing the Anti-Judaism from the New Testament*, 9–20, at 9–16.

[41]Simon Schoon, "Escape Routes as Dead Ends: On Hatred towards Jews and the New Testament, Especially the Gospel of John," *Anti-Judaism and the Fourth Gospel: Papers of the Leuven
Colloquium, 2000*, ed. Reimund Bieringer, Didier Pollefeyt and Frederique Vandecasteele-Vanneuville (Assen: Royal Van Gorcum, 2001), 144–58, at 145.

[42]Graham Keith, *Hated Without a Cause: A Survey of Anti-Semitism* (Carlisle, England:
Paternoster Press, 1997), 2–6. (The author insists on the necessity of differentiating between
antisemitism and theological polemics against Judaism as a religion.) John G. Gager, *The Origins
of Anti-Semitism* (Oxford: Oxford University Press, 1983), 8. (The author speaks of the difference between anti-Semitism and Christian anti-Judaism, that is, disagreements with Judaism on
religious or theological grounds.) E. H. Flannery, "Anti-Judaism and Anti-Semitism: A Necessary
Distinction," *Journal of Ecumenical Studies* 10 (1973): 581–88, at 583. (The author insists that anti-
Judaism, in contrast to antisemitism, is a purely theological phenomenon that rejects Judaism as
a path to salvation, but not the Jews as a people.)

re-envisioning either of these two traditions, or
their theological self-understanding. As one modern scholar put it:

> In the past horrible injustices and pogroms have
> been directed toward Jews on the basis of their
> being "Christ killers." Christians should be the first
> to speak out against such evils. On the other hand,
> we should not succumb to some politically correct
> desire to rewrite the Gospel accounts in order to
> refute this charge. We cannot rewrite what took
> place in the past.[43]

Saint Stephen, Bulgarian
icon, 17th century

The polemic with the Jews, which Jesus himself
began in his preaching and parables, ended with his
death on the cross after the verdict of the Jewish Sanhedrin. This polemic
was continued by his disciples and followers—the apostles of the first century, the Apostolic Fathers of the second century, and the Fathers of the
Church of the later centuries. As a rule, this polemic was in no way motivated by enmity against any specific ethnic group. First and foremost it
had a doctrinal character. The Fathers of the Church accused the Jews of
the same things that Jesus did: that they did not believe in God, that they
rejected the prophets that he sent them, that they then rejected and killed
his own beloved Son, and then continued to reject the apostles that he
sent, one after another. Stephen and James, mentioned by Chrysostom,
were victims of Jewish persecution. This persecution would have continued, had not the Jews themselves become a persecuted nation after their
exile in AD 70.

If we do not read the parable of the wicked tenants as a direct accusation of the Jewish people, what sort of alternative interpretations are possible? Several have been offered by modern secular scholars who reject
Jesus' authorship and ascribe the composition of this parable to the early
Church. One of them claims that "Since the parable provides no ready
identification models, no clear metaphorical referencing," and therefore

[43]Robert H. Stein, *Jesus the Messiah* (Downer's Grove, IL: InterVarsity Press, 1996), 238.

"an audience is left in a precarious position: *In the plot the kingdom fails and the inheritance is in doubt.*"[44] Others suggest the parable "may well have been a warning to absentee landowners expropriating and exporting the produce of the land."[45]

Still others believe this parable is a shocking story of a successfully perpetrated murder,[46] in which Jesus simply tells a disturbing and tragic story, but without applying it to anyone in particular.[47]

It seems to us that not much effort is needed to see that as soon as any commentator tears himself away from the *terra firma* of the Gospel's original context and stands on the shifting sands of speculation and guesswork, he loses the most important key to understanding the meaning of the parable.

> Despite seemingly tireless and ultimately fruitless efforts to find significant meaning in the parable of the wicked vineyard tenants, shorn of its New Testament Gospel context or when authenticity is denied, all that is left is banality. . . . These decontextualized approaches leave us with a parable that there is no real reason to tell or to preserve. . . . We are better off by far to take more seriously the earliest context we have . . . than the doubtful contexts found in later sources or in the imaginations and speculation of modern scholars.[48]

Such a context is, without a doubt, the conflict between Jesus and the spiritual elite of Israel—a conflict that is vividly expressed in all four Gospels.

According to the great Russian hierarch of the twentieth century St John (Maximovitch), "Those who do not come to the feast of the Lord inevitably will go to the feast of Herod, where the righteous man is always murdered."[49] This choice was made by those Jews who rejected the Messiah.

[44]Scott, *Hear Then*, 252–53.

[45]Bruce J. Malina and Richard L. Rohrbaugh, *Social-Science Commentary on the Synoptic Gospels* (Minneapolis: Fortress Press, 1992), 110.

[46]Crossan, *In Parables*, 96.

[47]*The Five Gospels: The Search for the Authentic Words of Jesus*, ed. Robert Walter Funk and Roy W. Hoover (Sonoma, CA: Polebridge Press, 1993), 101.

[48]Evans, *Fabricating Jesus*, 132

[49]Cited in Shargunov, *Evangelie dnya*, 2:108. Translated by DNK.

This rejection could not have been a passive and indifferent act of ignoring his presence, as we see in the answers of those called to the feast in Luke's version. It can only take the form of active opposition to the Messiah, to everything he said and did, which eventually led to his murder, and later to the murders of his apostles.

St John (Maximovich)

The Wedding Feast as an Image of the Eucharist

The parable of the wedding feast precedes not only Jesus' prophecies of the destruction of Jerusalem and the second coming, but also the Last Supper. This forces us to turn to the connection between the image of the wedding feast and the Eucharist that the Church formulated at an early stage. Early Christian art envisions this parable as a symbolic precursor of the most important sacrament of the Church: in catacomb paintings, the wedding feast is one of the most common depictions, and many liturgical texts make this connection, as do the Fathers of the Church in their commentaries.

The parable's image of the wedding feast reminds one of analogous images found in the Old Testament, including in the wisdom literature:

> Wisdom hath builded her house; she hath hewn out her seven pillars; she hath killed her beasts; she hath mingled her wine; she hath also furnished her table; she hath sent forth her maidens; she crieth upon the highest places of the city, "Whoso is simple, let him turn in hither." As for him that wanteth understanding, she saith to him, "Come, eat of my bread, and drink of the wine which I have mingled. Forsake the foolish, and live; and go in the way of understanding." (Prov 9.1–6)

In Christian tradition, this text is read as a prototype of the Eucharist, while the Biblical figure of Wisdom is an allegory for the Son of God. This text from Proverbs is also read by the Orthodox Church at all feasts of

Sophia: the Wisdom of God,
Icon, 1600

the Mother of God. This combination of the themes of the Eucharist and the Mother of God is characteristic of the Eastern Christian theological tradition. It was reflected in many works of the fathers, including their commentaries on the parable of the wedding feast.

The classical example of this is the *First Ethical Discourse* of St Symeon the New Theologian (11th century). It begins with the question of whom God took as bride for his only-begotten Son. To this question, Symeon answers, keeping in mind that the Virgin was a descendant of David: "It is the daughter of one who rebelled against him, one who committed murder and adultery. That is to say, he procured for himself as a bride the daughter of an adulterer and a murderer." God sent the archangel Gabriel to her, and by his word "the personal, co-essential, and co-eternal Word of God the Father entered wholly into the womb of the maid, and, by the descent and cooperation of his coessential spirit, took on flesh endowed with intelligence and soul from her all-pure blood, and became man. He was united without confusion with our corruptible and wretched nature and essence who is himself beyond nature and super-essential."[50] This is the mystical wedding of God: he took on our flesh, and gave us divinity.

Symeon continues, "For each of the faithful and sons of light this same marriage is performed in a like and scarcely diverging manner. How? In what way? By uniting himself to us in an all-pure and undefiled marriage, God imparts to us something greater than our own powers allow." This occurs thanks to faith in the Son of God, which grows in the heart of a person like a seed, and thanks to the Eucharist, through which the Son of God enters into man:

> But since it was once and for all that the Word of God became flesh from the Virgin, and was born, bodily, in manner inexpressible and

---

[50]St Symeon, *First Ethical Discourse* 9 (PPS 14:53–54).

The Eucharist,
Fresco,
14th century

transcending thought, and, since it is not possible that he should take flesh once more and be born of each of us, what then are we talking about? This: that the same undefiled flesh which he accepted from the pure loins of Mary, the all-pure Theotokos, and with which he was given birth in the body, he gives to us as food. And when we eat of it, when we eat worthily of his flesh, each one of us receives within himself the entirety of God made flesh, our Lord Jesus Christ, Son of God, and son of the immaculate Virgin Mary, the very One who sits at the right hand of God the Father. . . . He is no longer among us as an infant, and so known only according to the flesh. Rather, he is present in the body bodilessly, mingled with our essence and nature, and deifying us who share his body, who are become flesh of his flesh and bone of his bone. . . . Thus, while from his immaculate mother he borrowed her immaculate flesh, and gave her in return his own divinity—O strange and new exchange!—he takes no flesh from the saints, but he does make them sharers of his own, deified flesh. . . . Even so we too . . . become sons of his mother, the Theotokos, and brothers of

The Eucharist, Botticelli, 1495

Christ himself, as through the all-immaculate and ineffable marriage which took place with and in her. . . . This is the mystery of the marriages which the Father arranged for his only-begotten Son, who with him is co-everlasting and of equal dignity. . . . [51]

Such an interpretation was a culmination of many centuries of development for this eucharistic reading of the parable of the wedding feast, beginning with the earliest centuries of Christian thought. It belongs to the allegorical tradition of interpretation, which can lead one far away from the literal meaning of the text. To a contemporary secular scholar, such allegories, as a rule, seem strained, even artificial. Yet they continue to exist in the liturgical tradition of the Church as a fruit of theological thought that helps to reveal to the faithful the profound levels of meaning in the texts of the Gospels, which were intended from the beginning not to be read solely literally.

The Person Without a Wedding Garment

Let us now examine the part of the parable that is absent in Luke's account. In Matthew, another character makes an appearance: someone who is not properly dressed for a wedding. This part of the parable, when read literally, leads to a natural question: why was a person who was invited to a wedding feast cast out for not wearing the right clothing? The answer usually refers to a custom according to which each invited guest was given clothing appropriate to the feast as he entered. Thus, the person's lack of proper clothing meant that he rejected the king's gift,[52] and so this person's action was in line with the others who were called, but ignored the invitation outright.

[51]St Symeon, *First Ethical Discourse* 10 (PPS 14:56–60).

[52]William Hendriksen, *Exposition of the Gospel According to St. Matthew* (Grand Rapids, MI: Baker Book House, 1973), 797–98; Simon J. Kistemaker, *The Parables of Jesus* (Grand Rapids, MI: Baker Book House, 1980), 104.

Immediately preceding this episode are these words: "So those servants went out into the highways, and gathered together all as many as they found, both bad and good: and the wedding was furnished with guests." In Luke's version, the master commands that only the poor, maimed, halt, and blind be called to the feast. The difference between Matthew and Luke is significant. If Luke's version referred to people who came to the feast in spite of their low social status, Matthew includes a category

The Communion of the People, K. V. Lebedev, 19th century

of guests based on (lacking) moral qualities. The one who entered without proper clothing evidently belongs to the "bad," who, though they entered the bridal feast, were not worthy of it.

In this episode, we again see a reference not so much to the history of Israel as to the history of the New Testament Church. If we accept that the two groups of servants symbolize the prophets and the apostles, then naturally the entire story of the man who entered the feast with improper clothing refers to the period of church history after the resurrection of Christ. In that case, its meaning can be explained as follows: just as in the Old Testament period, some of those called by God rejected their calling, so too in the time of the New Testament there will be similar people. This is how ancient commentators generally understand this episode. Gregory the Great explained the parable this way to his community in Rome in the late sixth century:

> But since you have already come into the house of the marriage feast, our holy Church, as a result of God's generosity, be careful, my friends, lest when the King enters he find fault with some aspect of your heart's clothing. . . . What do we think is meant by the wedding garment, dearly beloved? For if we say it is baptism or faith, is there anyone who has entered this marriage feast without them? A person is outside because he has not yet come to believe. What then must we understand by the wedding garment but love? That person enters the marriage feast, but without wearing a wedding garment, who is present

Angel, P Cavallini,
Fresco, 1295–1300

in the holy Church, and has faith, but does not have love.[53]

A bit earlier in that same homily, Gregory speaks of the fact that in the Church, there are both good and evil people. "She brings them all forth to the faith, but does not lead them all to the liberty of spiritual grace successfully by changes in their lives, since their sins prevent it." In the Church on earth, people are "mixed together," but in the end they will be divided. The Church accepts "citizens of both parts . . . now without distinguishing them, but separates them later when they leave this life."[54]

Thus, the second part of the parable in Matthew's version leads listeners away from the question of the relationship between God and his chosen people. The entire first part was dedicated to what occurred outside the wedding feast: the servants invited the guests, they refused to come, and the servants find new guests to invite. The second part, in contrast, occurs at the wedding feast itself. Here it turns out that the fate of a single person can mirror the fate of the entire nation: in spite of the fact that he was not only invited but actually came and entered the feast, he was found unworthy and was cast into outer darkness.

The phrase "there shall be weeping and gnashing of teeth" occurs four times in the Gospel of Matthew and once in the Gospel of Luke. Jesus first uses this phrase in the account of the healing of the centurion's servant, which ends with these words: "Many shall come from the east and west, and shall sit down with Abraham, and Isaac, and Jacob, in the kingdom of heaven. But the children of the kingdom shall be cast out into outer darkness: there shall be weeping and gnashing of teeth" (Mt 8.11–12; Lk 13.28). The second time, he repeats it in his interpretation of the parable of the net: "The Son of Man shall send forth his angels, and they shall gather

---

[53]Gregory the Great, *Forty Homilies on the Gospel* 38.9 (PL 78:1287); *Forty Gospel Homilies*, 346–47.

[54]Gregory the Great, *Forty Homilies on the Gospel* 38.7 (PL 78:1285); *Forty Gospel Homilies*, 344.

out of his kingdom all things that offend, and them which do iniquity; and shall cast them into a furnace of fire: there shall be wailing and gnashing of teeth" (Mt 13.41–42). The third time is here, in the parable of the wedding feast. The fourth time it will be used in the parable of the talents, applied to the worthless servant: the master will "appoint him his portion with the hypocrites: there shall be weeping and gnashing of teeth" (Mt 24.51).

The King of Kings,
Icon, 19th century

Judging by these examples, Jesus used this phrase several times when speaking about the fate of sinners after death. But only in the first example does the phrase refer to Israel. In the other cases, it has a more universal character, indicating all who choose not to believe in Jesus, who will not follow his commandments, who will oppose God, who will sow temptations and do evil, who will not use their talents for good but instead will bury them in the ground. In all cases, he refers to a person's conscious decision. This decision is what determines his fate after death.

This is also how one should understand the phrase "many are called, but few are chosen." These words are another refrain that appears in Jesus' teaching, including both versions of the parable of the wedding feast (Mt 22.14; Lk 14.24). Those who are called include those to whom in various times and in different circumstances the voice of God spoke. Those who are chosen are those who heeded the voice of God.

The Apostle Peter, who heard these words directly from the lips of Jesus, wrote, "Wherefore then rather, brethren, give diligence to make your calling and election sure; for if ye do these things, ye shall never fall, for so an entrance shall be ministered unto you abundantly into the everlasting kingdom of our Lord and Savior Jesus Christ" (2 Pet 1.10–11). Here calling and election are side by side: those who are called and chosen are all the members of the Church. The Apostle Paul calls the members of the Church the chosen of God (Rom 8.33; Col 3.12; Tit 1.1). In Revelation, John the Theologian speaks of the Lamb of God as "Lord of lords, and King of kings, and they that are with him are called, and chosen, and faithful" (Rev 17.14).

Thus, Jesus' words that many are called, but few are chosen, even in the first generation of the Church, received a single interpretation: the called are those whom God invites to the wedding feast, while the chosen are those who remain there. The call is carried out through preaching that resonates with people, leading to their faith in Jesus Christ as God and Savior and their eventual baptism. Election refers to the entire experience of Christian life, including participation in the Eucharist.

The image of the wedding feast is found throughout the Orthodox liturgical cycle, including in the prayer rule before communion. In one of the hymns of Holy Week, which is sung several days in a row (including on Holy Thursday, which commemorates the institution of the Eucharist at the Last Supper), we hear the words: "Thy Bridal Chamber I see adorned, O my Savior, but I have no wedding garment that I may enter, O Giver of Light, enlighten the vesture of my soul and save me."[55] The image of the person who is bound hand and foot and cast out of the wedding feast is one of the leitmotifs permeating the penitential prayers and hymns of Great Lent and Holy Week.

4. The Ten Virgins

The parable of the ten virgins follows the parable of the wise servant, and this begins the last trilogy of parables in Matthew (Mt 24.45–25.30). After the parable of the ten virgins, the parable of the talents follows. All three of these parables form part of a larger sermon focusing on the theme of Christ's second coming.[56] In Matthew's account, this is Jesus' final public sermon, spoken two days before the final Passover.

---

[55]"Bridegroom Matins" of Holy Week, Exapostilarion. Translation in *The Bridegroom Services of Holy Week*, prepared by David Anderson, John Erickson, and V. Rev. Paul Lazor (Syosset, NY: Department of Religious Education, Orthodox Church in America, s.d.).

[56]Concerning the general context of this parable, cf. A. Puig i Tàrrech, *La parabole des dix vierges* (Rome: 1983), 19–29.

The Parable of the Ten Virgins, Miniature from the Rossano Gospels, 6th century

The sermon is immediately preceded by a prophecy of Jerusalem's destruction. When the disciples pointed out the temple's fine construction, Jesus tells them, "See ye not all these things? Verily I say unto you, there shall not be left here one stone upon another, that shall not be thrown down." Later, when they are alone with him on the Mount of Olives, the disciples ask Jesus, "Tell us, when shall these things be? And what shall be the sign of thy coming, and of the end of the world?" (Mt 24.2–3). The disciples do not yet know that the destruction of Jerusalem will occur during their own lifetime, while the second coming would be delayed for millennia. In their consciousness, the two events were connected, and both filled their hearts with terror. They can sense that Jesus will soon abandon them, and they had already heard him prophesy the coming calamities and persecutions many times. They also heard him promise that he would come again, not to continue his mission, but to bring the history of mankind to a close.

What interests them most is *when* all this will occur. Jesus' answer is reminiscent both in form and content of Old Testament prophecies, which, as a rule, provide no dates for future events, and the events themselves are often described figuratively or metaphorically. Prophecies combine different time periods, intertwining with each other, laying them one on top of another, creating a single picture of coming events that produces a singular effect upon the listener—either terror or hope, but with no concrete details or times.

Jesus speaks of the signs of his coming, but he refuses to assign a date and time: "But of that day and hour knoweth no man, no, not the angels of heaven, but my Father only" (Mt 24.36). Throughout this sermon, a theme will emerge: a call to vigilance, to constant readiness to meet this second coming: "Watch therefore, for ye know not what hour your Lord doth come" (Mt 24.42).

From direct prophecies, Jesus continues to speak in the language of parables or similes. He compares the time that precedes the end of the age with the state of the fig tree at the end of spring: "Now learn the parable of the fig tree: when his branch is yet tender, and putteth forth leaves, ye know that summer is nigh" (Mt 24.32). The suddenness of the second coming is illustrated by the example of a thief who unexpectedly breaks into a person's house (Mt 24.43). All these similes are sometimes included in lists of parables, especially since the simile of the fig tree is indeed preceded by the word *paroimia* ("parable"). Nevertheless, these similes are not full-fledged parables. They serve an illustrative function, as does his reference to Noah: "in the days that were before the flood they were eating and drinking, marrying and giving in marriage, until the day that Noah entered into the ark, and knew not until the flood came, and took them all away; so shall also the coming of the Son of Man be" (Mt 24.38–39).

In this whole episode, there are three full parables. All of them naturally fit the general tone of the sermon, and all have an eschatological character. They begin immediately after the words: "Therefore be ye also ready: for in such an hour as ye think not the Son of Man cometh" (Mt 24.44). The first in this trilogy is the parable of the faithful servant (Mt 24.45–51). We have already examined this parable together with its analogue in the Gospel according to Luke.

The story of the second parable, the ten virgins, is based on the particular wedding customs practiced in Palestine in Jesus' time:

> Then shall the kingdom of heaven be likened unto ten virgins, which took their lamps, and went forth to meet the bridegroom. And five of them were wise, and five were foolish. They that were foolish took their lamps, and took no oil with them. But the wise took oil in their vessels with their lamps. While the bridegroom tarried, they all slumbered and slept. And at midnight there was a cry made, "Behold, the bridegroom cometh; go ye out to meet him." Then all those virgins arose, and trimmed their lamps. And the foolish said unto the wise, "Give

us of your oil, for our lamps are gone out." But the wise answered, saying, "Not so, lest there be not enough for us and you. But go ye rather to them that sell, and buy for yourselves." And while they went to buy, the bridegroom came; and they that were ready went in with him to the marriage, and the door was shut. Afterward came also the other virgins, saying, "Lord, Lord, open to us." But he answered and said, "Verily I say unto you, I know you not." (Mt 25.1–13)

In many ancient manuscripts, including the Codex Sinaiticus, the parable ends with the phrase: "Watch therefore, for ye know neither the day nor the hour."[57] In other manuscripts, the words "wherein the Son of Man cometh" are added to resonate with Matthew 24.44 ("Therefore be ye also ready: for in such an hour as ye think not the Son of Man cometh"). John Chrysostom, who wrote his

The Dread Judgment and the Parable of the Ten Virgins, Unknown artist of the Flemish school, 15th century

commentary on the Gospel of Matthew at the end of the fourth century, did not work with a manuscript that included this addition. Nevertheless, Jerome included it in his Vulgate Bible. We cannot exclude the possibility that the phrase was present in one of the versions of the original text, but for some reason was left out in a subsequent version.

The ten virgins are characterized by the term *parthenoi*, which can be translated either as "virgins" or "young women." These are not grown women who decided to remain unmarried, these are the friends of the bride: young women who have not yet been given away in marriage.[58] The text in no way stresses virginity,[59] though subsequent Christian commentators bring attention to the theme.

---

[57] Aland, *Synopsis*, 412.

[58] Concerning the meaning of the term *parthenos*, see Puig i Tàrrech, *La Parabole*, 145–52.

[59] D. Buzy, "Les dix vierges," *Revue apostolique* 39 (1923–25): 73; Erich Klostermann, *Das Matthäusevangelium* (Tübingen: Mohr Siebeck, 1971), 200.

The Ten Virgins,
Tintoretto,
16th century

According to the conventions of the time, the wedding feast usually began in the evening. Before the beginning of the feast, the groom would take the bride from her home, where she awaited his coming together with her friends. The scene this parable describes took place, according to some scholars, in the home of the groom's parents,[60] or in the home of the bride's parents,[61] while some believe that the events begin at the home of the parents of the bride, and continue in the home of the parents of the groom.[62] The third possibility seems to best fit what we know about bridal rites of Palestine in the first century:

> The wedding guests were entertained in the bride's home until late evening. There they waited for the bridegroom, whose coming was announced by messengers. Some time after nightfall (in this parable, about midnight) the groom came to claim his bride and to take her to his father's home, where the wedding ceremony and other festivities took place. Both the coming of the bridegroom to the bride's home and

[60]Robert Gundry, *Matthew: A Commentary on His Handbook for a Mixed Church under Persecution*, 2nd ed. (Grand Rapids, MI: Eerdmans, 1994), 498; Donald Senior, *Matthew* (Nashville, TN: Abington Press, 1998), 274.

[61]B. T. D. Smith, *The Parables of the Synoptic Gospels: A Critical Study* (Cambridge: Cambridge University Press, 1937), 100; Eduard Schweizer, *The Good News according to Matthew* (Atlanta: Westminster John Knox Press, 1975), 467.

[62]Manson, *The Sayings*, 242–43; R. H. Smith, *Matthew* (Minneapolis: Augsburg, 1989), 293.

the procession to his father's home were accompanied by bright lights, especially by torches.[63]

The Catalonian Catholic theologian A. Puig i Tàrrech, the author of the most detailed examination of the parable of the ten virgins, paints a different picture. After sunset, when the bride has been prepared for the wedding, a procession made up of her parents, relatives, and friends sets out for the groom's house with lamps, songs, and dances. This procession moves slowly along the roads and streets to the house of the groom who awaits the bride in his home. When the bridal procession approaches the groom's house, he comes out to meet them, together with his parents and friends, and he greets the bride to raucous applause and joyful exclamations from all who are in attendance. After this, both processions enter the house of the groom to take part in the wedding feast.[64] But this description does not explain why the groom might be so long detained that the virgins had time to rest and fall asleep.

In some Greek manuscripts of Matthew, as well as in Latin and Syriac translations of this Gospel, the ten virgins process out to greet the bride and groom. In this version, the main action of the parable would begin and end, it seems, in the house of the parents of the groom, where the bride and groom then return later. In that house, however, it would not have been the virgins who awaited not the groom, but the friend of the bridegroom (Jn 3.29) and the sons of the bridechamber (Mt 9.15). Therefore, the generally accepted reading of the parable, in which they come out to greet the groom, is probably the most likely to reflect actual Palestinian wedding rituals.

Usually parables that use some detail to compare to the kingdom of heaven use the present tense: "The kingdom of heaven is likened unto a man . . ." (Mt 13.24), "The kingdom of heaven is like to a grain of mustard seed . . ." (Mt 13.31), "The kingdom of heaven is like unto leaven . . ." (Mt 13.33), "the kingdom of heaven is like unto treasure hid in a field . . ." (Mt 13.44). But the parable of the ten virgins uses the future tense: "Then shall

---

[63]Newman and Stine, *A Translator's Handbook*, 765.
[64]Puig i Tàrrech, *La parabole*, 206–207.

The Parable of the Ten Virgins, Peter Bruegel the Elder, 16th century

the kingdom of heaven be likened unto ten virgins . . ." This underlines the eschatological character of the parable: it speaks of what will take place at the second coming of Christ.

The content of the parable of the ten virgins is similar to other eschatological parables, including the parable of the wise servants who await the return of their master from the wedding feast (Lk 12.35–38). In both cases, the action occurs at night; a wedding feast is mentioned; all await the return of a main character; he comes late; those who await him must be ready to greet him at any moment. The plot of the parable of the wise servants is summarized thus: "Let your loins be girded about, and your lights burning . . . blessed are those servants, whom the lord when he cometh shall find watching. . . . Be ye therefore ready also: for the Son of Man cometh at an hour when ye think not" (Lk 12.35, 37, 40). These same words can also be used to summarize the parable of the ten virgins, with a single divergence: here these words are addressed to women, not men. We can also examine the parable of the wise servants as a direct continuation of the story begun in the parable of the ten virgins (the master of the house could easily have done the same thing he did in the former parable after his return from the wedding feast).

Two other parables are parallels to the parable of the ten virgins, with similarities in themes and plot: the parable of the wise servant in Matthew

The Parable of the Ten Virgins, Francken, 1616

(Mt 24.45–51) and the parable of those awaiting the return of the master in Mark (13.33–37).

The turning point of the parable of the wise servant is the unexpected arrival of the master (he came home earlier than expected); in the parable of the ten virgins, however, the opposite is true (he comes late). This tarrying plays an important role in the parable, framing the entire narrative. It is the reason that the virgins fall asleep, allowing their lamps to start going out.[65]

The image of the lamp is important. As a rule, these lamps were made of clay with a wick inside, fed by olive oil.[66] The foolish virgins' lack of oil did not stem from the fact that they had no oil to begin with, but rather that they did not take any additional oil as a precaution. Naturally, they poured oil into their lamps when they started, but they did not anticipate that the groom might be late. The wise virgins did anticipate this possibility, and so they not only poured oil into their lamps, but they also took some additional oil with them.[67] While the virgins rested and slept, their lamps continued to burn. When the voice was heard in the middle of the night announcing the coming of the bridegroom, they only had to trim their wicks and add a bit of oil. Here it became clear that the lamps of the foolish virgins were about to go out, and they had no extra oil with them.

[65]Snodgrass, *Stories with Intent*, 516.

[66]Jülicher, *Gleichnisreden,* 2:448; Senior, *Matthew*, 275. Some scholars believe that here the lamps are actually torches prepared from the wood of a tree and fed also by olive oil. Cf. Jeremias, *Parables*, 174; Gundry, *Matthew*, 498. The term *lampas* (lamp) can be used to mean both.

[67]Bailey, *Jesus through Middle Eastern Eyes*, 272.

The Ten Virgins,
Peter von
Cornelius, 1813

In the Old Testament, oil is a rich symbol indicating, in part, that God is the source of spiritual light: "For thou wilt light my lamp; O Lord my God, thou wilt enlighten my darkness" (Ps 17.28). Like a traveler walking at night, a man is directed on his journey by the word of God: "Thy law is a lamp unto my feet, and a light unto my paths" (Ps 118.105). According to the wise Solomon, "the commandment is a lamp; and the law is light; and reproofs of instruction are the way of life" (Prov 6.23). At the same time, "the spirit of man . . . searching all the inward parts of the belly" is also "the candle of the Lord" (Prov 20.27).

The burning of a lamp is a symbol of righteousness, while its dimming is a symbol of iniquity: "The light of the righteous rejoiceth, but the lamp of the wicked shall be put out" (Prov 13.9); "Yea the light of the wicked shall be put out, and the spark of his fire shall not shine. The light shall be dark in his tabernacle, and his candle shall be put out with him" (Job 18.5–6); "For there shall be no reward to the evil man; the candle of the wicked shall be put out" (Prov 24.20). Proverbs praises the virtuous wife who "riseth also while it is yet night, and giveth food to her household, and a portion to her maidens . . . she girdeth her loins with strength, and strengtheneth her arms. She perceiveth that her merchandise is good; her candle goeth not out by night" (Prov 31.15, 16–18).

In the prophets, the lamp acquires an eschatological symbolism. The burning of a lamp becomes a symbol of the glory of God and the salvation of Israel: "For Zion's sake will I not hold my peace, and for Jerusalem's sake I will not rest, until the righteousness thereof go forth as brightness, and the salvation thereof as a lamp that burneth" (Is 62.1). Quenching the light of a lamp symbolizes divine wrath: "Moreover I will take from them the voice of mirth, the voice of gladness, the voice of the bridegroom, and the voice of the bride, the sound of the millstones, and the light of the candle" (Jer 25.10).

The Parable of the Ten Virgins, William Blake, 1825

All this rich symbolism is present in the parable of the ten virgins. The lamps that are lit are a symbol of spiritual intensity and vigilance, readiness to greet the Son of Man who may come in any watch of the night. The lights that are going out, on the contrary, are a symbol of a lack of preparedness for this meeting, of carelessness and irresponsibility.

It is through the filter of this rich symbolism that we should understand the final scene in which the foolish virgins try to enter the house, but the bridegroom says, "I know you not." Some modern scholars see merely the reflection of the crude mores of a patriarchal society. According to them, the wise virgins do not show the necessary solidarity with their foolish sisters, thereby not fulfilling the commandment of love for neighbor; thus, the final scene reveals the ugly face of a society in which women are seen as worthy only of subjugation and marrying off.[68] Others, on the contrary, see in this parable a confirmation that Jesus considered equality between men and women to be important: having first told the parable in which the wise and foolish male servants act, he then continues with an analogous parable in which the main characters are women.[69]

It seems to us that to seek in this parable for a particular perspective on women's place in society is missing the point. The parable is not speaking about the customs of women, nor of the relationship of men toward

[68]Schotroff, *The Parables*, 31.
[69]Bailey, *Jesus through Middle Eastern Eyes*, 273.

women, nor of the place of women in society. The two groups of women in the parable merely symbolize two different ways of responding to one's responsibility before God, just as in the previous parable an analogous role was played by male servants. The only kind of equality that can be read into this parable is this: every person, regardless of gender, bears responsibility before God for his or her life and actions. Some show themselves to be wise, others foolish; some keep their lamps burning, others let theirs burn out; some remember the dread judgment, expect it, and prepare for it, others live as though there will never be a judgment at all.

The dialogue between the foolish virgins and the bridegroom is purposely told in a tone reminiscent of Jesus' other sermons, beginning with the Sermon on the Mount and ending with his final teaching before the Last Supper:

> Not every one that saith unto me, "Lord, Lord," shall enter into the kingdom of heaven, but he that doeth the will of my Father which is in heaven. Many will say to me in that day, "Lord, Lord, have we not prophesied in thy name? And in thy name have cast out devils? And in thy name done many wonderful works?" And then will I profess unto them, "I never knew you. Depart from me, ye that work iniquity." (Mt 7.21–23)

> When once the master of the house is risen up, and hath shut to the door, and ye begin to stand without, and to knock at the door, saying, "Lord, Lord, open unto us," and he shall answer and say unto you, "I know you not whence ye are." Then shall ye begin to say, "We have eaten and drunk in thy presence, and thou hast taught in our streets." But he shall say, "I tell you, I know you not whence ye are. Depart from me, all ye workers of iniquity." (Lk 13.25–27)

> Then shall he say also unto them on the left hand, "Depart from me, ye cursed, into everlasting fire, prepared for the devil and his angels. For I was hungry, and ye gave me no meat; I was thirsty, and ye gave me no drink; I was a stranger, and ye took me not in; naked, and ye clothed me not; sick, and in prison, and ye visited me not." Then shall they

also answer him, saying, "Lord, when saw we thee hungry, or athirst, or a stranger, or naked, or sick, or in prison, and did not minister unto thee?" Then shall he answer them, saying, "Verily I say unto you, inasmuch as ye did it not to one of the least of these, ye did it not to me." And these shall go away into everlasting punishment, but the righteous into life eternal. (Mt 25.41–46)

All these teachings refer to the end of human existence, which always—openly or in subtext—is present in Jesus' preaching.

The parable of the ten virgins has a rich history of interpretation in the patristic tradition. Among the Greek Fathers of the Church, interpretations often focus on the similarity between the words *eleos* ("mercy") and *elaion* ("oil"). Based on this, the oil in the lamp is understood to represent works of mercy that one group exhibited, but the other did not.

John Chrysostom said, "But by lamps here, he means the gift itself of virginity, the purity of holiness; and by oil, humanity, almsgiving, succor to them that are in need." In the image of the tarrying bridegroom he sees "that the time intervening will not be short, leading his disciples away from the expectation that his kingdom was quite immediately to appear." As for the image of the sleeping virgins, he mentions that death is like sleep. The lack of oil in the lamps of the foolish virgins then symbolizes their avarice: "nothing can be more foolish than they who are wealthy here, and depart naked there, where most of all we have need of humanity, where we want much oil." As for the wise virgins, they symbolize the fact that "no man can protect us there, if we are betrayed by our works, not because he will not, but because he cannot."[70]

Augustine's commentary is in many ways similar to Chrysostom's. He understood the lamps to symbolize good deeds, and oil to symbolize love. The fact that all fell asleep indicates that all—foolish and wise alike—can expect death. The lack of oil in the lamps of the foolish virgins symbolizes the lack of love in their hearts.[71] The lamps of the wise and foolish virgins, in fact, burned with different flames:

[70]John Chrysostom, *Homilies on the Gospel of Matthew* 78.1 (NPNF[1] 10:470–71).
[71]Augustine, *Homily* 43(93).2–8 (PL 38:574–77; NPNF[1] 6:401–403).

Observe then, beloved, before those virgins slept, it is not said that their lamps were extinguished. The lamps of the wise virgins burned with an inward oil, with the assurance of a good conscience, with an inner glory, with an inmost charity. Yet the lamps of the foolish virgins burned also. Why burnt they then? Because there was yet no want of the praises of men. But after that they arose, that is in the resurrection from the dead, they began to trim their lamps, that is, began to prepare to render unto God an account of their works. And because there is then no one to praise, every man is wholly employed in his own cause, there is no one then who is not thinking of himself, therefore were there none to sell them oil; so their lamps began to fail, and the foolish betook themselves to the five wise. . . . They sought for what they had been wont to seek for, to shine that is with others' oil, to walk after others' praises.[72]

The cry at midnight is unanimously interpreted as the final trumpet that the Apostle Paul speaks of (1 Cor 15.52; 1 Thess 4.16).[73] Moreover, according to Hilary of Poitiers, who used the Vulgate for his interpretation, "The bridegroom and the bride is our Lord God in the body. For as the Spirit is wedded to the flesh, so the flesh is to the Spirit. When the trumpet sounds the alert, we go out to meet only one spouse: the two have become one now that the humility of the flesh has passed over to spiritual glory."[74] The tarrying of the bridegroom is the time allotted for repentance; the trimming of the wicks is the return of the souls into their bodies, and their radiance is the proof of virtue contained in the vessels of our bodies.

In terms of allegorizing, Cyril of Alexandria goes the farthest afield. He interprets the virgins to be the leaders of nations, that is, the clergy. The five virgins are five stages of life: infancy, childhood, youth, maturity, old age. The fact that all five set out with their lamps lit shows that all souls were illumined by God through natural law. The virgins' sleep is the death of the

---

[72]Augustine, Homily 43(93).10 (PL 38:577–78; NPNF[1] 6:404).

[73]John Chrysostom, *Homilies on Matthew* 78.1 (NPNF[1] 10:470–71); Hilary of Poitiers, *Commentary on Matthew* 27.4 (SC 280:204; FOC 125:260–61); Epiphanius the Latin, *Homily on the Gospels* 36 (PLS 3:892–93); Cyril of Alexandria, *Commentary on the Gospel of Matthew* 280 (TU 61:251).

[74]Hilary of Poitiers, *Commentary on Matthew* 27.4 (FOC 125:260–61).

*The Parable of
the Ten Virgins,*
Ernest Karlovich
Lipgart, 1886

body, their awakening is the resurrection from the dead and the final judgment. The dimming of their lamps is the state of the soul when it begins to darken as though it were about to go out, and begins to go mad.[75]

The hymns of the Orthodox Church also interpret the parable of the ten virgins, especially during the services of Holy Week (Tuesday). Its imagery appears in many different hymns and prayers, including the troparion that is sung at Matins in the first three days of Holy Week:

[75]Cyril of Alexandria, *Commentary on the Gospel of Matthew* 280 (TU 61:251).

Behold the Bridegroom comes in the middle of the night; and blessed is the servant whom he shall find watching, but unworthy is he whom he shall find sleeping. Beware, therefore, O my soul, do not be weighed down by sleep, lest thou be given over to death and shut out of the Kingdom. But rouse thyself crying: "Holy, holy, holy art thou, O God. Through the Theotokos have mercy on us."[76]

This hymn connects the image of the ten virgins with imagery from the parable of the vigilant servants (Mt 24.43–51; Lk 12.35–48). All these parables contain an exhortation to spiritual vigilance, sobriety, and expectation of the final judgment, a call to prayer and repentance. The authors of the liturgical texts elicit their most important lesson without excessive allegory.

Jesus expressed this lesson in a single, short exhortation: "be vigilant" (or "watch/be watchful," *grēgoreite*). He repeated this same imperative three times in the parable of the servants awaiting the return of their master (Mk 13.33, 35, 37), then twice in the garden of Gethsemane (Mt 26.38, 41; Mk 14.34, 38). There it has a literal meaning, since the disciples, like the ten virgins, fell asleep while their Teacher was praying so intensely that he sweat blood (Lk 22.44). This example once again proves how closely the elements of the parables intertwine with real events.

5. The Talents and Minas

We have come to the parable that concludes all parables in Matthew and Luke. In Matthew's account, it ends the final trilogy of parables that began with the parable of the wise servant and continued with the parable of the ten virgins:

For the kingdom of heaven is as a man travelling into a far country, who called his own servants, and delivered unto them his goods. And

[76] *The Bridegroom Services of Holy Week*, 25.

unto one he gave five talents, to another two, and to another one: to every man according to his several ability; and straightway took his journey. Then he that had received the five talents went and traded with the same, and made them five other talents. And likewise he that had received two, he also gained two others. But he that had received one went and dug in the earth, and hid his lord's money. After a long time the lord of those servants cometh, and reckoneth with them. And so he that had received five talents came and brought five other talents, saying, "Lord, thou deliveredst unto me five talents: behold, I have gained beside them

The Parable of the Talents,
Miniature, 15th century

five talents more." His lord said unto him, "Well done, thou good and faithful servant: thou hast been faithful over a few things, I will make thee ruler over many things. Enter thou into the joy of thy lord." He also that had received two talents came and said, "Lord, thou deliveredst unto me two talents: behold, I have gained two other talents beside them." His lord said unto him, "Well done, good and faithful servant; thou hast been faithful over a few things, I will make thee ruler over many things: enter thou into the joy of thy lord." Then he which had received the one talent came and said, "Lord, I knew thee, that thou art an hard man, reaping where thou hast not sown, and gathering where thou hast not strawed, and I was afraid, and went and hid thy talent in the earth. Lo, there thou hast what is thine." His lord answered and said unto him, "Thou wicked and slothful servant, thou knewest that I reap where I sowed not, and gather where I have not strawed. Thou oughtest therefore to have put my money to the exchangers, and then at my coming I should have received mine own with usury. Take therefore the talent from him, and give it unto him which hath ten talents. For unto every one that hath shall be given, and he shall have abundance, but from him that hath not shall be taken away even that which he hath. And cast ye the unprofitable servant into outer darkness; there shall be weeping and gnashing of teeth." (Mt 25.14–30)

The parable is similar in content in Luke, but it is ascribed to the final part of Jesus' journey to Jerusalem, specifically, his visit to Jericho. The other two synoptic Gospels also refer to this visit. According to Matthew, Jesus heals two blind men there (Mt 20.29–34); according to Mark, there is only one blind man (Mk 10.46–52). In Luke's account, the healing of the blind man occurs at the approach to Jericho (Lk 18.35–43), while in Jericho proper another event occurs that is not found in Matthew or Mark: the encounter with Zacchaeus, the chief tax collector and a very rich man. Jesus enters his house, in spite of the complaint of the people who say that he entered the house of a sinful man. In answer to Zacchaeus' promise to give away half of his property to the poor and to return fourfold to all whom he had swindled, Jesus utters a phrase with eschatological resonance: "This day is salvation come to this house, forsomuch as he also is a son of Abraham" (Lk 19.9).

It is in Zaccheus' house that Jesus tells a parable similar to Matthew's parable of the talents, told in Jerusalem. The parable in Luke has a prologue and an epilogue, which mention Jerusalem:

> And as they heard these things, he added and spake a parable, because he was nigh to Jerusalem, and because they thought that the kingdom of God should immediately appear. He said therefore, "A certain nobleman went into a far country to receive for himself a kingdom, and to return. And he called his ten servants, and delivered them ten pounds [*mnas*], and said unto them, 'Occupy till I come.' But his citizens hated him, and sent a message after him, saying, 'We will not have this man to reign over us.' And it came to pass, that when he was returned, having received the kingdom, then he commanded these servants to be called unto him, to whom he had given the money, that he might know how much every man had gained by trading. Then came the first, saying, 'Lord, thy pound hath gained ten pounds.' And he said unto him, 'Well, thou good servant: because thou hast been faithful in a very little, have thou authority over ten cities.' And the second came, saying, 'Lord, thy pound hath gained five pounds.' And he said likewise to him, 'Be thou also over five cities.' And another came, saying, 'Lord, behold, here is

The Parable of the Talents, Willem de Poorter, 17th century

thy pound, which I have kept laid up in a napkin. For I feared thee, because thou art an austere man: thou takest up that thou layedst not down, and reapest that thou didst not sow.' And he saith unto him, 'Out of thine own mouth will I judge thee, thou wicked servant. Thou knewest that I was an austere man, taking up that I laid not down, and reaping that I did not sow. Wherefore then gavest not thou my money into the bank, that at my coming I might have required mine own with usury?' And he said unto them that stood by, 'Take from him the pound, and give it to him that hath ten pounds.' (And they said unto him, 'Lord, he hath ten pounds.') 'For I say unto you, that unto every one which hath shall be given; and from him that hath not, even that he hath shall be taken away from him. But those mine enemies, which would not that I should reign over them, bring hither, and slay them before me.'" (Lk 19.11–27)

As in other cases when two similar texts are found in two different Gospels, scholars like to speculate about which of the two belongs to the "historical Jesus" and which is an editorial alteration of the original text. Several possible answers to this "conundrum" are offered:

1) Jesus told two different parables that are similar in content;

2) Jesus told one parable, but it was written down differently by two evangelists;

3) Both evangelists took the parable from the hypothetical "Q source," but each edited it differently to reflect the needs of his community;

4) There are two literary prototypes (indicated by the letters L and M), which acted as sources for the two evangelists.

The first version is already considered obsolete by the whole scholarly community.[77] Even the search for an authentic source for the sermons and parables of Jesus by means of separating it from editorial additions in the Gospels has largely lost its luster among scholars. Many have returned to older hypotheses, coming to the understanding that the original text was most likely what came down to us historically, not some secret prototype that no one has found. And if we use the Gospels as the original text, then the answer to the "conundrum" is clear: Jesus told not one, but two parables in two different places. They are similar in content, but different in form.

The commonality of content is quite evident and requires no commentary. As for the differences in form, they are significant and deserve special attention. In Matthew, the currency in question is a talent, and in Luke—the mina ("pound" in the KJV). In Matthew, the lord simply travels to a far country and then returns, while in Luke he goes to receive a kingdom and comes back as a king. In Matthew, there are three servants: one receives five talents, another two, another one. In Luke, there are ten slaves, each of whom receives a single mina, but only three of the ten are then called to answer for their dealings. In Matthew, the wise servants describe a two-fold increase: the first makes ten out of five, the second makes four out of two. In Luke, one of them increases ten-fold, the second increases his capital five times. Matthew does not describe the reward for the wise servants in detail: they were faithful in small things, so they will be given great rewards. In Luke, the rewards are specified: one receives ten cities to rule over, the other five. The foolish servant in Matthew buries his talent in the ground; in Luke, he wraps it in a handkerchief.

[77] Fitzmeyer, *Luke*, 1230.

The differences in terminology are also significant. Unlike some parables that are almost identical in all three synoptic Gospels—for example, the sower, the mustard seed, and the wicked tenants—in this case, different terminology is used to describe even superficially similar elements.

All these differences prove the first hypothesis: Jesus told two different parables in two different places. They are similar in content, but very different in form. To ascribe such significant differences merely to the editor's pen is an unwarranted stretch.

By comparing the accounts in Matthew and Luke, it becomes clear that on the way to Jerusalem, Jesus began to speak of his second coming (Lk 17.20–37) when he answered questions about when the kingdom of God would come. The theme of one's fate after death appears in several parables Jesus told on the way to Jerusalem: the rich fool (Lk 12.13–21), the vigilant servants (Lk 12.35–40), the unjust steward (Lk 12.41–48), the foolish steward (Lk 16.1–9), the rich man and Lazarus (Lk 16.19–31), the workers in the vineyard (Mt 20.1–16). The parable of the ten minas ends this series. Yet the theme of the second coming and the fate of mankind after death continues in other sermons and parables Jesus told in Jerusalem (Mt 21.33–22.14; 24.3–25.46). There is nothing strange in the fact that two parables with similar content were told both on the way to Jerusalem and in Jerusalem proper.

As we have already mentioned before, the term "talent" in the Greco-Roman world was a unit of weight roughly equal to 42.5 kilograms. In Jesus' time, it had come to refer to a unit of currency equal to six thousand denarii.[78] The talent was the largest unit of currency in circulation. The Greek term *mina*, translated in the KJV as "pound," corresponds to the Hebrew *mane* and the Aramaic *mene*.[79] It equaled one hundred shekels, or one hundred Attic drachmas, and was sixty times less valuable than the talent.[80]

The situation in the parable that Luke records was well known to Jesus' audience. In 40 BC, Herod the Great traveled to Rome to receive the rights of kingship from Mark Anthony and Octavian, who were engaged in a

[78]Hultgren, *Parables*, 23.

[79]George Abbott-Smith, *A Manual Greek Lexicon of the New Testament*, 2nd ed. (Edinburgh: T & T Clark, 1929), 294.

[80]Fitzmeyer, *Luke*, 1235.

power struggle in Rome.⁸¹ His son Archelaus took a similar journey in 4
BC to receive his kingship from Octavian, who was emperor of Rome by
that time. Josephus describes this journey in great detail. Archelaus traveled to Rome by sea, together with a large group of friends and relatives,
and he left the administration of the government to his brother Philip.
But Antipas, another of Herod's sons, simultaneously rushed to Rome as
well, intending to present his own candidacy to the emperor. Archelaus
presented the will of Herod the Great, as well as other documents intended
to support his claim. The emperor summoned a council where he heard
arguments for and against Archelaus' claim. Finally, Archelaus fell at the
feet of Caesar, and then the emperor told him to rise, saying he considered
him worthy of the throne.⁸²

Nevertheless, a final decision was not made at the council. In the mean-
time, a delegation of Jews arrived in Rome, intending to petition against
the continuation of the kingship over Judea in general, but also against
Archelaus' claim in particular. In support of their petition, they cited the
lawlessness of his father, Herod the Great:

> They declared that he was indeed in name a king, but that he had taken
> to himself that uncontrollable authority which tyrants exercise over
> their subjects, and had made use of that authority for the destruction
> of the Jews, and did not abstain from making many innovations among
> them besides, according to his own inclinations; and that whereas there
> were a great many who perished by that destruction he brought upon
> them, so many indeed as no other history relates, they that survived
> were far more miserable than those that suffered under him; not only
> by the anxiety they were in from his looks and disposition towards
> them, but from the danger their estates were in of being taken away by
> him. That he did never leave off adorning these cities that lay in their
> neighborhood, but were inhabited by foreigners; but so that the cities
> belonging to his own government were ruined, and utterly destroyed
> that whereas, when he took the kingdom, it was in an extraordinary

⁸¹Josephus, *Wars of the Jews* 1.14.2–4; *Works of Josephus,* 565.
⁸²Josephus, *Antiquities of the Jews,* 17.9.1–7; *Works of Josephus,* 465–68.

flourishing condition, he had filled the nation with the utmost degree of poverty; and when, upon unjust pretenses, he had slain any of the nobility, he took away their estates; and when he permitted any of them to live, he condemned them to the forfeiture of what they possessed. And besides the annual impositions which he laid upon every one of them, they were to make liberal presents to himself, to his domestics and friends, and to such of his slaves as were vouchsafed the favor of being his tax-gatherers, because there was no way of obtaining a freedom from unjust violence without giving either gold or silver for it. That they would say nothing of the corruption of the chastity of their virgins, and the reproach laid on their wives for incontinency, and those things acted after an insolent and inhuman manner; because it was not a smaller pleasure to the sufferers to have such things concealed, than it would have been not to have suffered them. That Herod had put such abuses upon them as a wild beast would not have put on them, if he had power given him to rule over us.[83]

Finally, the emperor sought to mollify all sides. He "appointed Archelaus, not indeed to be king of the whole country, but ethnarch of the one half of that which had been subject to Herod, and promised to give him the royal dignity hereafter, if he governed his part virtuously. But as for the other half, he divided it into two parts, and gave it to two other of Herod's sons, to Philip and to Antipas, that Antipas who disputed with Archelaus for the whole kingdom." Some of the lands passed to Herod's sister Salome, and another part was added to Syria.[84]

All these events were well known. Jesus' audience would have swiftly associated the lord who goes to a far country with Archelaus or another claimant to the throne of Judea who would have to travel to Rome in hopes of receiving an imperial mandate to rule. As for the citizens that hate him and send an embassy with the words "We will not have this man to reign over us," they call to mind the Jews' embassy, which asked the emperor not to appoint Archelaus over them. It is easy to see Herod

---

[83]Josephus, *Antiquities of the Jews* 17.11.2; *Works of Josephus*, 472.
[84]Ibid., 17.11.4; *Works of Josephus*, 473.

The Parable of the Talents,
Engraving, 1712

the Great himself—whose cruelty was universally acknowledged—in the image of the "austere man" who "takes up what [he] laid not down, and reaps what [he] did not sow."

It is also worth noting that in Luke's account Jesus tells the parable in the house of a publican, a person who collected taxes on behalf of the Romans. The listeners in Zacchaeus' house could have been different sorts of people, probably most were his friends. In the second telling, in Jerusalem, only the disciples were present. In that version, the parable's societal recriminations are basically missing; the theme of receiving the kingdom is absent; all that remains is the departure of a certain lord in an unknown direction for unknown reasons.

In the Gospel according to Luke, a prologue precedes the parable. It describes the context for the parable's telling in these words: "because he was nigh to Jerusalem, and because they thought that the kingdom of God should immediately appear." Who are "they"? Obviously, the disciples. During the entire long journey to Jerusalem, Jesus spoke to them about the kingdom of God, and they naïvely assumed that Jesus was going to Jerusalem to establish his kingdom. They still believed that it was possible to conflate the idea of a Messianic kingdom of Israel on earth with the kingdom of heaven that Jesus constantly preached. Even after his death and resurrection, the first question they ask is: "Lord, wilt thou at this time restore again the kingdom to Israel?" (Acts 1.6). Their expectations of earthly kingship were still mingled with their understanding of the second coming of Christ and the end of the world. When they heard many predictions about this, they failed to understood even a fraction of what Jesus was actually saying, and they asked, "Tell us, when shall these things be? And what shall be the sign of thy coming, and of the end of the world?" (Mt 24.3). It is clear that Jesus' prophecies gave them hope, but at the same time, they were filled with confusion and terror; they did not know what to expect, nor when it would be.

To answer these expectations and concerns, Jesus told them the parable of a lord who traveled to a far country. This journey to a far country (the land of the dead, so to speak) was what awaited him. He knew this, and frequently predicted this journey, comparing himself with the prophet Jonah, who remained in the belly of the whale three days and nights (Mt 12.39–40; Lk 11.29–30). He had to undertake this journey to receive a kingdom from his Father.

Jesus knew that there were those who did not want him to be king over them—the scribes and Pharisees, the political and intellectual elite of Israel. They accused him of sowing where he did not reap, of taking up what he did not lay down, considering themselves to be the lawful heirs of Abraham and Moses, and Jesus to be an impostor whose claim to their spiritual authority was lawless. Their actions within the parable remind the listener of the wicked tenants who hoped that once they had disposed of the vineyard owner's servant and then his own son, they would receive the inheritance of the vineyard. This is the context that best describes the parable as told in Luke's Gospel.

Continuing this analogy, we can see the disciples of Jesus in the servants who were told to take care of their master's property. Two of them, each of whom received a mina, put it into circulation, and it brings good returns, either five-fold or two-fold, depending on their abilities. But one of the ten hides the mina in a cloth. Could this figure not suggest Judas? After all, he was in charge of the money box (Jn 12.6), and he would become the only one of the apostles to go against his Teacher, conspiring with those who had no desire to have him as king over them. The other apostles, on the contrary, each according to his abilities, would fulfill the mission that Jesus laid upon them.

John Chrysostom compared the parable of the talents, as recorded in Matthew, with the parable of the minas in Luke:

> And if in Luke the parable of the talents is otherwise put, this is to be said, that the one is really different from the other. For in that, from the one capital different degrees of increase were made, for from one pound one brought five, another ten; wherefore neither did they obtain

the same recompense; but here, it is the contrary, and the crown is accordingly equal. For he that received two gave two, and he that had received the five again in like manner; but there since from the same beginning one made the greater, one the less, increase; as might be expected, in the rewards also, they do not enjoy the same. But see him everywhere, not requiring it again immediately. For in the case of the vineyard, he let it out to husbandmen, and went into a far country; and here he committed to them the talents, and took his journey, that you might learn his long-suffering. And to me he seems to say these things, to intimate the resurrection.[85]

Thus Chrysostom sees Christ himself as the main character of the parable. Other ancient commentators agree with this interpretation. Gregory the Great asks, "Who is the man who sets out for foreign parts but our Redeemer, who departed to heaven in the body he had taken on?"[86] St Cyril of Alexandria believes that the departure of the master corresponds to Christ's ascension to heaven, that his property is those who have come to believe in him in all cities and countries, and the servants are those whom Christ crowns with the glory of priesthood.[87]

The christological reading of this parable, which dominates among ancient commentators, is also shared by some modern scholars.

Jesus, the nobleman, gives gifts to his disciples for them to use in his service. He anticipates returning to God and being enthroned. In God's good time he will return to his servants to deal with the faithful and the unfaithful. Judgment is pronounced against the master's determined enemies, but that judgment is not enacted.[88]

Some other contemporary scholars dispute this christological reading. N. T. Wright calls such an interpretation stereotypical and untrue, since, according to his point of view, in most of Jesus' parables the king, lord, or master of the house symbolizes the God of Israel, not the Son of Man.

[85]John Chrysostom, *Homilies on Matthew* 78.2 (NPNF[1] 10:471–72).
[86]Gregory the Great, *Forty Gospel Homilies* 18 (PL 76:1106; *Forty Gospel Homilies*, 127).
[87]Cyril of Alexandria, *Commentary on the Gospel of Matthew* 283 (TU 61:252–53).
[88]Bailey, *Jesus through Middle Eastern Eyes*, 407.

He who is like the Son of Man with a sword in his mouth, standing in the midst of seven lamps, The Revelation of John the Theologian, Illustration from the Bamberg Apocalypse, 11th century

He believes that the master's return after a long absence perfectly fits the context of God's return to Zion, and the idea of the second coming is more reminiscent of a post-resurrection innovation than the particularities of Jesus' own preaching.[89]

Leaving aside this quite dubious argument to the conscience of its author, we will only note that if we are to accept the idea of the second coming of Christ as a "post-resurrection innovation" invented by the apostles, then a significant amount of Christ's own words in the Gospels must be declared inauthentic. We believe that the idea of the second coming is so central to Jesus' preaching that it requires no proof. A significant portion of Jesus' final teachings to his disciples is dedicated to the second coming; in it, Jesus frequently speaks of the "coming of the Son of Man" (Mt 24.27, 37, 39) and not once does he speak of God's return to Zion. The prophecy that the Son of Man will come is an important motif of Jesus' preaching, beginning from his first teaching of the apostles (Mt 10.23) and ending with his

[89]Wright, *Jesus and the Victory of God*, 574–76.

last (Mt 24.44; 25.13, 31). As for these prophecies that the Lord will return to his people, to his city, and to his temple—this we find nowhere.

How are we to understand the talents that the lord gives to his servants? Ancient commentators understood the talents to symbolize various virtues,[90] or the physical senses, activity, and knowledge,[91] or in general "each person's ability, whether in the way of protection, or in money, or in teaching, or in whatever thing of the kind."[92]

With time, however, the most widely-accepted interpretation became the notion that the talents represent the individual abilities that God gives to each person. This understanding has so firmly entered the common lexicon that the word "talent" itself, which was initially only a unit of weight, then a unit of currency, eventually acquired in many modern languages (including modern Greek) the figurative meaning of "ability," "gifts," "creative potential," and now is used only in that sense.

In accordance with such an interpretation, the main meaning of the parable is that every person receives from God certain abilities and potential that he is called to realize. In Luke's version, Jesus uses two verbs that are similar in meaning: *pragmateuō* (to put into circulation) and *diapragmateuō* (to receive profit). In Matthew's version, we find two expressions: *kata tēn idian dynamin* ("each according to his strength") and *ērgasato en autois* ("put them to use" or literally "worked with them"). All these expressions put together stress a single idea: each person has particular abilities—some have more, some have less, each according to his measure. God gives them initial capital that each must put into circulation. At the dread judgment, God will settle accounts based on how much initial capital each was given. Only those who made a profit from this initial capital through good deeds done for their neighbors will be

[90]Origen, *Commentary on the Gospel of Matthew* 66–67 (GCS 38²:153–58).

[91]Gregory the Great, *Forty Gospel Homilies* 18 (PL 76:1106; *Forty Gospel Homilies*, 130–31). Based on this interpretation, Gregory explains why the single talent of the lazy servant was given to the one that already had ten, not to the one who had four: the one who had ten was a person who labored in physical asceticism, and in spite of his many fruits, he needed additional ones in knowledge (this is symbolized by the one additional talent) more than the one who had four, for that servant was subtle in both internal and external activity.

[92]John Chrysostom, *Homilies on the Gospel of Matthew* 78.3 (NPNF¹ 10:472).

justified. As St John Chrysostom said, "For this end God gave us speech, and hands, and feet, and strength of body, and mind, and understanding, that we might use all these things, both for our own salvation, and for our neighbor's advantage."[93]

The figure of the servant who hid his mina in a cloth or buried his talent in the ground illustrates the same thought, only in reverse. This image is similar to others that Jesus uses: the prodigal son who foolishly wasted the money his father gave him (Lk 15.12–16), the rich fool who imagined that he could use all of his riches on himself (Lk 12.16–20), the foolish servant who believed that his master would not return home soon (Mt 24.48–49). But if the story of the prodigal son ended well because he offered repentance, then the fate of those who consciously opposed God's will is more tragic. They will receive the harshest conviction at the dread judgment.

Why does the one who failed to put his money into circulation have his money taken from him in both parables? What is the meaning of the phrase "For I say unto you, that unto every one which hath shall be given, and from him that hath not, even what he hath shall be taken away from him"? This phrase is present in both versions of the parable, and in some sense expresses its main idea.

The saying has two parts. The first stresses that man cannot remain neutral with God. He either moves forward or falls backward. As for the mission that God lays upon each individual person, one cannot simply choose to play a waiting game: a person either does what God expects of him or not. Whoever does not fulfill God's will, fulfills the will of his enemy. Whoever does not serve God serves the devil. In another place, Jesus says, "He that is not with me is against me, and he that gathereth not with me scattereth abroad" (Mt 12.30).

The second part of the saying points to the fact that a man's spiritual riches grow exponentially if he puts his talents to God's service and the service of his neighbor. The more income he accrues, the more it grows. The image of money giving a plentiful return on investment ends up as an image similar to leaven in flour (Mt 13.33). Just as the dough rises because

[93]Ibid.

The Parable of the Talents, Jan Leychen, 1791–1826

of the presence of leaven, a person's spiritual capital grows when he puts his talents into circulation.

Finally, the question of one's intentions is crucial: does someone use his talents for personal enrichment, to fulfill carnal desires, for distractions and passions, or does he become a fellow-laborer with God (1 Cor 3.9), using his abilities for God's work?

God seeks allies and fellow-laborers. Having come to earth, he chose those whom he wanted to attract to his mission. Some of those he called abandoned everything and followed him (Mt 19.27; Mk 10.28; Lk 5.11; 18.28). Others left him sorrowfully, for they had much wealth (Mt 19.22; Mk 10.22; Lk 18.23). For such people, those riches became the talent that they buried into the earth. They did not enter into the joy of their Lord, and he did not make them masters of many cities, as he did the apostles, who founded churches in each city that they entered and became their spiritual leaders. This is how the parable of the talents and minas came to pass in the lives of those who were their direct audience—the apostles of Jesus Christ.

6. Awaiting the Master of the House

All that remains to examine is a short parable: Jesus' last parable in the Gospel according to Mark. It is part of a larger sermon that Jesus gave as he left the temple of Jerusalem, while sitting on the Mount of Olives. We find an analogous parable in the Gospel according to Matthew, which includes the following call to vigilance: "Watch therefore: for ye know not what hour your Lord doth come. But know one thing, that if the goodman of the house had known in what watch the thief would come, he would have watched, and would not have suffered the house to be broken up" (Mt 24.42–43). In Mark's version, this challenge grows into a separate parable:

> Take ye heed, watch [*agrypneite*] and pray: for ye know not when the time is. For the Son of Man is as a man taking a far journey, who left his house, and gave authority to his servants, and to every man his work, and commanded the porter to watch [*hina grēgorē*]. Watch ye [*grēgoreite*] therefore: for ye know not when the master of the house cometh, at even, or at midnight, or at the cockcrowing, or in the morning, lest coming suddenly he find you sleeping. And what I say unto you I say unto all, watch [*grēgoreite*]. (Mk 13.33–37)

Compared to the parables that we mentioned before, this parable may seem incomplete, especially its beginning, which is almost exactly the same as the beginning of the parable of the talents and minas in Matthew and Luke, but without the detailed story. One could even read this as a kind of sketch of other full parables, where the master not only leaves his property to his servants, but returns, asking for their report.

In the parable in Mark, the servants are only mentioned once, after this they play no role whatsoever. Nevertheless, there is a subplot in this parable, connected with the appearance of a person who is absent in other parables: the porter or doorkeeper (*thyrōros*). Palestinian homes were

The Parable of the Faithful Servant, Jan Leychen, engraving

usually separated from the street by an enclosure and a gate, where a porter was supposed to stand guard. The safety of the house depended in large part on the porter's vigilance.[94]

Naturally, the figure of the porter has a symbolic meaning, which reminds us of various Old Testament figures such as the prophet who stands on the watch tower (Hab 2.1) and the guard who is asked how much time of the night is left, and who answers, "the morning cometh, and also the night" (Is 21.11–12). The porter or guard is a person who stays awake at night while others sleep. He is vigilant as he guards the house in expectation of the master's return.

The words "at even, or at midnight, or at the cockcrowing, or in the morning" refer to the four watches of the night,[95] according to the Roman system of keeping time. It is not coincidental that this division of time is found in Mark's Gospel, since tradition holds that he wrote his Gospel for the Christians of Rome. According to the Jewish system of keeping time, the night was divided into three watches, as we see in Luke: "And if he shall come in the second watch, or come in the third watch, and find them so, blessed are those servants" (Lk 12.38).

In these words and in other nocturnal images that Jesus used in his eschatological teaching, some commentators see an indication that the

[94]Smith, *Synoptic Gospels,* 105.

[95]T. W. Martin, "Watch During the Watches (Mark 13:35)," *Journal of Biblical Literature* 120 (2001): 685–701.

second coming will happen at night.[96] It is more likely, however, that the night is a metaphor for earthly life, just as the day is a symbol of Christ's coming.

Comparing the second coming to a thief's sudden appearance made an impression on early Christians. The apostles Peter and Paul develop this theme more fully in their epistles:

> But the day of the Lord will come as a thief in the night, in which the heavens shall pass away with a great noise, and the elements shall melt with fervent heat, the earth also and the works that are therein shall be burned up. Seeing then that all these things shall be dissolved, what manner of persons ought ye to be in all holy conversation and godliness, looking for and hasting unto the coming of the day of God, wherein the heavens being on fire shall be dissolved, and the elements shall melt with fervent heat? (2 Pet 3.10–12)

> But of the times and the seasons, brethren, ye have no need that I write unto you. For yourselves know perfectly that the day of the Lord so cometh as a thief in the night. For when they shall say, "Peace and safety," then sudden destruction cometh upon them, as travail upon a woman with child, and they shall not escape. But ye, brethren, are not in darkness, that that day should overtake you as a thief. Ye are all the children of light, and the children of the day; we are not of the night, nor of darkness. Therefore let us not sleep, as do others; but let us watch and be sober. (1 Thess 5.1–6)

The image of the porter is not apparent in the apostolic epistles. However, this image unexpectedly appears in the Eastern Christian teaching concerning sobriety (*nēpsis*) as spiritual vigilance. In Evagrius Ponticus' classic work on prayer, he says, "Stand on guard and protect your intellect from thoughts while you pray. Then your intellect will complete its prayer and continue in the tranquility that is natural to it."[97] These words reflect a specifically Eastern Christian understanding of prayer as a work of the

[96]Cf. Marcus, *Mark*, 921–22.

[97]Evagrius, *On Prayer: One Hundred and Fifty-Three Texts* 173 (PG 79:1181; *Philokalia* 1:64).

*The Path
to Christ,* detail,
M. V. Nesterov,
1910

mind, which drives away all extraneous thoughts and images: "Watchfulness is a continual fixing and halting of thought at the entrance to the heart.
In this way predatory and murderous thoughts are marked down as they
approach and what they say and do is noted; and we can see in what specious and delusive form the demons are trying to deceive the intellect."[98]

The verbs *agrypneō* and *grēgoreō*, used in the parable, are both translated as "to watch," but in Christian ascetic literature, these verbs received a
much fuller meaning. These are the verbs that indicate the specific practice
of prayer during the night vigil.[99]

This practice of prayer was known to early Christian authors.[100] It
found wide circulation in the monastic traditions of both East and West.
Isaac the Syrian, in his *Ascetical Homilies*, speaks of prayer at night as more
worthy than all activities of the day. Prayer in night vigil is a sweet work

[98]Hesychius, *On Watchfulness and Holiness Written for Theodoulos* 1.6 (PG 93:1481–84;
Philokalia 1:163).

[99]Lampe, *A Patristic Greek Lexicon*, 24, 324.

[100]For example, Hippolytus of Rome, *Apostolic Tradition* 2, trans. Alistair Stewart, PPS 54
(Yonkers, NY: St Vladimir's Seminary Press, 2015), 69; Origen, *On Prayer* 12 (PG 11:453, PPS
29:137–38); Cyprian of Carthage, *On the Lord's Prayer* 36 (PPS 29:92–93); Eusebius, *Church History* 2.17.21–22 (NPNF² 1:119); Jerome, *Epistle* 22.37 (PL 22:421).

during which the soul senses eternal life, casting off the works of darkness, and putting on the gifts of the spirit.[101] John Cassian writes of prayerful vigilance at night, beginning from the eve of Saturday and continuing to the fourth call of the roosters. He mentions this practice as typical of the East from the beginning of the Christian faith, in imitation of the apostles. Cassian recommends that all monasteries in the West follow this practice as well.[102]

The practice of praying at night in Christian literature and in monastic tradition is only one example of how Jesus' call to vigilance received very specific practical application. Yet this call is not directed to monastics alone: "And what I say unto you I say unto all: watch." This challenge is universal, retaining its relevance for all times and for all Christians.

---

[101]Isaac the Syrian, *Homily 64* (*Ascetical Homilies*, 447–62, at 449); *Homily 65* (*Ascetical Homilies*, 436–67, at 466).
[102]John Cassian, *The Institutes* 3.5.8–9 (PL 49:140–45; NPNF² 11:215–16).

CONCLUSION

Nearly all the parables of Jesus have passed before us, from the very first—in which the kingdom of heaven was revealed through simple images such as the sower, the seed, the mustard seed, the leaven—to the last. They are all united by a call to spiritual vigilance and expectation of his second coming. These parables revealed to us a series of images, analogies, and metaphors, all of which are called to represent the reality of the spiritual world, using earthly concepts and symbols. They allowed us a glimpse behind the curtain of the mystical kingdom of heaven that Jesus spoke of from the beginning to the end of his public ministry.

Thanks to the richness of imagery and the multilayered meanings of Jesus' parables, they have thrilled their readers for centuries and they continue to delight countless people. "Hearing or reading these wise parables of the Gospel, one is amazed at the marvelous exactness, simplicity, and beauty of the images that Jesus chooses," in Patriarch Kyrill's words.[1] Pope Benedict XVI wrote, "There is no doubt that the parables constitute the heart of Jesus' teaching. While civilizations have come and gone, these stories continue to touch us anew with their freshness and their humanity."[2]

We saw that the interpretation of parables has occupied the thought of theologians, priests, and secular scholars for many centuries. Various methods of interpretation have been proposed, from the most radically allegorical, which tends not to leave one stone upon another of the original text, to the literal, which limits the meaning of each parable to historical context or narrow moralization. Neither of these methods was found to be satisfactory.

[1]Metropolitan Kyrill, *Slovo Pastyrya: Bog i chelovek: Istoriya spaseniya* [The word of the shepherd: God and man: The history of salvation] (Moscow: 2004), 195. Translated by DNK.

[2]Benedict XVI (Joseph Ratzinger), *Jesus of Nazareth: From the Baptism in the Jordan to the Transfiguration*, trans. Adrian J. Walker (New York: Doubleday, 2007), 291.

The Church preserves the teachings of Jesus, and she is their most authoritative interpreter. Over the centuries the Church developed an exegetical tradition that allowed many generations of Christians to understand the meaning of parables, to apply them to their own life's circumstances, to distill from them various moral lessons and spiritual instructions. Without jumping to excessive allegorizing or extreme literalism, such interpreters as John Chrysostom applied Jesus' parables to situations relevant for their own contemporaries, helping them read the parables not as theoretical presentations (which they never were) but as calls to action.

Nevertheless, no single ecclesiastical community can "privatize" Jesus and his teaching, declaring themselves to be the exclusive owners of the rights to his inheritance. Jesus is greater than the Church, because he is God himself, who came to earth in human flesh. The meaning of his person and teaching are so universal and all-encompassing that they go beyond the borders of the Church. Jesus belongs to the entire world and to every person. He has something to say to every human being, both to those who are already in the Church and those who are on the path to it and those who are far from it and from any religious affiliation at all.

Jesus is broader than the Church, just as God is broader than religion. God acts beyond the limits of religion: he is not a religious phenomenon at all. God allows himself to act upon those who believe in him, but also on those who do not admit his existence or his right to interfere in their affairs. He ignores this unbelief and acts however he sees fit. Wherever it is possible, he honors the free will of every human being. But if he considers it necessary, he can intervene in the life of a person without invitation, when that person does not expect him in the least, as he did with Saul on the road to Damascus (Acts 9.1–8).

As for those who consider themselves to be close to God, he can hide his face from them as well. This is what happened in Jesus' own time, when he unexpectedly invaded the lives of those who followed the law of Moses and awaited the coming of the Messiah. In his face, they failed to see the face of God incarnate. In his words they failed to hear the "words of eternal life" (Jn 6.68). They remained blind and deaf to his teachings and parables,

The Hunters in the Snow, Peter Bruegel the Elder, 1565

while thousands of other people had their eyes and ears opened by these same teachings and parables.

The parables of Jesus belong not only to the Church and not only to believers. They belong to all mankind. They are capable of saying something new to each person. Other than the literal or figurative meaning, which is studied and will continue to be studied by scholars and commentators, these parables have something else that attracts people beyond these meanings. They have a message, a story, an image, a mood, they have "breadth, and length, and depth, and height," and through them is revealed "the love of Christ, which passeth knowledge" (Eph 3.18–19). In order for the parables to have that effect, it is by no means necessary to understand their meaning. One can simply listen to them as one listens to music, to read them as one reads poetry. One can encounter them as one does the visual arts.

When a person walks into a gallery in a museum, walking past various paintings and scenes of city or village life, various portraits or still-lives, as a rule, he does not ask himself the question: "What does it mean?" "What is the meaning of that image?" "How should I read that painting?" Every visitor to Vienna's Museum of Fine Art thinks different things as he stands before Peter Bruegel the Elder's famous painting *The Hunters in the Snow.* An artist will pay attention to the color scheme, the way the paint is applied to the canvas, the expressiveness of the images, the uses of perspective. A historian might pay attention to the way the people are dressed, to the weapons they use in the hunt, to the breed of hunting dog, to other elements of everyday life. A person who is neither artist nor historian might find something else entirely. It suggests a certain mood or allows him to translate his thoughts to the sixteenth century, to sense the atmosphere of a life separated from his own by five hundred years.

If we speak of Jesus' parables in terms of content, we believe that the eternal worth of these stories is, first of all, that they help people better understand God, approach him, love him. In these parables, God appears as a supreme Lord who has absolute power over his subjects. He gives to each what he considers necessary, then he demands an account from each about how his gifts were used. He harshly punishes those who oppose his will and who fail to fulfill his commands. At the same time, he also appears as a longsuffering Father, plenteous in mercy. He runs to the prodigal son, embraces him and kisses him. God is dispassionate, but he is not without feeling. He is in heaven, but he is not far from earth. He is all-powerful, but he is ready to make way for the will of man when he considers it useful. God loves man as his own creation, his own child, and every parable reveals this truth in a slightly different way.

Second, the parables speak about Jesus. As their author, he is also the main character of many of the stories. The parables of Jesus are God's letter to mankind, and the one who reads that letter aloud is one who is simultaneously God and man. Jesus does not separate himself from God, and all the qualities and characteristics that he ascribes to God belong to him as well. In the parables, he reveals himself not only as the wise Teacher, but also as the Good Shepherd who goes out of his way to find the lost sheep, who then finds it and bears it on his own shoulders, and rejoices at its recovery. He reveals himself as the one whom God sent into his vineyard to gather the fruits and as one who was obedient to the will of the Father, even at the cost of his own life: "He made himself of no reputation, and took upon him the form of a servant, and was made in the likeness of men, and being found in fashion as a man, he humbled himself, and became obedient unto death, even the death of the cross" (Phil 2.7–8).

Third, the parables speak of the kingdom of heaven, revealing it as a reality invisibly present in human life, like leaven in a lump of dough. Like a small mustard seed, it ripens and grows inside a person imperceptibly, but then transforms into a tree in whose branches the birds find refuge. Like a pearl of great price, for which a person is ready to sell everything he has, it pushes all earthly attachments out of a person's soul, uniting him with heaven and showing him a direct path to God.

Finally, the parables speak of how a person must relate to other human beings. He is called to forgive them as the father forgave his prodigal son, as God forgives his debtors. He is called to react to another's calamity as the good Samaritan responded when he saw the man who had been attacked by robbers. He must love as one to whom much has been forgiven. He must see people through God's eyes, to look deeply into their souls and to see the image of God in them.

Jesus told the parables in a specific historical context, but their significance goes far beyond that limit. They have universal meaning, and two thousand years after they were told, they are still as expressive as they were for Jesus' contemporaries, plunging the thoughts of the reader into the bottomless depths of faith.

ABBREVIATIONS

ANF   The Ante-Nicene Fathers. Edited by Alexander Roberts and James Donaldson. Buffalo, 1885–1887. 10 vols. Repr., Peabody, MA: Hendrickson, 1994.

CSCO   Corpus Scriptorum Christianorum Orientalium. Leuven: Peeters Publishers, 1903–.

CSEL   Corpus Scriptorum Ecclesiasticorum Latinorum. Vienna, 1866–2012. Berlin: De Gruyter, 2012–.

FOC   The Fathers of the Church Series. 127 vols. Washington: Catholic University of America Press, 1962–

GCS   Die Griechischen Christlichen Schriftsteller.

NPNF¹   The Nicene and Post-Nicene Fathers, Series 1. Edited by Philip Schaff. New York, 1886–1889. 14 vols. Repr., Peabody, MA: Hendrickson, 1994.

NPNF²   The Nicene and Post-Nicene Fathers, Series 2. Edited by Philip Schaff and Henry Wace. New York, 1890. 14 vols. Repr., Peabody, MA: Hendrickson, 1994.

PG   Patrologia Graeca. Edited by J.-P. Migne. 162 vols. Paris, 1857–1886.

Philokalia *The Philokalia: The Complete Text.* Compiled by St Nikodimos of the Holy Mountain and St Makarios of Corinth. Translated by G. E. H. Palmer, Philip Sherrard, and Kallistos Ware. 4 vols. London: Faber and Faber, 1983–1999.

PL   Patrologia Latina. Edited by J.-P. Migne. 217 vols. Paris,
            1844–1864.

PPS   Popular Patristics Series. Crestwood, NY [Yonkers, NY]: St
            Vladimir's Seminary Press, 1996–

SC   Sources chrétiennes. Paris: Les Éditions du Cerf. 1942–

TU   Texte und Untersuchungen zur Geschichte der altchristlichen
            Literatur. Leipzig: Hinrichs, 1883–1941; Berlin: De Gruyter,
            1942–.

BIBLIOGRAPHY

1. The Old and the New Testaments

Biblia Hebraica Stuttgartensia. Ediderunt K. Elliger et W. Rudolph: Adjuvantibus H. Bardke et al. Textum Masoreticum curavit H. P. Rüger. Stuttgart: Deutsche Bibelgesellschaft, 1990.

The Holy Bible. King James Version. Standard text ed. Cambridge: Cambridge University Press, 1995.

Novum Testamentum graece. 28th revised edition. Eberhard Nestle, Ewrin Nestle, Kurt Aland, et alii, editors. Stuttgart: Deutsche Bibelgesellschaft, 2012.

Septuaginta, id est Vetus Testamentum graece iuxta LXX interpretes. Editio minor. Edidit Alfred Rahlfs. Duo volumina in uno. Stuttgart: Deutsche Bibelgesellschaft, 1979.

Synopsis quattuor Evangeliorum. Locis parallelis evangeliorum apocryphorum et partum adhibitis. 13th rev. ed. Kurt Aland. Stuttgart: Deutsche Bibelgesellschaft, 1988.

2. Liturgical sources

Bridegroom Services of Holy Week, The. Prepared by David Anderson, John Erickson, and V. Rev. Paul Lazor. Syosset, NY: Department of Religious Education, Orthodox Church in America, s.d.

Great Book of Needs, The. Translated by St Tikhon's Monastery. Vol. 1. South Canaan, PA: St Tikhon's Seminary Press, 2009.

Lenten Triodion, The. Translated by Mother Mary and Kallistos Ware. South Canaan, PA: St Tikhon's Seminary Press, 2002.

Paschal Service, The. Edited by John Erickson and V. Rev. Paul Lazor. Introduction by V. Rev. Paul Lazor. Syosset, NY: Orthodox Church in America, Department of Religious Education, repr. 1986.

406   THE PARABLES OF JESUS

Synaxarion of the Lenten Triodion and Pentecostarion, The. Translated by Sera-
    phim Dedes. Introduction by Roman Braga. Edited by David Kidd and Mother
    Gabriella. Rives Junction, MI: HDM Press, 2005.

3. Works of the Fathers and Teachers of the Church

Ambrose of Milan. *Commentary of Saint Ambrose on the Gospel according to
    Saint Luke*. Transleted by Íde M. Ní Rian. Dublin: Halcyon Press, 2001.

_____. *De poenitentia*. PL 16:465–524. English: *Two Books Concerning Repen-
    tance*. NPNF² 10:329–359.

Amphilocius of Iconium. *Homily 4: On the Sinful Woman*. PG 39:65–89.

Anastasios of Sinai. *Anastasii Sinaïtae: Quaestiones et responsiones*. Edited by M.
    Richard and J. Munitiz. CCSG 59. English: *Questions and Answers*. Translated
    by Joseph A. Munitiz. Turnhout: Brepols Publishers, 2011.

Augustine. *Homilies on the Gospel of John*. PL 35:1379–1976; NPNF¹ 7:7–452.

_____. *De consensu evangeliorum*. PL 34:1041–1230. English: *On the Harmony of
    the Gospels*. NPNF¹ 6:79–236.

_____. *Questions on the Gospels*. CCSL 44B.

_____. *Sermones 1–50*. CCSL 41. *Sermones 51–340*. PL 38:332–1484. *Sermones
    341–396*. PL 39:1473–1718. English: *Sermons on Selected Lessons of the New
    Testament*. NPNF¹ 6:245–545.

Clement of Alexandria. *Stromata*. ANF 2:299–568.

Cyprian of Carthage. *De dominica oratione*. CSEL 3.1:187–205. English: Tertullian,
    Cyprian, and Origen. *On the Lord's Prayer*. Translated and introduced by
    Alistair Stewart-Sykes, 65–93. PPS 29. Crestwood, NY: St Vladimir's Semi-
    nary Press, 2004.

Cyril of Alexandria. *Commentary on the Gospel of Matthew*. TU 61:153–269.

_____. *Fragments. Commentarii in Matthaeum*. *[Fragmenta]*. TU 61:153–269.

_____. *S. Cyrilli Alexandriae arhiepiscopi Commentarii in Lucae Evangelium
    quae supersunt syriace e manuscriptis apud Museum Britannicum*. Oxford,
    1858. English: *Commentary upon the Gospel of St. Luke*. Translated by R.
    Payne Smith. Oxford: Oxford University Press, 1859.

Diadochos of Photiki. *One Hundred Texts on Spiritual Knowledge and Discrimi-
    nation*. PG 65:1200. *Philokalia* 1:253–296.

Epiphanius the Latin. *Interpretatio evangeliorum.* Cited as *Commentary on the Gospels.* Pages 936–94 in Patrologiae latinae supplementum. Vol. 3. Turnhout: Brepols, 1963.

Eusebius of Caesarea. *Historia ecclesiastica.* PG 20:45–905. English: *Church History* 2.17.21–22 NPNF² 1:81–387.

Evagrius Ponticus. *De oratione capitula.* PG 79:1165–1200. English: *On Prayer: One Hundred and Fifty-Three Texts. Philokalia* 1:55–71.

Gregory Palamas. *Homilia quadraginta una.* PG 151:9–550. English: *Saint Gregory Palamas: The Homilies.* Translated by Christopher Veniamin. Dalton, PA: Mount Thabor Publishing, 2016.

Gregory the Great. *Homiliarum xl in euangelia libri duo.* PL 76:1075–1312. English: Gregory the Great. *Forty Gospel Homilies.* Translated by Dom David Hurst. Cistercian Studies Series 123. Kalamazoo, MI: Cistercian Publications, 1990.

———. *Homilies on Ezekiel.* English: Saint Gregory the Great. *Homilies on the Book of the Prophet Ezekiel.* Translated by Theodosia Tomkinson. Etna, CA: Center for Traditionalist Orthodox Studies, 2008.

Gregory the Theologian. *Oratio 4: Contra Julianum imperatorem prior invectiva.* SC 309:86–293. English: *Julian the Emperor, Containing Gregory Nazianzen's Two Invectives and Libanius' Monody with Julian's Extant Theosophical Works.* Translated by C. W. King. London: George Bell and Sons, 1888.

Hesychios the Priest. *De temperantia et virtute centuriae duae ad Theodulum.* PG 93:1479–1544. English: *On Watchfulness and Holiness Written for Theodoulos. Philokalia* 1:162–198.

Hilary of Poitiers. *Commentary on Matthew.* Translated by D. H. Williams. FOC 125. Washington: The Catholic University of America Press, 2012.

Hippolytus of Rome. *De traditione apostolica.* SC 11. English: *On the Apostolic Tradition.* Second edition. Translated by Alistair Stewart. PPS 54. Yonkers, NY: St Vladimir's Seminary Press, 2015.

———. *Refutation of All Heresies.* ANF 5:9–153.

Ignatius of Antioch. *The Letters.* SC 10. Ignatius of Antioch. *The Letters.* Translated by Alistair Stewart. PPS 49. Yonkers, NY: St Vladimir's Seminary Press, 2013.

Irenaeus of Lyons. *Adversus haereses libri quinque.* PG 7a:437–1117, 7b:1119–1125; SC 263–264, 293–294, 210–211, 100, 152–153. English: *Irenaeus Against Heresies.* ANF 1:315–567.

Isaac of Nineveh (Isaac the Syrian). *Homilies.* Edited by Sebastian Brock. CSCO 554. Leuven: Peeters, 1995. Isaac of Nineveh (Isaac the Syrian). *"The Second Part," Chapters IV–XLI.* Translated by Sebastian Brock. CSCO 555. Leuven: Peeters, 1995.

Isaac the Syrian. *The Ascetical Homilies of Saint Isaac the Syrian.* Boston: Holy Transfiguration Monastery, 2011.

Isidore of Pelusium. *Letters.* PG 78:177–1674.

Jerome. *Commentariorum in Matthaeum.* CCSL 77. English: St Jerome. *Commentary on Matthew.* Translated by Thomas P. Scheck. FOC 117. Washington: The Catholic University of America Press, 2008.

_____. *Epistulae.* CSEL 54–56. English: *The Letters of St. Jerome.* NPNF2 6:1–296.

John Cassian. *De institutis coenobiorum.* PL 49:53–476. English: *Twelve Books on the Institutes of the Coenobia.* NPNF² 11:201–290.

John Chrysostom, *Homilies on the Gospel of Matthew.* NPNF¹ 10.

_____. *Homiliae septem de Lazaro.* PG 48:963–1054. English: John Chrysostom. *On Wealth and Poverty.* Translated by Catharine P. Roth. PPS 9. Yonkers, NY: St Vladimir's Seminary Press, 2020.

_____. *Homilies on the Gospel of John.* NPNF¹ 14.1–334.

_____. *Sermo catecheticus in pascha.* PG 59:721–724. English: *Catchetical Homily.* Pages 45–47 in *The Paschal Service.* Syosset, NY: Orthodox Church in America, Department of Religious Education, repr. 1986.

_____. *St John Chrysostom on Repentance and Almsgiving.* Translated by Gus George Christo. FOC 96. Washington: Catholic University of America Press, 1988.

John Climacus. *The Ladder of Divine Ascent.* Boston: Holy Transfiguration Monastery, 2012.

Justin Martyr. *Dialogue of Justin, Philosopher and Martyr, with Trypho, a Jew.* ANF 1:194–270.

Lactantius. *The Divine Institutes.* ANF 7:9–223.

Macarius the Egyptian. *The Fifty Spiritual Homilies of St Macarius the Egyptian.* Translated by A. J. Mason. London: SPCK, 1921.

Maximus the Confessor. *Quaestiones et dubia.* PG 90:786–855. Also CCSG 10. English: *St. Maximus the Confessor's Questions and Doubts.* Translated by Despina D. Prassas. DeKalb, IL: Northern Illinois University Press, 2010.

Origen. *Commentariorum series in evangelium Matthaei*. GCS 38.2. English: *Commentary on the Gospel of Matthew*. ANF 9:413–512.

_____. *Commentarius in Ioannem. Fragments on John*. GCS 483–574.

_____. *Commentary on Matthew*. ANF 9:413–512.

_____. *De oratione libellus*. PG 11:415–562. English: Tertullian, Cyprian, and Origen. *On the Lord's Prayer*. Translated and introduced by Alistair Stewart-Sykes, 111–214. PPS 29. Crestwood, NY: St Vladimir's Seminary Press, 2004.

_____. *Homilies on Luke, Fragments on Luke*. Translated by Joseph T. Lienhard. FOC 94. Washington: The Catholic University of America Press, 1996.

Symeon the New Theologian. *First Ethical Discourse*. In St Symeon the New Theologian. *On the Mystical Life: The Ethical Discourses*. Vol. 1, *The Church and the Last Things*. Translated by Alexander Golitzin. PPS 14. Crestwood, NY: Saint Vladimir Seminary Press, 1995.

_____. *One Hundred Theological and Practical Chapters*. SC 51bis. In Symeon the New Theologian. *The Practical and Theological Chapters and the Three Theological Discourses*. Translated by Paul McGuckin. Cistercian Studies 42. Kalamazoo, MI: Cistercian Publications, 1982.

_____. *The Epistles of St Symeon the New Theologian*. Edited and translated by H. J. M. Turner. Oxford: Oxford University Press, 2009.

Tertullian. *Adversus gnosticos scorpiace*. CCSL 2:1067–1097. English: *Scorpiace* [*Against the Gnostics*]. ANF 3.633–48.

_____. *De pudicitia*. CCSL 2:1279–1330. English: *On Modesty*. ANF 4:74–101.

_____. *De virginibus velandis*. CCSL 2:1207–1226. English: *On the Veiling of Virgins*. ANF 4:27–37.

Theodore of Mopsuestia. *Fragmenta comentarii in Evangelium Matthaei*. [Fragments on Matthew]. TU 61:96–135.

Theophylact of Bulgaria. *The Explanation of the Holy Gospel According to Luke*. House Springs, MO: Chrysostom Press, 2007.

4. Other Sources

Abbott-Smith, George. *A Manual Greek Lexicon of the New Testament*. Second edition. Edinburgh: T & T Clark, 1929.

Albright, W. F. and C. S. Mann. *Matthew: Introduction, Translation and Notes*. London: Doubleday & Company, Inc., 1971.

Alfeyev, Hilarion. *Jesus Christ, His Life and Teaching.* Vol. 1, *The Beginning of the Gospel.* Yonkers, NY: St Vladimir's Seminary Press, 2018.

_____. *Jesus Christ, His Life and Teaching.* Vol. 2, *The Sermon on the Mount.* Yonkers, NY: St Vladimir's Seminary Press, 2019.

Bailey, Kenneth E. *Finding the Lost: Cultural Keys to Luke 15.* St Louis, MO: Concordia Publishing House, 1992.

_____. *Jesus through Middle Eastern Eyes.* London: SPCK, 2008.

_____. *Through Peasant Eyes: More Lucan Parables, Their Culture and Style.* Grand Rapids, MI: William B. Eerdmans Publishing Company, 1980.

Bailey, Mark L. "Guidelines for Interpreting Jesus' Parables." *Bibliotheca Sacra* 155:617 (1998): 29–38.

Barnard, L. W. "To Allegorize or Not to Allegorize?" *Studia Theologica* 36 (1982): 1–10.

Baum, G. *The Jews and the Gospel: A Re-Examination of the New Testament.* Westminster, MD: The Newman Press, 1961.

Beavis, Mary Ann. "The Foolish Landowner (Luke 12:16b–20): The Parable of the Rich Fool." In *Jesus and His Parables: Interpreting the Parables of Jesus Today,* ed. V. George Shillington, 55–68. Edinburgh: T&T Clark Ltd., 1997.

Belliotti, Raymond Angelo. *Jesus the Radical: The Parables and Modern Morality.* Lanham, MD: Lexington Books, 2013.

Benedict XVI (Joseph Ratzinger). *Jesus of Nazareth: From the Baptism in the Jordan to the Transfiguration.* Translated by Adrian J. Walker. New York: Doubleday, 2007.

Black, Matthew. "The Theological Appropriation of the Old Testament by the New Testament." *Scottish Journal of Theology* 39 (1986): 1–17.

_____. *An Aramaic Approach to the Gospels and Acts.* Second edition. Oxford: Clarendon Press, 1957.

Blomberg, Craig. "The Miracles as Parables." Pages 327–59 in *Gospel Perspectives.* Vol. 6, *The Miracles of Jesus.* Edited by David Wenham and Craig Blomberg. Sheffield: Sheffield Academic Press, 1986.

_____. *Interpreting the Parables.* Second edition. Downer's Grove, IL: IVP Academic, 2012.

Borg, Marcus. *Jesus: Uncovering the Life, Teachings, and Relevance of a Religious Revolutionary.* San Francisco: HarperSanFrancisco, 2006.

Borovsky, Irvin J. "Introduction." Pages 9–20 in *Removing the Anti-Judaism from the New Testament*. Edited by Howard Clark Kee and Irvin J. Borovsky. Philadelphia: American Interfaith Institute, 1998.

Boucher, Madeleine I. *The Parables*. Wilmington, DE: Michael Glazier, Inc., 1981.

Boys, Mary C. "Beyond 'Removing' Anti-Judaism: The Theological and Educational Task of Reframing Christian Identity." Pages 88–102 in *Removing the Anti-Judaism from the New Testament*. Edited by Howard Clark Kee and Irvin J. Borovsky. Philadelphia: American Interfaith Institute, 1998.

Braun, Willi. *Feasting and Social Rhetoric in Luke 14*. Cambridge: Cambridge University Press, 1995.

Brunt, P. A. *Italian Manpower, 225 B.C.–A.D. 14*. London: Oxford University Press, 1971.

Bultmann, Rudolf. *History of the Synoptic Tradition*. Translated by John Marsh. Oxford: Basil Blackwell, 1963.

Buzy, D. "Les dix vierges." *Revue apostolique* 39 (1923–25).

Cadoux, A. T. *The Parables of Jesus: Their Art and Use*. London: Clarke, 1930.

Calvin, John. *Institutes of the Christian Religion*. Translated by Henry Beveridge. London: Arnold Hatfield for Bonham Norton, 1599. Electronic edition: Bellingham, WA: Logos Bible Software, 1997.

Carlston, Charles E. *The Parables of the Triple Tradition*. Minneapolis: Fortress Press, 2007.

Casey, Maurice. *Jesus of Nazareth: An Independent Historian's Account of His Life and Teaching*. London: T&T Clark International, 2010.

Chilton, Bruce. *A Galilean Rabbi and His Bible: Jesus' Own Interpretation of Isaiah*. London: SPCK, 1984.

Crossan, John Dominic. *In Parables: The Challenge of the Historical Jesus*. Sonoma, CA: Polebridge Press, 1992.

Crouzel, Henri. *Origène*. Paris: Lethielleux, 1985.

Davies, W. D. and Dale C. Allison. *A Critical and Exegetical Commentary on the Gospel according to Saint Matthew*. Vol. 1. London: T & T Clarke, 1988.

Dodd, C. H. *Historical Tradition in the Fourth Gospel*. Cambridge: Cambridge University Press, 1976.

———. *The Parables of the Kingdom*. London: James Nisbet and Company, 1935.

Doerksen, V. D. "The Interpretation of the Parables." *Grace Journal* 11 (Spring 1970): 3–20.

Donahue, John R. *The Gospel in Parable*. Minneapolis: Fortress Press, 1988.

Donne, John. *Selections from Divine Poems, Sermons, Devotions, and Prayers.* Mahwah, NJ: Paulist Press, 1990.

Dostoevsky, Fyodor. *Crime and Punishment.* Translated by Constance Garnett. London: Heinemann, 1914.

_____. *The Brothers Karamazov.* Translated by Richard Pevear and Larissa Volokhonsky. New York: Knopf Doubleday Publishing Group. 1991.

Drury, John. *The Parables in the Gospels: History and Allegory.* London: Crossroad Publishing Company, 1985.

Evans, Craig A. *Fabricating Jesus: How Modern Scholars Distort the Gospels.* Downer's Grove, IL: InterVarsity Press, 2006.

_____. *Jesus and His Contemporaries.* Leiden: E. J. Brill, 1990.

_____. *Matthew.* Cambridge: Cambridge University Press, 2012.

Finley, M. I. *Ancient Slavery and Modern Ideology.* New York: The Viking Press, 1980.

Fitzmyer, Joseph A. *The Gospel According to Luke, I–IX.* Garden City, NY: Doubleday, 1981.

Flannery, E. H. "Anti-Judaism and Anti-Semitism: A Necessary Distinction." *Journal of Ecumenical Studies* 10 (1973): 581–88.

Ford, Richard Q. *The Parables of Jesus: Recovering the Art of Listening.* Minneapolis: Augsburg Fortress, 1997.

Funk, Robert Walter, and Roy W. Hoover, eds. *The Five Gospels: The Search for the Authentic Words of Jesus.* Sonoma, CA: Polebridge Press, 1993.

Funk, Robert Walter, Bernard Brandon Scott, and James R. Butts. *The Parables of Jesus.* Sonoma, CA: Polebridge Press, 1988.

Gabdullina, V. I. " 'Bludnii syn' kak model' pobedenija: evangel'skii motiv v kontekste biografii i tvorchestva F. M. Dostoevskogo" [" 'The Prodigal Son' as a model of behavior: a gospel motif in the context of the biography and works of F. M. Dostoevsky"]. *Vestnik Tomskogo gosudarstvennogo pedagogicheskogo universiteta* [Bulletin of Tomsk pedagogical state university] 6 (2005): 16–22.

Gager, John G. *The Origins of Anti-Semitism.* Oxford: Oxford University Press, 1983.

Gale, A. M. *Redefining Ancient Borders: The Jewish Scribal Framework of Matthew's Gospel.* New York: T & T Clark International, 2005.

Gathercole, Simon. *The Gospel of Thomas: Introduction and Commentary.* Vol. 2. London and Boston: Brill, 2014.

Goodacre, Mark. *Thomas and the Gospels: The Making of an Apocryphal Text.* Grand Rapids, MI: Eerdmans Publishing Company, 2012.

Green, Joel B., Howard Marshall, and Scot McKnight, eds. *Dictionary of Jesus and the Gospels: A Compendium of Contemporary Biblical Scholarship.* Second edition. Downers Grove, IL: InterVarsity Press, 2013.

Gundry, Robert. *Matthew: A Commentary on His Handbook for a Mixed Church under Persecution.* Second edition. Grand Rapids, MI: Eerdmans, 1994.

Hare, Douglas R. A. *The Theme of Jewish Persecution of Christians in the Gospel According to St Matthew.* Cambridge: Cambridge University Press, 1967.

Haufe, G. "Παροβολη." In *Exegetical Dictionary of the New Testament.* 3 vols. Edited by Horst Balz and Gerhard Schneider, 3:12–16. Grand Rapids, MI: Eerdmans, 1990–1993.

Hedrick, Charles W. *Many Things in Parables: Jesus and His Modern Critics.* Louisville, KY: Westminster John Knox Press, 2004.

Hendriksen, William. *Exposition of the Gospel According to St. Matthew.* Grand Rapids, MI: Baker Book House, 1973.

Herzog, William R. *Parables as Subversive Speech: Jesus as Pedagogue of the Oppressed.* Louisville, KY: Westminster John Knox Press, 1994.

Hultgren, Arland J. *The Parables of Jesus: A Commentary.* Grand Rapids, MI: Wm. B. Eerdmans Publishing Co., 2002.

Hunter, A. M. *Interpreting the Parables.* Philadelphia: Westminster Press, 1961.

Ireland, Dennis J. *Stewardship and the Kingdom of God: An Historical, Exegetical, and Contextual Study of the Parable of the Unjust Steward in Luke 16:1–13.* Leiden: E. J. Brill, 1992.

Izmestieva, N. S. "Ob odnom evangel'skom siuzhete u F. M. Dostoevskogo ('Vozbrashchenie bludnogo syna' v romane *Podrostok)*" [On a gospel story by F. M. Doestoevsky, "The return of the prodigal son," in the novel *A Raw Youth*]. *Vestnik Udmurtskogo universiteta* [Bulletin of Udmurt University] 5 (2006): 35–46.

Jeremias, Joachim. "Palästinakundliches zum Gleichnis vom Säemann (Mark 4:3–8)." *New Testament Studies* 13 (1966–1967): 48–53.

_____. *The Parables of Jesus.* New York: Charles Scribner's Sons, 1972.

Johnston, Robert M. and Harvey K. McArthur. *They Also Taught in Parables: Rabbinic Parables from the First Centuries of the Christian Era.* Grand Rapids, MI: Zondervan, 1990.

Jones, Ivor H. *The Matthean Parables: A Literary and Historical Commentary.* Leiden: E. J. Brill, 1995.

Jones, Peter Rhea. *The Teaching of the Parables.* Nashville, TN: Baptist Sunday School Board, 1984

Jülicher, Adolf. *Die Gleichnisreden Jesu.* 2 vols. Freiburg: J. C. B. Mohr (Paul Siebeck), 1888–89.

Kasper, Walter. "Foreword." Pages x–xvii in *Christ Jesus and the Jewish People Today: New Explorations of Theological Interrelationships.* Edited by Philip A. Cunningham, Joseph Sievers, Mary Boys, and Hans Hermann Hendrix. Grand Rapids, MI: William B. Eerdmans Publishing Company, 2011.

Keener, Craig S. *The Gospel of Matthew: A Socio-Rhetorical Commentary,* Grand Rapids, MI: William B. Eerdmans Publishing Company, 1999.

Keith, Graham. *Hated Without a Cause: A Survey of Anti-Semitism.* Carlisle, England: Paternoster Press, 1997.

Kelber, Werner H. *The Kingdom in Mark: A New Place and a New Time.* Philadelphia: Fortress Press, 1974.

Kim, Seyoon. "Jesus—the Son of God, the Stone, the Son of Man and the Servant: The Role of Zechariah in the Self-Identification of Jesus." Pages 134–48 in *Tradition and Interpretation in the New Testament: Essays in Honor of E. Earle Ellis.* Edited by Gerald F. Hawthorne and Otto Betz. Grand Rapids, MI: William B. Eerdmans Publishing Company, 1987.

Kissinger, Warren S. *The Parables of Jesus: A History of Interpretation and Bibliography.* Metuchen, NJ: Scarecrow Press, 1979.

Kistemaker, Simon J. *The Parables of Jesus.* Grand Rapids, MI: Baker Book House, 1980.

_____. *The Parables: Understanding the Stories Jesus Told.* Grand Rapids, MI: Baker Academic, 2002.

Klauck, H. J. *Allegorie und Allegorese in synoptischen Gleichnistexten.* Münster: Aschendorff, 1978.

Kloppenborg, John S. *The Tenants in the Vineyard.* Tübingen: Mohr Siebeck, 2010.

Klostermann, Erich. *Das Matthäusevangelium.* Tübingen: Mohr Siebeck, 1971.

Kyrill (Metropolitan). *Slovo Pastyrya: Bog i chelovek: Istoriya spaseniya* [The word of the shepherd: God and man: The history of salvation]. Moscow: 2004.

Lambrecht, Jan. *Out of the Treasure.* Leuven: Peeters Press, 1991.

Lampe, G. W. H. *A Patristic Greek Lexicon.* Oxford: Clarendon Press, 1961.

Léon-Dufour, Xavier. *Life and Death in the New Testament: The Teachings of Jesus and Paul.* Translated by Terrence Prendergast. San Francisco: Harper & Row, 1986.

Lermontov, Mikhail. *A Hero for Our Time.* St Petersburg, 2008. In Russian.

Levine, Amy-Jill. *Short Stories by Jesus: The Enigmatic Parables of a Controversial Rabbi.* New York: HarperOne, 2014.

Lischer, Richard. *Reading the Parables.* Louisville, KY: Westminster John Knox Press, 2014.

MacArthur, John. *A Tale of Two Sons: The Inside Story of a Father, His Sons and a Shocking Murder.* Nashville, TN: Thomas Nelson, 2008.

Malina, Bruce J., and Richard L. Rohrbaugh. *Social-Science Commentary on the Synoptic Gospels.* Minneapolis: Fortress Press, 1992.

Manson, T. W. *The Teaching of Jesus: Studies of its Form and Content.* Cambridge: Cambridge University Press, 1967.

Marcus, Joel. *Mark 1–16: A New Translation with Introduction and Commentary.* New Haven and London: Yale University Press, 2000.

_____. *Mark 1–8: A New Translation with Introduction and Commentary.* New Haven: Yale University Press, 2000.

Martin, T. W. "Watch During the Watches (Mark 13:35)." *Journal of Biblical Literature* 120 (2001): 685–701.

Meier, J. P. "The Historical Jesus and the Historical Samaritans: What can be Said?" *Biblica* 81 (2000): 202–232.

Minear, P. A. "A Note on Luke 17:7–10." *Journal of Biblical Literature* 93 (1974): 82–87.

Morris, Leon. *The Gospel according to Matthew.* Grand Rapids, MI: William B. Eerdmans Publishing Company, 1992.

Nave, Guy D. *The Role and Function of Repentance in Luke-Acts.* Leiden: Brill, 2002.

Newman, Barclay M. and Philip C. Stine. *A Translator's Handbook on the Gospel of Matthew.* London, New York, Stuttgart: United Bible Societies, 1998.

_____. *A Handbook on the Gospel of Matthew.* New York: United Bible Societies, 1988.

Nygren, Anders. *Agape and Eros.* Philadelphia: Westminster Press, 1953.

O'Collins, Gerald. *Jesus: A Portrait.* Maryknoll, NY: Orbis Books, 2008.

Olmstead, Wesley G. *Matthew's Trilogy of Parables: The Nation, the Nations and the Reader in Matthew 21:28–22:14*. Cambridge: Cambridge University Press, 2003.

Orton, D. E. *The Understanding Scribe: Matthew and the Apocalyptic Ideal*. London: T & T Clark, 1989.

Peisker, C. H. "Konsekutives *hina* in Markus 4:12." *Zeitschrift für die neutestamentliche Wissenschaft* 59 (1968): 126–27.

Perrin, Norman. *Jesus and the Language of the Kingdom: Symbol and Metaphor in the New Testament Interpretation*. Minneapolis: Fortress Press, 1976.

Philaret of Moscow. "Beseda v Nedelyu o bludnom syne i na pamyat svyatitelya Aleksiya." [Homily for the Sunday of the Prodigal Son and the Commemoration of St Alexis], 12 February 1856. In *Pribavleniya k Tvoreniyam sv. Ottsov* [Supplements to the works of the holy fathers] 15 (1856): 23–32.

Popovich, Justin. *Tolkovanie na evangelie ot Matfeya* [Commentary on the Gospel of Matthew]. Pages 5–466 in *Sobranie tvorenii* [Collected works]. Vol. 5 Moscow: Palomnik, 2014.

Puig i Tàrrech, Armand. "Interpreting the Parables of Jesus, a Test Case: The Parable of the Lost Sheep." Pages 253–89 in *Gospel Images of Jesus Christ in Church Tradition and in Biblical Scholarship*. Edited by Christos Karakolis, Karl-Wilhelm Niebuhr, and Sviatoslav Rogalsky. Tübingen: Mohr-Siebeck, 2012.

_____. "Metaphors, First Context and Jesus Tradition." *Biblische Notizen* 159 (2013): 73–120.

_____. " "The Parable of the Tenants in the Vineyard." *Biblische Notizen* 158 (2013): 85–112.

_____. *La parabole des dix vierges*. Rome: Biblical Institute Press, 1983.

Rowe, Robert D. *God's Kingdom and God's Son: The Background to Mark's Christology from Concepts of Kingship to the Psalms*. Leiden: Brill, 2002.

Sakharov, Nikolai. "Kratkii obzor metodiki sovremennogo tolkovaniya pritchei Khristovykh v sinopticheskikh Evangeliyakh" [A brief review of the methodology for the modern interpretation of the parables of Christ in the Synoptic Gospels]. *Sbornik trudoe kafedry bibleistiki MDA* [Proceedings of the department of biblical studies of the Moscow Academy of Sciences] 1 (2013): 187–222.

Sanday, William. *Essays in Biblical Criticism and Exegesis*. Sheffield: Sheffield University Press, 2001.

Schoon, Simon. "Escape Routes as Dead Ends: On Hatred towards Jews and the New Testament, Especially the Gospel of John." Pages 144–58 in *Anti-Judaism and the Fourth Gospel: Papers of the Leuven Colloquium, 2000*. Edited by Reimund Bieringer, Didier Pollefeyt and Frederique Vandecasteele-Vanneuville. Assen: Royal Van Gorcum, 2001.

Schottroff, Luise, and Wolfgang Stegemann. *Jesus and the Hope for the Poor.* Maryknoll, NY: Orbis Books, 1986.

Schottroff, Luise. *The Parables of Jesus.* Minneapolis: Ausburg Fortress, 2006.

Schweizer, Eduard. *The Good News according to Matthew.* Atlanta: John Knox Press, 1975.

Scott, Bernard Brandon. *Hear Then the Parable.* Revised edition. Minneapolis: Fortress Press, 1989.

Senior, Donald. *Matthew.* Nashville, TN: Abington Press, 1998.

Shargunov, Aleksandr. *Evangelie dnya* [The Gospel of the day]. Two vols. Moscow: Sretensky Monastery, 2008.

Smith, B. T. D. *The Parables of the Synoptic Gospels: A Critical Study.* Cambridge: Cambridge University Press, 1937.

Smith, Charles William Frederick. *The Jesus of the Parables.* Philadelphia: The Westminster Press, 1948.

Smith, R. H. *Matthew.* Minneapolis: Augsburg, 1989.

Snodgrass, Klyne R. *Stories with Intent: A Comprehensive Guide to the Parables of Jesus.* Second edition. Grand Rapids, MI: WIlliam B. Eerdmans Publishing Co., 2018.

_____. *The Parable of the Wicked Tenants.* Tübingen: Mohr Siebeck, 1983.

Stein, Robert H. *An Introduction to the Parables of Jesus.* Philadelphia: The Westminster Press, 1981.

_____. *Jesus the Messiah.* Downer's Grove, IL: InterVarsity Press, 1996.

Stern, Frank. *A Rabbi Looks at Jesus' Parables.* Oxford: Rowman & Littlefield Publishers, Inc., 2006.

Suggs, M. J. *Wisdom, Christology and Law in Matthew's Gospel.* Cambridge, MA: Harvard University Press, 1970.

Tannehill, R. C. *Luke.* Nashville, TN: Abingdon, 1996.

Turner, Nigel. *Grammatical Insights into the New Testament.* London: T&T Clark International, 2004.

van Tilborg, S. *The Jewish Leaders in Matthew.* Leiden: Brill, 1972.

Velimirovich, Nikolai. *Tvoreniya* [Collected works]. Three vols. Moscow, 2010.

Vermes, Geza. *The Authentic Gospel of Jesus*. Oxford: Allen Lane, 2003.

von Albrecht, M. *Istoriya rimskoy literatury ot Andronika do Boeziya i ee eliyanie na posleduyushchie epokhi* [The history of Roman literature from Andronicus to Boethius and its influence on later eras]. Moscow: Greko-Latinskii Kabinet Y. A. Shichalina, 2004.

Weir, S. "A Bridal Headdress from Southern Palestine." *Palestine Exploration Quarterly* 105 (1973): 101–109.

Wenham, David. *The Parables of Jesus*. Downers Growe, IL: InterVarsity Press, 1989.

White, K. D. "The Parable of the Sower." *Journal of Theological Studies* 15 (1964): 300–307.

Wierzbicka, Anna. *What Did Jesus Mean?: Explaining the Sermon on the Mount and the Parables in Simple and Universal Human Concepts*. Oxford: Oxford University Press, 2001.

Wilkinson, J. "The Way from Jerusalem to Jericho." *The Biblical Archaeologist* 38.1 (1975): 10–24.

Williams, James G. *Gospel against Parable: Mark's Language of Mystery*. Sheffield: Almond Press, 1985.

Wright, N. T. *Jesus and the Victory of God*. Minneapolis: Fortress Press, 1997.

Wright, Stephen I. *Jesus the Storyteller*. London: SPCK, 2014.

_____. *Jesus the Storyteller*. Louisville, KY: Westminster John Knox Press, 2015.

Young, Brad H. *Jesus and His Jewish Parables: Rediscovering the Roots of Jesus' Teaching*. New York: Paulist Press, 1989.

_____. *Jesus the Jewish Theologian*. Grand Rapids, MI: Baker Academic, 1993.

_____. *The Parables: Jewish Tradition and Christian Interpretation*. Grand Rapids, MI: Baker Academic, 2012.